**EUROPEAN
INDUSTRIAL
RELATIONS**

EUROPEAN INDUSTRIAL RELATIONS

by
INDUSTRIAL DEMOCRACY IN EUROPE (IDE)
INTERNATIONAL RESEARCH GROUP

CLARENDON PRESS · OXFORD
1981

Oxford University Press, Walton Street, Oxford OX2 6DP
London Glasgow New York Toronto
Delhi Bombay Calcutta Madras Karachi
Kuala Lumpur Singapore Hong Kong Tokyo
Nairobi Dar Es Salaam Cape Town
Melbourne Wellington
and associate companies in
Beirut Berlin Ibadan Mexico City

Published in the United States by
Oxford University Press, New York

British Library Cataloguing in Publication Data

Industrial Democracy in Europe (IDE)
International Research Group
European industrial relations.
1. Employee's representation in management
– Europe.
I. Title
331.89'14   HD5660.E9   80-41055
ISBN 0-19-827254-5

Typesetting by Hope Services, Abingdon
and printed in Great Britain by
Richard Clay (The Chaucer Press) Ltd.,
Bungay, Suffolk

FOREWORD

The study on Industrial Democracy in Europe (IDE) is an international collaborative effort to assess the effects of national schemes for employee participation on a comparative basis. The variations of industrial democracy systems in twelve countries provided the natural experimental setting to investigate how their formal rules and regulations for participation affect the distribution of influence and power in organizational decision making. Thus, a deliberate attempt was made to go beyond the traditional legal comparativism in industrial democracy studies and relate formal norms systematically to organizational processes: participation, influence and power in the first place, social and economic consequences in the second.

Some 25 social scientists from about 20 major institutions of higher learning in the various countries collaborated in the conduct of this research. In many ways it became for all of us a significant experience of collective learning. Hence, the published products of the joint research have no individual authors. We decided to opt for a collective authorship which best reflects the style of collaboration of the group as a whole over the past years. The way we worked together made it impossible to attribute a specific idea or the origin of a concept to a given individual alone.

The first two publications on this study are interrelated. The first, *Industrial Democracy in Europe,* presents the conceptual framework, methods, and findings of the IDE study. The second, *European Industrial Relations,* provides a qualitative description of the various legal and socio-economic country contexts that were considered to be relevant in a study of industrial democracy. In that sense the present publication describes the national background and *'couleur locale',* the former the systematic international comparison. Together they should best serve other researcher colleagues, practitioners of participation in industry and the interested public.

IDE International
Research Group

ACKNOWLEDGEMENTS

The IDE International Research Group is indebted to many institutions that have supported its efforts. The International Institute of Management of the Science Center Berlin has carried the load of supporting the first planning seminars and has lent crucial support to the international project by covering costs of the international co-ordinating team (Bernhard Wilpert and the assistance of Wolfgang Potratz and Jörg Rayley at various phases of the research) and part of the associated overheads. Of particular importance to the whole project was always the interest and unfailing support it enjoyed from Walter Goldberg, then director of the International Institute of Management.

A major grant of the Thyssen Foundation (Cologne) has facilitated most of the IDE meetings and the necessary *ad hoc* assistance in the international co-ordination efforts. A supplementary grant by the Ford Foundation (New York) made it possible to hire Gabriele Freidank as assistant for co-ordination.

Various national funding agencies have helped to cover part of the *sur place* expenditures at various plenary sessions. They have thus been of critical support at different stages of our research: Maison des Sciences de l'Homme (Paris), Nuffield Foundation (London), Boris Kidrić Foundation (Ljubljana), Histadrut (Israel).

For each of our meetings we gratefully acknowledge the hospitality of the host — usually the home institution of the national research team.

The research of each sub-study was supported by national or international funding agencies or research institutions:

Belgium: The Fonds voor Kollektief Fundamental Onderzoek and the Laboratorium voor Toegepaste Psychologie (Ghent University)

Denmark: Handelshøskjolen in Copenhagen and Arhus, Handelshøgs-koleafdelingen in Søderborg, Odense University Center, Association for Young Businessmen's Education, Den Lettstedska Fonden' (Sweden) and the Danish Social Science Research Council

Finland: Finnish Academy, Foundation for Economic Education, Jenny and Antti Wihuri's Foundation, Helsinki School of Economics; Research Foundation of the Finnish Cooperative Banks

France: CORDES and CRESST

Italy: Consiglio Nazionale delle Ricerche (C.N.R.), Istituto di Statistica e Ricerca Sociale 'C. Gini'-Universita di Roma, Instituto per la Formazione et l'Addestramento Professionale — I.R.I. (I.F.A.P.)

Israel: The Technion Research Foundation, Israel; Government, Ministry of Labour; Israeli Institute for the Advancement of Labour Relations

Netherlands: The Netherlands Organization for the Advancement of Pure Research and the Free University (Amsterdam), State University at Leyden

Norway: The Department of Labour and Municipal Affairs and the Work Research Institutes

Sweden: The Bank of Sweden Tercentenary Foundation, Svenska Handelsbanken Foundation for Social Science Research, Swedish Institute of Management, Economic Research Institute, Stockholm School of Economics, Swedish Work Environment Fund, Swedish Social Science Research Council and the companies participating in the research

UK: The Anglo-German Foundation for the Study of Industrial Society.

West Germany: The International Institute of Management of the Science Center Berlin

Yugoslavia: Raziskovalna Skupnost SR Slovenije

Initially, drafts of chapters were written around a common but not inflexible framework and were then circulated around the other national groups by the contributors involved. Further revisions and updating over the course of the project were necessary and these were finally compiled by Malcolm Warner into the form presented here. The introduction to the volume was written by Malcolm Warner, considerably assisted by the critical role of Cornelis Lammers and Veljko Rus, and many valuable suggestions from other IDE-team members.

The Belgian chapter was written by Pol Coetsier and Marnix Ryckaert; the Danish chapter by Reinhard Lund with detailed comments and suggestions from Flemming Agersnap and Palle Bruus. The Finnish chapter was prepared by Juhani Kauhanen and Oiva Laaksonen with suggestions from Timo Kaupinen, Matti Pekkanen, Matti Savola, and Heikki Urmas. The French contribution was written by Janine Goetschy and Dominique Martin; the German contribution by Bernhard Wilpert, with the assistance of Gabriele Freidank, Jörg Rayley and Wolfgang Potratz; the British chapter by Malcolm Warner, with the useful comments of Malcolm G. Wilders and John H. Teal. The Israeli chapter was developed by Eliezer Rosenstein and Itzhak Gur-Lavie from an earlier version. The Italian report was written by Riccardo Peccei and Titta Vadala, with the assistance of the Italian team in the compilation of statistical material. The chapter on the Netherlands was drafted by Erik Andriessen on the basis of comments made by Pieter J. D. Drenth, Gerko Hamming, Cornelis Lammers and Jan Verdam, J. van Putten and W. J. Wijnberg. The description of the Norwegian industrial relations system was written by Thoralf Ulrik Qvale with suggestions from Torild Skar, Lars Christian Berge, Thomas Sandberg, Knut Veium, and Harry O. Hansen; the Swedish chapter by Thomas Sandberg with the assistance of Roger Molin and Nils-Gunnar Rudenstam. Lastly, the description of the Yugoslav system was written by Vesna Pusić and Veljko Rus. The final set of conclusions for the volume was prepared by Cornelis Lammers with critical suggestions by many members of the IDE team. The institutional affiliations of the international IDE team are listed below:

Belgium:	Pol Coetsier, Professor of Psychology and Marnix Ryckaert, University of Ghent.
Denmark:	Flemming Agersnap, Professor of Organization, School of Economics and Social Science, Copenhagen.
Finland:	Oiva Laaksonen, Professor of Organisation, Helsinki School of Economics.
France:	Dominique Martin, Centre de Recherches en Sciences Sociales du Travail, Sceaux.
West Germany:	Jörg Rayley, Technische Universität Berlin. Bernhard Wilpert, Associate Research Fellow, International Institute of Management, Science Center Berlin and Professor of Psychology, Technische Universität Berlin.
Italy:	Francesco Consoli, Universita Degli Studi di Roma. Riccardo Peccei, London School of Economics.
Israel:	Eliezer Rosenstein, Associate Professor, Israel Institute of Technology, Haifa.
Netherlands:	Eric Andriessen, IVA-Institute of Social Research, Tilburg. Pieter J. D. Drenth, Professor of Psychology, Free University Amsterdam. Cornelis J. Lammers, Professor of Sociology, State University at Leyden.
Norway:	Thoralf U. Qvale, Research Fellow, Work Research Institutes, Oslo.
Sweden:	Thomas Sandberg, University of Uppsala, Bengt Stymne, Professor of Organization Theory, Stockholm School of Economics.
U.K.	Peter Abell, Professor of Sociology, University of Surrey, Guildford, Surrey. Frank Heller, Senior Staff; Tavistock Institute of Human Relations, London. Malcolm Warner, Professor and Research Co-ordinator Joint Graduate Programme, Administrative Staff College, Henley-on-Thames; and Brunel University.
Yugoslavia:	Vesna Pusić, University of Zagreb. Veljko Rus, Professor of Sociology, University of Ljubljana.

Corresponding Members:
Professor Walter Goldberg, International Institute of Management, Germany; Professor Theo Pirker, Germany; Professor Jean-Daniel Reynaud, France; Professor Stanley E. Seashore, USA; Professor William H. Starbuck, USA.

Associate Researchers:
Gabriele Freidank, international co-ordination; Janine Goetschy, France; Itzhak Gur-Lavie, Israel; Wolfgang Potratz, Germany; Titta Vadala, Italy; Malcolm Wilders, Great Britain.

International
Co-ordination: Bernhard Wilpert

CONTENTS

1

INDUSTRIAL DEMOCRACY IN EUROPE –
POSSIBLE CONJECTURES AND EXPLANATIONS

1. PLAN OF THE VOLUME

In this volume we consider the relationship between Industrial Relations and Industrial Democracy in Europe with reference both to existing and to possibly future sets of insitutions and processes. We aim first to examine the framework of the present system of collective bargaining in their national settings, and we invite the reader to make comparisons between national systems as these suggest themselves, both by explicitly displaying an initial set of conjectures and, later suggesting patterns, communalities, and contrasts after the national chapters have been presented. In the final chapter, we shall try to see whether the conjectures now to be set out can help to organize the largely institutional background data from the respective countries into a more strictly comparative framework, and provide a comparison of seven national systems inside the European Community with five outside.

This volume covers nearly all the countries of the European Community and includes several beyond its frontiers, although not too far outside its periphery. Inclusion of specific countries in the study depended on research collaborators being readily available. At bottom, the main interest of the study was 'scientific' and academic, although it was also directed to policy-making.

2. COUNTRIES AND SYSTEMS COVERED

While the accompanying volume, *Industrial Democracy in Europe* (IDE, 1980), will analyse the main findings from a systematic, interdisciplinary *quantitative* perspective, we hope here to set the scene for the wider understanding of such analytical and empirical relationships. The following twelve chapters will describe and discuss in a *qualitative* vein the Industrial Relations System and the attempts to institutionalize Industrial Democracy in Belgium, Denmark, Finland, France, Great Britain, Holland, Israel, Italy, Norway, Sweden, West Germany, and Yugoslavia. The political, economic, and social context of each system will be outlined and its current debate about Industrial Democracy presented.

In the twelve countries concerned, there is neither a *common* Industrial Relations System, nor an identical Industrial Democracy arrangement. The countries range from those in which less than one in five workers is unorganized (for example, Sweden), to those where the proportions are reversed (for example, France); where work councils are required by statute (for example, West Germany) to where they are voluntary (for example, Great Britain); where workers sit on boards as of right (for example, Denmark) to where they as yet do not (for example, Finland); where there is *de jure* workers' control (for example, Yugoslavia) to where it is often arguably *de facto* (for example, Great

Britain); where there are many self-governing collectives (for example, Israel) to where these are rare (for example, Belgium); where there are many semi-autonomous work-group experiments (as for example, in Norway) to where these are minor and peripheral (as, for example, in France); where the trade union federation is unitary (say, in Germany) to where there are denominational federations (as, say, in Holland); from where union bargaining has traditionally been highly developed (for example, Great Britain), to where it has basically not been officially part of the system (as in Yugoslavia); from where large-scale heavy industry dominates (as in Germany), to where it is limited (for example, in Denmark); from where the socialized sector is central (as in Israel), to where it is limited (for example, Belgium); from where strikes are very frequent (say, in Italy), to where they are less frequent (for example, in Sweden).

The twelve countries all have industrial democracy institutionalized to some degree but not all have statutory works councils, although many are moving towards this model. The German experience is prominent (see Wilpert, 1975). Belgium, France, and Holland initiated such councils in the immediate post-war period (Garson, 1975: 163). Britain shrinks from anything other than 'single-channel' representation although it is more common in larger firms (Clarke *et al.*, 1972: 72-3). The Scandinavian countries too have favoured the 'voluntaristic' Anglo-Saxon model, although this may be changing. Yugoslavia is *sui generis* with its workers' self-management system; Israel is also a special case, but with, for example, a considerable degree of worker representation at plant council level among other devices (see also, IDE, 1980, ch. 2).

There is a wide range of employee representation on boards of companies. Germany has the well-known co-determination legislation, with (almost) parity representation on top boards of large companies since 1976. In Holland, works councils may veto candidates to the supervisory board. Belgium, too, has been fairly strongly critical towards co-determination from both unions and employers' sides. In spite of the recent proposals, Great Britain has neither supervisory boards nor workers' representatives on the top policy bodies of private companies, but a few innovations have appeared in the public sector. Norway, Sweden and Denmark have a minority board-representation law on German lines. In Yugoslavia, the 'Commission of Workers' Countrol' supervises policy decision-making. Israel has a 'Joint Management' system in Histadrut enterprises, for example.

The variety of forms of participation is both fascinating and challenging. There exist different statutory arrangements within multi-national companies operating in some or all of these countries. Each country, in turn, has a different record of industrial conflict; whether one or another Participative Structure causes a given level of disputes or *vice versa* is yet unproven. Do low-conflict countries give birth to developed participation arrangements, or do high levels of strikes 'necessitate' such laws? Or are the two phenomena interactive and mutually reinforcing? Can we distinguish between factors which cause the institutionalization of such arrangements and their subsequent functioning? Is the type of Industrial Relations System a pre-condition for this functioning? Indeed, to which forces in advanced societies are Participative Structures in the main a response? It is to this final and fundamental question that we now specifically address ourselves.

3. THE ANALYTICAL FRAMEWORK

Conjectures

The relationship between the Country-Contextual variables (C-CON) of the model which forms the basis of the international study and one of the central variables, that is Participative Structure (PS), will be the focus of the discussion to be elaborated here (see IDE International Research Group, 1976). We have said we will present the qualitative dimension but we also hope to offer the statistical background of this relationship. The chapters to be presented will in fact discuss all the relevant background factors which influence and constitute the Industrial Relations System (IRS) in each country of which the Participative Structure (PS) is a reflection or a consequence. The historical factors prior to 1945 will *not* be discussed except *en passant,* but the political, economic, social, and related factors affecting the Industrial Relations System since that date will be commented upon in the appropriate degree of specificity. The County-Contexts (C-CON) will be reviewed as determinants of the respective Participative Structure (PS): hence the hypothesized causal explanation, that context determines structure, to simplify the relationship for the purposes of discussion.

The links between the IRS and PS can be perhaps better understood if we consider Clegg's view that:

Some trade unionists and theorists see collective bargaining as constituting industrial democracy, as providing the most effective means whereby workers can share in the government of industry. But other trade unionists, managers and theorists regard collective bargaining as a limited form of industrial democracy. In their view it needs to be supplemented by one or more other forms if workers are to enjoy as large a share in industrial decision making as they should. There are also those who hold that industrial democracy can exist only where complete workers' control has been achieved.

Most of the proposals for supplementing collective bargaining fall under one or other of two headings. Either they advocate additional joint bodies of managers and workers' representatives empowered to discuss matters of joint concern which are not subject to collective agreements; or they propose the inclusion of workers' representatives on the boards of companies. (1977: 83)

Each IRS is itself generally shaped by the C-CON variables and in so far as PS legislation is largely post-war, we can posit the following: that context shapes the IRS which in turn is a necessary condition for the PS to function. The last variable may even be seen as, in effect, part of the IRS. In some countries where legal PS is hardly existent such as in Great Britain, we are basically only looking at custom and practice as part of the IRS. In Clegg's formulation (1977: 83), there is a common denominator to *all* the national arrangements, in so far as all have collective bargaining processes, and many have supplemented these in the ways he suggests, although at different times, for different reasons, and to different degrees. Implicit in this argument is a scale ranging from (at one end) bargaining to (at the other) complete workers' control, with intermediate steps of additional 'joint bodies' and 'workers' representatives' on boards.

In order to deal with the twelve national sets of national participative arrangements which follow, we need a number of conjectures, if not hypotheses, to enable a critical analysis to be made. Although this volume is intended to provide a qualitative feel for the phenomena which we hope to analyse in a more statistical manner in the accompanying volume, we need to go beyond a series of mere descriptive cameos, revealing though they may be individually. A framework combining industrial relations theory and inter-organizational analysis may be needed.

Sets of Relationships

What then are the possible conjectures which might establish a potential set, or sets, of relationships between the variables involved (see Poole, 1978), which would be applicable to the whole group of twelve nations studied, or indeed to a wider collection of similar countries? All are, for example, more or less advanced industrialized societies with many accompanying characteristics in common — many belong to the European Community, with fairly comparable political arrangements. Several belong to the North Atlantic Treaty Organisation for their collective security. All the countries, even with the political difference involved in the case of Yugoslavia (and the neutrality of that country, together with Sweden and Finland), belong to the Organization for Economic Cooperation and Development. Indeed, advanced industrialized states share common problems and dilemmas for the individual. As a political analyst has observed (Camps, 1972:41):

Today, at all levels of society, a pervasive organisational problem is how to combine efficiency with an adequate sense of participation. . . . and as government has become larger and remote and less personal (and with the advent of the computer less personal in a new sense) any effective participation by the individual has become, in fact, extremely difficult. And the situation tends to feed on itself: as the individual loses the feeling that he can effect what happens he loses his sense of responsibility, or opts out, and a bad situation is made worse.

However, have some of these advanced countries been able to cope better than others and devised political and industrial forms of participation which help to reduce such 'alienation'? Progress has been slow, according to Vanek (1975:1), for 'the process of economic democratization or economic participation trails considerably behind the process of political democratization and political self-determination'. To what degree is this, in fact, the case?

Possible Explanations: The Political

The first conjecture which we can consider is that the development of participative structures depends on an appropriate 'political' background. By this we mean the exercise of 'political' will or leadership, even ideology, over a sustained period of time, at least from 1945, and operating because the greater 'political' advance (in a sense to be defined below) the more developed the degree of participation structure will consequently have become. What we mean by politically 'advanced' is a controversial matter, but the factors here are likely to be a high degree of political mobilization (see Lipset, 1960), high voter-turn out, vigorous opposition parties, etc. in the pluralist model, or in another model, the consequences of political revolution as in the Yugoslav case (Warner, 1975).

Why should this be the case, even if it were true? The most plausible argument would run as follows: the development of democracy in the *economic* sphere (or the industrial, for the purposes of this discussion) follows albeit with a lag that in the political sphere. The more 'advanced' the political arrangements, the more industrial democracy is likely to be demanded, accepted and institutionalized, for example, via ideological pressures.

Has the political 'myth', used in the anthropological sense, of European harmonization been a 'strong inducement to change national laws regarding labor participation' (Garson, 1975:162) because of the efforts of the Commission to develop a European Companies Statute? The political impetus for such a change has been implicit in the notion of the so-called Fifth Directive, and a starting point for our own discussion of Industrial Democracy in Europe (see IDE International Research Group, 1976). This represents a political explanation in itself, and one worthy of later discussion, although many countries have introduced elements of their PS before harmonization was mooted.

The Economic Explanation

An alternative, but not necessarily contradictory explanation is the economic one, although it may be a special economic 'meliorist' one. Here we might suggest that the degree of participative structure depends on the level of economic development, other things being equal. This might take the form of the 'industrialism' thesis, and that as countries become more industrialized, and hence alike, they develop similar economic and political institutions. A great deal of sociological work seems to rest on this assumption, and has spilled over into the industrial relations and management literature (see Weinshall, 1977).

This could perhaps take a 'convergence' form (see Kerr *et al.,* 1961, for the original formulation), and arguing for growing similarity in Europe. Hence the higher the GNP, the greater the 'demand' for institutionalized participation may be. If we included a subsidiary factor, education, perhaps as an intervening variable, it might be plausible. It might even be said that the richer the economy, the more it could 'afford' participation (on the 'supply' side of the equation), assuming that the latter was regarded as having costs *vis-à-vis* production, although a PS might not necessarily follow in any highly developed form, e.g. Switzerland. Or can we say that in such economies the advanced technology requires people to be 'involved', otherwise they may make costly mistakes? Although less likely, self-management (as in the Yugoslav case) *can* develop in a less developed economy, with small organizations and a liberal market. Or can we argue that only in more advanced economies, with bigger firms, greater investment in human resources, and more educated, far-seeing managers (and trade union leaders), that participation is accepted? This might be called the optimistic 'co-determination' conjecture: and here the Danish or Swedish models might spring to mind.

A Social Explanation

A further explanation may be called a social or sociological one. It would argue

PS is dependent on the level of social advance, other things being equal. But as S itself may be a function of E, then it is little different from the preceding one. None the less, we might try to relate PS to the social differentiation in the countries concerned and consider the *distribution* as well as the *level* of GNP for example, both of which would distinguish 'Nordic', for example, from 'Latin' Europe perhaps. Or, as a further complication, we could argue that social stability might be indicated by the rate of inflation: higher inflation leading to less social stability. We might also consider the *degree* and *rigidity* of social stratification.

Social differentiation may relate to differing experiences of urbanization, rate of immigration, occupational traditions, and so on. The older the industrial culture, the greater the differentiation. Here Britain may be set apart from the other states. Again, conversely, more recently industrialized nations, such as Yugoslavia and Israel, may be in turn different from the others. The presence of a long standing communitarian and/or egalitarian tradition may be relevant. The size of the population and its dispersion may be of some relevance *vis-à-vis* the strength of fellow-feeling in the community.

There is possibly a *cultural* explanation, parallel to the above, where we may argue PS is determined by the value-system. For example, the Scandinavian *versus* the Latin distinction may be a good illustration, where the degree of labour management co-operation in the former enables the stable institutionalization of conflict regulation in an *inter-organizational* context.

The Organized Labour Explanation

Variants of each of these and intervening variables are also possible. One such version is the Organized Labour explanation which would argue that PS depends on the strength of Organized Labour in a country, other things being equal.

This might take the form of a critical mass of Organized Labour leading to Labour or Socialist parties being in office for a long time, as until recently in Sweden, or of a strong labour movement coexisting previously with Christian Democratic hegemony as in West Germany.

The relevant variables here to consider are, for example, the proportion of the labour force which is unionized, the age and number of unions, whether there is a united trade union movement, as is the case in possibly eight of our set of countries (as opposed to denominational union confederations), and so on.

Is it possible that a strong trade union movement is a substitute to, rather than a concomitant or cause of, a developed PS system? What is the role of grass-roots, possibly informal trade union workshop organization as in the case of the British shop-steward movement, or other continental plant-steward representation (see Carew, 1976:56–82).

The Informational Explanation

An informational explanation is another possibility, and this links the amount of information, or knowledge available, to the degree of participation. Hence the more education, newspaper circulation, etc., the greater the degree of PS, other things being equal. This variable may possibly be a function of E, or P, or both.

This thesis is well-presented in a broader sense by a political scientist:

With increasing economic and technological development resources become available which makes it possible to begin to re-adjust the balance of political skills between elite and mass. It is probably not by sheer coincidence that, in the political development of European nations, expansion of the electorate tended to be linked with the expansion of public education: a literate citizenry could keep in touch with national-level politics via the 'printed mass media'. (Inglehart, 1972:347)

It requires no great leap to transfer this conjecture from the realm of political to industrial democracy (see IDE, 1980, ch. 11).

Explanations over Time

It should by now have become fairly clear that no simple argument will in itself explain the level of PS (see also Garson, 1977:214-30) and that it will probably depend on several factors; and these may vary over time, as we shall now consider. Variants of most conjectures may thus be presented as operating in a time-dimension (see, for example, Sorge, 1976), in which the economic (possibly even Marxist) 'cyclical' explanation may be cited whereby the degree of participation varies with the state of economy and that PS varies with the changing level of economic activity, as does industrial conflict (see Shalev, 1978:1-21, for example). A version of this (as seen by Brannen *et al.*, 1976: 258-9) argues that:

The general trend of worker and trade-union demands during the course of this century has been related to the 'sphere of consumption', that is to economic demands. In a situation of boom and prosperity following 'crisis' the normal institutions of collective bargaining are revitalised and the institutions of partici-pation fade into disfavour. The demands for workers' control fall away. Where economic goals are achieved there is little support either for radical reconstruc-tion or the forms of participation (e.g. joint consultation) which have little bearing on financial rewards. Where slump follows 'crisis' a similar situation obtains. With reduced power it becomes important to employ the conventional vocabulary which is more acceptable to a relatively more powerful management and expresses workers' concerns more directly, while vocabularies of workers' control seem of doubtful relevance when the employment situation is fragile.

This at least is a theory of sorts, although perhaps less clear than it might be as we shall see in a moment. The evidence to be presented from the twelve countries to be discussed may help us see the degree to which this kind of 'grand theory' is apposite.

In the view of these writers (and also more recently Ramsay, 1977) Worker Participation, in the form of joint consultation and in the pejorative sense used by its critics, increases during periods of recession and diminishing profit rate, as the 'crises of capitalism' call for workers to acquiesce in consultative arrangements to raise productivity (see Ramsay, 1977:493-4). This tentative explanation is presented as probably Anglo-centric, with Britain seen as a 'type case' (Brannen *et al.*, 1976:245-6), but these critics imply that the 'cyclical' nature of participation can in fact be regarded in the context of industrial society generally.

Again, we may argue that the non-pejorative form of industrial democracy (from the Left's viewpoint, that is) is workers' control, and this probably varies *de facto* and positively with the state of employment, and hence output; because a tight labour market leads to the progressive erosion of managerial prerogatives. To directly relate the reality of workers' control to the tightness of the labour market is probably more accurate than the formulation (in Brannen *et al.*, 1976: 258-9) which is ambiguous, although conceding its 'doubtful relevance' when employment is 'fragile' (1976:259).

Suppose we combine the two notions; we may now conjecture that consultation (PS_c and workers' control (PS_w) co-vary conceivably in opposite directions, and we would expect that they are negatively correlated with each other. But as institutions change slowly, we may find that the previous recession's PS_c co-exists with this boom's PS_w. Indeed, we might look for evidence for the degree to which PS_w becomes institutionalized, and hence acquires a degree of quasi-permanence. This explanation, of course, may be combined with those relying on political, labour, social and other factors.

Is it possible to argue (as for example, Garson, 1974:9) that co-determination 'is increasing in popularity as an experiment and seems to have established expectations leading to demands for more extensive forms of worker participation in management'? Indeed are not all schemes of participation/co-determination/control/self-management increasing, in differing degrees of lineality, the awareness of workers experiencing these opportunities (See Qvale, 1973) with perhaps an 'experimental' Hawthorne-type effect thus created? This is perhaps too sweeping a conjecture, and it remains to be seen whether it is a better predictor than the 'cyclical' supposition. The reader can examine the evidence for this in the chapters presented, and then the concluding synthesis in the last chapter.

4. FINAL REMARKS

The various explanations we have discussed need to be combined and we need to see how far the IRS is the decisive conditioning variable here. At the same time, the degree to which PS is necessarily dependent on the IRS is debatable. Indeed, some observers may go on further than looking at the IRS in seeking an exclusive and coherent explanation of participative behaviour (see IDE, 1980, ch. 10).

A theory of Industrial Democracy of this type has been argued by Clegg (1977:97-8) as follows:

So long as adequate arrangements are made for collective bargaining within the plant, collective bargaining may be regarded as a satisfactory form of industrial democracy. But where regional or industry agreements fail to provide for plant bargaining, there are demands for alternative arrangements to allow workers to exercise some influence over those matters which concern them and which cannot be adequately regulated in regional or industry agreements.

Prevailing union attitudes towards industrial democracy (1977:86 ff.), may be based in the differences in the respective national bargaining patterns. Where industrial democracy could be extended by national agreements this was done, as in the case of Britain and Sweden; where it could not, as in the case of France and Germany, it 'had to be extended by statute or not at all' (1977:92). This is perhaps to compress and simplify, but we can see if it is falsified as we review the twelve national *systems,* and the *organizations* which comprise them.

The preceding argument does not explicitly review the political, economic, and social characteristics of the respective countries, and these we would argue weigh heavily upon the industrial relations structure and process, and indeed there are feedback mechanisms which also operate. National backcloths of course vary: that 'in different nations the labour movement should present itself under a wide range of organisational forms and adopt many different modes of behaviour is therefore no cause for surprise' (Kendall, 1975:309). None the less, we may posit the main difference between systems is where the primacy of PS legislation is used to settle questions regarding the workers' job relations rather than via collective action. Again, inter-organizational analysis may provide the key.

To sum up, different levels of conjecture are possible: but they may be premature. This volume is essentially a background briefing for the reader *vis-à-vis* the accompanying volume based on the Industrial Democracy in Europe fieldwork data, using (within each national system) the plant as the unit of analysis, and covering a wide range of organizations, groups, and individuals. It is true that we hope here to suggest ways in which the PS data may be patterned but its major role is to assist understanding of the main IDE findings. We now turn to the national systems, moving from North to South.

REFERENCES

Brannen, Peter, Eric Batstone, Derek Fatchett, Phillip White (1976), *The Worker Directors: A Sociology of Participation.* London: Hutchinson.
Camps, Miriam (1972), 'European unification in the 1970s'. In Michael Hodges (ed.), *European Integration.* Harmondsworth: Penguin Books.
Carew, Anthony (1976), *Democracy and Government in European Trade Unions.* London: George Allen and Unwin.
Clarke, R. Oliver, Derek Fatchett, and Ben C. Roberts (1972), *Workers' Participation in Management in Britain.* London: Heinemann Educational Books.
Clegg, Hugh (1977), *Trade Unionism under Collective Bargaining: A Theory Based on Comparisons of Six Countries.* Oxford: Blackwells.
Garson, G. David (1975), 'Recent developments in workers' participation in Europe'. In Jaroslav Vanek (ed.), *Self-Management: Economic Liberation of Man.* Harmondsworth: Penguin Books.
―― (1977), 'Paradoxes of Worker Participation'. In G. David Garson (ed.), *Worker Self-Management in Industry: the West European Experience.* New York: Praeger.
Inglehart, Ronald (1970), 'Public opinion and regional integration'. In Michael Hodges (ed.), *European Integration.* Harmondsworth: Penguin Books.
IDE-International Research Group (1976), 'Industrial democracy in Europe (IDE). An international comparative study'. *Social Science Information,* 15.
―― (1980), *Industrial Democracy in Europe.* Oxford: OUP.

Kendall, Walter (1975), *The Labour Movement in Europe.* London: Allen Lane, Penguin Books.

Kerr, Clark, John T. Dunlop, Frederick Harbison and Charles Myers (1961), 'Industrialism and world society'. *Harvard Business Review,* January–February.

Lipset, Seymour Martin (1960), *Political Man.* Garden City, New York: Double-day.

Poole, Michael (1978), 'Industrial Democracy: A Bibliography Review of Ideas, Institutions and Research'. Paper given to SSRC Conference on Institution-alization. University of Sussex, 8–11 September.

Qvale, Thoralf (1973), 'Participation and conflict: some experiences from a Norwegian industrial democracy programme'. Paper given to the International Industrial Relations Association 3rd World Congress, London.

Ramsey, Harvie (1977), 'Cycles of control: worker participation in sociological and historical perspective'. *Sociology,* 11.

Shalev, Michael (1978), 'Lies, Damned Lies and Strike Statistics'. In Colin Crouch and A. Pizzorno, *The Resurgence of Class Conflict in Western Europe since 1978.* Vol. I. London: MacMillan.

Sorge, Arndt (1976), 'The Evolution of Industrial Democracy in Countries of the European Community'. *British Journal of Industrial Relations,* 14.

Vanek, Jaroslav (ed.) (1975), *Self-Management: Economic Liberation of Man.* Harmondsworth: Penguin Books.

Weinshall, Theodore D. (ed.) (1977), *Culture and Management.* Harmondsworth: Penguin Books.

Warner, Malcolm (1975), 'Whither Yugoslav self-management?' *Industrial Relations Journal,* 6.

Wilpert, Bernhard (1975), 'Research on Industrial Democracy: the German case'. *Industrial Relations Journal,* 6.

2

THE NORWEGIAN INDUSTRIAL RELATIONS SYSTEM

INTRODUCTION

1.1. General Situation and Background

From being among Europe's poorest countries around the turn of the century, Norway ranked in 1966 as eleventh out of 120 countries in GNP per capita, and as thirty-fifth in terms of total GNP. During the next 10 years, the economy has developed even more rapidly with the prospect of making the country one of the richest in the world in wealth per head. GNP per capita in 1975 amounted to 7.058 US$ (UN, 1975). Industralization started late in Norway. The economy was largely based until this century upon traditional primary industries (paper and pulp, farming, fish, mining) and grew slowly without disrupting the population pattern to the same extent in more advanced European countries. With only 2 per cent of the surface cultivated and the rest dominated by forests, steep valleys, mountains, lakes, glaciers, and fiords, communication was difficult, and centralized political and economic power was generally unfeasible. The pattern of small scale farming, forestry and fishing by independent (self-owning) farmers and fishermen living along the 2,650 km.-long coast and in the valleys, and of minor industries in small centres had generally remained unchanged until the development of the huge hydro-electric resources after 1910. (At the turn of the century only 12 per cent of those above 25 years were employed in industry, 4 per cent in construction and 0.3 per cent in mining (Lorenz, 1974).) Norway has an area of 324,000 sq. km. (excluding Svalbard, etc. which has an area of another 62,000 sq. km.) giving a population density of 13.1 persons per sq. km., which is among the lowest in the world. For a Western European country, the proportion of the labour force still employed in the primary industries remains relatively high (Table 2.1).

Norway was for 400 years in a union with Denmark with the Danish king as the sovereign. In the wake of the Napoleonic wars, Norway broke out of this union and achieved its own, at that time very progressive, constitution before joining a looser union with Sweden in 1814. The relationship with Sweden became gradually more strained towards the end of the nineteenth century, and in 1905 Norway broke away. A Danish prince was invited to become King of Norway after a referendum over the choice between kingdom and republic. Norway remained neutral in the First World War, but became involved in the Second when occupied by German forces in 1940. The Norwegian king and government then moved to London, and after the war Norway joined NATO. In the period after the Second World War there has been general agreement across larger political parties on foreign policy (including the NATO membership) with the sudden exception over the question of membership in the European Community.

Table 2.1
Labour force by industry. Percentages of people employed

	1930	1950	1973	1976
Agriculture, forestry, fishing, hunting	35.8%	25.9%	11.4%	9.3%
Manufacturing, construction, mining, power supply	26.5%	36.5	33.9	34.4
Transport, communications	8.3	10.1	9.9	9.3
Trading, catering	10.5	10.8	14.1	15.9
Public and private services	18.6	16.2	30.7	26.5
Banking, financing, insurance, business services	–	–	–	4.6
Others	0.3	0.5	0.0	0.0
	100.0	100.0	100.0	100.0

Sources: Seierstad, 1975, *Statistical Yearbooks 1974, 1977.*

1.2. Political Power

The Norwegian parliamentary system dates back to 1884, but the last remains of royal power did not disappear until the break-up of the union with Sweden in 1905. This event and the introduction of voting rights (for men in 1898 and women in 1913) undermined the basis for the alliance between the liberals (V) and the workers. Since 1887, the labour movement had its own party, DNA, but until 1905 this had been overshadowed by the liberals and the fight against the union with Sweden. However, industrialization grew rapidly after the turn of the century, and DNA's votes increased three-fold from 1906 to 1912.

After the First World War, the revolutionary wing of DNA gained majority in the party and several years of infighting and splitting-up followed. However, in 1927 the labour movement again was united in one party, and at the parliamentary elections of that year it became the largest political party with 34.1 per cent of the votes, taking over government. For the first time in Norwegian political history, the main dividing line no longer went between the Conservatives (H) and the Liberals (V), but between the Labour Party and the bourgeoisie.

In 1928, after only two weeks in office, the new Labour Government was defeated. Seven years later the Labour Party again took office, this time in a coalition with the bourgeois Agrarian Party (B). This event marked a turning-point in DNA's politics which changed from the revolutionary 'taking control over the means of production' to the social-democratic strategy of 'stimulating, co-ordinating and checking' the private industries without interfering with owner-ship, at least not initially (Furre, 1972).

The recession in the 1930s created large scale unemployment and industrial unrest, with strikes and lock-outs, when soldiers were used against workers' pickets. The Labour Party launched the 'work for all' policy and created a strong alliance between industrial workers, small independent farmers and fisher-men. Their backing soon gave a clear parliamentary majority and kept the Labour Party in government for 28 years. This composition of the party's support explains the direction of its socio-political policies which attempted to retain a balanced development between town and country (Brox, 1966). The Labour Party then lost its absolute majority, but remained in office with the help of the two members from a young left-wing Socialist Party (SF). However, these two joined the bourgeois parties in the voting against the Labour Govern-ment's handling of a dispute over a serious accident in a state-owned coal mine.

A bourgeois coalition government with a conservative Prime Minister was established and ruled for 28 days. (There are no provisions in the Norwegian constitution for dissolving Parliament and calling new elections within the four-year periods.) The Labour Party was back and ruled until 1965 when the bourgeois parties for the first time since the early 30s got a clear majority in Parliament and assembled a coalition government with a Christian People's Party Prime Minister. This conservative/liberal majority shrunk to one seat in 1969.

In 1971, the coalition government had to resign after the Centre Party (former Agrarian Party) Prime Minister had 'leaked' a confidential document on the continuing EEC-membership negotiations to the leader of the 'People's Movement against EEC'. Then a minority Labour Government held office until the EEC referendum in 1973. This government, which supported full member-ship, resigned when it was defeated at the referendum, and a bourgeois minority government took over until the parliamentary election in 1973. Since then the Labour Party has held office with the support of the left-wing socialists. The last election took place in September 1977, and gave a majority for all the socialist of just one seat — the left-wing losing 14 seats — but the Labour Government was able to stay in office with the support of the remaining two left wing socialists.

The election of 1977 shows a return to the situation before the EEC referen-dum as far as the socialists are concerned. In addition, the socialist/non-socialist distinction has become clearer following the loss of votes given to the central/liberal parties. The long-term trend in favour of the conservatives which started in the 1950s has continued, reflecting the urbanization process and the absolute and relative expansion of the service sector. The Conservative Party in 1977 received its strongest support since 1930 (41 seats, around 26 per cent), while the ultra-conservative party which appeared in 1973 was eliminated. There appears to be a polarization in parties with the Labour Party, on the one hand, and the Conservative Party on the other, and a corresponding weakening of the 'green alternative' of the centre/liberal parties.

The Labour Government has always had strong backing from the trade unions, and there is a regular tradition of at least one cabinet minister being a union official. Much of the Labour Government's support comes from workers in primary industries, agriculture, and fishing. To maintain this support the government has developed these industries by strengthening their national organizations: thus purchasing, processing, sales, and distribution of raw materials and products in these areas are mainly handled through producer co-operatives or state monopolies. These bodies are generally controlled by the farmers and fishermen, and are accepted as legitimate participants in national policy-making processes.

In the post-war period, Labour and the centre/conservative parties have agreed upon foreign policy (including the NATO membership) and also upon the main guidelines for national policy: economic growth, full employment, and the development of the welfare state. Main dividing issues between the bourgeois and socialist parties have been in economy, i.e. the level of direct state control over the industry (state-ownership), level and principles of taxation, and wealth distribution. Cultural issues such as language and education are very central in Norwegian politics, but do not create clear dividing lines between *parties*. This is particularly so over drinking laws and abortion and religious matters. In recent years a 'green line' has been achieved within the centre (liberal) parties, and there has also been some co-operation with the new Socialist Party in support of its criticism of the centralist growth policies of the Conservative and Labour parties. Table 2.2 indicates the support given to the political parties in elections after 1945.

1.3. Recent Political Events of Nationwide Significance

The first indication of a less stable political situation appeared in 1961 when the left-wing of the Labour Party broke away and formed a new Socialist Party (SF) campaigning mainly against NATO membership and nuclear armaments. In addition SF wanted to impose stricter control on industry and criticized the Labour Government for abandoning income and wealth equality. Although Norway still is among the capitalist countries with the smallest economic differences among groups and classes, the development towards more equality stopped around 1950 (Seierstad, 1975).

Towards the end of the 1960s populistic ideas emerged within the SF, campaigning against the Labour Party's pragmatic, productivity-orientated policies. At this stage SF consisted of intellectuals, members from the Labour youth organization, and a substantial number of local unionists and workers. After SF voted against the Labour Government in 1963, thus bringing in a bourgeois coalition government, Norwegian politics has been much more unstable. The mere demonstration of an alternative government had a substantial effect and this manifested itself in the 1965 election. The great shock, however, came in the EEC referendum in 1972 when a majority went against the established leadership and created a split through all parties except the extreme left and right wings. The new dividing lines went between the centre and the periphery geographically, between top and bottom within the labour movement, between the young and the old generation in general, and between farming/fishing on one

Table 2.2
Parliamentary Elections in Norway (1945-1977 (% votes cast)

	1945	1953	1965	1973	1977
Labour Party (DNA)	41	46	43	35	43
Communist Party (NKP)[1]	12	5	1	−	0,4
Socialist Party (SF/SV)	−	−	6	11	4
Liberals (V)[2]	14	10	10	2	3
Centre (Agrarian) (SP)	8	9	9	7	9
Christian People's Party (Kr.F.)	8	10	8	12	12
Conservative (H)	17	18	20	17	25
Others	−	−	2	15[3]	4[4]
Total	100	98	99	99	100

Source: Statistical Yearbook, 1946-1977.

[1] The Communist Party merged with Socialist Peoples Party and the Labour Information Committee against EEC (DNA members) to form the new Socialist Party (SV) after the EEC referendum. The Communist Party, however, partly refused to phase out its own organization, so it still exists as a separate, but smaller, party.

[2] Also this party was split on the EEC-issue, and a new liberal party (DNF) won representation in the Parliament for one period (1973-7).

[3] A new ultra conservative party (ALP), demanding less taxation and state control, got 5 per cent of the votes and 4 seats in 1973, but only 2 per cent and no seats in 1977.

[4] Includes a number of small parties (DNF, ALP, etc.).

side and industry on the other (Valen, 1976). Apart from the clear economic interests of the primary industries to remain outside EEC, the arguments against were based on nationalistic, ecological, democratic and related values. This was obviously a reaction to the centrally controlled growth policies which had dominated the political scene since the 1930s.

The tactical co-operation between large farmers' organization and the left wing of the labour movement against EEC membership could not continue for long beyond the referendum, and, as demonstrated, there has been a return to the old parties and dividing lines. Within the labour unions the reaction to centralization still remains, particularly in the demand for decentralization within their own organizations. The rules, procedures, selection processes, etc. of the labour movement, however, do not allow for any rapid adjustment to political and other changes; indeed, they actually call for what Fivelsdal and Higley (1970) term 'organizational disaster'.

Following the strikes in the Swedish iron-mines around 1970, there was a series of unofficial strikes in Norwegian plants the following years indicating similar unrest. A study (Karlsen, Qvale and Lange, 1971) of the Norwegian strikes showed they were caused by specific dissatisfaction over payment and the working environment, and general dissatisfaction over the problems met when trying to improve conditions through the trade union channels. The very high degree of centralization in the collective bargaining procedures and hence the lack of local involvement and influence therefore was the primary target for criticism. The centralization process has still continued in subsequent years, though union and political leaders have been trying to respond to the local demands by their centrally initiated programmes for the democratization of industry (board representation), for the improvement of working conditions (new Working Environment Act), as well as by general social and economic policies. None the less the reaction against the system of central collective bargaining is increasing in strength, for instance, the campaign against the comprehensive package deal in 1978.

The discovery from 1967 of North Sea oil and gas reserves, which are very large in relation to the demand of the economy and the population, created a new political situation by giving the government unexpected financial resources to solve the country's social and economic problems. In 1977, however, the position had to be reconsidered, as it became clear to the government that the effects of the international recession would negate the contribution from the oil and gas. At this stage, however, the Labour Government had been re-elected after a period of the highest growth in private consumption ever registered.

1.4. The Economic Situation

The Norwegian economy is highly dependent upon foreign trading which is between 40 and 50 per cent of the GNP. The country has always been capital-importing, and has balanced its import surplus by incomes from its large merchant marine. Since 1976 Norway actually has been a net exporter of oil, and from 1977 has been also exporting large quantities of gas to the Continent and Britain; it is expected that both resources will give an immediate increase in revenue from abroad of nearly 10 per cent. The expected oil incomes have enabled the Government and the private companies to borrow to support industry and to expand private consumption, and this had partly protected the economy from the world depression. However, a very rapid increase in the costs of the off-shore installations, large delays in the development of oil and gas, a disastrous decline in shipping, and serious problems for the traditional export industries have forced the government to review the situation. Table 2.3 gives the growth rate of wage costs and workers' yearly incomes for the period 1970-6.

Table 2.3
Yearly increase in wage costs per hour and workers yearly incomes 1969-1976 (adult workers, average for men and women) (%)

	1970	1971	1972	1973	1974	1975	1976
Company wage costs	12.2	14.4	10.7	13.2	17.9	19.5	15.6
Workers yearly income[1]	10.6	11.4	7.7	10.0	16.5	20.1	12.0

Source: NOU, 1977:17.
[1] Excluding sick benefits.

By 1977, Norway was one of the world's most expensive countries in terms of labour costs, and a Swedish devaluation made this seem even more serious for the export industries. One effect has been a reversal of the 1977 decision of the central union to decentralize collective bargaining in 1978. For the first time since the war, the government is uncertain whether full employment and net growth in incomes can be achieved. Since the government did not expect any improvement in 1978, it stopped a major part of the subsidies and loans given to industries to sustain employment. By January 1978, foreign debts reached 100 billion N.kr. From September 1978 the government introduced a total pay and price freeze which lasted until 1980.

The population has increased by about 10 per cent in the last 20 years reaching 4 millions around 1975. In 1964 37.6 per cent of the adult population (over 16) was employed in paid work. This increased to 42.4 per cent in 1975. A special feature in Norway has been the relatively large proportion of women who are not in paid work (in 1972 59 per cent of the women in the age group 16-74 were not economically active), although there has been a rapid increase in female employment since 1960 (Skard, 1978).

Registered unemployment has been low (in the region of 1-1.5 per cent as yearly average) in the whole period since 1945 (Table 2.4). This amounts to less than 20,000 people. In fact, there have been long periods of labour shortage, and this has been the limiting factor on growth in certain sectors. Before 1970, there has been very little foreign labour, and after 1975 there has been a complete stop on immigration. The figures in Table 2.4 are lower than the real unemployment because large groups are not registered, mainly young school-leavers who have not had paid work earlier and thus are not entitled to unemployment benefits, women who would take paid work if alternatives were available (an estimated 140,000 (Skard, 1978)), and partly disabled people who receive a social support.

Table 2.4
Registered unemployment in Norway (%)

1964	0.9
1975	1.3
1977	1.1
1978 (to June)	1.2

Source: Directorate of Employment.

Yet there has been a high degree of stability in the employment situation, mainly due to the government's policy of full employment and to the structure of the Norwegian economy which has dampened the national effects of international recessions.

During the period 1865-1965 the growth rate of the GNP has had an average of 2.6 per cent, and 3 per cent if we consider the part of this period within this century (Table 2.5). For 1945-62 the growth was 4.7 per cent (yearly average). (Statistisk Sentralbyrå, 1965.)

We can see the rapid growth in GNP in the last decade. This reflects both the effect of oil finds, the tremendous increase in oil prices which benefits Norway, the short boom in international tanker operations in the early 1970s, the increased value of energy in general etc. (Norway has the largest per capita

Table 2.5

Gross domestic product in million N.kr. and growth rate in fixed prices

GNP	(Million N.kr.)	Growth rate (%)	
1960	36,101	5.8	
1965	47,815	5.7	
1970	79,694	3.4	2.0[1]
1971	89,098		4.6[2]
1972	98,397		5.2
1973	111,854		4.1
1974	129,728		5.2
1975	148,701		4.2
1976	169,419		5.8
1977	189,475		4.1

Source: Statistical Yearbooks 1966-1977, Central Bureau of Statistics 1978.
[1] Figure for 1970 recalculated on basis of new formula.
[2] For 1971 a new formula was adopted (standard national account).

production of electric energy in the world, the energy production in 1975 amounting to around 19,000 KWh per capita. A substantial part of Norwegian industry is based on cheap hydro-electric energy (production of metals and alloys), and this part is not hit by the international recession to the same extent as for example, the mechanical industry. The rate of inflation has been moderate in the post war period, although it reached a peak around 1976-7 with a yearly average around 10 per cent.

1.5. Social Stratification, Social Policy and Living Conditions

Norway is commonly described as a relatively egalitarian society (Torgersen, 1975). Class distinctions are less obvious than in other industrialized countries. There was no creation of an important, dominating class or aristocracy during the nineteenth century and when industrialization accelerated around 1900, the Norwegian society consisted then mainly of independent small farmers and fishermen. The poor soil, steep hills and narrow valleys did not make large scale farming/land-owning widespread. Industrialization did not disrupt the population pattern to the same degree as happened earlier in Europe; and urbanization and the creation of slums were less dominating. (Thorsrud & Emery, 1969). A very high level of migration (between 1836 and 1915, around 750,000 Norwegians left for the USA) in the latter half of the nineteenth century partly explains the relative absence of a large proletariat.

During the interwar period the new working class grew rapidly amidst poor material conditions, and the same revolutionary attitude developed here as in the rest of Europe. The revolution, however, did not occur. Instead the Labour Party, when taking over the Government in 1935, aimed at transforming society through reform. This pragmatic reformism has dominated Norwegian politics since the Second World War.

The most important social reform introduced by the Labour Government in the 1930s was the expansion of the education system. Seven years' compulsory free education (starting at the age of seven) was introduced in 1936. In 1946 all primary and secondary schools were standardized to give education of equal quality for all youth. In particular Norway has no private-school system outside the public one.

Keynesian economics has dominated the Labour Party and Government since it took office in the 1930s. This has been so strong that many critics argue that most other socialist ideas have been sacrificed or given low priority to economic growth within the framework of a mixed economy with increasing state consumption. The development in government and private consumption over the last four years is shown in Table 2.6 from which may also be seen the relatively large military expenditure of the country.

Table 2.6
Domestic product: private and government consumption at 1970 prices
M. N.kr.

	1972	1973	1974	1975	1976
Private consumption	47.692	49.301	51.288	54.160	57.555
Growth rate private (%)	3.1	3.4	4.0	5.6	6.3
General government consumption	13.412	14.001	14.465	15.203	15.896
civilian	10.652	11.198	11.729	12.259	12.969
military	2.760	2.803	2.736	2.944	2.927
Growth rate government (%)	3.9	4.4	3.3	5.1	4.6

Source: Statistical Yearbook 1977.

Apart from the changes in the school system, most social reforms were delayed until the late 1950s because of the need for reconstruction of the country after the war. There was broad political backing for this policy. The trade unions too were strongly oriented towards increasing productivity, and there was a high level of local and central co-operation on productivity measures. Collective agreements were designed to help the introduction of 'time and method' studies, piece-rates became widespread, and a large number of shop stewards etc. were trained in the use of such techniques. A strong US influence was behind this development ideologically; and the Marshall Plan financed productivity work.

In the late 1950s, the development of a comprehensive social security system started. In 1967 Parliament introduced the public pension and social security system, securing a minimum standard of living to all Norwegians. Membership is compulsory. The contributions are partly paid by the employers. The state's expenses on health and social security has increased by a yearly average of 17 per cent in the period 1961–73. No other public sector had such rapid growth.

To create employment and economic activity in the most depressed districts, Parliament in the late 1940s agreed to build a state owned steel works in the north, and an aluminium smelter on the west coast. Later, the state has been less directly involved in establishing new industries, and has until the 1970s, left the creation of new hydro-electric plants to private national and international enterprises. Then there was a reversal, and the state bought back a number of internationally owned plants to secure national control over energy and oil resources. A state-owned company is to take an increasing role in the development of the Norwegian continental shelf resources.

By 1960, the situation in the school system was still characterized by 90 per cent of the pupils/students being within the primary and secondary schools (Lindbekk, 1975). At this stage, the 9-years basic schooling was being introduced while the relative share of the budget given to vocational schools was going down. By the mid-1970s all schools below university level were in principle integrated into one system which allowed for various combinations of practical and theoretical subjects and thus gives opportunities for different educational/vocational career-paths. The expansion of university education in Norway came late compared with other countries (Table 2.7).

Table 2.7

Persons 16 years and over by highest education completed (number of years at school) (%)

	1950	1960	1970	1975
Primary school, continuation school, & other at same level (7–9 years):	83.6	79.5	69.7	63.8
Secondary school (10–12 years):	13.4	16.3	23.7	27.5
University level (13 years or more):	3.0	4.2	6.6	8.7

Source: Central Bureau of Statistics 1975–1978.

In order to secure a wide-based (both politically and geographically) press, and to give smaller political parties a chance to operate at the national level, newspapers and parties receive considerable public support. Radio and television services are completely controlled by a state monopoly again reflecting the Norwegian concern for democratic control over media and anti-pluralism.

The distribution of income and wealth in the nation is assumed to be relatively equal. About 9.7 per cent of wage earners and 8.6 per cent of the self employed in 1974 had net incomes below N.kr. 19,900 and 1.4 per cent of wage earners and 4.6 per cent of the self employed had net incomes above N.kr. 100,000 (St. meld, nr. 61), according to taxation statistics. Computed as income per household, this pattern remains. Taxation and social policy have been aiming at levelling inequalities in the whole post war period (progressive taxation, social benefits and tax deductions according to economic need, etc.) (Table 2.8).

2. NATIONAL INDUSTRIAL RELATIONS SYSTEMS

2.1. The legal basis and main ramifications

Legal regulations in industrial relations were first introduced in 1892 with the Factory Inspection Act. This act was amended and extended several times until

Table 2.8
Development in taxation and transfers in % of gross national product.

	Gross taxation	Transfers from public to private	Net taxation
1968	38.5	16.0	22.5
1970	41.0	19.4	21.6
1972	46.4	21.2	25.2
1974	45.8	21.0	24.8
1975	47.1	21.7	25.4
1976	46.4	22.3	24.1
1977	46.1	20.9	25.2

Source: St. meld. 61.

it was replaced by the Workers' Protection Act in 1936, which in turn was modified in 1956 and completely replaced by the new law about workers' safety and work environment in 1976/7.

The first local contracts were signed in the 1870s, in 1907 the first national agreement was reached between metal trades workers and employers, while the Basic Agreement (national collective agreement) between the Federation of Trade Union (LO) and the Confederation of Employers (NAF) goes back to 1935. This agreement is regarded as the constitution of Norway's industrial relations. It has been extended and changed continuously and is now covering a wide range of issues. In addition to the Basic Agreement each union/employers' association has its collective agreement covering special issues and payment. In 1915 the Labour Disputes Act settled the question of the legal character of collective agreements. It rules that where an employee and an employer had a private contract in a plant where a collective agreement existed, the latter was supreme (Norwegian ILO Committee, 1975).

Traditionally, collective bargaining and the trade unions' system of local representatives, company-level union committee, national unions, and the confederation have been considered as the central basis for workers influence, and as the dynamic force behind the development of industrial relations. It still cannot be disputed that this system is very important for the functioning of other parts of the industrial relations system as well. After 1965 there have been periods of rapid reform, and new legislation seemed to dominate over extending the scope of collective agreements. Partly, agreements and legal rules supplement each other, as is the case with the new Working Environment law; and partly, the new laws draw new groups of employees (notably white-collar) into the picture but to some extent leave sanctioning to courts and governmental agencies (see IDE, 1980, ch. 11).

2.2. Trade unions history and principle of organization

The first workers' society was established in 1848, and 51 years later (1899, one year later than Sweden and Denmark) the national confederation, the LO, was created. On this occasion representatives of 74 organizations with a total membership of around 15,000 were gathered, but only 1500 of these initially became members. Until 1905 the LO lived under the shadow of the struggle for national independence. Shortly after the union with Sweden was broken the Iron and Metalworkers' Union and the Printers' Union joined LO and took over its leadership. At this stage, LO's enduring key principles; reliance on industrial rather than regional unions and concentration of power in the central administration, were established (Norwegian ILO Committee, 1975).

Contact between the LO and the labour movements' political wing, the Labour Party (DNA), has been very close from the start. Two members of the party's Central Committee were also members of the LO's Secretariat, and the LO had two members in the party's Central Committee. The Labour Party has since its start in 1887 mainly been based on collective membership. At the LO's founding meeting in 1899, many wanted compulsory Labour Party membership for all LO's members. The decision, however, was to leave this question to the individual unions. The reason was mainly the influence of the Liberal Party (V) among workers. Still, the link between the LO and DNA was strong and has remained so with the exception of the 1920s when the Labour Party was split.

In 1963, 600 local unions, each averaging about 5,000 members, were collective members accounting for about 40 per cent of LO's total membership. Since then, collective membership has been drastically reduced, and today only an estimated 10 per cent of LO's 630,000 members are also collective members of the Labour Party. LO's membership, however, had been growing fast: in 1906 there were 16,000; in 1907, 35,000; in 1912, 53,000; and in 1919, 144,000. The depression in the 1920s reduced the membership, which did not reach the 1919 level until 1931. In 1938, the right to be organized was legally guaranteed, and this led to an increase from 172,500 to 344,800 members in one year. After the Second World War there was rapid growth until 1955, but since then the average growth in membership has been around 1 per cent per year.

The low growth during the last decade reflects a decline in overall unionization. In 1965, 60.6 per cent of men and 33.1 per cent of women were members, while the figures in 1975 were 55 and 31.4 per cent (Karlsen, 1977). This means that the increase in total membership in this period is mainly women. Growth in employment has been in the secondary and tertiary sectors, and here the men are reluctant to join the LO, but rather choose independent associations.

In 1923, the LO Congress made a decision to speed up the process away from the craft-based structure and towards an industry-based one. This process has been slow, but there has been a steady reduction in the number of unions, usually through mergers (like the recent one when the diminishing Bricklayers union joined the Building Industry Workers Union) so that the total number of unions within the confederation today is 35. Following the development of North Sea oil- and gas-based industries, the LO launched a new Petrochemical Workers Union intended to cover all hierarchical levels and groups in this new sector. So far this union has not been very successful in competing with independent staff associations. This illustrates one of the LO's major problems: to extend operations to new areas covering new professions and particularly white collar employees outside the public sector. The LO's activities and membership are concentrated around the traditional industries and public employment, and only the latter sector is growing (Tables 2.2 and 2.3).

The Norwegian trade union federation is among the western world's most centralized, and has been moving towards more centralization since the beginning. Its central bodies, the Congress which meets every fourth year, the General Council and the Executive Board, make all policy decisions as well as maintaining strict control over the national unions which only have autonomy in internal matters, and in the settlement of local disputes. National unions have basically the same structure as the LO. 'As a rule national unions maintain strict control over its local branches. Invariably, it is the national union which conducts negotiations and conclude collective agreements, although important decisions made by the executive board of the union must be approved by the general council or by a referendum among the members'. (Norwegian ILO Committee, 1975.)

The Federation's central position is illustrated by the following:

A collective agreement cannot be terminated, new demands cannot be presented, a strike cannot be called without the approval of the Executive Board. When several unions are simultaneously engaged in bargaining, the federation invariably leads the negotiations. If a strike involves more than one union, the federation assumes command of the walkout, and no individual union may reach a settlement without the approval of LO's executive board. (Norwegian ILO Committee, 1975.)

In the late 1960s and the 1970s, new dimensions have been added to the central negotiations through extensive Labour Government involvement in the central collective bargaining ('package deals'). These include the use of subsidies, change in taxation levels, pricing of food, etc. to obtain a particular target in net spending power within the current forecast of economic growth and an acceptable rate of inflation. This development also clearly examplifies the LO's move towards using the corporatist link rather than direct bargaining.

2.3. Industrial conflicts and conflict-settlements

With the exception of the period between the two world wars, there has been little open conflict in Norwegian industry. From 1921 to 1939 26 million days were lost, 7.5 million days in one year alone; while the figure in the post-war period never has exceeded 1 million days in a single year. From 1950 to 1975, around 2 million working days were lost (Petersen, 1975) (Table 2.9).

Table 2.9
Registered strikes

	1949	1950	1955	1960	1964	1970	1975
No. of conflicts	47	30	22	12	3	15	22
No. of workers striking	9,010	4,399	9,971	656	230	3,133	3,282
No. of days lost	104,759	42,310	108,087	2,417	1,310	47,204	12,473

Source: Statistical Yearbooks 1967-1977.

Two years in the last 15 years' period, however, differ: 1961 with 423,082 days lost, and 1974 with 318,433 days lost. The number of unofficial strikes has been increasing, and some of these have occured in the public sector.

The principle of peace for the duration of a collective agreement goes back to the Labour Disputes Act, 1915. There is a distinction between 'conflicts of interest' and 'conflicts of rights'. The latter are disagreements about claims raised in connection with an existing collective agreement. Such disputes cannot be settled by work stoppage, but must be dealt with by the Labour Court whose word is final. Disputes of interests are submitted to a state mediator if agreement cannot be reached through direct bargaining. If all conciliation efforts fail, the parties can launch work stoppages.

In practice, this means that official strikes and lock-outs only take place after the expiration of a collective agreement. Stoppages for political demonstrations, however, may legally take place also within the period of duration of the agreement, but these have been infrequent. (The last large one occurred in 1970 when 500,000 workers staged a short work stoppage against the government's economic policy.) It is generally assumed that the link between the LO and the largely governing Labour Party explains some of the change towards industrial peace in the post-war period.

Another part of the explanation is derived from the legal framework covering industrial relations and the degree of centralization of the two main labour market organizations. The 1915 Labour Disputes Act established a system of mediation in conflicts of interests. Thus work stoppages in practice are always forbidden until mediation had been tried, and there is a 'cooling-off period' of four days before a strike or lock-out can take place. After mediation has started, another four days will pass before a work stoppage may take place. The ballot and its rules increase the chances of success for mediation. The national bargaining parties may use several sorts of ballots to cover the groups involved in the new agreement. Votes from the LO and the non-LO groups may be pooled, for example, before counting, for a simple majority. The national leaders agree on the need to avoid open conflicts because of the effects on the economy; the rules of the Labour Disputes Act have been adhered to, numerous amendments have been made to it with the single aim to find peaceful solutions to industrial disputes.

The provisions for compulsory arbitration, however, have been less in favour. After the Second World War, Wage Boards were in operation until 1952, when free collective bargaining again became the main principle. This did not lead to any increase in trade disputes. The ILO Committee (1975) explains this by referring to the responsible attitude of the organizations and the vulnerability of the Norwegian economy to strikes and lock-outs. In each single case a law must be passed by Parliament. None the less, compulsory arbitration was used by the government 56 times in the period 1952–1975 to settle disputes. Conflicts in transport and power supply have fairly frequently been resolved through compulsory arbitration. In the years 1964 and 1966 major parts of the biannual central collective bargaining also were submitted to legislation, but generally the number of wage earners affected by arbitration yearly has been modest and, as demonstrated, been concentrated to key sectors where stoppages have wide economic consequences. In the larger, manufacturing industries, with strong unions, arbitration has been very little used. In the spring of 1978 all national collective agreements were submitted to compulsory arbitration reflecting the employers' reluctance to meet wage demands in a deepening major economic recession. The pay and price freeze introduced by the Labour Government during the autumn of 1978 was intended to curb inflation, restore Norwegian industry's competitiveness, and thus to secure employment. This suspension of free collective bargaining rights has been accepted by the LO central bodies as well as by Parliament.

2.4. The Confederation of Employers (NAF)

The first confederation of employers of any size emerged in 1871, but was mainly preoccupied with protecting their crafts until the 1880s when the confederation became involved in the fight against demands of workers and their emerging trade unions. In 1896 a union of crafts and industry was formed and in 1900 the NAF was established. This was not a direct reaction to LO which was created the year before, but the conclusion of a process which started 20 years earlier (Ousland, 1975). In 1902 the NAF's members were 876 companies with 34,000 workers; and in 1920 the number had increased threefold and the number of workers doubled. By 1978 the number had reached to 9,100 companies with 377,000 employees, making the NAF by far the largest employers' confederation. It covers all the major employers, plus a very large number of small enterprises (if a company has less than four employers, membership is free). During 1977, numerous small employers joined in connection with new legislation on sick pay to workers. There are some other confederations of employers, but these are smaller and do not compete with the NAF.

According to the NAF's constitution, it is to act as a defence against the demands from employees — but it is also intended to work for 'good and lasting relations between employers and workers'. This should be done through considering fair demands from workers and their unions and rejecting unreasonable ones (Petersen, 1950). In 1975 the main objective for the association was formulated as securing a realistic development in payments in industry (Petersen, 1975). In the first period NAF was drawn into bargaining only when conflict had emerged locally. Today, NAF takes over and leads all local bargaining immediately when disagreement arises.

Conflict between LO and NAF culminated in 1931 with the 'Great Lock-out', and from then on the relationship has been changing towards peaceful solution of disputes. This is very much due to the ideological reorientation in LO in the 1920s and 1930s. After the October 1917 Revolution, the DNA was more left than other European sister-parties, and, in joining the third International in 1919, was the only social-democratic party that did not split over this issue (Bull, 1968). The NAF fought with all possible means against the LO whose aim was the immediate take-over of industry. Lock-outs, the use of the 'Prison Law' (a law making picketing an offence punished by prison), and calling in the police and the army against striking workers were among the more drastic methods used by the NAF. When the take-over of the means of production by the labour movement ideologically was postponed, co-operation rather than extended conflicts was accepted — 'there seems to be an emerging understanding also among workers that the employer as such has a function' wrote Petersen (1950), a conservative economist.

In the period from 1950 to 1975 the process towards a higher level of co-operation rather than conflict has continued. The development of participation in productivity committees and industrial democracy are used as examples of the changing atmosphere at company level. Joint participation by the two labour market organizations in national committees and boards is seen as indicative of the same process at the national level (Petersen, 1975).

2.5. The development of industrial democracy

Within the Norwegian Labour movement, the issue of industrial democracy has been on the agenda since the 1880s (Berg, et al., 1977). Until the First World War, however, most attention was being paid to organizing the workers in unions and to establish the basic rights of the unions and their members (job security, the right to bargain and make contracts, the rights of the shop stewards, the working conditions, payment, etc.). Around 1920, a law introducing workers' councils (originally a communist proposal based on the soviets in USSR) was passed, but never had any impact. The workers' councils as eventually defined by the new law would act as joint information bodies without the decision-making power of the soviets. After the Second World War productivity committees, used in the USA and Britain during the war, were introduced as part of the basic agreement. But the union leaders maintained that the new committees, which had advisory power, were seen as an important step towards socialism (Gullvåg, 1955; Lorenz, 1974).

During the 1950s and 1960s, the basic agreement was supplemented and expanded in the area of joint information and consultation (works councils, department councils, etc.). Since 1948, workers in some state-owned enterprises have nominated one member of the board of directors, but the general debate about industrial democracy did not reappear until the late 1950s. Then the LO and the Labour Party set up a joint committee to draft a proposal. In 1963 the committee's report was published recommending changes in four areas: (1) workers' representation in a new policy-making body in between the owners (share-holders) and the board of directors; (2) strengthening of the joint consultation system; (3) further education of workers to enable them to participate; and (4) redesigning the 'out-lived, undemocratic organizational set-up' of the industrial enterprises (Felleskomitéen LO/DNA, 1965).

At the same time, the LO together with the Employers Confederation jointly initiated research into industrial democracy. The first phase of this consisted of a study of experience of board-level representation in Norway and abroad. Thorsrud and Emery (1964, 1969) who carried out the study were negative about board representation as a means of increasing the employees' influence over the enterprise. Their critique was mainly centred around the strategic aspects of industrial democracy. They claimed that board-representation seemed to have little effect as seen by the average union member, that structural changes in the ownership of industry and in the environment made *management's* (rather than the boards') decisions more central for the workers, and finally that board-membership created a problematic role-conflict for the employees' representatives. Thorsrud and Emery suggested an alternative strategy that could be tested experimentally in different sectors. The main idea was to work up from the shop floor — starting with concrete changes in the work situation in production (increased workers autonomy, training, technological and related changes, etc.) to allow workers to have a higher degree of control over the production process. Such changes were seen as a first step in a strategy of reform which later was expected to have ramifications both at higher managerial and union level, as well as outside the sector (the family, the local community, and the educational system). The suggestions were approved, with leaders of the national organization helping in the selection of companies for the experiments, and a series of projects were carried out in the period 1965-9 (Thorsrud & Emery, 1969, Emery & Thorsrud, 1976). At this stage the policy-makers thought that the results were very promising and decided that a general diffusion of ideas and solutions should take place in industry supported by aid from centre (training, information, consultancy, and research). A very slow 'low-profile' diffusion process has been going on since then, while the political discussion in the early 70's again has been concentrated among *legislation* for board-level representation and improved working environment.

In the 1960s the bourgeois coalition government and its majority in Parliament stopped the reform process but with Labour back in power a number of new laws have been passed. From 1973 employees have had the right to minority (one-third) representation at the board level in manufacturing industries. The new Working Environment Act from 1977, which replaces the old Workers' Safety Act, calls for higher standards in a number of areas, including the psychological, social, and political areas that were originally taken up in the experiments in the 1960s. Participation by the employees in the implementation of the new act is compulsory and represents a new trend in Norwegian legislation. Greater influence over decisions affecting one's own working conditions is seen both as a part of a good working environment as well as a necessary condition for improvements in the social and psychological field (Gustavsen, 1977).

Around 1972, the basic agreement was also modified to support the spread of ideas from these experiments. When this question came up for legislation there was broad political support in Parliament indicating a change in political thinking in the liberal and conservative parties as well. Other sectors — commerce, shipping, banking, insurance, newspapers, construction etc., which to a large extent are outside the LO-NAF area — have also been subjected to democratization in different forms after 1973. For the public sector (state, municipalities, etc.) a committee has submitted a proposal for increased employee participation. Another committee, to look into the question of local political representation in the governing bodies of industrial enterprises, presented its proposals in 1977 (NOU, 1977:28). The majority recommended participation on the boards of directors from the local communities plus improved communication between firms and local politicans. These proposals received very little support and are no longer on the political agenda.

2.6. Participation within companies

Traditionally participation by employees has been secured through national collective agreements until 1973 when the Company Act was changed to allow for board representation. Several bodies for participation are specified by the agreement for the private manufacturing industries. To set up a Works Council (W.C.) more than 100 employees are needed and should have ten members; if there are more than 400 employees, it should have fourteen. If one of the parties demands and the main organizations (unions, employers) agree, a W.C. may be established for less than 100 employees. Half of the members should be elected by management; the other half by the different groups of employees through their local unions. The Council has information and consultation functions and has no power to make decisions, the emphasis being on productivity and the well-being of employees; it may not deal with wage bargaining. In principle information on all important changes related to the employees should be given, but management may demand confidentiality in specific cases.

Department Councils (DC) may be established if more than 200 employees are involved. It is composed of, at the minimum, a manager, the local chief shop steward, and at least one representative from foremen/supervisors in the department. In addition the parties may decide to extend membership and may ask others to attend the meetings. It should deal with the same issues as the Works Council with special bearing on the department, and concentrate on budgets, plans, reports, and measures to improve production, but has only advisory power with the exception of matters that are related solely to the department, provided that management has agreed to transfer power.

Together, the local union representatives make up the local shop steward comittee, the counterpart of management at the plant level, where most of the conflicts are solved through direct negotiations. In larger establishments, there is usually a departmental shop-steward committee. There is also a central union committee at corporate level built up by chief shop stewards from each unit. (As mentioned the *regional* trade union system is not emphasized and is rather unimportant in matters concerning labour–management relations.) Local union leaders are automatic members of Departmental and Works Councils. Shop stewards have special protection against dismissal and have a number of special rights, for example the use of company time for union work, the right to demand meetings with management, etc. They are elected for one year by the local (plant-level) union members.

The old Accidents Prevention Act, last modified in 1956, specified Safety Committees and safety representatives, but did not make it compulsory to have workers' representatives in the committees, nor to channel all safety matters through them. This act was replaced by the Work Environment Act in 1977 which goes much further in securing employee participation. The employees have half of the seats, and every second year they also elect the chairman so that they have a majority over management's representatives. In addition, the power of the Safety Committee (now named Environment and Safety Committee) and safety representatives has been substantially increased.

Through the Company Act, employees since 1973 have the right to elect one third (at least 2) members of the Board of Directors (if more than 50 and less than 200 employees), and to elect one-third (at least 4) of the members of the new Corporate Assembly (CA) (if more than 200). The remaining two-thirds are still elected by the owners and shareholders. The CA has at least 12 members.

In this two-tier system the highest ranking one, the Corporate Assembly, is a new body, created with the purpose of electing the Board of Directors, to supervise this Board, and to have the final say in matters involving large investments (large in relation to the company's total assets) or significant changes in the size of the workforce. In these two areas shareholders cannot over-rule the decisions of the Assembly.

According to Norwegian legislation, day-to-day management is the responsibility of the general manager, whose functions and responsibilities are different from those of the board of directors. The board of directors is usually composed of external directors supposed to look after the interests of the shareholders (Gustavsen, 1972). The general manager takes part in the board meetings but until the employees themselves obtained board representation was not usually a board member. The idea of having the Corporate Assembly goes back to 1963 and the joint LO/DNA committee which wanted a new body to decide upon the long term policies of the company and to secure employee influence on these.

If there is local disagreement over the implementation of the rules of the Company Act giving board representation, a national Industrial Democracy (ID) Board (composed by representatives from LO, NAF and the Department of Labour) will settle the matter. Generally there has been little disagreement over the Act, but the ID Board has in a large number of cases made local adaptations if these have been supported by all parties. These adaptions have mainly concerned election rules so that employees in different locations all may be represented.

2.7. The main bargaining structure

According to the Basic Agreement disagreement should be settled through negotiations between the employer and the employees' elected shop stewards. If agreement cannot be reached, representatives from the unions and employers confederation are drawn into the local negotiations. If agreement still cannot be reached, negotiations between the central organizations will take place, but the main rule is that disputes should be settled at the lowest possible level. After having reached the highest level, the dispute may follow one of the channels: if it is a dispute over rights, i.e. the interpretation of rules or sometimes the spirit of the rules, the conflict will be referred to voluntary arbitration or to the Labour Court. On the other hand, if it is a dispute over interests, a solution is first sought through mediation, which then automatically gives a cooling-off period of 16 days. A proposal from the mediator may be voted on, with or without the recommendation of the parties. If rejected there are two possibilities, either a strike or a lockout (and new mediation after 30 days) or compulsory arbitration. In the latter case the National Payment Board is drawn in by the Government and a decision is made which constitutes the new agreement.

Union strength varies between industries and sectors. The Iron and Metal Workers Union is usually considered the strongest and is traditionally well represented in top LO positions. All workers' unions, with the exception of those attached to mobile or temporary work-places have high membership rates, usually in the region of 90–100 per cent although membership in principle is voluntary. The LO-affiliated white-collar unions are weak in privately owned enterprises, while strong in the public services.

Politically, the LO is considered a legitimate interest party in all sectors of political life and, together with the Confederation of Employers, nominates representatives for national boards, committees, working parties, etc. (Rokkan, 1972). This can clearly be seen as a consequence of the social-democratic policy and of the simple non-pluralistic structure of Norwegian society. In the long periods of Labour majority, almost no political decisions would be made without the LO being at least consulted and giving its support. None the less, it has been losing strength in terms of relative membership as groups of non-organized and non-LO organized white-collar workers have been growing at a faster rate (Karlsen, 1977). State intervention in the settlement of disputes is fairly frequent. As mentioned, this takes the form of tripartite national collective bargaining and the use of compulsory arbitration to protect the public interest.

3. PROGRAMMATIC PERSPECTIVES, PROBLEMATIC ISSUES AND DEVELOPMENTS

Norwegian politics are generally pragmatic, and public, theoretical, political discussions are quite infrequent. Stability is the best characterization of the political situation particularly as the impact of the EEC debate and the referendum seems gone. The legitimacy of the national institutions is generally without challenge (Torgersen, 1975). The Labour Party won the 1977 election on a programme where full employment, social security, and moderate material growth were the central policies, and the liberals who attempted to introduce a 'green alternative' were almost wiped out. The left wing, which propagates among other things, reduced private consumption, strengthened control over industry, channelling of oil incomes to developing countries, and, most importantly departure from the traditional US–NATO orientation in foreign politics, suffered a similar reduction in popularity. These events indicate little change in central Norwegian politics, at least on a short-term perspective.

In industrial relations, it is very unlikely that a conservative/liberal majority in Parliament, and hence in government following the clear long-term trend in favour of these parties, would make much difference apart from probably slowing down the pace of legal reforms. Before the parliamentary election in 1977, the Conservatives promised to revoke the bank 'deprivatization' act before it became effective, but this issue did not play any major part in the election campaigns.

The impression of stability, however, is what is seen in observing the decision-making processes at the national level. In this chapter, we have mainly been concerned with the industrial relations in male-dominated manufacturing industries and the large centralized organizations involved in this sector. Among the Labour Party and LO leaders, there are few signs that any major developments will be initiated in industrial relations. It was agreed in 1977 to create a new

Labour/LO committee to look into a further democratization of industry, and there is some interest in a revision of sections of the legislation covering industrial relations (for example, the Industrial Disputes Act). Part of this interest is derived from the recent Swedish co-determination laws. Pressure for these reforms seems mild, and though experience with recent reforms like board representation is positive, no major shift in power distribution has followed (Engelstad and Qvale, 1977). Employee ownership is still being rejected by the LO leaders, but there is growing support for other alternatives to the capitalist forms. The Basic Agreement is continuously being amended, and in the most recent (1978) revision shop stewards' status is again being strengthened. The LO's leaders have announced their interests in increasing its involvement in further education, in leisure and recreation activities, and in finding new pension/ retirement arrangements etc. Any advance in this direction is likely to be delayed by the emerging recession. There are signs, though still unclear, that some of the larger manufacturing unions do want more autonomy from the LO.

In national collective bargaining, the main issues are the relative low wages in low profit industries, and the large wage-drift in the profitable ones. The problem of low pay is a threat to the solidarity within the LO, and high wage drift makes national collective bargaining over pay rather unimportant in other sectors. During 1978 there has been a growing consensus on the need to reduce national private consumption. The unions now put the highest priority on employment security, and seem to accept that only the lowest paid and the old-age pensioners can expect any relative improvement during the next few years. The Labour Government's recent attempts to attract foreign companies to Norway by offering partnerships in North Sea developments and/or oil deliveries are motivated by the need to create jobs when traditional industries like shipbuilding and seafaring fail.

There are certain trends indicating possible qualitative change in Norway. Although Norway seems a highly non-pluralistic society, populist traits are still observable, and seem to be increasing in strength. Reactions against central control from the districts, which are less depopulated than in most other industrial countries, is growing. In addition migration to the urbanized areas has now stopped. The disagreement over the pace and form of the development of the oil industry exemplifies the important centre-periphery discussion. Fear of negative impact on local communities and fishing and the risk for blow-outs etc. already has delayed oil explorations by several years. Local action groups with broad political backing are immediately formed when the question of the location in an area of hydro-electric, thermal or nuclear power plants arises.

More clearly within industrial relations, we find the reactions against bureaucratization of the trade unions' own organization. The left-wing socialist party is developing its alternative to the policies of the Labour Party by emphasizing local bargaining and rights to take action (e.g. strikes) rather than the existing, centralized conflict resolution and the use of the corporative channels. So far, the Labour movement and the establishment have no reply to this critique apart from claiming there is more to gain through central political action than through increased local activity.

Probably the clearest indicator of change is seen in the feminist movement, gaining momentum over the last decade, and very strongly representing alternative values and strategies to those of the central established organizations. Women have won around 25 per cent of the seats in Parliament and in municipalities, and their participation in education is now level with that of men. The challenge from this group is not reflected in the labour market organizations, the large parties or in the composition of central bodies such as policy-making committees, boards, etc. (Skard, 1979). Together with the relative weakening of the LO despite its increase in corporate power, and the emergence of large, independent staff associations who so far largely have been kept outside central politics, women may constitute the strongest national dynamic factor in the industrial relations area in the future.

In the short term, however, the present sudden interruption of national economic growth, which had lasted the whole post-war period, may have serious impact on industrial relations. It is reasonable to assume that the continuing centralization of control in the country and within the labour market organizations has been a factor both in Norway's economic growth and in the relatively equal distribution of welfare within the nation. In a lasting recession, the policies of the Labour Party which linked trade unions to state intervention in collective bargaining will create serious tensions within the unions, and between farmers and industrial workers. Signs are already to be seen.

REFERENCES

Aubert, V. (1975), 'Sosiale klasser og lag'. In Ramsøy, N. R. & Vaa, M. (eds.), *Der norske samfunn*. Oslo: Gyldendal.
Berg, P. O., Eskild, A. & Webster, R. (1977), *Reglene om bedriftsdemokratiet*. Oslo: Tiden.
Brox, O. (1966), *Hva skjer i Nord-Norge?* Oslo: Pax.
Bull, E. (1968), *Norsk Fagbevegelse. Oversikt over fagorganisasjonens historie*, 2.utg., Oslo: Tiden.
Central Bureau of Statistics (1946-1977), *Statistical Yearbooks*. Oslo.
    (1969), *Historical Statistics, 1968*. Oslo.
    (1965), *The Norwegian Post War Economy*. Oslo.
    (1972), *Nasjonalregnskapet 1954–1970*. Oslo.
    (1975), *Education background of the Population*. Oslo.
    (1978), *Statistisk Ukehefte S.U.* Nr. 5. Oslo.
    (1978), *Statistisk Ukehefte S.U.* Nr. 16. Oslo.
Emery, F. E. & Thorsrud, E. (1969), *Form and content in industrial democracy*. London: Tavistock.
Emery, F. E. & Thorsrud, E. (1976), *Democracy at work*. Leiden: Nijhoff.
Engelstad, P. H. & Qvale, T. U. (1977), *Innsyn og innflytelse i Styre og Bedrifts-forsamling*. Oslo: Tiden.
Felleskomitéen/LO/DNA (1965), *Instilling om demokrati i arbeidslivet*. Oslo.
Fivelsdal, E. & Higley, J. (1970), 'The Labour Union Elite in Norway'. In Ruin, O. (ed.): *Scandinavian Political Studies*. Vol. 5. Oslo: Universitets-forlaget.
Furre, B. (1972), *Norsk Historie 1905–1940*. Oslo: Det norske samlaget.
Galtung, J. (1968), 'Norge i verdenssamfunnet'. In Ramsøy, R. R. & Vaa, M. (eds.), *Det norske samfunn*. Oslo: Gyldendal.
Gullvåg, H. (1955), Posisjon og innstillinger hos industriarbeidere. Nordisk Psykologis monografiserie. nr. 6., Oslo.

Gustavsen, B. (1972), *Industristyret.* Oslo: Tanum.

Gustavsen, B. (1977), 'A legislative approach to job reform in Norway'. *International Labour Review,* 115: No. 3.

Higley, J., Field, G. L. & Groholt, K. (1976), *Elite Structure and Ideology.* Oslo: Universitetsforlaget.

Karlsen, J. I., Naess, R., Ryste, Ø., Seierstad, S., Sørensen, B. Aa. (1975), *Arbeidsmiljø og vernearbeid.* Oslo: Tiden.

Karlsen J. I., Qvale, T. U., & Lange, K. (1971), *Tariffstridige aksjoner.* Oslo: Work Research Institutes.

Karlsen, J. E. (1977), *Hva skjer i fagbevegelsen?* Oslo: Tiden.

Kommunal Og Arbeidsdepartementet (1977), 'Oversikt over tvungne og frivillige lønnsnevnder'. Oslo: KAD (mimeo).

Lindbekk, T. (1975), 'Utdannelse'. In Ramsøy, N. R. & Vaa, M. (eds.), *Det norske samfunn.* Oslo: Gyldendal.

Lorenz, E. (1974), *LO – 75 år.* Oslo: Pax.

Norwegian ILO-Committee (1975), 'Labour Relations in Norway'. Oslo: The Norwegian Joint Committee in International Social Policy.

NOU (1977), 'Kommunal representasjon i bedriftene'. Norges Offentlige utredninger 1977: 28. Oslo: Universitetsforlaget.

OECD, National accounts of OECD countries.

OECD (1976), Main Economic Indicators. February.

Ousland, G. (1974–5), *Fagorganisasjonen i Norge,* Vol. I–III. Oslo: Tiden.

Petersen, E. (1950), *Norsk Arbeidsgiverforening gjennom femti ar. 1900–1950.* Oslo: Norsk Arbeidsgiverforening.

(1975), *Norsk Arbeidsgiverforening 1950–1975.* Oslo: Norsk Arbeidsgiverforening.

Rasmussen, T. F. (1975), *The Economically active population in Norway.* Oslo: Central Bureau of Statistics.

Rokkan, S. (1972), *Numerical Democracy and Corporate Pluralism. Politisk aktivitet og struktur.* Oslo: Universitetsforlaget.

Seierstad, S. (1975), 'Norsk økonomi'. In Ramsøy, N. R. & Vaa, M. (eds.), *Den norske samfunn.* Oslo: Gyldendal.

Skard, T. (1979), 'Progress for women. Increased female representation in political élites in Norway'. In Epstein, C. F. & Coser, R. L. (eds.), *Access to Power: Cross-national Studies of Women and Elites.* London: Allen & Unwin (forthcoming).

St.meld.nr.61 (1976–7), Om inntektsforderling og skattepolitikk. Oslo: Finans og tolldepartmentet.

Thorsrud, E. & Emery, F. E. (1964), *Industrielt demokrati.* Oslo: Universitetsforlaget.

(1969), *Mot en ny bedriftsorganisasjon.* Oslo: Tanum.

Torgersen, V. (1975), 'De politiske institusjonene'. In Ramsøy, N. R. & Vaa, M. (eds.), *Det norske samfunn.* Oslo: Gyldendal.

United Nations (1975), *Statistical Yearbook.*

Valen, H. (1976), 'National conflict structures and foreign politics. The impact of the EEC issues on perceived cleavages in Norwegian politics'. *European Journal of Political Research.*

3

THE SWEDISH INDUSTRIAL RELATIONS SYSTEM

1. GENERAL SITUATION AND BACKGROUND

The Swedish Social Democratic Party was in government between 1932 and 1976, some years with a majority of its own in parliament and most of the time with a socialist majority. Despite this, the labour legislation regulating employee participation remained unchanged until the 1970s, the basic principle going back to the turn of the century. But during the 1970s, when the political position of the Social Democratic Party has been relatively weak, we have witnessed a flood of new labour legislation.

Our aim is to present the legal basis for employee participation, individual and collective, in decision-making in firms, and its historical background and its connection with the economic, social, and political development. Special regard is paid to the reorientation of industrial relations during the 1970s.

Some limitations must be explained. Firstly, labour legislation is dealt with generally. Regulations applying only to a few decision areas are omitted. Consequently, most of the rules included here have a procedural character involving the relationship between the actors–employer and employees and their respective organizations. Material rules directly prescribing the conditions within a decision area are left aside. Secondly, we have restricted ourselves to the 'private' sector, thus leaving aside regulations for those employed in public administration, education, and health services, with an emphasis on industry. Thirdly, we treat a situation valid in autumn 1980. Things may change rapidly. Sweden has serious external and internal economic problems and comprehensive debate about wage earners' funds and negotiations on a co-determination agreement for the privately owned firms and on a proposal for union meetings to be allowed during working hours are continuing. Lastly, we are aware that the distribution of material wealth and decision-influence between the employees and the employer are affected by many other factors than the legal.

1.1. Economic and Industrial Structure

Sweden is a large country with a small population; a little over 8 million and a population density of 20 inhabitants per square km. Population growth during the post-war years has been steady. The number of immigrants has been high both in absolute and relative numbers, averaging 30,000 respectively, a little below 1/2 per cent per year, with much higher figures mainly during the second half of the 1960s. (SCB, 1969b: 46-9; SCB, 1972b: 15; SCB, 1975: 86; SCB, 1976: 85; SOU, 1967: 18.)

During the post-war years, the gross domestic product has increased faster than at any other time. During the first half of the 1960s, the growth rate was especially high, while during the 1970s it has decreased noticeably.

Table 3.1
Gross domestic product, average growth per year 1861–1975 (percentage)

A		B	
1861–90	2.3	1950–5	3.0
1891–1915	3.6	1955–60	3.3
1921–40	3.5	1960–5	5.1
1946–65	4.3	1965–70	4.0
		1970–5	2.9

Source: A: Åberg, 1969: 17, 191. B: SOU, 1962–10: 86; SOU, 1975–89: 111.

Seen in a longer perspective Sweden, like other industrial countries, has gone through decisive structural changes. Table 3.2 shows how the importance of the agrarian sector has decreased all the time, and how the industrial sector has grown without interruption until the post-war years when it was outflanked by the service sector.

Table 3.2
Production and population in agriculture. industry, and other sectors 1910–1970 (in per cent)

		Agriculture	Industry	Others
1910	Production	25	32	43
	Population	49	32	19
1930	Production	13	43	44
	Population	39	36	25
1950	Production	12	49	30
	Population	20	41	39
1970	Production	4	46	50
	Population	8	40	52

Source: Jörberg & Krantz, 1975: 7.

The sectoral changes have taken place in a manner surprisingly smooth. The switch from agriculture to industry has, to a high degree, been supported by the agricultural, industrial, and labour policies of all governments. Immigration policy has also facilitated the growth of industry. The groups in the labour market have not only accepted but also pushed for this development. The change from goods to service production has been more controversial as it has implied a growth of the public sector, primarily the communal part. It is mostly after 1960 that the public sector has grown; 1960–75 the employment share of the sector increased from 12 to 25 per cent (SOU, 1975–89: 174). This growth has been pushed in the first place by the Social Democratic Party, generally accepted by the other political parties. However, there have been a few questions that have caused deep political conflicts.

As a small and highly industrialized country, Sweden is dependent on the international division of labour. This dependency has increased considerably during the post-war years: the import–export ratio of the gross domestic product now amounts to 1/3. Exports are to a large extent concentrated to a few large industrial firms. In 1975, the 10 largest export firms were responsible for 1/3 of total exports, the 25 largest firms for almost 50 per cent (SCB, 1976b; Veckans affärer, 1976: 24–33). Not only production but also capital has been internationalized during these years. Foreign-owned companies employed 42,000 people in 1970. This amounted to just under 5 per cent of the total number employed in industry; a much higher percentage exists in the chemical industry's subsidiary branches. At the same time Swedish-affiliated producing companies abroad employed 182,000 people, many of the large ones having more than half of their employees abroad. (Lundgren, 1975; Samuelsson, 1977; Swedenborg, 1973.)

The Swedish economic system must be considered a market economy. Within the agricultural sector, which is privately owned, pricing is controlled by agreement between the government and the farmers' organizations. Industry is not regulated to any noteworthy extent and public ownership is marginal. On the other hand, the service sector is subject to both public control and public ownership. There were tendencies both towards increased liberalism and towards socialism during post-war years. Direct control has been gradually removed while the public sector has grown and public responsibility for economic development has increased (Lindbeck, 1975: 255–8).

Within the industrial sector, there have also been considerable structural changes. The textile industry has decreased drastically and the machine industry increased its already high share and now accounts for approximately 45 per cent of industrial production. This change has been facilitated by both political and labour market parties. The selective labour market policy has aimed at switching employees from less to more productive branches. This has caused in turn the social and regional problems first noted during the 1960s. The Swedish trade union movement has been a unique driving force behind these structural alterations. Later, we will show how the takeover in 1932 of the Social Democrats meant that the trade unions paid more attention to the economic development.

The tendency towards concentration and centralization, which have been significant in most areas since the war (Dahlström, 1976:17), applies also to the size and structure of work-places. The average number employed in a work-place has increased from 34 to 75 with large branch differences. The average number of white-collar workers has increased twice as fast as that of blue-collar workers, which means just under 3 blue-collars to every white-collar in 1975 against just over 5 in 1945 (SCB, 1945: 120–1; SCB, 1956: 122–5; SCB, 1965: 127–9; SCB, 1974: 127–9). If we go from the work-place to the business, the concentration tendency here have been strengthened by amalgamation. After a quiet beginning in the 1950s, the number of mergers increased fourfold during the 1960s maintaining this level during the 1970s. During the 1960s, the merged firms accounted each year for 3 per cent of employment and production (Rydén, 1971: 56, 208-9). On average in 1970, the largest firm had 40 per cent of production in its industry, the 4 largest 70 per cent, and the 8 largest 80 per cent. Variation between branches was very large. Import competition varied significantly, but with an average for industry as a whole of 25 per cent (SPK, 1972: 5-6; SOU, 1968-5: 13-29, 51-113; Wibe, 1976: 16-26).

Owner-concentration is significant in industry, 90 per cent of which is privately owned, the remainder being small state and co-operative concerns. Though large firms are dominated by powerful private interests, these firms are vital to the Swedish economy. In 1963 the 17 foremost finance-families had majority or strong minority interests in 343 firms with at least 500 employees each; together those employed in these companies accounted for 55 per cent of all the employed in firms of this size. Firms where the 17 families had majority or strong minority interests represent 36 per cent of the industrial production. Certain ownership groups have disappeared from the scene and new ones have appeared since 1963, but the picture of increasing concentration is mostly the same. (SOU, 1968-7; Hermansson, 1962, 1979; Lindström & Nordin, 1977; LO, 1976a; Lundh, 1973; Odnoff, 1967; SIND, 1980: 5.)

The increased concentration within industry has not only been accepted but also encouraged by the government and the labour market parties. In 1970, however, the social democrats and the communists as well as the trade union movement started to advocate a reduction of the power of the employers to the advantage of the employees. One strategy during the 1970s has been to strengthen the rights of the workers at the expense of capital, and all the new labour legislation can be seen as an expression of this. Another strategy, which has been hotly debated since 1975, is to acquire influence by taking over capital through wage earners' funds.

Like the gross domestic product, industrial production has increased rapidly during the greater part of the post-war period. As seen from Table 3.3, the productivity increase was highest during the 1960s.

Table 3.3
Industrial productivity, average growth per year 1945-75 (percentage)

1950-5	1955-60	1960-5	1965-70	1970-5
2.3	2.7	7.1	7.3	4.6

Sources: SOU, 1962-10: 85-7; SOU, 1975-89: 205.

The elimination of less productive firms has been facilitated by the labour market policy. Capital investment per working hour increased substantially and the producitivity of capital has risen as well as the employees' level of education (SOU, 1975-89: 69-78, 195-210). What weight different factors have had is difficult to say, but they all have increased the intensity of labour utilization.

1.2. Living and Working Conditions

One-third of the population is concentrated in the three big urban areas Stockholm, Gothenburg, and Malmö. The three most northernly regions, with two-thirds of the surface, have not more than 20 per cent of the population. More than three-quarters of the population now live in the densely populated areas against one-half in 1930. Growth of population in these three urban areas is to a large extent a reflection of commercial and industrial development there (SCB, 1945: 14-5; SCB, 1975: 23; SCB, 1975b: 10).

The working life of men increased slowly until 1920 and then slowly diminished due to longer education in youth and earlier pension age and is now 87 per cent. The proportion of women in the labour force has risen since the beginning of the century, especially 1910-30 and 1950-70, and is now 72 per cent. Both figures refer to the age group 16-64 years (SCB, 1974b: 101; SCB, 1979b). The growth of women employed outside home has gone hand in hand with the growth of the service sector. Women are under-represented in goods production and over-represented in the service producing areas; within the public sector they are very much over-represented (SOU, 1975-89: 177). This growth is the result of an equalization between men and women, the development of the public child-care service, and the policy to facilitate womens' entrance into the labour market.

The gross domestic product per capita has grown to one of the highest in the world. At the same time a consecutive equalizing of income has taken place, irrespective if one counts before or after taxation, with or without social transfers (SOU, 1975-9: 324-9). The Swedes consider themselves having a relatively high level of welfare (Ahrne, 1976). In a comparative study of the Nordic countries, Allardt (1975) has shown that Sweden not only has the highest standard of living, but also the greatest accomplishment of community relations and self-realization. However, large groups of people are excluded from this welfare (Johansson, 1971).

Table 3.4

Gross national product per capita (dollars)

1960	1965	1970	1975
1,865	2,708	4,109	8,459

Source: UN, 1969, 1976.

Table 3.5

Class structure in 1930 and 1965 (percentage)

	1930	1965
Working class in a strict sense	41	39
Working class in a broad sense	55	53
Burgeoisie (and related groups)	4	3
Petite bourgeoisie (small business men, farmers)	31	14
Intermediate social groups	10	28

Source: Therborn, 1973.

The working class is nearly as large at the end of the period as at the beginning. The small business groups and the farmers have decreased while the intermediate social groups — technicians, teachers, medical and nursing personnel — have increased to a corresponding degree (cf. also SCB, 1976c: 52).

Allardt's investigation shows that experiences of social contradictions are rather strong in Sweden (Allardt, 1975: 132):

Probably this has its background in that the Swedish labour movement has a large and unitary strength in the social democrats' great dominance. The consciousness of contradictions and above all class differences has been maintained during the years. This implies that Sweden cannot to any great extent be regarded as a privatized community. Conflicts and unease are covered in political and most of all class terms.

In contrast to citizens in the other Nordic countries the Swedes believe that they are dealt with more equally (Allardt, 1975: 135). Himmelstrand (1977: 33) summarizes:

the Swedish working class, in subjective terms, is prepared for rather profound structural transformations of Swedish society, while at the same time indicating a sense of material affluence and a sense of trust in the system which will channel demands for societal change through union activity and democratic political participation. But also among the middle-class strata social consciousness exhibits a greater understanding of the structural contradictions of capitalism to suggest some degree of receptiveness to demands for structural transformatins of Swedish society.

Unemployment has, during the entire post-war period, been kept to a low level with an average of 1½ per cent. During economic recession it has risen to 2 per cent, twice to 2½ per cent. This is a result of the expansionist economic policy the Social Democratic governments have pursued since the 1930s, mostly supported by the opposition. During the 1970s it has been the non-socialist parties that have advocated and effected such an expansionist policy. The labour market policy has played an increasingly important role. In spite of this, differences remain concerning age, sex, and regions. Youth unemployment has been especially serious during recent years; 15.6 per cent of all those employed have been unemployed at least once during the last five years. The corresponding figure for the age group 16-24 years is 31.5 per cent and in the three most northernly regions 18.8, 18.2, 21.5 per cent respectively (SCB, 1976c: 151-4).

During the 1970s, the working week has been shortened to 40 hours. Of the full-time employed only 56 per cent work a maximum of 8 hours a day considering overtime, extra work, etc. If the breaks for lunch etc. and the journey to and from the work-place are included, then it is only 7 per cent of all full-time employed who work the maximum of 8 hours per day, while 62 per cent work 8-10 hours/day and 30 per cent more than 10 hours per day. Eighty per cent work during the daytime. Primarily parts of the service sector show lower figures. Seven and a half per cent have different kinds of shift work; in industry the corresponding figure for production workers is 22.5 per cent (SCB, 1976c: 118-24, 334, 348).

It has been shown that 5-10 per cent of the working population are troubled by heat, cold, draught, and bad ventilation and a further 15-20 per cent are to some extent. Within industry the figure is doubled; 15 per cent say they have very dirty work, also here the figure is doubled for industrial workers. Also with regard to noise, the conditions in industry are very bad compared to other work-places. Of industrial workers, 50 per cent have unsuitable working positions. For all employed, the figure is 20 per cent lower. Forty per cent of industrial workers, and 20 per cent of all employed, regard their work as monotonous. On the other hand, 20 per cent of the industrial workers consider their job as a strain psychologically against 30 per cent for all employed. The job, not the branch of industry, appears to be decisive. (SCB, 1976c: 194-6, 212-13, 219, 250-1.)

On the influence a worker has on arranging working hours, deciding rest periods, appointing an immediate boss, deciding the holiday period, selection of work-mates, respectively 60, 42, 81, 27, and 69 per cent of all the employed say that they have no influence. For industrial workers, the situation is even worse: on the five questions 78, 62, 86, 47, and 80 per cent respectively say that they have no influence. With the exception of one area, the difference is almost 20 per cent. Higher appointments, as expected, mean more influence. Influence becomes negative when the work-place becomes larger. The lower the appoint-ment and the larger the work-place, the higher the proportion of the employed showing an instrumental attitude to work. Amongst industrial workers the fre-quence is 55 per cent against 30 per cent for all employed. (SCB, 1976c: 270-5, 279-81, 285-7.)

Even if the workers' protection laws, with roots far back into the nineteenth century, is the oldest labour legislation, the working conditions at the work-place have mostly been neglected by the government, by the political parties, and to a surprisingly large extent also by the labour market parties. It was not until the 1960s that the Swedish Confederation of Trade Unions (LO) became active in the work environment area and in a series of studies indicated bad work-ing conditions in different branches of industry. In 1970 an official investigation was initiated, in 1974 the 1949 Workers' Protection Act was amended and in 1978 a new Work Environment Act came into force. Once the development started at the end of the 1960s, it has proceeded rapidly and the labour market parties have in the whole agreed on the steps necessary to take. (LO, 1966b; SOU, 1972-86; SOU, 1976-1, 2 and 3.)

1.3. Political System

The political system consists of three levels: local community, regional council and central government. Even if the local and regional self-government rests on a long and solidly rooted tradition, it is indisputably the government which is the most important poltical element. Its significance has increased parallel to the centralization and concentration in other parts of society.

Since 1970 the parliament had contained one chamber, in the old parliament the second chamber played the decisive role. The government is elected on a parlia-mentary basis. Most central administration is carried out by boards which have, a very independent position vis-a-vis both parliament and government. Also on the regional (county) level the governmental administration plays a decisive role. On the local level the administration is carried out by communal bodies, often within the framework of detailed government instructions. The importance of the local and regional levels lies in the conditions they create for different types of activities and employment, though they have very little to do with specific conditions at the work-places.

Political development has been exceedingly stable since the beginning of the nineteenth century, which 'effectfully contrasts with Sweden's quick and, during earlier periods, rather leaping economic development' (Allardt, 1975: 71).

During the whole post-war period, the Social Democrats have been the largest party with between 42.7 and 50.1 per cent of the votes. Only in 1968 they have reached a majority of their own in the electorate. Together with the communists the social democrats have reached a majority of votes, with the exception of 1956-60 and from 1973 onwards. Nor have the social democrats had a majority of their own in parliament (including the second chamber until 1970), with the exception of 1945-8 and 1968-70. As is seen from Table 3.6 the communist vote meant that the non-socialist parties have had a majority only in 1956-8, before they gained a majority in 1976. The parliamentary election in 1973 resulted in a dead-heat between the non-socialists and the socialists.

Table 3.6
Parliament from 1945 (number of seats in the second chamber 1945-70, in the single chamber 1970-9)

	Conservatives	Centre party	Liberals	Social democ.	Communists	Non-social.	Socialists
1945-8	39	35	26	115	15	100	130
1949-52	23	30	57	112	8	110	120
1953-6	31	26	58	110	5	115	115
1957-8	42	19	58	106	6	119	112
1959-60	45	32	38	111	5	115	116
1961-4	39	34	40	114	5	113	119
1965-8	33	36	43	113	8	112	121
1969-70	32	39	34	125	3	105	128
1971-3	41	71	58	163	17	170	180
1974-6	51	90	34	156	19	175	175
1976-9	55	86	39	152	17	180	169
1979-	73	64	38	154	20	175	174

Source: SCB, 1976: 406.

Though the social democrats only twice had a majority of their own in parliament, they continued in office until the change of government in 1976. The years 1951-7 they were in coalition with the Centre Party (which explains why there was not a non-socialist government in 1956-8), while at all other times they have been able to rely upon the communists who prefer a social democratic government to a non-socialist one.

2. NATIONAL INDUSTRIAL RELATIONS SYSTEM

2.1. The Labour Market Organizations

As mentioned, 90 per cent of firms are privately owned. Most of them are members of the employer organization, the Swedish Employers' Confederation (SAF). The few state-owned firms are organized in the Collective Bargaining Board for State-owned Enterprises, and the few co-operative-owned firms in the Collective Bargaining Organization for Co-operative Employers. In contrast to the employers, the employees are not organized according to these three sectors, but most of the blue- and white-collar workers are organized by the Swedish Confederation of Trade Unions (LO) and the Swedish Central Organization of Salaried Employees (TCO).

The LO was founded in 1898 on the initiative of the Social Democratic Workers' Party (which was mainly founded by trade unions in 1889). Then 24 national unions, most of which were craftmens' unions, joined the LO. These organized over 50,000 workers. At that time, the LO was a rather loose organization. The local level had significant independence. In tbe beginning of the 1930s the statutes of the national unions which concerned members deciding on wage agreements and strikes differed. In 1933 the boards of the national unions were given the right to decide themselves on collective agreements and conflict measures. Thus the public voting changed from decisive to advisory. The unions who wished to remain within the LO were forced to accept these new regulations. In 1941 a new regulation was introduced stipulating that the LO shall decide on conflict measures which involve or can involve (e.g. through lock-outs) more than 3 per cent of the members. The LO was at the same time given the right to decide on whether the yearly wage negotiations should be carried out centrally. Summing up, the national unions' position towards the LO has weakened and, at the same time, the national unions' position towards the local branches, clubs, and private members has strengthened. Moreover, on national union and LO levels the employed union representatives do most of the work. The local level has no formal influence on the choice of the union representatives who work on national union and LO levels. (Hadenius, 1976.)

The LO is today the controlling organization for over 2.0 million workers, of which 1.4 million are employed in private firms (SCB, 1978: 254). On the average, 90-5 per cent of the workers are members. Within commerce, service, and forestry membership is relatively low, while within industry it is almost 100 per cent (Elvander, 1969: 50). Most of the unions within the LO organize their members according to the principles of the industrial union. There were 44 national unions in 1960; today the number of unions connected with the LO is down to 24 through mergers. The national unions are comprised of 1,900 branches (7,900 in 1960) formed of work-place organizations (called 'clubs'). Parallel with these organizations are LO districts and LO local trade councils, co-ordinating the branches of different unions within a geographical area. Their primary tasks are to exert union pressure, give information, and organize educational activities. These are carried out on intimate terms with the Social Democratic Party. Besides the LO, there are the syndicalists, who set up the Central Organization of Swedish Workers with 18,000 members (SCB, 1978: 254). The organization was created in 1910 after the LO's defeat during the general strike a year earlier. (Andersson, 1979; Elvander, 1969; Hadenius, 1976.)

In the beginning of the 1930s the first central organizations of commercial, clerical, and technical employees were formed. These merged in 1944 into Swedish Central Organization of Salaried Employees (TCO). Unions connected with the TCO organize 1,050,000 white-collar workers of which about 500,000 are employed privately (SCB, 1978: 254). Around 70 per cent of the privately employed white-collar workers are members of trade unions. Membership varies markedly between different branches of commerce and industry. While 90 per cent of clerks employed by insurance companies and banks are union members the proportion of those in commerce and service and in industry's is much less: 50 and 75 per cent respectively (Elvander, 1969: 48).

The TCO is organized roughly on the lines of the LO and has 24 national unions. These are in turn formed of regional branches to which work-place clubs belong. The membership-strong unions within TCO are organized according to the principles of the industrial union. This is the case, for example, with the Swedish Union of Clerical and Technical Employees in Industry (SIF) with 240,000 members. There are also TCO unions which are organized on the principles of the professional union, for instance the Swedish Foremens and Supervisors Association with 70,000 members. There is another central body for salaried employees, the Swedish Conferderation of Professional Associations (SACO/SR) with 190,000 salaried employees, of which approximately 30,000 are in private employment (SCB, 1978: 254). The SACO/SR apply, in contrast to the LO and the stronger unions in the TCO, the principles of the professional union. Otherwise, the SACO/SR is formed in the same way as the LO and the TCO. (Andersson, 1979; Elvander, 1969.)

To be able to meet organized workers with a co-ordinated front, the employers in 1902 merged in the Swedish Employers' Confederation (SAF). The organization of the SAF was centralized, extending full powers to the top echelons. Even today the highest level of the SAF has a greater authority in decisions concerning collective agreements or conflict measures in comparison to the LO and the TCO.

There are 39 employer unions connected to SAF. These provide for 36,000 private firms with a total of 1,335,000 employees, of which 810,000 are blue- and 525,000 white-collar workers (SCB, 1978: 255). Approximately 47 per cent of all the employed in Sweden work in firms that are connected to the SAF. The proportion within the private sector is much higher: 88 per cent.

Some of the characteristics of the Swedish labour market have already been observed, but will now be described in more detail. Centralization is one such feature. Influence on both the employer and employee sides resides in a few dominating organizations. All negotiations and agreements of any importance are subject to these top organizations. Both different kinds of resources and the right of decision are concentrated at the highest level. The first central wage agreement between the LO and SAF was reached in 1940 and since the middle 1950s there have only been centralized wage negotiations. The role of the national unions is to adjust the central agreements to the specific branches. Also within the individual firms, discretion in wage negotiations is very limited.

Not only the wage but also the collaboration agreements have been negotiated between the LO and the SAF.

The intimate connection between the LO and the social democrats is most striking. During the social democrats' long period of office, the LO has manifested an obvious public responsibility which among other things has implied that it actively assented to the policy of continuous rationalization. It is remarkable that it was not before the 1970s that the LO used the Social Democratic Party to introduce new labour legislation. In contrast to the LO, the TCO is politically neutral.

The state of affairs between the LO and the SAF during the post-war years has varied between conflict and compromise. The three periods when polarization has been the greatest have occurred during the planned economy debate up until 1950, the pensions conflict of 1956–60, and the changes in labour legislation from 1970, much strengthened by the 1975 proposal of the LO creating wage earners' funds. Between these frosty periods, the relations have mostly been characterized by compromise, especially during the 1960s when the level of welfare was rising fast.

Because the central bodies sometimes have been at odds does not mean that all areas of mutual interest are involved, nor does it mean that local relations necessarily have been chilly. One way to indicate the state of relations between the labour market parties is to study the number of strikes and working days lost. The number of strikes has been low during the whole post-war period and with the exception of a few years, the number of working days lost has also been low. Towards the end of the 1960s, the number of wild-cat strikes noticeably increased. These can often be seen as a reaction against the attitude of the local employer and against the limitation imposed by central wage negotiations.

2.2. The role of Public Powers

The government's economic, industrial, and labour market policies have provided opportunities for different kinds of activities and employment though the government has shown little interest in the conditions at the work-place. It was not before 1949 that the National Board of Occupational Safety and Health was formed and most of the safety protection activity has always occurred at regional and local level.

During the post-war period, and especially in the 1960s and 1970s, the government's employment and industrial policies have come to include a lot of selective measures designed to stimulate economic activity in de-populated areas and in stagnating industries. The growth of those selective measures has considerably increased the number of contacts between the government's central and regional administration and the firms. This is especially true for the biggest companies and some ministries.

The public sector has few instruments to plan and control economic activity. One such is the Act on Public Representation on the Boards of Banking and Insurance Companies. Another, very controversial, one is the Act on Public Representation on the Boards of Companies and Foundations. From the beginning in 1973, the law was valid for the biggest investment companies and foundations. In 1976 it was extended by the social democratic government to include 60 companies and 10 foundations. However, the non-socialist governments have not appointed representatives for any new companies and in 1979 the law was restricted to 30 companies and 10 foundations.

It is remarkable that Sweden almost completely lacks the co-operation at the branch and/or regional basis between employers, unions, and the state, which exists in many other countries. The creation of trade councils was suggested by the social democratic government after the war but was rejected by industry. It was later revived at regular intervals, primarily by the LO; it was from this proposal that the LO's wage earners' funds came (Åsard, 1978).

Until 1970 most of the labour legislation were practically unchanged for decades, and the labour market parties themselves regulated conditions by agreements rather than by law. The laws had a procedural character. The material content resulting from these laws was ultimately determined by the relative strength of the labour market parties.

At the beginning of the 1970s the role of the government changed. The LO and TCO demanded that those employed should be represented on company boards and that employers' right to direct work should be eliminated. With only a very tepid response from the employers, the LO and the TCO voted to solve the problems with new laws. This began a period of intensive legislation resulting in new or changed laws on Working Hours (1970), Board Representation for the Employees (1973, 1976), Worker's Protection (1974 replaced by one on Work Environment in 1978), Labour Conflicts (1974), Employment Protection (1974), Shop Stewards (1974), and Co-determination at Work (1977).

As stated earlier, this legislative work is a result of a strong reorientation in the trade union movement, and primarily in the LO around 1970, which was first manifested at the LO congress of 1971. This reorientation followed, during the second half of the 1960s, growing awareness of bad working conditions and explicit mistrust of union members.

Though the state has become more active as an employer during the last decade the number of state-owned firms is too small to be significant.

2.3. Basic Industrial Relations Rules

In this section, we deal with the most important labour legislation and agreements. These include the Act on Co-determination at Work (replacing in 1977 the 1936 Act on Right of Association and Negotiation, the 1928 Act on Collective Agreements, and the 1920 Act on Mediation in Labour Conflicts), 1974 Act on Labour Conflicts (which replaced the 1928 Labour Court Act). The Basic Agreement is discussed though it is to be cancelled — as all other central collaboration have already been — when the parties reach a co-determination agreement. A very short outline is included about the development of acts and agreements.

After a serious industrial conflict, the first nation-wide agreement was reached in 1905. The agreement, besides covering wage levels, also contained rules of how negotiations concerning the interpretation and the application of the agreement should be carried out, and, further, rules for how new agreements should be depicted.

The role of the trade unions at the work-place at this time was unclear and active union members were often pestered. In the SAF's statute there was a provision (§ 23) that no affiliated organization or private firm could come to an agreement with its employees without there being in it a paragraph which specified that the employer alone had the right to direct work and to employ and dismiss the workers. In 1906, an agreement was reached between the LO and the SAF, the so-called December Compromise, which involved the acceptance of the LO of the employer's right to establish paragraph 23 in all agreements. The SAF undertook to respect the employee's right of association. The employer's right to dismiss employees freely became restricted in 1938, in 1964, and especially in 1974. The conditions of power in the labour market during the whole of this century are based on the December Compromise, even after the introduction of the Co-determination Act in 1977 which makes it possible for the unions to demand a co-determination agreement restricting the employer's right to direct work.

Parallel to the labour market parties' efforts to regulate their joint problems themselves, official investigations occurred to legally handle the many and extensive labour conflicts. In 1906 came the Act on Mediation in Labour Conflicts. After many abortive attempts and much disagreement, further laws, the Act on Collective Agreement and the Labour Court Act, were accepted in 1928. In 1936 the Act on Right of Association and Negotiation was introduced without the previous confrontation. This was a codification of the conditions that prevailed since the agreements of 1905 and 1906. It came into force primarily to give the growing group of salaried employees the same position as the workers already had.

In 1935 an official commission appointed by the social democratic government recommended a new Labour Peace Obligation Act and that the terms in the act should be left to the labour market parties to negotiate. This, after discussions between the SAF and the LO, resulted in the Basic Agreement of 1938. This agreement restricted even more the earlier, though legal, possibilities for the parties to rely on conflict measures in the first instance. After the Basic Agreement the Work Council Agreement of 1946 was the second most important item of co-operation between the SAF and the LO. The Work Council Agreement was, of course, only one of many collaboration agreements, the rest being the Protection against Accidents at Work-places (1942, 1951, and 1967), the Apprentice Training (1944), and the Time and Motion Study (1948, 1972) agreements.

The 1970s have involved a thorough transformation of the labour legislation. The basic provisions are now collected in the Co-determination Act. The rights of association, to strike, and to apply a lock-out are, moreover, constitutionally binding. The right to strike, however, belongs to the union and not the private individual.

The right of association involves the right to belong to and make full use of membership in an employee union. The right of association belongs to the private employer and employee, and not to an organization as such. It applies only to those already employed. Those looking for jobs can be refused employment on the grounds that they are members of a certain union. The right of association only gives protection against measures taken on the grounds of membership in a union (positive right of association), and not against measures taken on the grounds that someone is not a member of a certain union (negative right of association). There is no legal protection against a stipulation in a collective agreement that all employees in a particular firm must belong to a particular union. However, the SAF has not so far permitted its members to introduce conditions such as these. The employers outside the SAF, not least the union-owned firms, have sometimes used such stipulations, primarily against syndicalists. The right of association can be used by supervisors as well as white-collar workers. Earlier, supervisors could be forbidden to belong to the same union as their subordinate personnel, but a clause of that sort is not included in the Co-determination Act.

The Act on Shop Stewards (1974) includes rules which give the union stewards better employment security, a stronger position at the work-place, and better working conditions, such as the right to take time off etc. All these make it easier for the shop steward to look after the union's assignments.

The right of negotiation belongs to single employers as well as to unions of employees and unions of employers. To the right to negotiate for one party there is equally an obligation for the other party to enter into negotiations. However, this obligation to negotiate does not involve an obligation to reach an agreement. Ultimately, an agreement can only be reached failing a successful negotiation, by the use of conflict measures. There are no restrictions in the Co-determination Act which excludes matters that cannot be negotiated, though this was true of earlier legislation as well. Labour unions, through negotiation and agreement can also influence decisions concerning labour and company management, which was not the case before when it was accepted from 1906 that negotiations between employer and union could deal with wages and general conditions of employment only. At present, when negotiations between the parties result in a collective agreement, both the contracting parties and their organization members are bound by it.

There is an important distinction between conflicts of interests and judicial conflicts. A judicial conflict applies to a dispute arising over the interpretation and application of a decision which has been reached under an agreement, while conflict of interests applies to a dispute over conditions which are not controlled by an agreement. According to the Co-determination Act, it is forbidden for the parties (when the agreement is in force) to take industrial action in judicial disputes; this peace obligation applies to both the contracting parties' organizations and the private members.

When interests are at stake, however, the parties do have the right to take conflict measures. A typical conflict of interests is when the parties negotiate for a new agreement where a party retains the right to take action during the existing contract period in questions of co-determination following a failure to reach agreement on the subject. There are, of course, rules which limit the rights of the parties to take industrial action during non-contracting periods. In the old Basic Agreement it was forbidden to use such action against a neutral third party or as a way of retaliation; nor was it legal to use it against someone who, in earning his living, employed only his family (except in certain conditions), or against someone for religious, political, or similar reasons. Anti-social conflicts were also forbidden. Furthermore, the Basic Agreement ruled that a course of procedure must be followed before conflict measures could be taken. The new Co-determination Act stipulates that conflict measures are forbidden even in non-contracting periods if it is against the constitution of the organization in question. On the employee side, this means that the decision on conflict measures must be made at the national union or LO levels.

When negotiating parties cannot reach a collective agreement, the rules of mediation in labour conflicts (in the Co-determination Act) become applicable. The government supplies a specially appointed conciliator. The conciliator can be summoned by a party in labour dispute or he can intervene on his own initiative if a conflict has broken out or threatens to break out. The law prescribes that at least one week's warning must be given before industrial action begins. Moreover, the parties are obliged to appear before the conciliator for final negotiations. Failure to appear before him can result in the imposition of a monetary penalty by the Labour Court. In order to settle extensive disputes, the government can instead appoint a conciliation board.

If a judicial conflict cannot be solved by negotiations, it is referred to the Labour Court for settlement. The members of the Labour Court are, on the one hand, independent of the parties' interests, and, on the other hand, representatives for them. The decision of the Labour Court cannot be contested. A conflict cannot be taken to the Labour Court until all previous agreed measures have been exhausted, i.e. local negotiation, national union negotiation, Labour Court. Rules which apply to the Labour Court can be found in the Act on Labour Conflicts. The main purpose of this act is that important and significant cases from the viewpoint of labour legislation shall be dealt with by the Labour Court.

2.4. Management Prerogatives

Legally the distribution of influence between the employer and the employees has been determined by the same principle since the beginning of the century. The employer has the right to take decisions alone in all questions if not otherwise prescribed in laws and/or collective agreements. This was established in the December Compromise in 1906. As a consequence of this, all questions except wages and employment conditions were excluded from bargaining and subject to the employer's exclusive decision. This very restricted area of negotiable questions remained even after the 1936 Act on Right of Association and Negotiation had specified the right of negotiation to include 'the relation between employer and employees' (section 4; cf. also Adlercreutz, 1975: 17, 75).

While procedural rules undisputably have favoured the employer, there have been material rules limiting the employer's discretion in areas like workers' protection, working hours, holidays, employment protection, and time off for studies and union work. Moreover, the Work Council Agreement forced the employer to inform and consult the union in some questions.

The restricted right of negotiation was, in the early 1970s, the main reason for the trade-union movement to demand far-reaching changes in the labour legislation (LO, 1971a; Schiller, 1974). Consequently, the 1977 Act on Co-determination explicitly stipulates that all questions may be regulated in collective agreements. But as long as such co-determination agreements have not been reached, it is still the employer who has the right to take decisions (Bill 1975/76-105: 245). And like all collective agreements, the co-determination agreements must ultimately be achieved with the help of conflict measures.

But even in the absence of a co-determination agreement, the Co-determination Act limits the employer's prerogatives through information and consultation obligations and the union's right of interpretation. We treat those rules in the next section. As a prelude, however, the following quotations from the bill (1975/6-105: 195-6) do give an impression of the intentions behind the 1977 Co-determination Act.

The Act shall be interpreted as an expression of the opinion that it is no longer the employer alone who can make decisions, but that decision-making shall be divided between employer and employee through negotiation and agreement.

Therefore the proposed Act includes special rules that collective agreement should be established in questions of influence and special means for reaching such collective agreements. The employees shall also have the right of interpretation in conflicts about work duty and influence issues. The rest of the legislation gives the employees a stronger right of negotiation where extended rights of co-determination have not been agreed upon, and the right to information. These rights shall apply to all questions which deal with the relations between employer and employee, also questions concerning both labour management and company management. The stronger right of negotiation shall give the employed a more equal standing with the employer.

2.5. Information and Consultation Rules

Beginning in 1946 the work councils were the first and the only measure for information and joint consultation and were therefore the primary element in industrial democracy. The coming into force of the Act on Co-determination at Work has led to the abolition of the Work Council Agreement as well as the other collaboration agreements. According to the agreement, the employer or the union could, at work-places with at least 50 employed, demand that a work council should be established. The union held the majority of seats in the council. In many firms, the work council was enlarged by a series of subcommittees dealing with different questions. In the larger firms, one could also find a work council for the whole business group. The work councils were mostly of little significance as a means for power-sharing as their competence were very restricted and they met too seldom. The work councils were such that any collaboration was on the employer's own terms (Adlercreutz, 1975: 104).

In 1976 the work council organization was extended by the creation of a sub-committee on economic questions on which the union representatives had an unlimited right to information concerning the economic status of the firm. At the same time the union was given the right to appoint a workers' economic consultant, who had an unlimited access to economic information. These two measures were in force for only one year before all collaboration agreements were cancelled in favour of the new Act on Co-determination.

The Act on Co-determination prescribes an unconditional and unlimited obligation for the employer to inform the local union. 'The employer shall keep the union, with whom he has a collective agreement, continuously informed about the production and economy of his business and also about the guidelines for his policy on personnel. The employer shall moreover give the union an opportunity . . . to examine books, accounts and other documents . . .' (section 19 of the Act). The union itself appoints the information receiver(s). If the employer wants certain information to be kept secret, he must bargain about this. Even secret information may be sent on to the union board by the receiver. (Sections 20-2.)

The Act on Co-determination also stipulates an unconditional obligation for the employer to negotiate with the local union before important changes occur or whenever the union so demands even though the employer has the right of decision. (Sections 11-12.) If the local parties cannot come to an agreement, the local labour union can demand negotiations between the two national organizations. If the parties cannot even then come to an agreement, the employer can carry out his decision. Only in exceptional cases can the employer be not obligated to postpone the execution of his decision during the negotiations.

These information and consultation rights apply only to unions who have a collective agreement with the employer. However, other unions do have the same right to negotiations about work or employment conditions for their members. This contributes to the unity of the trade union movement. Of equal importance is that negotiations must be carried out under a peace obligation; no conflict measures may be used. Thus, the only argument for the union is arguments, while the employer must postpone the decision during both the local and the central negotiations.

The Act of 1976 on Board Representation for the Employees gives the right of employees of companies with more than 25 employees to elect two delegates on the board. (The Act of 1973 was applicable to firms with more than 50 employees.) It is the right of unions who have a collective agreement with the company and who represent more than half of the employees to elect these two members of the board. If any of the workers' or the salaried employees' unions have more than 80 per cent of the employed tied to the collective agreement, this union have the right to elect both delegates. In other cases, the two largest unions elect one delegate each; smaller unions can elect a deputy member of the board. Principally they have the same position, responsibility and duties as other members of the board.

2.6. Co-Determination Rules

The traditional bargaining questions have been wage levels and employment conditions. Due to the centralized character of the wage negotiations, the local wage negotiations have been restricted to the distribution of local 'pools of money'. Local wage negotiations are carried out not only in connection with the local application of the central wage agreement but also when, for example, changes in the rate of production or rationalization measures necessitates a new wage level. All these local negotiations are carried out under the obligation to maintain industrial peace.

The strongly centralized bargaining system, with little discretion for local parties, from time to time causes tensions between the national organizations and the local employer and union. The higher rate of wild-cat strikes during the 1970s can partly be explained as a reaction against the central wage agreement in firms where it is obvious that the employer could afford wages higher than those stipulated in the central agreement. But at the same time, a certain degree of centralization is necessary for the unified wage policy.

As indicated earlier, one of the main objectives behind the 1977 Act on Co-determination was to make all questions negotiable and give the employees opportunity to gain influence through a co-determination agreement. Official investigations preceding the law gave examples of questions that now can be dealt with in negotiations and agreements. To 'labour management' belongs choice of working methods and working equipment, production change, distribution of work within a group, planning of working premises, rationalization measures, flexibility of working hours, personnel training, personnel statistics, transfer of staff, promotion. To 'company management' belongs production policy and volume, purchasing, selling, advertising, production expansion and reduction, investment, allocation of profit, incurring of debts, budget, etc.

To make the employer more interested in a co-determination agreement, the law gives the union the right to use conflict measures in every question where the union has raised demands during the negotiations but where the employer has refused to include the question in the co-determination agreement. The idea is that the employers are so interested in industrial peace that they are willing to give up some influence in order to avoid strikes. Whereas only the union can demand a co-determination agreement, both parties have surviving conflict rights. (Sections 32, 44.)

The Co-determination Act came into force on 1 January 1977. In connection with the wage negotiations in the autumn 1976, the LO and the PTK (which is a cartel of the national unions within the TCO and SACO/SR which organizes salaried employees within the private sector) presented their demands on a co-determination agreement. The SAF too presented a proposal. In spring 1977 the LO and PTK had developed and co-ordinated their demands and presented them jointly. The SAF had in the meantime to explain their own proposal.

The two proposals were very different. The LO/PTK proposal enumerated the questions where one wanted different degrees of influence while the SAF proposal dealt with the way to organize co-determination. While the first raised far-fetched claims, the second, if anything, retained the status quo.

By autumn 1980 the four-year-old negotiations between the LO/PTK and SAF have still not produced an agreement for the privately owned firms. After several earlier proposals, the LO/PTK in October 1979 and the SAF in January 1980 presented two very similar proposals. In the main they are identical but it has not been possible to reach agreement on some essential points.

The proposals stipulate three areas where the local unions can demand a greater influence; planning, personnel and organization of work. Some guidelines are given for the local agreements but most questions are left to the local parties: the degree, form and content of co-determination. The LO/PTK demand short- and long-range plans for those areas while the SAF wants a less formalized system. Within the personnel area even the proposed central agreement contains detailed rules for how to handle recruitment, introduction, education etc. The SAF-proposal especially emphasizes the individual worker and the work group; the shop steward plays an important role.

The proposals contain special rules for small businesses where direct influence is said to be more important. Co-determination is also extended from the single work-place to the whole business group. In questions of importance for more than one unit within the group, information and negotiation can take place between the group management and a group of union representatives. The stipulations in the Act on Shop Stewards are also extended to facilitate union activity within the whole business group.

According to both proposals, the local union can engage consultants at the firm's expense (the SAF will restrict this right to firms with more than 50 employees). Both parties get equal rights to engage researchers; however the proposals differ in cases in which the parties cannot reach an agreement. During the negotiations with the SAF, the LO/PTK were able to reach a co-determination agreement with the employer associations for state- and co-operative-owned firms. This agreement is similar to the original LO/PTK proposal in many respects. Even if the state- and co-operative-owned firms are few, this co-determination agreement is important as it is the first one covering an industrial and commercial sector.

The co-determination agreements for the state-owned firms (March 1979) and the co-operative-owned firms (April 1979) are basically the same. The greater part of the agreement contains a list of questions where the local unions can demand negotiations with the employer to introduce co-determination. The three headings are planning, organization, and personnel with an emphasis on company management and personnel policy. Work organization and computer systems are held to be less important.

It does not stipulate any specific degree of influence, regarding this as a bargaining issue for the local parties. If the local parties cannot reach an agreement, there will be negotiations between the national unions. If these central negotiations too are without result, the employer decides the contents on planning and organization in the agreement. Though the contents will be based on the result of the negotiations, ultimately it is the employer who decides the scale of his employees' influence within planning and organization. With personnel questions, the third and last step is to refer the issue to a central co-determination council with the task to help the parties to reach an agreement. Clearly the position of the employees is stronger here. The organization of co-determination is equally an issue for the local parties. However, a guiding principle seems to be that co-determination shall be exercised jointly. If one cannot agree on a question, this can be subject to a local or, if necessary, a central negotiation.

A separate co-determination agreement has been reached for the banking companies (March 1979). For this quite homogeneous group of firms it has been possible to include rather detailed stipulations about the organization of co-determination. The basic principle is to integrate co-determination with ordinary organization of the banks. Also here an issue can be referred to a local and, if necessary, a central negotiation.

The agreement contains a long list of questions where co-determination is of special importance. Among these are organization and computer-system design, work organization, planning and budgeting, personnel policy, and mergers. The degree of influence for the union is not specified in the central agreement but in the local agreements for each bank.

Another separate co-determination agreement was signed for the insurance companies (August 1979). Like the banking agreement, the main principle is to integrate co-determination with ordinary organization. The local club is given the right to appoint at least two representatives for the bodies dealing with company management and also shop stewards for labour management issues. If no agreement is reached in this way, one of the parties can call for negotiations under the Co-determination Act. The questions mentioned as of special importance for co-determination are similar to those in the banking agreement.

2.7. Union and Worker Prerogatives

The Act on Workers' Protection of 1974 gave safety representatives, elected by the unions, the right to interrupt work considered to be dangerous. This was the first time that the employees' side took over the right of decision supported by legislation or by agreement. The Act on Co-determination gives the employees' side the right to veto the employer's use of contractors if 'the measures proposed by the employer can be considered as disregarding the law or the collective agreement or that the measures otherwise are in conflict with what is generally approved' (section 39). The veto right belongs to the national union and must be preceded by a local negotiation.

Previously, when the employer and the union disagreed on the interpretation and application of a certain regulation, the employer always had a temporary right to settle the conflict. The union had to bring the dispute before the Labour Court, and until its judgement was given, the employer's interpretation was valid. The 1974 Act on Shop Stewards for the first time gave the union the right to interpret the law and the employer the right to bring the issue to the Labour Court if he wants a change in the union's decision.

According to the 1977 Co-determination Act, the union has the right of interpretation in a question of co-determination or work duty until the issue has been settled by the Labour Court. In disputes about the interpretation of wage agreements, the employer has the right to decide but must start negotiations and ultimately bring the issue to the Labour Court. If he fails to do this, the union's interpretation is valid. (Sections 33–7.)

3. PROGRAMMATIC PERSPECTIVES, PROBLEMATIC ISSUES, AND DEVELOPMENTS

3.1. 1970s – A Decade of Reorientation

During the 1970s the body of Swedish industrial relations legislation, most of which had been in force for many decades, has been replaced by a series of new laws and quite a few agreements. The reason for this development is the drastic change in trade union policy around 1970.

The Swedish working class movement is strong in politics and in the trade unions. Since the 1930s its guiding principle has been to increase production and to use this increase to get a more even distribution of wealth. Despite the Social Democrats being in office since 1932, the working class movement did not use its political position to change the conditions of working life to any significant extent. And as the trade unions gave priority to wage increases, the distribution of power between the employer and the employees remained not only unchanged but also unquestioned till the end of the 1960s. At that point management's powerful position was attacked and in the early 1970s new labour legislation was demanded. This change is explained by the growing criticism among the trade union members of past attitudes and policies.

From the early 1930s to the late 1960s the dominating goal in Sweden's economic policy was to facilitate the growth of the more productive industries and companies even if this caused a successive elimination of less productive units. Thus rationalization measures were not only accepted but also promoted. From the 1940s structural changes were speeded up by the LO's wage policy, i.e. the same pay for the same job irrespective of the profitability of individual firms and industries. Then the selective labour-market policy – formulated by trade-union economists – helped people to get new jobs in more productive units. Also the rationalization and intensification of individual jobs were accepted.

The aim to increase growth was successfully reached during the 1960s, but at a high price. In industries and firms the traditional symptoms of dissatisfactory labour relations were seen in this decade: absenteeism, personnel turnover, and recruiting difficulties. More importantly, regions became depopulated as people had to leave work-places and companies. Intensified production both diminished influence and satisfaction for the workers and made it more difficult for many to get and to hold a job. There was a substantial increase in immigration bringing segregation problems both to the work-places and to residential areas.

These problems had existed to some extent earlier but the very rapid structural changes and rationalization during the 1960s compounded them. It is said, too, that the welfare-state and the benefits of social security reached a point where people felt they were not forced to accept bad conditions of work. People discovered that economic growth which had been pushed by the labour market parties and the government almost unanimously, demanded a price they were not willing to pay. One can also point to the intense debate in the late 1960s questioning the traditional distribution of power and wealth.

We have shown that the trade union movement not only accepted but also promoted the structural changes. The first signs of a hesitation can be found in a report to the LO congress 1961 (LO, 1961a) demanding better employment security. A deeper survey into the price people had to pay for the growth of welfare can be found in two reports to the LO congress of 1966 (LO, 1966a; LO, 1966b). However, no solution to the problems was presented then; and for a few years it was the Liberal Party alone that demanded the most far-reaching changes towards industrial democracy.

It was not until 1969, when evidence of a decline of confidence among union members was registered, that a reorientation started within the labour movement. The LO congress 1971 was the definitive turning-point. Two reports (LO, 1971a; LO, 1971b) both demonstrated an awareness of the problems and proposed solutions. The LO congress formulated a large number of demands for greater influence for both the individual employee and the union. Those demands lead to official investigations and new or revised labour legislation.

That a change in union policy occurred in 1971 was indeed remarkable; but to formulate a policy is one thing, to accomplish it quite another. So, even allowing the traditionally strong position of the trade union movement, the quick realization of the proposed labour legislation is equally remarkable. However, it does seem that new factors have arisen to weaken the position of the unions. As most of the factors will be valid also in the future, we will devote some space to them.

In 1968 the social democrats for the first time in the post-war period reached a majority of their own in the electorate. Since then they have successively lost a substantial part of their voters, so that in the 1979 election they polled only 43.5 per cent of the electorate. This can be explained, not by structural changes in the electorate but by a number of certain issues. First the non-socialist parties during the 1970s have advocated and carried through an expansionistic policy in contrast to the social democrats' more restricted one. This change of the social democrats' traditional policy has made it difficult for them to use the employment argument as before.

Second is the ecological issue which has meant a conflict with the traditional growth philosophy of the Social Democratic Party and of the LO. Furthermore, this issue cuts across party boundaries. The prime example is nuclear energy, where the Social Democrats have advocated the same alternative as the Conservative and Liberal Parties and the capital owners — and consequently these parties lost voters to the Centre and Communist parties. This issue, and the debate about wage earners' funds, were the main factors behind the Social Democratic defeat in 1976.

The nuclear power question went on to split the non-socialist parties as well, and after only two years in office the first non-socialist government for 44 years had to resign. It was succeeded by a minority liberal government. Thus it is more the weakness of its competitors than its own strength that has improved the position of the Social Democratic Party towards the end of the decade. But in the election in autumn 1979, the non-socialists again defeated the socialist parties, with a margin of only a few thousand of votes. The non-socialist parties now have organized a new government with a stronger support in parliament.

The position of the trade union movement should remain strong in the future. The LO has compensated the declining number of industrial members by organizing the employees in the service sector. There has even been a debate about limiting the number of national blue-collar unions to one for industry and one for service in order to increase the unions' organizational strength.

The white-collar unions are steadily increasing in size. The coming into force of cartels between most TCO (and sometimes LO and SACO/SR) national unions within a certain sector has further strengthened their position. During two recent wage negotiations in the private sector, the LO and the PTK (the white-collar union cartel) have bargained jointly towards the SAF without any major tensions.

The economic recession, especially in 1977 and 1978, has been an obstacle to the unions. But even if unemployment has been high in Sweden's experience, the number of people in the labour force has increased. The non-socialist parties have been credited for this increase. It is understandable that the non-socialist parties have been trying to satisfy many union demands since a large proportion of their voters comes from the wage earners' class (Petersson, 1977: 14).

Finally, it is worth repeating that during four decades from the 1930s when the Social Democrats were at their most powerful, there was no serious attempt to improve the status of the trade unions and working conditions; but, paradoxically, during the 1970s when the Social Democrats' positions was weakened, far-reaching changes in labour legislation were demanded by the trade unions themselves (see also IDE 1980, 322).

3.2. The State of Co-determination

The Co-determination Act was a result of union demands and was approved in parliament by a huge majority. Both politicians and unions leaders exaggerated the importance of the new law and made people expect immediate and radical changes. But the changes have generally been few and small. Though central co-determination agreements were achieved for smaller parts of industry, commerce and service, there are as yet only a few local agreements for single firms.

In the absence of co-determination agreements, the only alternative has been to stick to the law. A few studies have been published of the application of the co-determination act (Björklund, Molin, & Sandberg, 1979; Dahlström & Sterner, 1978; Hart & Sterner, 1978; Lennerlöf & Hellberg, 1979). One common finding is the variations in the use and the consequences of the law. Another is the state of co-determination has been affected more by the economic recession, mergers, temporary dismissals of employees, reorganization than by the new law. In some firms, existing elaborated co-determination systems, in being before the new law, have disappeared.

The obligation for the employer to inform and bargain with the union – on his own initiative in important issues or where the union itself demands – seems to be fulfilled in most cases. Compared with the old rules in the Work Council Agreement, the new rules are not only more far-reaching but have also been much more strictly practiced. But if the employer is determined to have it his way, after using information and negotiation procedures, he can take the decision he wants. However, the local and the central negotiation that may follow give the union time to work out an alternative proposal. And the employer can be eager to avoid the time-lapse unavoidable during a central negotiation, and therefore be willing to compromise.

A serious limitation in the Co-determination Act is the lack of regulations for business groups. The information and consultation rules apply only to the single firms even if the important information and decisions are to be found elsewhere in the group.

The way the contacts between the employer and the union are handled differ widely. There is an obvious tendency away from the joint bodies with limited discretion towards direct negotiations and union representation in one or two management bodies. In a company it is possible to find, beside the supervisory board with its two union representatives, a management group including the chairman for the blue-collar, supervisor, and white-collar union clubs. This group can meet every second week or once a month. In between different managers can contact the union representatives to inform them or to start a negotiation. The work council has mostly been abolished but several of its committees are still working (though the agreement on work councils is no longer in force).

One can also notice a tendency to centralize the contacts between management and unions. In many firms, even rather big ones, most contacts are handled by just a small number of managers and union representatives. In these firms middle managers and supervisors often complain about being over-ruled and not even informed. In a few of the firms studied, elaborated systems for shop-floor participation have vanished; in others, they have developed further. The reason is not the Co-determination Act *per se* but a decision to follow the law literally or to emphasize the intentions of the law. Though local co-determination agreements are still lacking, it is a fact that the ordinary employee says he cannot see any changes in his work situation connected with the Co-determination Act.

It is not only on a national level that the co-operation between blue- and white-collar unions has become more intimate. In many of the firms studied, a growing awareness of the necessity to act jointly towards the employer is to be observed. In a few cases, the local clubs have fulfilled the LO-PTK agreement and have established a local co-determination council with the aim to formulate a joint policy in co-determination questions.

3.3. A New Act on Shop Stewards?

In 1976, when Parliament had approved the Co-determination Act, a new public commission was appointed with the task to investigate some remaining questions. These came under four headings: (1) an extension of the right to perform union activities within working time paid by the company; (2) the right for the unions to arrange information meetings for all employees within paid working time; (3) the right for the unions to engage consultants paid by the company; and (4) the right for the unions to let researchers investigate problems within the company.

In 1977, the commission agreed that these four rights should be granted. The union reaction was as positive as the employer reaction was negative. The issue certainly caused a lot of trouble for the new non-socialist government and it took a year before the three parties could agree upon a joint proposal (the same day as the coalition government resigned due to the conflict on nuclear energy). The government proposal was rather restricted compared with the commission's conclusion and now the reactions of the unions were extremely negative. The new liberal minority government tried to modify the proposal so that it could be approved by the LO and TCO but both organizations refused, evidently waiting for parliament elections and a social democratic government which would carry through the original commission proposal.

In the meantime the right for unions to engage consultants paid by the company has been settled within both the state- and the co-operative-owned firms through the co-determination agreements. In a separate agreement in June 1972 covering the co-operative-owned firms, the employer and the unions were given the same rights and duties regarding research within the company. If one side wants research to be carried out, it must first negotiate with the other party. If a local agreement cannot be reached, a central negotiation between the national unions can be resorted to. Failing a solution there, the respective national union has the right to decide that the research can be performed.

It is no coincidence that one and the same issue is dealt with in the proposals for a new act on shop stewards and for co-determination agreements. This shows the desirability to integrate all those prescriptions in the Co-determination Act in order to get more clear and consistent rules.

3.4. Wage Earners' Funds

We have noticed that in contrast to many other countries Sweden has very little institutionalized collaboration between the public powers, employers, and unions on an industrial or regional basis. The LO congress 1951, 1961, and 1966 all rejected proposals for branch funds before the 1971 congress decided to let the question be investigated. The main motives behind the proposals were to complement the wage policy, to stimulate capital formation, to increase labour's share of the production cake, and to increase the influence of the unions. Despite those fundamental goals, the proposals attracted very little attention, even in 1971. (Åsard, 1978: ch. 3.)

Between 1971, when the LO investigation started, and 1975, when the first version was published, the main purpose for the wage earners' fund changed several times. The emphasis changed from capital formation in 1971 to the wage policy in 1973 and then to equalization in the distribution of wealth and power in 1975. In 1976, when the definitive report was presented to and approved by the LO congress, all the motives mentioned were included. (Åsard, 1978: ch. 4.)

The 1976 report demanded that every privately owned firm should use 20 per cent of its profit to issue shares, which should be owned by the wage earners collectively through one central fund for the whole country. The central fund should be headed by a board appointed by the national unions. The right to nominate members of the company boards should be reserved to the local unions as long as the wage earners' fund owned no more than 20 per cent of the shares. After that the right should be switched over to a number of branch funds, appointed by the national unions. (LO, 1976a: chs. 4-7.)

The initial proposal in 1975 already caused a very negative reaction from the SAF and the non-socialist parties which led to the election campaign in 1976. The wage earners' fund proposal was one of the most important factors behind the socialist defeat in the election. Equally important was the bad co-ordination between the militant LO and the defensive Social Democratic Party. In 1978, in an effort to overcome a rather difficult political position, the LO and the Social Democratic Party presented a joint proposal. In this, only privately owned firms with at least 500 employees would be included. The wage earners' shares would be administered by one central fund, appointed by Parliament and not the national unions as in the earlier proposals. The right to nominate members of the company boards would be divided between the local unions and regional committees as long as the wage earners' fund owns no more than 40 per cent of the shares. Over that limit, the right would belong to the regional committees. (LO-SAP, 1978.)

The co-ordination between the two organizations, the rather modified proposal, and references to a public commission has made the issue less topical in the 1979 election campaign. We are now waiting for one or more proposals from the public commission and the LO and social democratic conferences in 1981. Wage earners' funds will probably be one of the main issues in the 1982 election.

REFERENCES

Public material
UN (1969) and (1976), *Statistical Yearbook.*
SCB (National Central Bureau of Statistics: Statistiska centralbyrån) (1945–78), *Statistical abstract of Sweden.*
    (1969b), *Historical statistics of Sweden Part 1.*
    (1972b), *The effect of post-war external migration on population trends in Sweden.* Forecasting information 1972: 14.
    (1974b), *Population, education and labour market in Sweden.* Forecasting information 1974: 8.
    (1975b), *Population and housing census Part 3: 3.*
    (1976b), *National accounts 1963–75.* Statistical reports SMN 1976: 7.4.
    (1976c), *Living conditions. Report no. 2.*
    (1978b), *Yearbook of labour statistics.*
    (1979b), *Labour force survey 1979: 1.*
SIND (National Board of Industry: Statens Industriverk) (1980–5), Agandet i det privata näringslivet.
SOU (Reports of Official Commisions of Enquiry, Statens offentliga utredningar) (1962–10), *Sveriges ekonomi 1960–1965.*
    (1967–18), *Invandringen.*
    (1968–5), *Industrins stuktur och konkurrensförhållanden.*
    (1968–7), *Ägande och inflytande inom det privata näringslivet.*
    (1971–5), *Svensk ekonomi under 70-talet med utblick mot 80-talet.*
    (1972–86), *Bättre arbetsmiljö.*
    (1975–81), *Demokrati på arbetsplatsen.*

SOU (Report of Official Commisions of Enquiry, Statens offentliga utredningar) (1975-89). *Långtidsutredningen 1975.*
(1975-90), *Arbete åt alla.*
(1976-1), *Arbetsmiljölag.*
(1976-2), *Bakgrund till förslag om arbetsmiljölag.*
(1976-3), *Rapporter i psyko-sociala frågor.*
SPK (National Price and Cartel Office: Statens pris- och kartellnämnd) (1972), *Koncentrationen inom svensk industri 1967-1970.*
BILL (1975/76: 105), *Arbetsrättsreform: Lag om medbestämmande i arbetslivet.*

Organizational material
BAO-SBMF (1979), *Avtal om medbestämmande i bank.*
FFO-FTP (1979), *Avtal om medbestämmande i försäkringsbranschen.*
KFO-LO/PTK (1979), *Medbestämmandeavtal.*
LO (Swedish Confederation of Trade Unions: Landsorganisationen) (1941), *Fackföreningsrörelsen och näringslivet.*
(1951), *Fackföreningsrörelsen och den fulla sysselsättningen.*
(1961a), *Fackföreningsrörelsen och företagsdemokratin.*
(1961b), *Samordnad näringspolitik.*
(1966a), *Fackföreningsrörelsen och den tekniska utvecklingen.*
(1966b), *Individen och den industriella miljön.*
(1971a), *Demokrati i företagen.*
(1971b), *Låglön och välfärd.*
(1976a), *Kollektiv kapitalbildning genom löntagarfonder.*
(1976b), *Solidariskt medbestämmande.*
LO/PTK (1977), *Förslag till medbestämmandeavtal.*
LO/SAP (1978), *Löntagarfonder och kapitalbildning.*
SAF (Swedish Employers' Confederation: Svenska arbetsgivareföreningen) (1977), *Förslag till huvudavtal.*
SFO-LO/PTK (1979), *Medbestämmandeavtal.*

Literature
Åberg, Y. (1969), *Produktion och produktivitet i Sverige 1861-1965.* Uppsala: AWE.
Adlercreutz, A. (1975), *Arbetsrätt.* Lund: AWE/Geber.
Ahrne, G. (1976), *Den gyllene kedjan.* Stockholm: Prisma.
Allardt, E. (1975), *Att Ha Att Älska Att Vara — Om välfärd i Norden.* Lund: Argos.
Andersson, K.-O. (1979), *Arbetsmarknadshandboken.* Stockholm: Pogo.
Åsard, E. (1978), *LO och löntagarfondsfragan.* Stockholm: Rabén & Sjögren.
Björklund, L., Molin, R., Sandberg, T. (1979), *Makt och MBL.* Uppsala: Department of business administration (mimeo).
Dahlström, E. (1976), *Efficiency, satisfaction and democracy in work. Ideas of industrial relations in post-war Sweden.* Gothenburg: Department of sociology. A shortened version appeared in *Acta Sociologica* 1977, 1.
    Sterner, M. (1978), *Scan väst.* Gothenburg: Department of sociology (mimeo).
Elvander, N. (1969), *Intresseorganisationerna i Sverige.* Lund: Gleerup.
    (1974a), 'In search of new relationships: parties, unions and salaried employees' associations in Sweden'. *Industrial and Labour Relations Review* vol. 28, 1.

Elvander, N. (1974b), 'The role of the state in the settlement of labor disputes in the Nordic countries: a comparative analysis'. *European Journal of Political Research*, 2.

(1974c), 'Collective bargaining and income policies in the Nordic countries: a comparative analysis'. *British Journal of Industrial Relations* vol. 12, no. 3.

Forsebäck, L. (1976), *Industrial relations and employment in Sweden*. Stockholm: Prisma.

Hadenius, A. (1976), *Facklig organisationsutveckling*. Stockholm: Rabén & Sjögren.

Hart, H., Sterner, M. (1978), *Berol kemi*. Gothenburg: Department of Sociology (mimeo).

Hermansson, C. H. (1962), *Monopol och storfinans*. Stockholm: Rabén & Sjögren.

(1979). *Kapitalister i monopol*. Stockholm: Arbetarkultur.

Himmelstrand, U. (1977), 'Socialism and social liberalism in the context of Swedish societal change'. Uppsala: Department of Sociology (mimeo). ·

(1980), *et al.*, *Beyond welfare capitalism. Issues, actors and forces in societal change*. London: Heinemann (forthcoming).

Högberg, G. (1973), 'Recent trends in collective bargaining in Sweden'. In *Collective bargaining in industrialised market economies*. Edited by ILO, Geneva.

Ingham, G. (1969), *Strikes and industrial conflict. Britain and Scandinavia*. London: Macmillan.

Johansson, S. (1971), *Politiska resurser*. Stockholm: Allmänna förlaget.

Johnston, T. L. (1962), *The bargaining process in Sweden*. London: Allen and Unwin.

Jörberg, L., Krantz, O. (1975), *Ekonomisk utveckling i de nordiska länderna 1914–1970*. Lund: Department of economic history (mimeo).

Karlsson, L.-E. (1973), 'Industrial democracy in Sweden'. In Hunnius, G., Carson, D., Case, J. (eds), *Workers control*. New York: Vintage.

Korpi, W. (1978), *The working class in welfare capitalism*. London: Routledge & Kegan Paul.

Lennerlöf, L., Hellberg, P. (1979), *Medbestämmandet enligt lag. Vad blev det?* Stockholm: PA-rådet.

Lindbeck, A. (1975), *Swedish economic policy*. London: Macmillan.

Lindström, S., Nordin, S. (1977), *Ven äger storföretagen?* Stockholm: Tiden.

Lundh, L.-G. (1973), 'Ägande och kontroll under senkapitalism'. *Häften för kritiska studier*, no. 8.

Lund, R. (1976), 'Contemporary developments in industrial relations: The Scandinavian countries'. Odense: Graduate school of business (mimeo).

Lundgren, N. (1975), *Internationella koncerner i industriländer*. Stockholm: Allmänna förlaget.

Odnoff, J. (1967), *Samhallsekonomi som spel*. Stockholm: W&W.

Öhman, B. (1974), *LO och arbetsmarknadspolitiken efter andra världskriget*. Stockholm: Prisma.

Von Otter, C. (1976), 'Schweden: Neue entwicklungstendenzen im Verhältnis von Gewerkschaften, Unternehmen und Staat'. *Gewerkschaftliche Monatshefte*, no. 9.

Petersson, O. (1977), *Väljarna och valet*. Stockholm: Liber.

Rydén, B. (1971), *Fusioner i svensk industri*. Stockholm: IUI.

Samulesson, H.-F. (1977), *Utländska direkta investeringer i Sverige.* Stockholm: AWE.

Schiller, B. (1974), *LO, paragraf 32 och företagsdemokratin.* Stockholm: Prisma.

Schmidt, F. (1972), 'The role of trade unions and employers' associations'. In Aaron, B., Wedderburn, K. (eds), *Industrial conflict. A comparative legal survey.* London: Longman.

—— (1976), *Facklig arbetsrätt.* Lund: Norstedts.

—— (1977), *Law and industrial relations in Sweden.* Stockholm: AWE.

—— (1978), *Löntagarrätt.* Lund: Norstedts.

Swedenborg, B. (1973), *Den svenska industrins investeringar i utlandet 1965–1970.* Stockholm: IUI.

Therborn, G. (1973), *Om klasserna i Sverige 1930–1970.* Lund: Zenit.

Veckans Affärer (1976), no. 40.

Wibe, S. (1976), *Monopol och monopolkapitalism? Häften för kritiska studier,* no. 7–8.

4

THE DANISH INDUSTRIAL RELATIONS SYSTEM

1. GENERAL SITUATION AND BACKGROUND

Introduction

At the turn of this century, the central organizations of the Danish workers and employers were formed. They negotiated a general agreement which settled the major issues of the employers' prerogative to direct work and the workers' right to organize and bargain collectively for higher wages and shorter hours. Shop stewards were elected, to an increasing extent at company level, during the first decades of this century to represent the workers' interests. The state supplemented this machinery to smooth the opposing interests of workers and employers by establishing a state conciliator and a Labour Court. Nevertheless, major strikes and lock-outs took place during the 1920s and 1930s which reminded the public that the conflict between labour and employer continued. The background for this conflict was the recurrent economic crises, the worst of which was the one in the 1930s, when one third of the workers were unemployed. The political scene was influenced to an increasing degree by the Social Democrats who elected the Prime Minister in 1924-26 and 1929-42, but the labour movement was unable to achieve a majority at national level.

Against this background, developments after the Second World War showed new tendencies regarding the role of the state in industrial relations, with a changed relationship between workers' and employers' organizations and attempts towards industrial democracy. A precondition was an economic change from stagnation to growth. Denmark has during the 30 years 1945-75 experienced a considerable growth in the standard of living, but at a very uneven pace. After a short reconstruction period 1945-9, the rate of annual growth of real national income fell to approximately 2 per cent during the 1950s (Hansen, 1977; Economic Secretariat, 1976). This fall was the result of unfavourable terms of trade, especially for agricultural products, the raising abroad of tariff barriers, and the lack of reinvestments during the war years.

The years after 1958 and until 1973 saw an extremely rapid rate of annual growth of real national income of approximately 5 per cent. A conscious national policy of furthering manufacturing industry was carried out by the government, and the external conditions were improved. On this basis a completely new industrial climate was created with more inventive developments in all spheres: technology, organization, worker–management relations, social welfare, education etc. Another result of this rapid growth was that resources were drawn into the public sector and housing, and manufacturing investment lost momentum. Thus, a re-evaluation of the Danish economic situation was necessary in 1972. The international oil crisis in 1973, then combined with a crisis in the Danish construction industry, changed the climate drastically, and at present Denmark has high unemployment and a big deficit in the balance of payments.

1.1. The status-quo of political power

The Folketing (the Danish parliament) is the only representative body of the political parties at the national level. According to the principle of parliament-arism, as it is practiced in Denmark, the government cannot have a majority in the Folketing when the latter is against it on critical issues. So, the Folketing completely dominates the government.

In the post-war period 1945-75, Danish Governments have had Social Demo-cratic prime ministers during two thirds of the period, but usually as minority governments. The main opposition parties have been the Farmers' party and the Conservatives. Until the end of the 1960s these three parties and the Social Liberals accounted for 80-90 per cent of the votes. During this time the welfare state was firmly established.

Table 4.1.
Voting results of some elections of Folketing (per cent)

	1945	1957	1966	1975	1977
Social democrats	32.8	39.4	38.2	30.0	37.0
Farmers' party	23.4	25.0	19.3	23.3	12.0
Conservatives	18.2	16.6	18.7	5.5	8.5
Social liberals	8.1	7.8	7.3	7.1	3.6
Communists	12.5	3.2	0.8	4.2	3.7
Socialist people's party			10.9	5.0	3.9
Left wing socialists				2.1	2.7
Georgists (justice party)	1.9	5.3	0.7	1.8	3.3
Progress party				13.6	14.6
Others	3.1	2.7	4.1	7.5	10.7
Percentage voting	86.3	83.7	88.5	88.2	88.7

Sources: Borre *et al.*, 1976: 11; Høgh, 1965: 106 and *Statistical Yearbook*, 1977.

In the 1970s the picture has changed. Opposition parties to the right and left of these four older parties have arisen and articulated a deeply felt dissatisfaction among the population with the achievements made since the war. From the left, the establishment is criticized for not having passed beyond the welfare state, and from the right public expenditures to maintain the welfare system is attacked. Moreover, political scientists now see the Danish political system divided not only along the usual left–right dimension, but also along a new dimension of support–criticism of the political system. This new dimension is mirrored by less stability among the electorate with more than ten parties to choose.

The consequences of this political situation have been fewer possibilities for action on the part of the Social Democratic party and the trade unions and the increasing difficulty for workers and employers to keep the political parties away from problems in the labour market with less autonomy.

1.2. Recent political events of nationwide significance

The major political questions after 1973 have centred around the energy crisis, balance-of-payments deficits, inflation and unemployment. It has been difficult to deal equitably with the various opposing interests of the many social groups. The political parties have only succeeded in making short-term compromises on the economic policy but they have not agreed upon a long term policy. The current situation is one of political impotence (Hansen, 1977: 210).

The entry of Denmark into the EEC in 1972 was decided on by a referendum which showed 57 per cent of the electorate in favour of membership (Hansen, 1977: 209). The result was that membership added to the problems in manufacturing and fishing industries, although improving conditions in agriculture. The opposition against entry has not succeeded in making withdrawal from the EEC a political issue in the national elections of 1977.

1.3. Economic situation

About one half of the around 5 million inhabitants of Denmark is economically active, that is, 1.5 million men and 1 million women (Economic Secretariat, 1977: 113).

The rate of unemployment declined from 1945 to about 10 per cent of insured wage earners in the 1950s, and during the 1960s nearly full employment and labour shortage became a matter of course (Olsen, 1962: 214; Kjerkegaard, 1976: 145). After 1973 unemployment returned as in most other countries, so the unemployment rate is once more above 10 per cent of the insured wage earners or 4-5 per cent of the work force (Economic Secretariat, 1977: 113).

The economic trend in Denmark was characterized by growth from 1945 to 1974, but from 1974 to 1975 the real national product dropped for the first time (cf. Table 4.2). During the next two years growth continued (Economic Secretariat, 1977: 99), but not at the rate achieved in the 1960s. At that time there was no spare capacity, and prices increased markedly. An even stronger upward movement of prices took place after the oil crisis in 1973.

The balance of payment has been a major determinant of Danish economic policy, and in the 1970s it has placed a limit on the means of fighting unemployment. In the 1950s the balance of payment changed from a deficit to a surplus, but in the 1960s deficits were recorded again, and after the oil crisis this deterioration became even more drastic.

1.4. Social stratification, living conditions, and social policy

More than 90 per cent of Danish companies are privately owned. In the food industry, co-operative firms play an important role with dairies and slaughterhouses being owned by farmers' co-operatives. In commerce, workers' and farmers' co-operatives run retail shops covering a major part of the retail business. The public sector is limited to railways, post and telecommunication, and social, educational and administrative institutions.

A shift in the structure of trade during the 1950s and the 1960s has changed Denmark from an agricultural to a manufacturing country, and further changes during the 1970s have put the service sector and the white collar people in front. The tertiary sector now accounts for approximately half of the urban

Table 4.2.
Economic indicators. Selected years 1947–1975

	1947	1955	1965	1970	1975	
GDP (current market prices) mill. kr.	17,292	31,269	76,065	127,944	227,241	
GDP (1955 market prices) mill. kr.	24,093	31,269	49,857	61,450	68,274	
Price index based on GDP at market prices[1]	36	50	76	100	167	
	1970	1971	1972	1973	1974	1975
GNP at factor cost mill. kr.	112,257	123,443	138,619	158,055	180,851	201,582
GNP (1955 factor cost prices) mill. kr.	55,916	57,834	60,137	61,537	62,157	60,579
Index of real GNP	100	103	108	110	111	108

Note: GDP (gross domestic product) is the value of the national production of goods and services with deduction for raw material and intermediate products. This value is measured in market prices i.e. included indirect taxes and price subsidies.

GNP (gross national product) at factor cost is equal to GDP at market prices minus interests and dividends paid to foreign countries and minus taxes plus price subsidies.

[1] This price index is based on indexes of GDP at current market prices and 1955 prices. The index is influenced by indirect taxes and price subsidies.

Sources: Statistical Yearbooks and other official statistics.

work force. The number of skilled workers has declined since the mid-1960s, and amounts only to approximately 15 per cent, leaving one-third of the labour force as non-skilled workers (Economic Secretariat, 1977: 113).

The functional income distribution has been constant, but this does not say anything about possible changes in the distribution of personal income. General information is lacking on this point, but more specific data are available. Comparison between some groups of salaried employees and workers in the 1960s and 1970s shows, for instance, that the ratio between salaried and workers' wages increased during the 1960s, but has since then decreased. This can be seen from Table 4.3. Among the workers, a tendency towards a smaller differential between skilled and unskilled men during the last ten years is indicated, and female workers have experienced a continuous improvement during the post-war years, approaching wage levels of unskilled male workers.

The general standard of living is among the highest in the world as measured by the GDP per capita. Government services expenditure has increased from 13 to 22 per cent of GDP at factor cost from 1965 to 1975. A major reason for this is the strong expansion of Danish social welfare measures i.e. improved pension schemes for old age and disability, better health insurance providing for free hospitalization, sick benefits, and medical services, maternity aid, etc. Another reason for the increased government expenditure is the expansion of education. The average length of the educational period has extended; and in 1972 nine years at school was made compulsory. The number of high-school students has grown to one-quarter of the relevant age group, and 17 per cent of an age group are admitted to the universities (Kjerkegaard, 1976: 124). Despite better educational conditions, many educational problems are still unsolved, as highlighted by the statistics (Kjerkegaard, op. cit.). First, about one quarter of an age group gets no education after the nine years of school. Secondly, workers' children are still under-represented among the high-school and university students. Thirdly, an increased investment in vocational training in comparison with the high-school and university education is essential to establish the necessary supply for the labour market. Fourthly, more adult education is needed to lessen the discrepency in the amount of teaching given to young and older generations. These and other educational problems are discussed by the central educational council of the ministry of education, and a report stating alternative goals and methods for reforms up to 1990 was prepared during the years 1975-8 (Det centrale Uddannelsesråd, 1975 & 1978). A majority of the council members favoured 12 years of education for everybody after 1990 and improvements to deal with the deficiences enumerated above. Moreover, the council stated that the educational system can qualify young and adults for the democratization of working life (Det centrale Uddannelsesråd, 1975, p. 339).

Table 4.3.
Social stratification

Index of life incomes, selected occupations compared with smith/ machine worker	1960	1970	1975	
Clerk, state employed	95.9	106.5	99.6	
Public-school teacher	113.7	133.0	116.3	
High-school teacher	124.6	153.9	136.0	
Female office clerk, privately employed	71.5	77.4	74.6	
Female office clerk, state employed	83.4	94.5	87.9	
Policeman	97.8	114.7	109.6	
Smith/machine worker	100.0	100.0	100.0	
Differentials between average wages	1945	1955	1965	1975
Skilled workers	116	119	117	110
Non-skilled workers	100	99	97	96
Women workers	86	70	76	86
All workers	100	100	100	100

Source: Statistical Yearbooks; Det Økonomiske Rad, 1977.

2. THE DANISH INDUSTRIAL RELATIONS SYSTEM

The main facets of the Danish industrial relations system are captured by focusing on (1) the agreements and laws regulating the behaviour of the workers' and employers' organizations at the national level; (2) the employee–management relationship at the company level centering around participation; (3) public powers influencing the system; and (4) stating industrial relations actors' views on current problems.

2.1. Legal basis and main ramifications of overall Industrial Relations system

National laws and nationwide agreements

The legal basis for the establishment of trade unions and employers' organizations has been the general constitutional right to form associations, and state interference with the labour market organizations as such has been weak until the 1930s. It was workers' and employers' organizations which themselves elaborated a contractual, collective framework to regulate their joint relationships. This, according to labour law experts, has contributed to a peaceful development of the labour market (Rise & Degerbøl, 1973: 21).

In 1899, the newly established organizations, that is, the Danish Federation of Trade Unions (now LO) and the Employers' Confederation (DA) negotiated an agreement which first gave the employers 'the right to direct and distribute work', second contained a mutual recognition of the two parties' organizations, and third regulated the right to strike and lock-out by establishing a warning period and the number of bodies which could decide upon conflicts. This agreement was regarded for more than half a century as the constitution of the labour market. On the initiative of the Federation of Trade Unions the agreement was renegotiated in 1960 and 1973, but the main principles were upheld. The most important extension of this so-called Main Agreement was rules for handling grievances about unjustified dismissal of individual workers.

A joint LO and DA committee formed in 1908 agreed upon Standard Rules for Handling Labour Disputes which were made compulsory by law in 1934. According to these rules, any disagreement in the period between renegotiations of new terms of wages etc. shall be solved by mediation at the local level or in case of a dispute of rights eventually by arbitration. The distinction between disputes of rights and disputes of interests dates back to the 1908 joint committee. Disputes of interests cover demands for a change in wages and other working conditions, and they should be solved by collective agreements. During the agreement period a peace obligation exists for both parties. This practice was explicitly included in the Main Agreement of 1960 and repeated in 1973. In case of disagreement about the interpretation of the agreement, that is, a conflict of rights the issue shall be solved by arbitration, failing mediation at the local level.

An alleged breach of agreement is sent for a decision by the Labour Court, established by law in 1910 following a proposal from the two federations. The Labour Court consists of 12 members elected by the employers' and the workers' organizations, and 1 chairman and 3 vice chairmen elected by the 12 members. This law was altered in 1973 to take account of union dissatisfaction with the Court's handling of illegal strikes by establishing more flexible sanctions.

The third fruit of the joint committee of 1908 was a law on state conciliation in case of a failure to get the collective agreements renegotiated. The state conciliators and mediators are appointed by the minister of labour after recommendation from the Labour Court. State conciliators and mediators have the right to intervene during collective bargaining under specified conditions.

This structural framework for industrial relations in Denmark has been extended by government involvement since the 1930s. From 1933 and onwards the government and the Folketing, often by passing a law, dictated the terms of agreement when one or both parties have not accepted the state conciliator's proposal. In 1936, the two national federations themselves established certain procedural rules for negotiation of new agreements and voting rules ('package-voting') which furthered a centralization of collective bargaining. The rules have been changed but the feature of centralization has prevailed. Thus, bargaining issues are always divided into general and specific ones. The former are negotiated by the national Confederation of Employers' Associations and the Federation of Trade Unions.

Another aspect of the general IR framework is an agreement of 1947 (re-negotiated in 1964 and 1970) between the Trade Union Federation and the Employers' Confederation which created co-operation committees in firms above a certain size (now 50 employees). The co-operation committee consists of one half management representatives and one half employee representatives chosen from shop stewards. This committee aims at increased competitiveness and greater job satisfaction.

In 1973 the company act was amended to secure employee representatives at company board level. This law was passed unanimously by the Folketing. The representation consists of two seats elected through direct elections. It is a condition that a majority of the employees must in advance have expressed their acceptance of the representation. In about half of the cases, the representation comprises one worker and one salaried employee, for example a middle manager (Dansk Arbejdsgiverforening, 1975: 6). Finally, the law on Work Environment (previously called the Factory Act and Workers' Protection Act) has included since 1954 provisions for the election of work safety representatives among the workers. In addition, the workers' and employers' organizations work together with the state to contribute to unemployment insurance, employment service, training, and social benefits. The Danish unemployment insurance scheme is organized by unemployment insurance associations closely allied with the trade unions. The costs are to a small extent paid by the wage-earners, but mainly refunded by the state. The employment service is supplied by state employment service offices. These offices are supervised by committees consisting of state representatives and representatives from the employers' and workers' organizations. Vocational training is organized by the Ministry of Labour and the Ministry of Education. Trade unions and employers' organizations have a determining influence in most of the committees regulating vocational training. The supply of social benefits is mainly a state and municipal function, but in special laws the Federation of Trade Unions and the Employers' Confederation take part in the administration. This is the case with the Law on Labour-market Supplementary Pension Scheme and the Law on Daily Sickness Benefits.

Organizational principles of unions and employers' associations

Trade unions were established during the last quarter of the nineteenth century in conjunction with the expansion of manufacturing firms. The skilled workers formed craft unions which have survived until the present day. Around the turn of the century the unskilled male workers organized themselves in a general union which today gathers one quarter of the total membership of the Danish trade union movement. Some skilled unions have amalgamated after World War II, and the total number of national unions within the Trade Unions Federation, the Landsorganisationen (LO) is about 40.

The highest body in the LO is the congress which consists of the head councils of the unions and some other representatives and meets every fourth year. The congress elects the president, vice president, treasurer, 5 secretaries and an executive committee (Buksti & Johansen, 1977: 31). This committee of 22 is the highest body in the LO and includes the president of the LO and the presidents of the metal workers' union and the general workers' union (Auken, 1970: 123, 142; Wechselmann, 1975: 224-5). Two representatives of the Social Democratic party can (and do) join the executive committee.

The national unions comprise around 1800 local unions bound to a certain geographical area. Members elect the president of the local union and a committee to take care of the daily business for a period of one year. Every 3-5 years the members elect representatives to the congress of the national union. The congress usually elects the leaders, the head council and the president, and eventually the vice-president and the treasurer. An executive committee may be elected by the congress or the head council. Some unions elect their leaders by referendum (see Buksti & Johansen, 1977).

At the firm level, workers of each craft as well as the unskilled workers form clubs and elect club committees which in larger firms combine into a joint club. The chairman of the club acts as shop steward. In firms where there is no club, the workers will in any case have chosen a shop steward who has certain rights and responsibilities according to the collective agreement. The average constituency of the shop steward is approximately 50, and the median average length of tenure is two and a half years (Lund, 1963). The shop stewards and club representatives will have more or less formal relationship to the local union.

Around 85 per cent of the skilled workers and 70 per cent of the unskilled workers are organized (Plovsing, 1973: 13). About one half of the salaried employees are organized, but there are great variations between various groups of employees, and they are divided among many organizations. The National Union of Commerce and Office Employees (HK) is the second largest member of the LO. Another large group of salaried employees is the Federation of Danish Civil Servants and Salaried Employees (FTF); it is not a member of the LO, and by contrast to the HK, acts as a politically neutral organization. Another difference between the two organizations is that HK has most of its members in the private sector while FTF has more public employees. FTF also organizes employees at supervisor levels whereas HK only includes subordinate employees. After several years of mutual conflict, HK and FTF negotiated a jurisdictional agreement in 1969 (Blum & Ponak, 1974). Larger separate organizations cover academic people and supervisors and technical superordinate employees.

The Confederation of Employers' Association, the Dansk Arbejdsgiverforening, was established in 1896 to counter the demands of trade unions. The Confederation consists of about 180 associations (in 1977, see Buksti & Johansen, 1977: 135) each of which covers handicraft, manufacturing, building

Table 4.4.
Danish labour market organizations: Selected years 1945-1975

	1945	1955	1965	1975
Danish Federation of Trade Unions (LO)				
Number of national unions	72	71	66	44
Number of local branches	3,432	3,632	3,466	1,812
Total membership	579,422	693,204	833,980	953,318
The Federation of Danish Civil Servants and Salaried Employees (FTF)		88,465	132,113	210,190
Academics' Central Organization				44,047
Other organizations for higher level employees		56,541	70,016	68,266
Danish Employers' Confederation (DA)				
Number of members	19,658	23,628	22,712	20,943
Number of associations	246	259	223	180
Number of workers employed	222,000	332,323	400,035	291,685

Source: Statistical Yearbooks.

and construction, transport, commerce, and office work. Some of the branches are divided into special associations for the major geographical areas.

Therefore, the number of associations far excedes the number of national unions. The percentage of organized employers is rather small as seen by the number of employed workers in relation to the total manual working force. Nevertheless, the agreements which the Confederation negotiates with the trade unions are directly or indirectly determining the employment conditions both in the private and the public sector. The Confederation is highly centralized because the associations have no right to decide wages, hours, etc. which is the authority of the Confederation. The highest body is the general assembly. This elects the general council which meets four times a year, and an executive committee which usually meets twice a month.

The Confederation has a large staff of specialists many of whom come from an academic background. These take care of statistics regarding working conditions, training of employers and supervisors, and represent the Confederation in national and international committees.

Influence potential on government

The Danish labour market organizations have a close relationship to the political forces of the country. The Danish LO is represented on the executive board of the Social Democratic party, and this party is represented on the executive board of the LO. When the Social Democrats are in government, as they have been most of the time since the 1930s even though they have never had a majority in parliament, the LO and the government have informal talks on a continuous basis (Auken, 1972: 164-5).

In general, it cannot be said whether the Social Democratic party or the LO is the dominating element. It depends on the issue, or the coalition possibilities in parliament. The Employers' Confederation has no similar close relationship to anyone party or government. Yet, there is an informal relationship between employers' officials and non-Socialist members of parliament. Lately, there have also been formal meetings between the DA and the non-Socialist parties prior to major political–economic decisions. Both top organizations are represented in a wide range of state committees on labour and social matters, and economic policy are not decided upon by parliament without prior talks with the two organizations. This integration of labour market organizations and public policy means that the organizations no longer act as pressure groups but have been made part of a pluralistic system with more or less corporative features (Dahlerup *et al.*, 1975: 328).

Previously, when the Danish Employers' Confederation and the LO made a compromise on an issue, they could expect that the government would bring in the necessary legislation, but as has been mentioned, this may not be the case now, because of the number of parties in parliament. For example, the proposed act on vocational training and economic compensation to the apprentices of 1977, where the Folketing opposed the LO–DA compromise and carried through its own line.

The Industrial climate

The general increase in strikes in many countries during the 1960s has also been experienced in Denmark even though the figures (strike days per 100 employees) are lower than in, for example, the United Kingdom (Hyman, 1972: 32).

It is generally felt that many reasons cause the increase in the number of un-official strikes. Besides protests against special legislative measures regarding tax increases, protests against wage differentials and the piece rate system are important factors. To this must be added the dynamics of higher expectations from better educated employees and the activities from left wing political groups who favour action on the firm level. Public opinion may also contribute to unofficial strikes, for example, during the spring 1974 when an opinion poll counted 40 per cent of the electorate as thinking that the unofficial protest strikes were supported by the workers in general (Avisarbogen, 1974: 24/5). The unofficial strikes put a certain pressure on the relations between the LO and the Employers' Confederation, but have not stopped the efforts of these two to find joint solutions to the general problem of labour relations.

Regarding accidents and other work environment indicators, statistics are not reliable. The number of accidents registered by the Factory Inspectorate was 25,000 in 1974, but the number of work accidents with more than three days' absence may be about 70,000. Work accidents with 1-3 days' absence may hit 2 million people each year, but the exact figure is not known (Arbejdsmil-jøgruppen, 1973: 43).

The understanding of the adverse effects of inferior working conditions has been increased by recent investigations into various aspects of the working environment. These investigations have shown that about one third of the LO members suffer the inconvenience from noise and draughts. Furthermore, 25-30

Table 4.5.
Strikes and lockouts in Denmark: Selected years 1945–1977

	1945	1955	1965	1970	1973	1974	1975	1976	1977
Number of stoppages (more than 100 lost days)	35	13	37	77	205	134	147	204	228
Number of strikers or lockouts	8,526	6,257	14,194	55,585	337,100	142,352	59,128	87,224	36,305
Lost days (1000)	66	10	242	102	3,901	184	100	210	230

Source: Statistical Yearbooks: Nyt fra Danmarks Statistik, 98/1978.
Note: in contrast to earlier decades, the new feature is that it is now unofficial strikes which are flourishing, but because of their short term nature they do not count much in the statistics on loss of working days (see Table 4.6).

Table 4.6.
Number of lost working days during five-year periods within the areas of the Employers' Confederation (1000) days)

Period	Official stoppage	Unofficial stoppage
1950–4	0	43
1955–9	1,054	59
1960–4	2,107	113
1965–9	221	92
1970–4	3,612	448
1975–7	11	502

Source: DA, *Annual Reports.*

per cent of LO members mention symptoms such as pains and stress (Arbeidsmil-jøgruppen, 1974: 13 & 16). From the point of view of the industrial climate , however, it is important to notice that most LO members express satisfaction with their supervisor, their work tempo, their relations with their colleagues, and content of work (Arbejdsmiljøgruppen, 1974: 64 & 207).

2.2. Participation in companies
Main legal basis

In Danish firms the employer has 'the right to direct and distribute work' but there are formal limits to this right, and practice may differ between firms. Collective bargaining is one limiting factor but according to the topics negotiated it is only of modest importance in this respect. Workers' indirect participation in a small range of management decision-making takes place through their elected shop stewards. These representatives have as their main duties negotiations for wages and overtime pay, and also work safety and hygiene, now to be taken care of by special representatives in the firm (Hornemann Møller, 1968).

The establishment of co-operation committees has extended the workers' indirect participation in management decisions because management must allow them to influence the policies of day-to-day production and work planning, and in the implementation of major alterations in the enterprise. Furthermore, the committees have the right to exercise co-determination in formulating principles which govern the organization of local work, safety and welfare conditions, and staff policy. Research shows that the committees actually cover a wide range of issues, but only one third of employees connect various improvements with the work of the co-operation committees (Martini Jørgensen, 1971).

The employee representatives at board level of joint stock companies since 1974 give workers and salaried employees the possibility for indirect participation in major policy decisions. But from the first it appears that these representatives have not yet been very active, and the employees do not know much about what is going on (Westenholz, 1976: 5).

Since the 1950s, the Employers' Confederation has extended the training of managers in modern methods of management and co-operation and this has contributed to an increased direct participation of workers in management's day-to-day decisions. This development has also become mandatory according to the joint agreement on co-operation and co-operation committees. Besides referring to workers' rights according to collective agreements and to participation through shop stewards and co-operation committees, this agreement also contains the following principles, under the heading, 'Day-today co-operation in all enterprises':

Management of the enterprises should be carried out in such a manner as to inspire, to the widest possible extent, co-operation in order to ensure competitive ability of enterprises and job satisfaction. The widest possible delegation of responsibility and authority to individual members or groups of members is necessary in order to ensure that employees are given a say in arranging their own work situations and influencing the decision-making in the enterprises. Methods of management according to these principles should be applied through every stage in the internal organization of the enterprises.

In a few special cases, the unions and the employers' association have formally agreed upon experiments with semi-autonomous work groups e.g. within the metal industry, but several other experiments have taken place under the auspices of the co-operation committee in question (Agersnap et al., 1974).

2.3. Unity/disunity of representation

When the co-operation committees were established in 1947, it was at once incorporated into the agreement that the shop stewards should become the workers' representatives in the committee and other workers were eligible only in cases where the number of representatives to be elected exceeded the number of existing shop stewards. In this way rivalries between the committee and the shop steward were excluded.

Regarding the new board representatives, no similar restrictions are found; and the trade unions have taken no clear attitude. Some have argued for shop stewards at the board to secure co-ordination of workers' interests, while others have suggested the shop stewards would get involved in role-conflict. The first elections in 1974 and the beginning of 1975 have shown that approximately half of the elected worker representatives are shop stewards (Dansk Arbejdsgiver-forening, 1975: Table 4).

Between the trade unions and the shop stewards, no publicly recognized conflict of a widespread nature is found; but investigations have shown that there are deep differences of opinion as to whether the shop steward is to represent the workers' or the local union's interest at the firm level. In case of conflict between these interests workers, shop stewards and managers think that the shop steward should give priority to the workers' interests at the firm level whereas the union officers want the shop stewards to try to reconcile the two interests. All groups agree that the shop stewards take the workers' side in case of conflict with the union (Hornemann Møller, 1969).

The relationship between manual workers and salaried employees is positive in Denmark. There is no antagonism between subordinate and superordinates, and election of representatives to the company boards have shown that in many cases an open or tacit agreement between all employees has secured the representation of both subordinate and superordinate employees. Nevertheless, at the level of the co-operation committee supervisors and middle management are rather passive and no support of workers' points of view can be expected from them. This may also be a reflection of the structure of the Danish committees according to which one half of the members represent the responsible management and the technical and commercial employees who are not members of a trade union, and the other half representing the remaining groups of employees. Regarding subordinate white-collar employees, manual workers have helped them in their recent drive towards an increase in the number of organized white-collar employees within HK.

2.4. Main bargaining structure

The major bargaining issues are settled at the national level. The two top organizations, LO and the Employers' Confederation, negotiate the general issues e.g. general wage increases and holidays; and the national unions and employers' associations try to agree on their specific interests regarding wage differentiation within the industry, rules of dismissal according to seniority, etc. What is left for local negotiations between the shop stewards and the employer at the plant level, depends very much upon the wage system. In case of a system of minimum wage rates, combined with additional payments to workers with special qualifications and working conditions as found in the metal industry, local bargaining at plant level takes place several times during the agreement period to adjust wages to local productivity increases. Where so-called normal wage rates exist the possibility for wage negotiations depends upon the local employer and the employment situation. During the full employment period of 1960s, it became more and more common that the normal wage rates were adjusted once or twice a year to the increases in the average level, as disclosed by wage statistics published by the unions and the Employers' Confederation.

In firms where piece rates exist, there is always the possibility of those rates being negotiated again when work methods and production change. Negotiations caused by a cost-of-living clause are not usual, because there is a cost-of-living clause in the collective agreements imposing an automatic relationship between increases in prices and increases in wages.

It appears that during the 1960s, a quarter of the growth in money wages was due to the collective bargaining rounds every second year, a quarter caused by the cost-of-living clause, and the rest was due to the wage slide carried through by local bargaining. The result was that the skilled workers got relatively less during the collective bargaining at the national level, but more at the firm level, whereas the unskilled workers got more at the national level to catch up with what they had lost at the firm level, with the added intention of lessening differentials. Actually such a decrease took place during the period 1963–74 because of a wage policy at the national level and an improvement of employment situation (Landsorganisation, 1975a). To some extent, the bargaining issues at the local and the national level differ from each other. At the local level, more welfare issues are considered, but as some of these may be of interest to all parties, e.g. sick insurance, they become national issues and are made a legislative matter. Especially during the 1950s, many social issues were brought to the national level for the first time through this process (Agersnap et al., 1960: 186).

Role and strength of unions in bargaining

The power balance between unions and the Employers' Confederation has not changed during several decades. Both sides have large conflict-funds and are able to supplement them with support from abroad. Furthermore, neither part is torn by internal rivalries. But a few modifying comments can be made to this picture. During the late 1960s and early 1970s, a certain tendency on the part of the unions to press for political solutions when not being able to convince the Employers' Confederation could be seen because of the strong political position of the Social Democrats and left-wing parties. The most extreme victory for the unions was the decision by parliament in 1972 to make the employers responsible for daily sickness and accident benefits from the first day of absence. A right-wing turn in the Folketing has now stopped this tendency in union policy.

At the firm-level, the workers may have pushed their demands further than before because of full employment during the 1960s, and the management more often gave in to the regret of the Employers' Confederation. But this situation too has changed as unemployment increased to more than 5 per cent of the labour-force during the middle of the 1970s.

Enforcement and sanctioning possibilities

The Standard Rules of 1910 and the Labour Court work effectively to maintain the system of collective agreements, but the more radical groups of the Danish labour movement demand during the existing agreements the right to bargain to the point of strike action and reject the Labour Court. The consequences of an unreasonable dismissal of a worker or a shop steward is a fine imposed on the employer, and even though the shop stewards have a possibility of staying in the firm, this is not usually the decision taken by the Labour Court. Here the workers' threat of striking may be more effective. To interpret the agreement on co-operation committees and serve as the body responsible for dealing with breaches of it, a co-operation board has been established by the two top organizations, but only a few cases have been brought before it. Finally it should be noticed that it is common that matters which have been raised as grievances during the existing agreement are incorporated in the bargaining period.

2.5. The role of public powers in the Danish Industrial Relations System
The company level

At the company level, the state authorities interfere with the worker-management relationship to an increasing extent.

First, in case of strikes the police has in recent years taken a more active role in securing access to the companies by non-strikers. The question about so-called physical blockades has been a touchy one giving rise to debates in the Folketing (Folketingstidende, 30/10 1975; Folketingets forhandlinger, 8/3 1978) and much resentment in the trade union movement.

Second, the machinery for the state's supervision of the work environment has been extended as a result of the work environment law of 1975. More technical and medical personnel has been involved in the state's supervision of labour conditions, and frequent visits to the places of work are planned. Special state campaigns to improve working conditions are to be run in co-operation with company committees of worker representatives, supervisors and employers (Arbejdstilsynet, 1977). Whether the state will expand participation above or below the board, is yet to be seen.

The national level

Nationally, the state interferes with the labour market to settle disputes, runs an employment service, gives vocational training, and awards social benefits. But the corporative nature of the relationship between the labour market organizations and the state at the national level is most clearly mirrored in the state's attempts to maintain an incomes policy since the 1960s (Auken & Buksti, 1975).

In 1963, a coalition government of Social Democrats and Social Liberals succeeded in carrying out a so-called general solution regarding changes in work incomes, trade incomes and public expenditures for the following year. The collective agreement between LO and the Employers' Confederation was adjusted and renewed for two years. Later incomes policies had the character of declarations by the government on the economic situation. However, in 1974-5 once more an ambitious effort at an incomes policy was made, but owing to a deep political split up in the Danish Parliament, the co-ordination of collective agreements, financial policy, social expenditures, and limits on trade income was relatively modest.

In August 1976, the Social Democratic minority government under pressure from a non-Socialist majority carried through an economic policy which contained control of prices and personal incomes, reductions of planned public expenditures, an increase of indirect taxes, and a limit of 2 per cent for wage increases during the next round of collective bargaining (November 1976 to March 1977). Whereas the Employers' Confederation welcomed this sort of an incomes policy, the LO rejected the policy as such, but confirmed its trust in the Social Democratic government and accepted to formulate its demands within the framework set up by parliament. Therefore LO furthered demands only for a special wage increase for the lowest paid, improvements for shift workers and other workers having hard working conditions, and an extension of the educational fund. Some of these demands were accepted and two thirds of the workers voted for the draft settlement prepared by the conciliator, though two thirds of the employers voted against it. Then the Social Democratic minority government took action, and in the Folketing Social Democrats, Conservatives, and three Centre parties passed a law giving statutory effect to the settlement against votes from parties to the left and right of this coalition (Metal, 4 & 6/1977).

In August 1977, the government got broad political support to a combined plan to limiting demand for higher indirect taxes and stimulating employment by subsidies etc. during the period 1977-80, but the weakness of this compromise was that no clear solutions to the balance of payment and unemployment problems were secured (Metal 14/1977: 9; Economic Secretariat, 1977: 42).

3. PROGRAMMATIC PERSPECTIVES, PROBLEMATIC ISSUES, AND PROSPECTIVE DEVELOPMENTS

3.1. Programmatic perspectives

In December 1973 a Danish government commission published a major review for the next 15 years 1972-87 (PP-II, 1973). Even though the energy crisis, the increase in unemployment, and the balance-of-payment problems in the last few years have changed the Danish outlook in several ways, this report also pointed to some fundamental questions covering the labour market and industry which have to be solved, and presented arguments which still may be shared by a majority of the Danish population.

In the short and long range perspective it is necessary to change Danish trade or industry structure to increase exports of goods and services. This means organizational changes in the interrelationships between industry and the state, and greater mobility in the labour market. Pressures for a lowering of costs will accelerate technological changes. However, this sort of reasoning is the standard way of economists' thinking and nothing is said about the viewpoints of the ordinary citizens and their reactions to structural unemployment. How to legitimize the societal changes of the coming years will become a major problem.

According to the Danish LO's congress 1975 the major demand of the trade unions is greater though responsible control of the society. Among the methods mentioned is economic democracy (Landsorganisationen, 1975: 26-7). The idea of economic democracy is to secure capital for new investments at the same time as the wage-earners get their share of the capital growth and the accompanying economic influence.

The LO has proposed a 'wage-earners investment and profit (dividend) fund' financed by a duty on all employers. This proposal has been criticized for being too centralized and giving the LO top too much power. The LO proposal was favoured by the Social Democratic government in 1973, but failed in parliament. The opponents on the left and the right have their own proposals, and it is generally felt that it is necessary to start some kind of economic democracy.

The employers' side has expressed a positive attitude towards an extension of industrial co-ownership at the company level, but the employers are against collective funds controlled by the unions. The employers also prefer voluntary agreements as against compulsory arrangements (Dansk Arbejdsgiverforening & Industriradet, 1972: 18 & 32-3).

In 1977, a committee with representatives from the labour market organizations was established by the Danish government. The aim is to evaluate different economic democracy models, and it is to be expected that these deliberations will become an important part in future collective bargaining rounds (Finanstidende, No. 7, 1977).

3.2. Main implications of the system

Issues mainly addressed by the system

The Danish labour market organizations have been developed to influence wages and hours of work, social security measures, vocational training, and the participation of the employees.

On the union side, according to the 1975 LO congress, the immediate task is to fight unemployment. The LO has proposed several employment measures including public steering and financing of housing. The LO also intends to intensify its work on those other matters which go beyond the traditional wage negotiations, beginning with the building up of a regional organization and a strengthening of its training of union people.

On the employers' side, the major problem is competitiveness in home and foreign markets. With the profit motive as the incentive, the employers maintain that higher Danish production and greater exports are the only way out of unemployment and balance of payment difficulties. They favour an incomes policy, with wages co-ordinated with the national economic policy and giving production and employment the priority over wage increases (Industriradet, 1977).

The divergent views between unions and employers are not astonishing, but it is new that they are so explicitly expressed. This may, of course, result in future confrontation, but it does heed to a better understanding of the problems and to compromises.

Public reactions to the system

Unions and their methods are accepted by their members. Unions are found to be necessary and local and national bargaining are recognized as the most important ways of furthering the demands of the workers, whereas radical measures – sit-ins and general strikes, – are not accepted (Gundelach et al., 1969; Jørgensen & Lind, 1975). In the second half of 1974, opinion polls showed that a majority

(53-69 per cent) of the Danish population was in favour of autonomous negotiations between the LO and the Employers' Confederation, while 16 to 24 per cent of the population thought that parliament should determine the guide-lines within which negotiations should take place (Avisarbogen, 1974, 7/10, 14/12, & 31/12).

Conclusions

Political changes since 1970 have strengthened the non-socialist parties, and the economic situation since 1973 has weakened the labour movement because of rising unemployment and diminishing resources to introduce reforms. Both have checked the offensive for greater union influence in company decision-making.

Furthermore, the changes in industrial relations have created a gulf between national leadership and the local level. This, on the union side, results in different opinions on how to achieve industrial democracy. The national labour market organizations have grown more powerful and have now achieved a decisive influence in matters concerning employment and competitiveness in comparison with other countries. They now (reluctantly) feel forced to accept more responsibility for the general development of the national economy. They are no longer just the advocates of one of the parties, but have to show more objective attitudes and to push for less selfish goals. These changes of attitude are primarily felt in the top of the organizations and have yet to filter down to lower levels. It has, created of course, a certain amount of unrest and dissatisfaction in some local branches.

Since the agreements now are settled by big 'package deals' or eventually by law they do not carry in them the former obligation to adhere to the agreement to the same extent. Regarding the Labour Court, it is no longer seen only as a collective institution for clarifying misunderstandings etc., but also as a police court supporting the wealthy, the 'establishment'. Hence the rise in the number of unofficial 'wildcat' strikes and in the number of attacks on unions for being co-opted or petrified.

On the other hand, according to many Danes, the economic situation demands an incomes policy and investments which leads to economic democracy. It is to be expected that employee influence on ownership will stimulate participation in other decision-making areas at the company level, furthering industrial democracy.

At the same time, the tighter industrial relations system has moved some of the conflict away from the traditional management–worker disputes at the company level. Because of external pressures and differences, the local partners have become more aware of other factors which in turn leads to mutual beneficial solutions. This has led to a development of a new 'machinery', parallel to the traditional one for bargaining. These consist of the participation schemes comprising works council, representation on company boards, semi-autonomous work groups, and so on.

All in all, the growth in industrial democracy in Denmark is not an automatic one. But, the continuing experiments with incomes policies, economic democracy, etc. can be seen as an attempt to find an industrial relations system more democratic in nature and more suitable to a 'mixed' economy.

To sum up, Danish relations in the post-war period have been looked at in the context of industrial democracy. It is maintained here that changed political conditions and unemployment have weakened the demands of the trade unions. Industrial relations are put under pressure because of unofficial strikes, but they have not stopped the workers' and employers' organizations finding joint solutions. The period 1945–75 has seen a change towards extended participation schemes from the shop floor to the company board, but the employees do not take much interest in the working of the participating machinery. Against the background of the current balance-of-payment problems and high unemployment rate, the most animated discussion concerns attempts to introduce an incomes policy and economic democracy. These two solutions illustrate the tendency towards corporative features of the Danish industrial relations system. In both cases, however, opposing views of political parties, trade unions, and employers' associations make agreement on goals and methods extremely difficult. None the less, some sort of income-policy package deals including features of economic democracy are to be expected in the future if the past is an indication.

REFERENCES

Agersnap, Flemming, Finn Junge, Ann Westenholz, Palle Møldrup & Lisbeth Brinch (1974), 'Danish experiments with new forms of co-operation on the shopfloor'. *Personnel Review*, 3.

Agersnap, Torben, Pia Barfod, Reinhard Lund & Poul Milhøj (1960), *45 Timers Ugens Indførelse 1958–60*. København.

Agreement on Cooperation and Cooperation Committees between the Danish Employers' Confederation and the Danish Federation of Trade Unions (1970).

Arbejdsmiljøgruppen af 1972 (1973), *Arbejdsmiljø*. København. Rapport 1.

(1974), *Arbejdsmiljøundersøgelsen*. København. Rapport 2.

Arbejdstilsynet (1977), *Status og Planer 1977/82*. København.

Auken, Svend (1970), 'Tilrettelæggelsen af dansk fagbevægelses politik'. Økonomi og politik. 2.

(1972), 'Fagbevægelsen som politisk instrument'. In John Mølgaard, Jesper Due, & Jørgen Steen Madsen (eds), LO – Magt eller Afmagt. København.

Auken, Svend & Jacob A. Buksti (1975), *Indkomstpolitik i Danmark*. Aarhus Universitet.

Avisårbogen (1974).

Blum, Albert & Allen Ponak (1974), 'White collar unions in Denmark'. *Industrial Relations Industrielles*, 29.

Borre, Ole, Hans Jørgen Nielsen, Steen Sauerberg & Torben Worre (1976), *Vælgere i 70'erne*. Akademisk Forlag.

Buksti, Jacob A. & Lars Nørby Johansen (1977), *Danske Organisationers Hvem, Hvad, Hvor*. København.

Dahlerup, Drude, Carsten Jarlov, Lars Nørby Johansen & Ole P. Kristensen (1975), 'Korporatisme-begrebet og studiet af samspillet mellem politiske institutioner'. Økonomi og Politik, 4.

Dansk Arbejdsgiverforening (The Danish Employers' Confederation), *Annual Reports*.
    Pamphlet on Membership, Copenhagen. No date.
    (1975), Medarbejdere i Bestyrelsen — En Statistisk Undersøgelse. København.
Dansk Arbejdsgiverforening & Industrirådet (1972), Medarbejder — Medejer. København.
De Samvirkende Fagforbund i Danmark 1898-1923. (1922) København.
Det centrale Uddannelsesråd (1975), *Redegørelse for Arbejdet med en Samlet Uddannelsesplan frem til 1990*. København.
    (1978), *U-90*. Kobenhavn.
Det økonomiske Råd (1977), *Dansk Økonomi Maj 1977*. Kobenhavn.
Economic Secretariat of the Danish Government (1976), *Økonomisk Oversigt. Marts 1976*. København.
    (1977), *Økonomisk Oversigt. December 1977*. København.
Finanstidende. (1977), No. 7. 18 November.
Folketingstidende, Folketingets forhandlinger (fortryk). Published by the Danish Folketing. København.
Gundelach, Peter, Hans Hansen, Steen Martini Jørgensen, Olaf Rieper, Helge Tetzschner & Reinhard Lund (1969), *De Ansattes Indflydelse på Københavns Kommunes Arbejdspladser,* SFI studie 18. København.
Hansen, Svend Aage (1974), *Økonomisk Vækst i Danmark. Bd. II. 1914-1970.* København.
Hornemann Møller, Iver (1968), *Tillidsmænd i Industrivirksomheder.* København.
    (1969), *Tillidsmandsinstitutionens Effektivitet.* SFI studie 13. København.
    (1976), 'The Effectiveness of Shop Stewards and Supervisors', I & II. SFI studie 33. København.
Hyman, Richard (1972), *Strikes.* Fontana.
Høgh, Erik (1965), *Sociologi.* København.
Industrirådet (1977), *Industrien i Samfundet.* København.
Jørgensen, Henning & Jens Lind (1975), *Fagforeningen Set af Medlemmerne.* Fabrik- og Specialarbejdernes Fagforening. Odense.
Kjerkegaard, Else (ed.) (1976), *Levevilkår i Danmark.* Socialforskningsinstituttet & Danmarks Statistik. København.
Landsorganisationen i Danmark/The Danish Federation of Trade Unions, *Co-Ownership, Co-Determination.* Copenhagen. No date.
    (1976), *The Danish Trade Unions Movement.* Copenhagen.
    (1975a), *LO Gør Status.* København.
    (1975b), *LO's Kongres 1975.* Formand, Thomas Nielsens mundtlige beretning. København.
Lund, Reinhard (1963), 'Shop Stewards in Danish Industry'. *Journal of Industrial Relations, 3*.
Martini Jørgensen, Steen (1971), *Kommunale Samarbejdsudvalg.* København.
Metal (1977), 4 & 6. Published by the Metal Workers' National Union.
Olsen, Erling (1962), *Danmarks Økonomiske Historie Siden 1750.* København.
Plovsing, Jan (1973), *Funktionær. Organiseret eller Uorganiseret?* SFI pjece 2. København.
PP-II (1973), *Perspektivplan-redegørelse 1972-1987.* København.
Rise, Allan & Jens Degerbøl (1973), *Grundregler i Dansk Arbejdsret.* København.

Statistical Yearbooks, Statistical Tables, Statistical Inquiries, Nyt fra Danmarks Statistik. Published by Danmarks Statistik.

Westenholz, Ann (1976), *Lønmodtagerrepræsentation i Aktieselskabsbestyrelser.* Nyt fra Samfundsvidenskaberne. København.

5

THE FINNISH INDUSTRIAL RELATIONS SYSTEM

1. GENERAL SITUATION AND BACKGROUND

The Finnish social system and constitution originate in the period during which Finland was part of the kingdom of Sweden. In 1809, as a result of a war between Sweden and Russia, Finland fell under Russian domination as an autonomous Grand Duchy with her existing constitution, laws and institutions. In 1917 Finland became an independent republic. Intensive legislative work started from that year. The highest people's representative body is the 200-seat parliament. Representatives of the parliament are elected by universal suffrage every four years, most recently in 1979 (see Table 5.1).

1.1. Status Quo of Political Power

The country has four main political parties: the Democratic League of the People of Finland (which includes Communists), the Social Democratic Party, the Centre Party and, on the right, the National Coalition Party. In addition, between the Central Party and the National Coalitition Party, are two minor but notable parties: the Liberal Party and the Swedish People's Party in Finland. In 1958–62 and 1966–70, parliament had a left-wing majority, but at all other times the centre and right wing have had a majority. Excluding short periods, the Centre Party has had representatives in political government during the whole period of independence. The most frequent partners of the Centre Party in government have been the Liberal and Swedish parties, with a coalition of either the Social Democratic Party or the National Coalition Party. Since 1966, the latter has been in opposition.

In December 1975, stimulated by the recession, a broad-based government was formed. All the main parties excluding the National Coalition Party were represented. This coalition, however, fell in Autumn 1976 because of internal conflicts but in spring 1977 it returned to power.

The voting percentage has ranged between 73.5–85.1 per cent. The political power ratio in Finland has been quite stable during the last thirty years. The share of seats of the left-wing parties has been between 44 and 52 per cent, and the number of female representatives in Parliament is now 54, 27 per cent of the whole.

1.2. Recent Political Events

The great changes in Finnish society in the 1960s and 1970s, notably in the social structure and in the structure of the economy (with the diversification of the industrial base), have affected political life. These changes have brought

Table 5.1.

Parliamentary elections in Finland 1945-1979. Number of representatives in Parliament

			1945	1954	1966	1979
L W		Democratic League of the				
E I		People of Finland (incl.				
F N		Communists)	49	43	41	35
T G		Social Democratic Party	50	54	55	52
C						
E		Centre Party	49	53	49	36
N		Liberal Party	9	13	9	4
T		Swedish People's Party				
R		in Finland	14	13	12	10
E						
R W						
I I		National Coalition Party				
G N		(Conservatives)	28	24	26	47
H G		Others	1	–	8	16
T						
			200	200	200	200

Sources: Statistical Yearbook, 1976 and election results, 1979.

about a closer co-operation between the so-called centre parties, i.e. the Centre (Agrarian) Party, the Liberal Party, and the Swedish People's Party, as a counterbalance to the other dominating political group, the Social Democrats. The interests of the supporters of these groups — the agrarian population and civil servants on the one hand, and civil workers and other employees with small income on the other hand — differ considerably from each other, which greatly hampers the solving of problems. In the local government elections in October 1976, the key questions were incomes policy, employment, and taxation. In the last few years the heavy direct taxes, mainly due to a high inflation rate, have been regarded as unreasonable by nearly all parties. From the beginning of 1977, the tax on business turnover percentage was raised from 11 to 14 per cent, the progression and thus also the effect of the income tax and property tax were lightened respectively.

1.3. The Economic Situation

Population

The population of Finland, which is now about five millions (with 75 per cent of working age), has grown quite rapidly, especially just after the Second World War. In the 1950s and 1960s emigration to Sweden was quite considerable. Nowadays, it is estimated that about 300,000 Finns live in Sweden. Since 1955, the labour force has been allowed to move without any restriction in the whole of Scandinavia. In 1976, however, there were only 11,700 foreigners in Finland.

Finland has a Swedish-speaking minority of 6.6 per cent of the whole population, a reduction of 3.0 per cent since 1940. Fifty-eight per cent of the population is concentrated in the three south-western provinces, an area which is 16 per cent of the total. This concentration occurred mainly in the 1950s and 1960s, the result of the diminishing need for agricultural labour. Nearly half (48 per cent) the population are active and working.

Labour Market

Table 5.2.

Labour force by some industries (excluding people working in household economy)

	Manufacturing	Banking & Insurance	Total Labour Force	Outside agricultural sector
1948	353,900	10,200	1,635,500	56.0%
1955	401,100	16,300	1,798,000	64.1%
1965	460,100	29,100	1,980,900	73.3%
1975	609,000	42,800	2,272,100	85.2%

Source: Statistical Yearbooks 1948-76.

In the banking and insurance sector the growth of employees has been rapid since the 1960s. The proportion of women here is high, 65 per cent of the labour force. One-third of the industrial labour force is employed in the metal and engineering industry. The proportion of women in industrial labour is about one-third, but in the metal and engineering industry the proportion is 20 per cent (Kavonius, 1975).

In industry, 20 per cent of jobs employ 80 per cent of industrial labour. Companies in metal and engineering industry have more employees than industrial companies in general, and half of the companies with over 1,000 employees operate in the metal and engineering sector. Finland has paid much attention to labour policy during the last twenty years. It has taken various measures to ensure high employment. The main activities are as follows: retraining for employment purposes, employment agency services, guidance, etc. Unemployment has primarily been a result of structural change as the emphasis has moved from agriculture to service and manufacturing industries. The effect of the recession can, however, be seen in the figures for the last few years, with annual unemployment being 0.4 per cent in 1955, 1.4 per cent in 1965, 2.2 per cent in 1975, 4.0 per cent in 1976, and 6.1 per cent in 1977. During the years 1966-9 there was a changeover to a 40-hour week in Finland and now the average number of working hours is down to 38 hours per week.

Economic Growth

In 1945-51 there was heavy inflation in Finland and the exchange value of the mark was lowered three times in 1945 and twice in 1949. Further devaluations took place in a smaller scale in 1957, 1967, and 1977 (twice). From the year 1973 on, there has been on an average a 15 per cent inflation in Finland, peaking

Table 5.3.
Gross national product in million Fmk (at market prices)

	Million Fmk	Real GNP (1964 = 100)
1965	25,828	105
1970	43,592	132
1971	47,661	136
1972	54,909	145
1973	66,746	154
1974	84,174	160
1975	98,572	160
1976	109,218	163
1977	120,338	162

Source: Statistical Yearbook 1977.

in 1975 when the cost-of-living index reached 17.8 per cent and then fell to 14.4 per cent in 1976, 12.7 per cent in 1977, and 7.5 per cent in 1979.

1.4. Social Stratification and Social Policy

Social Stratification

There have been great structural changes in the Finnish labour force since World War II. The number of farmers and farm workers has shrunk considerably but the number of administrative and clerical employees has increased very much both in the private and in public sector. It is expected that in the future labour in services will grow rapidly and the proportion of industrial workers will remain at the same level.

Table 5.4.
Employed labour force in Finland by industries

	1950	1960	1970	1975	1977
Agriculture, forestry	45.8	35.5	20.3	14.8	13.1
Manufacturing	20.8	21.6	25.9	27.4	27.4
Construction	6.3	8.7	8.3	8.5	7.6
Commerce (Incl. Banking & Insurance)	9.5	13.6	18.9	20.4	20.3
Transport, Communication	5.4	6.3	7.1	7.2	7.5
Services	10.8	14.0	18.1	21.6	24.1
Unknown	1.4	0.3	1.4	0.1	0.0
	100%	100%	100%	100%	100%
Total	1,984,300	2,033,300	2,118,300	2,221,00	2,111,000

Sources: Statistical Yearbook 1977 and ETLA Suhdannekatsaus, Spring 1978.

The large increase in the percentage of employees' share in the net domestic product in the mid-1950s to the mid-1970s from 55.9 per cent to 71 per cent is a result of new social policy legislation (pension systems, insurance systems, etc.).

During the last ten years, the wage differences between wage earners and salaried employees have shrunk and at the same time progressive income taxation has equalized the disposable income per person. Also, the wage differentials between male and female have shrunk lately. The average earnings per month for industrial male workers was in 1976 Fmk 2,390 and for female workers Fmk 1,760.

Education

In Finland there is practically no illiteracy because of compulsory primary school attendance (for 6-8 years) since 1921. The largest school reform ever carried out in Finland was completed by the end of 1977, when a fully comprehensive system was installed. All children receive full-time free education between the ages of seven and sixteen at schools provided for by the public authorities. In 1945, 13,583 pupils were at university (37.0 per cent women); by 1975, this was up to 69,925 (49.0 per cent women).

According to a research study carried out by the Finnish Newspapers' Association, the Finns read on an average two newspapers daily. The total net circulation of newspapers issued 3-7 times a week amounted to 2,536,589, i.e. 537 copies per 1,000 inhabitants in 1976. According to the study, the Finns spend half an hour daily on reading newspapers, of which only about 20 per cent represented social democratic or communist views.

2. THE NATIONAL INDUSTRIAL RELATIONS SYSTEM

2.1. Legal Basis and Main Ramifications of Overall IRS

The Main Features of the Finnish Labour Market Organizations

The labour market organizations play a very central role in Finland. Their operations are aimed at improving conditions for their own members, but they also contribute to regulating social growth as well. The relations between the various organizations in the labour market have been forged by (1) following the principle of industrial union; (2) a high degree of organization; (3) a high degree of centralization in the whole labour market system, with (4) the principle of securing national settlements, and with (5) the government playing an active part. There are two remaining features in Finland's industrial relations which affects them: the split in the unions between Social Democrats and Communists; and the limited right of the public sector to strike.

History and Legal Basis of the Labour Market System

The Finnish constitution, dating from 1919 states the freedom of assembly and association which underlie Finnish industrial relations. The birth of trade unions at the end of the nineteenth century and the beginning of the 20th century created the necessary pressures for the initiation of legislation. After Finland won independence and the political and social turmoil had settled, parliament began to produce labour legislation rapidly, with a labour agreement act (1922), a work regulation act (1922), an apprenticeship act (1923), a collective bargaining act (1924) and a collective labour disputes arbitration act (1925) being passed. One purpose of this legislation was to promote the adoption of collective bargaining, but these were not applied in practice at that time. However, it was only under the pressure of the 'Winter War' in 1939 with the Soviet Union that the leaders of the labour market organizations started negotiations with the aim to produce a common declaration. The first General Agreement between the Central Labour Organizations was made in 1944.

The following period of industrial relations legislation came directly after the Second World War. An act concerning collective labour agreements was passed in 1946, an act concerning labour arbitration courts in 1946, and one concerning work councils in 1946. Some previous legislation in the labour field was also reformed. Labour legislation saw another period of development in the mid-sixties, and previous legislation was changed to meet improved conditions and a more developed collective bargaining system. The Labour Protection Act passed in the early 1970s is strongly aimed at securing the co-operation of employees, and thus reflects the present trend in this field; for example the employment contract act of 1970, the annual vacation act of 1973, and the act of 1970 concerning payments to employees on leaving employment.

The Labour Unions

The formation of trade unions in Finland coincided with the quickening of Finland's industrialization in the 1880s. Statutes restricting associations were eased. The first unions were created, formed on a craft and, usually, a local basis. With the growth of the unionization these craft unions were formed into industrial unions. The aim of the labour organizations was from the first the achievement of a collective bargaining system, but the small proportion of members and the lack of co-operation between organizations together with the fact that employers did not recognize the unions, prevented this. Union membership has risen considerably lately. In the whole of industry in 1975, 81 per cent of workers are in unions. The level is lower in the service industry and where female workers are in the majority. Membership among office workers, civil workers, and civil servants have risen sharply only recently, where in 1975 61 per cent of employees are in unions.

Table 5.5.
The unionization of wage-earners and salaried employees in 1965–1975 in Finland (%)

Year	Salaried Employees	Wage-earners	Total
1965	33	54	46
1975	61	81	73

Source: Timo Kauppinen, 1976: 24.

In addition to the growth in membership, the power of a labour market organization also depends on its finances. The position of the employees' unions was improved in 1968 by a so-called Stabilization Agreement enjoining employers to collect membership fees from their employees, which are tax-deductible. At that time this agreement was unique in the market economy countries.

In Finland, as well as in all the Scandinavian countries, the creation of trade unions on an industrial basis has replaced the former craft unions. However, the set-up in Finland differs from that in the other Scandinavian countries, and resembles the system in Britain. In the other Northern countries the political two-way or even three-way split within the labour union movement is not so distinctive as in Finland. There are in practice two local trade sections per working place in Finland: one section formed by the formally ruling political group, the other by those in opposition. These groups generally consist of Social Democrats and Communists.

Central Organization of Finnish Trade Unions (SAK) was established in 1907. This organization, whose membership (951,000) is the largest, plays a crucial role in the Finnish labour market system. The 28 Member Unions are made up of trades sections (about 5,800), and trades sections in the same district form local unions (about 145). The membership mainly consists of industrial workers and other manual workers, together with some office worker groups. The workers elect their representatives to unions by voting. These unions again appoint their representatives to the delegate assembly of the Central Organization of Finnish Trade Unions (SAK), which, meeting every five years, designs a policy for the next five-year period. As a supreme policy-making body for a union the delegate assembly elects for the Central Organization the general executive council, the board, and the union presidents. The general executive council, meeting once a year, evaluates the activities of the past year and fixes the amount of the membership fees to be collected from the member unions. According to the earlier rules, a member union was not allowed to start a strike without the permission of the Central Organization. According to the present rules member unions only have to advise the Central Organization of planned strikes within a fixed period to enable the leaders of the Central Organizations to participate in the settlement of disputes.

The organizing of office workers and civil servants began at the end of the 19th century. Professional unions often originated in idealistic organizations. The Confederation of Salaried Employees in Finland (TVK) was established in 1922. The membership of the TVK member organizations is 280,000.

The Finnish Professional Workers Central Organization (AKAVA) chiefly representing those with a university or other specialized training, was established in 1950 and now has 146,000 members. Its member organizations are mostly formed on the basis of members' training (e.g. the Union of Finnish Lawyers).

The Confederation of Technical Employee Organizations in Finland (STTK) was established in 1946 as a central body for organizations representing those in technical professions. Including engineers in the service of industry, technical foremen, etc. Members total some 89,000.

Employer Organizations

The organization of Finnish employers began in the printing industry in 1900, to be followed by the metal and engineering industry, which advocated the need for a central organization. This could not be achieved until 1907, the same year the workers' central trade union was formed. From the first employers' organizations were more closely united than corresponding trade unions. Employers are also grouped according to industry.

The Finnish Employers' Confederation (STK) was founded in 1907. Its members are companies in industry, building, transport and forwarding, and the employer associations they have formed. It has 31 member associations covering 4,400 industrial companies. There are 620,000 wage and salary earners working for the STK-member companies. The delegate assembly, the supreme policy-making body in the STK, elects the general executive council. At the delegate assemblies, large industrial employer organizations and major industrial companies have more power than smaller unions and companies, because the number of delegates is determined by the amount of wages paid by the STK member companies.

The Confederation of Commerce Employers (LTK) was established in 1945 after collective bargaining had begun. It chiefly operates as an employers' organization in the services industry. The seven member associations include various retail and wholesale organizations, banks and insurance companies. There are 5,200 member companies with 300,000 employees in their service.

In addition to the two organizations mentioned above, there are four smaller organizations or combined associations. Agricultural employers are represented in collective bargaining by the Federation of Agricultural Employers with 2,100 members covering with some 14,000 employees. Employers in the public sector have also begun to organize in recent years. As far as municipalities are concerned, the Local Authorities' Negotiating Commission acts as the employer in labour market matters of 250,000 officials and workers. As far as the State is concerned, collective agreements for 200,000 public employees are taken care of by the Department of Public Personnel Management. The Evangelic-Lutheran church has also its own central organization, the Church Negotiating Commission with 12,000 employees.

Collective Agreements and Incomes Policy

Since 1968, with the exception of two years, collective labour agreements have been based on national incomes agreements worked out between the central organizations and the Government (see Figure 5.1). These agreements last from one to two years. The aims of national agreements are to curb the growth of inflation and ensure the maintenance of employment, while raising the real incomes of employees and preserving the competitive ability of the country. Various State measures in relation to prices, agricultural incomes, taxation, labour and social policies have been linked with the national agreements. Likewise, a variety of social policy measures have been agreed to by the organizations.

General Agreements between the Central Organizations

In addition to the collective labour agreement for a certain time, 'general agreements', which are usually permanent co-operation agreements, are concluded between the labour market organizations. These agreements generally deal with issues that would elsewhere be regarded as falling within the scope of industrial democracy. But the general agreements concluded have increased co-operation between employers and employees at both the working-place and the organizational level. A number of equivalent agreements have been made in the public administration sector. The most important general agreement, made in the private sector are:

(1) The General Agreement (1944): this placed the negotiating contacts of the central organizations on a permanent basis, expressed the willingness of these bodies to conclude collective labour agreements, and defined the fundamental rights and duties of employers and employees.

(2) The Agreement on Protection Against Dismissal (1966) which aims, first, to ensure that employees will not be dismissed without a valid reason and, second, to define rules in the event of termination of employment.

(3) The Agreement on Shop Stewards (1969) which contains stipulations about the negotiating contacts between the employer and the employee as well as the special status of the shop steward in employment. The agreement specifies the tasks and rights of shop stewards as well as the negotiating procedure to be followed.

(4) The Agreement on Labour Protection (1969): this covers safety methods developed in the firm as a form of co-operation between employer and employee. This agreement is significant for the labour market organizations because it enables them to agree among themselves on those matters connected with industrial safety in which the law leaves to them freedom of action.

(5) The Agreement on Rationalization (1972) which covers the general principles to be applied in rationalization activity; particular emphasis is laid on the importance of co-operation between employer and employees. Features that are stressed in the agreement are planning and openness as well as the importance of training programmes in connection with rationalization.

(6) The Agreement on Training (1976) between the labour market organizations: this specifies how participation in training courses connected with one's occupation is to be implemented in practice during employment. It also states how loss of earnings and course costs are to be reimbursed. The agreement also covers training which results from co-operation agreements between employers and employees as well as covering the training provided to members within their own trade unions.

(7) The Agreement on Information (1970): this agreement is intended to promote the dissemination of correct information within the firm. It defines the aims, structure and methods of information activity and lists the areas falling within its scope.

(8) The Agreement on Work Place Welfare (1971): the Agreement defines the oulines for the growth of work-place welfare, the modes of operation and principles of welfare, and modes of co-operation which could be developed.

The Significance of the Labour Market System in Finnish Society

In recent years, the power of the labour market organizations has grown to such an extent that the Finnish Parliament has been obliged to enact laws which have been already agreed on by the labour market organizations. Labour market agreements concluded during the last few years have mainly been on incomes policy – salaries, prices, taxation, and agricultural incomes – and on various questions of social policy. In addition to employers' and employees' organizations, agricultural producers and representatives of the Government and even the Prime Minister and the President of Finland have attended these negotiations. The ever-increasing power of the labour market organizations has hampered traditional Finnish political decision-making, and it has brought into question the present institutional status of the labour market system in society.

The trend in the growth of membership in both employers' and employees' organizations has been the same. The correlation coefficient of the growth of memberships is 0.97. The development of unionization fluctuates: a period of rapid unionization of employees is always followed by a regression, benefiting employers' organizations. There seems to be a continuous effort to reach a balance (Kauppinen 1976: 56). In spite of the Agreement of 1923, according to which a member of a trade union may not be compelled to join either of the Socialist parties (the Social Democratic or the Communist Party), the trade unions and these parties have close mutual relationships. On the one hand, this means a growth of power of both the employees' organizations as well as the Socialist parties.

The Industrial Climate

The development of the relationships between the labour market parties can be studied in accordance with the 'conflict continuum' set out by Bernard (1952). At one end of the continuum opposing parties try to deal with their disagreements on interests and values by isolating and destroying the opposing party. At the other end the interests of the parties involved with the conflict become so much alike that the conflicting parties become equalized. The phases of the conflict continuum are the sequence: elimination, exploitation, equilibrium, coalescence, and last, assimilation.

When studying the development of the Finnish industrial relations from 1917 the following analogous periods can be noted:

(1) The conflict period of elimination in 1917–18, during which both parties tried to eliminate each other in war circumstances.

(2) The conflict period of exploitation in 1919–39. After the 1918 Civil War inequality in wealth and power between workers and the middle class remained the same. In labour struggles in the 1920s the conflict was even more vehement and generally the stronger party, the employers, tried to break strikes.

(3) The period of equilibrium in 1945–67, during which both labour market parties developed their organizations and their relative strength became equalized, but in the Labour parties and in the trade union movement Social Democrats and Communists struggled hard for power. In 1957 the central organization of employees dissolved into two parts for ten years (Savola, 1968: 84 ff.).

(4) The period of coalescence and partial assimilation from 1968 when the first incomes policy agreement in which the State participated was achieved. An increase in the power of the labour market system as a whole is typical of the period. The employee and the employer parties have to some extent coalesced in the face of the power of the State and have proposed many incomes policy agreements. The effects in terms of strikes are reflected in Tables 5.6 and 7.

Table 5.6
Active labour and labour disputes 1945–1975

	Active labour 1945–75			Labour disputes 1945–75								
	Employees			Whole country				Metal & Engineering Industry				Banks & Insurance
Year	Whole country	Metal engineering industry	Banks & Insurance	Labour disputes	Workers involved	% active labour	Work days lost	Labour disputes	Workers involved	% active labour	Work days lost	
1945		83,000		102	37,129		357,664	18	6,938	8.4	32,000	no disputes
1955	1,798,000	97,400	16,300	72	42,402	2.4	344,195	17	6,970	7.2	12,472	no disputes
1965	2,155,000	134,600	29,100	29	6,959	0.3	16,047	12	3,567	2.6	5,673	no disputes
1975	2,221,000	198,000	42,800	1,554	215,140	9.7	284,200	953	149,870	75.7	141,571	no disputes

Note: the system of collecting statistics was changed in 1971, so that figures for 1975 are not comparable with those for other years.
Source: see next table.

Table 5.7
Results of labour disputes, 1945-1975, in Finland

Year	Compromise		Employers won		Employees won		No result or unknown		Total	
	No.	%	No.	%	No.	%	No.	%	No.	%
1945	63	62	5	5	34	33	–	–	102	100
1955	25	35	29	40	12	17	6	8	72	100
1965	15	52	7	24	3	10	4	14	29	100
1975	633	41	37	2	1	0	883	57	1,554	100

Sources: Sosiaalinen Aikakauskirja, 1946, 1956, 1966. Tilastokeskus: työvoimatilasto-toimisto.

During the years of rapid economic growth (1969-74) Finland became accustomed to a considerable drift of wages above the agreed increases. For example, in 1972-3 the index of negotiated wage rates rose to 9.4 per cent and the wage drift 6.0 per cent. This was because various individual unions and work places made their own adjustments, which differed from the national settlement. Since the same wage drift was not possible in all fields, this led to some fields dropping behind, with consequent unrest among workers who suffered. Other causes for discontent were strong inflation and sharply progressive income tax. The development can roughly be illustrated as in Figure 5.1. Under the influence of inflation and heavy progressive taxation, salaried people have taken home less and less of the nominal salary increases agreed upon in collective bargaining agreements. This has meant stronger pressure from employees for salary increases beyond the collective bargaining agreement, and the employers have often agreed to these demands, especially when there was a shortage of labour. The sliding of wages is soon reflected in prices, and thus causes inflation. A circle is formed which is difficult to break.

A general change in value priorities and effective mass information has made people more aware of potential alternatives, and made them feel that their own opportunities have widened. This has resulted in increased work-place mobility, more absenteeism, and a more critical attitude towards the environment at both community and work place level. (cf. IDE 1980, ch. 5).

2.2. Participation in Companies

After the First World War the efforts in various European countries to establish Work Councils and similar co-operation organs met with a poor response from the Finnish trades union movement. Because of labour's weak position at the time and of sharp discrepancies between the employers' and workers' organizations, these collaborative efforts bore no fruit. In the changed atmosphere after the Second World War, however, a temporary law concerning work councils was passed in 1946.

The Work Council

The act, in force from 1949 required the creation of work councils in industrial plants where 60 persons had been regularly employed during the calendar year.

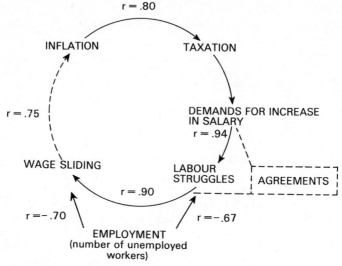

Source: Kähäri, 1976

Figure 5.1. *Correlations between inflation, taxation, employment, labour struggles, and wage drift, 1965-1974.*
Source: Kähäri, 1976.

The tasks of these councils were to give specified information to the employees' representatives about the company's operations, and to act as an advisory organ promoting production, work, discipline, safety, healthy conditions, a pleasant atmosphere, professional development, and industrial peace. There were representatives from the employer, the workers, and the salaried personnel according to the number of people employed.

Personnel in the plant	2	employer representatives
60-120	3	workers' representatives
	1	salaried-personnel representative
121-	3	employer representatives
	5	workers' representatives
	2	salaried-personnel representatives

Workers and salaried-personnel representatives were elected by secret ballot every second year. Everybody over eighteen years could vote and the candidate for election could be not less than 20-years-old.

The influence of work councils was, however, minimal because of the councils' advisory nature. In Finland work councils were active in 1,200 out of some 7,000 industrial plants. Personnel employed in these plants numbered 400,000, 20 per cent of the total labour force. The implementation of the Work Council Act was controlled by the National Board of Labour Protection under the Ministry of Social Affairs. A new act on co-operation within enterprises passed Parliament in spring 1978 (see below).

The Shop Steward System

The first general agrement between the two biggest national labour market organizations (SAK and STK) was drawn up in 1944 and renewed in 1946. A collective bargaining system between the organizations was begun, based on the General Agreement. Shop stewards appointed by the trades sections were organized as a result of the General Agreement too. The shop steward's sphere of activity was determined so as to include all matters concerning the application of any agreement between the labour market organizations. At company level the shop steward is the most important part in the participation system. It is through him that all problems concerning the working of the agreements, and nowadays a great number of other general issues in company industrial relations, are dealt with. The shop steward system was created first in the manu-facturing field but in the 1970's it has been extended to all industries and the governmental and municipal sectors. All employees, except some specialists and middle and top managers, are within the sphere of influence of the shop-steward system.

The Labour Protection Act

The Labour Protection Act, which came into force in 1974, stipulates that employer and employees must co-operate in dealing with the various matters connected with labour protection. At any work place where at least 10 persons are regularly employed, workers and staff must each select their own work protection representatives (for 2 years at a time). At a work place where at least 20 persons regularly work, a labour-protection committee of representa-tives from the employer (a quarter of the committee), workers and staff must be established. The task of this committee, a supervisory one, is to promote labour protection and health at the work place.

Other Participation Systems

In industry, but also in many other fields such as the banking sector, voluntary experiments have been made since the 1950s to increase participation above the current minimum legal limits. Results from these experiments have been con-tradictory. The experiments have mostly been initiated by the management of a company on the basis of the recommendations of the employers' confederation. Various democratic administrative systems are being put into practice in Finland to improve the conditions of living and to increase democracy, notably in pro-vincial administration, schools, industry, and participative administration of tenant houses. The major parties agree on the need to increase participation but they have been unable to agree on how the participation opportunities of the individual should be developed, that is, to what extent, in what form (direct or indirect), and within what schedule.

The New act on co-operation within enterprises

The agreement between the SAK, STK, and the State on a revitalization policy for the Finnish economy, made in December 1977, contained a proposal for a new law. It concerned the development of industrial democracy and was to be dealt with by the parliament in the immediate future. The act was actually passed in May 1978 and came into force in July 1979.

The new law included all enterprises with more than 30 employees. The negotiating parties are representatives from the employer, from the shop stewards, and from the work-protection committee. To deal with matters covering the whole work place, a smaller negotiation committee is then elected by proportional representation.

Matters to be negotiated are:

(1) Matters directly affecting the position of the work place personnel, such as essential changes in tasks, working methods and organization of work; permanent shifts from one task to another; and the timing of regular working hours as well as of rest and eating periods.

(2) Productive factors affecting work place personnel, such as essential machinery and instrument investments, arrangements of working space and changes in product choice and service; plans for rationalization at stated times; and the significant expanding, reducing, or terminating of the activity of the firm or the transfer of work to another place.

(3) The effects of points (1) and (2) on the number of personnel.

(4) Discussions of alternatives before notices of laying-off and redundancy are given.

(5) Principles and methods of recruitment, information gathered in connection with recruitment, and job orientation.

(6) Application of in-company information, including information leaflets, bulletin boards and information sessions. In addition, the employers have to present (a) accounts to employees, (b) a statement of the economic situation of the firm at least once during the financial year, and (c) a personnel scheme for at least one year.

(7) Budget plans connected with social activities and personnel training. The decisions, to be made within the limits of the budget in accordance with the opinion of the majority of the personnel representatives, cover granting of work-relation residences, arrangement of child care and meals at the work place, the use and planning of social premises at the work place, club and leisure activities as well as donations and contributions granted to employees.

(8) Work rules in the company.

(9) Budget plans connected with co-operative and professional training and organizing of co-operative training.

(10) Principles of the use of labour outside the company.

The Works Council Act of 1949 and the Work Regulation Act of 1922 were repealed simultaneously.

2.3. The Main Bargaining Structure and the Labour Court

The Main Bargaining Structure

As stated earlier, the principal procedure followed is negotiation at national union level, aiming at an overall solution, that is, a general formulation of the main lines covering all the parties in collective bargaining jointly. When a national solution between the central organizations and the Government is found, the member organizations begin to negotiate the actual labour agreements proper on the basis of it. If no national solution is arrived at, collective bargaining takes place directly at industrial union level. When the central organizations come to an agreement, the member organizations are left to decide on individual issues, i.e. the provision of wage increases awarded to some special groups. The member organizations are also granted a fixed period within which they may reject a national agreement, if union branches do not approve it. Agreement procedures differ somewhat from union to union. There may be quite considerable differences, for instance, in the degree of detail of wage stipulations. The proportion of collective bargaining done at company level is quite low.

In-Company Dispute Settlements

If a dispute concerning the contents of a collective agreement or its implementation arises at the work place, the persons involved in settling it will be the shop steward, representing the trade union, and a representative appointed by the employer. If negotiations at the work place fail to lead to a settlement, the matter is passed on to the employers' and employees' organizations in that industry. In the event of this too failing to produce agreement, the national organizations can provide their advisory opinions on how the dispute is to be resolved. If no settlement is reached through arbitration, either of the organizations can refer the matter to the Labour Court for settlement.

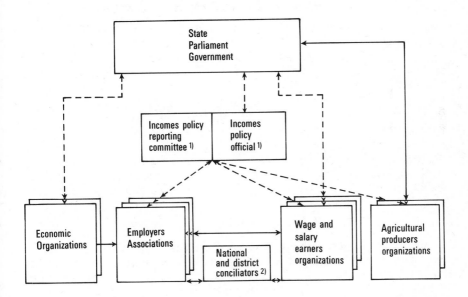

Figure 5.2. *Finnish incomes policy negotiation mechanism.*
   [1] Organ appointed by Government to produce impartial information for collective bargaining negotiations.
   [2] The task can also be described as that of a mediator according to OECD terminology.

The System of Conciliation

The object aim of the system of conciliation for labour disputes is to help the labour market organizations to reach a collective agreement when negotiations between the organizations have reached a dead end. This, however, does not mean an enforced agreement, since an organization may freely choose to reject or accept the result. For conciliation purposes, Finland has two national conciliators, whose tasks are both pre-emptive and connected with actual conciliation. In addition, five part-time conciliators take care of local conciliation tasks.

The Labour Court

This is a special court which in the final instance settles disputes arising out of a collective agreement in force or the consequences of a breach of the agreement. Three of its members are appointed by the organizations of wage-earners and salaried employees. Three others are appointed on the joint recommendation of the employers' organizations. The President of the Labour Court and two further members are required to be non-partisan.

3. PROGRAMMATIC PERSPECTIVES, PROBLEMATIC ISSUES, AND DEVELOPMENTS

3.1. Programmatic Perspectives

The Individual, the Organization, and Industrial Relations

As we have already seen, Finland did not have, until the new 1978 act on co-operation within enterprises, an effective and legal general participation system at work-place level which enabled the individual worker to take part in decision-making. But the worker employed in industry especially was not completely at the mercy of his employer's whim. Comparatively powerful trade unions were and are in the background to protect the worker, and, as we have seen, the agreements between employee and employer organizations have increased the workers' chance to influence matters at the work-place. With the growth of the labour market organizations, much decision-making, particularly concerning personnel, has been shifted outside the company to these organizations. Between them they agree on wage levels and working conditions. This trend is continuing and is beginning to have an increasing effect on office workers, who are not yet completely unionized.

Changes in Social Structure

Changes in social structure, especially in the relative proportions of different population groups, have a decisive effect on the power balance between labour market organizations. According to forecasts, changes in industrial structure in Finland will prove more rapid than in any other West European country in the 1970s. Those who earned their livelihood from agriculture and forestry in the 1950s were 46 per cent of the working population, but in 1977 they were only 13 per cent. It is predicted that by 1985 only 7 per cent will earn their living in this way. Labour in services, however, will grow from 48 per cent in 1975 to

55 per cent in 1985. If this is true, office worker organizations will be able to increase their membership and thus their power, with effects on both employee and employer organizations.

3.2. Main Implications of the System

As mentioned before, the participation system at the national level is quite well developed in Finland. Its main features will probably not change in the near future, but as the structure of the Finnish economy develops, the power relations between the different parties in the labour market will in turn change. The white-collar organizations of both employees' and employers' will grow more powerful.

The problem in the near future is to develop participation at company level according to the new act which came into force in July 1979. Many companies have, however, already encouraged their managers in participative leadership and have also created their own participation systems. However, these systems have often been based on other organizational principles than the new law, and these will have to be adapted to the new legislation.

In sum, in Finnish society, the labour market organizations are well developed and have a strong influence in labour relations and in social legislation through the incomes policy carried out during the last ten years. The collective bargaining system is a prominent feature in Finnish society as a way of ensuring employees' participation at the national level. The steadily increasing power of the labour market organizations is largely the result of first, the growth of their membership — in 1975 the unionization among salaried employees was 61 per cent and wage-earners 81 per cent — and, second, the improved financial position of the labour unions, and, third, the strong bonds with political parties. With the growth of the labour market organizations, much decision-making has been shifted outside the company level to the labour market organizations.

The industrial climate of Finland has been affected by (1) The conflicts between workers and the middle class which culminated in the 1918 Civil War and which are still reflected in the political and labour market systems; (2) the power struggles both between Social Democrats and Communists, and within the Communists themselves; (3) the relatively short life of governments, because of the great number of political parties, which creates uncertainty in political life and also in industrial relations.

Employees' participation in organizational decision-making has been under discussion in Finland for over ten years. At last, in spring 1978 a new act on co-operation within enterprises was passed in parliament. The main contents of the law were drawn up and agreed upon by the national labour market organizations in the end of 1977. The organization of the new co-operation system lies heavily on the old organs: shop stewards and work-protection delegates. The worker has not, however, been completely at the mercy of his employer. He is supported by powerful trade unions and by the many varied agreements made between the employees' and employers' organizations which have increased his ability to influence matters at his work-place.

REFERENCES

Bernard, Jessie (1952), *American Community Behavior*. New York: The Dryden Press.

Central Statistical Office of Finland (1968), *National Accounting in Finland in 1948-1964*. Helsinki: Valtion painatuskeskus.

(1974), *National Accounting in Finland in 1964-1974*. Helsinki: Valtion painatuskeskus.

Statistical Yearbook of Finland, 1945-1977. Helsinki: Valtion painatuskeskus.

Finnish Employers' Confederation (1976), *A Brief Outline of Labour Market Relationships in Finland*. Helsinki: Teollisuuden Kustannus Oy.

Haataja, Lauri; Hentilä, Seppo; Kalela, Jorma; Turtola, Jussi (eds), (1976), *Suomen työväenliikkeen historia*. Joensuu: Kansan Voima Oy.

Hautala, Heikki (1976), *Suomen talouselämän rakenne ja kehitystekijät*. Tapiola: Weilin & Göös.

Huuska, Väinö (1968), *Etujärjestöjen painostuspolitiikka Suomessa*. Porvoo: Politiikan tutkimuksia VIII.

Kauppinen, Timo (1976), *Työmarkkinajärjestöjen keskinäisistä voimasuhteista*. Helsinki: Työelämän suhteiden neuvottelukunta.

Kavonius, Marja (1975), 'Naisten asema työelämässä palkkauksen kannalta, Tasa-arvoasiain neuvottelukunta'. Helsinki: Valtioneuvoston kanslian julkaisuja, 1975: 4.

Koljonen, Niilo (1966), *Työntekijä ja yritysdemokratia*. Helsinki: Kustannusosakeyhtiö Tammi.

Koskinen, Pirkko K. (1973), *Työntekijöiden osallistumisesta päätöksentekoon yrityksessä*. Helsinki: Suomalaisen lakimiesyhdistyksen julkaisuja B: 166.

Kähäri, Pete-Veikko (1976), 'Inflaatio ja palkkaliukumat'. Helsingin kauppakorkeakoulu, hallinnon laitos (mimeo).

Leskinen Esko (ed.), (1973), *Työmarkkinajärjestöt*. Tapiola: Weilin & Göös.

Lilja, Kari (1977), *Työntekijöiden osallistuminen hallintoon teollisuusyrityksissä. Tutkimus työnantajapuolen toiminnan kehityksestä*. Helsinki: Helsingin kauppakorkeakoulu.

Lähteenmäki, Olavi (1969), 'Valtiollisen demokratian tunnusmerkkejä yritysdemokratiassa'. Turun yliopiston sosiaalipolitiikan laitoksen tutkielmia, B: 8 – 1969.

Ogburn, William F. & Nimkoff, Meyer F. (1964), *Sociology*. Boston: Houghton Mifflin Company.

Savola, Matti (1969), *Lakko työelämän ristiriitana*. Porvoo: Werner Söderström Osakeyhtiö.

Sosiaalinen aikakauskirja 1946, 1956 and 1966, Sosiaaliministeriön julkaisuja.

Suomen Työnantajain Yleinen Ryhmä (ed.), (1977), STK:n ja SAK:n yleiset sopimukset. Jyväskylä.

Tosi suomalainen, Päiviö Hetemäki 60 vuotta. (1973), Helsinki: Suomen teollisuuden keskusvaliokunta.

Työmarkkinaopas, (1976), Helsinki: Sanomapaino.

Urmas, Heikki (1975), *Työrauhajärjestelmä yhteiskunnan osajärjestelmänä*. Helsinki: Helsingin kauppakorkeakoulu.

Wiio, Osmo A. (1970), *Yritysdemokratia ja muuttuva organisaatio*. Tapiola: Weilin & Göös.

Virastodemokratiaan valtionhallinnossa, 'Virastodemokratiatoimikunnan mietintö', Komiteanmietintö 1973: 77. Helsinki: Valtion painatuskeskus.

Yleissopimus (1976), STK, TVK ja STL. Helsinki.
Yritysdemokratiakomitean mietintö (1970), Komiteanmietintö 1970: A3. Helsinki: Valtion painatuskeskus.
Yritysdemokratian sovellutuskomitean mietintö (1974), 'Komiteanmietintö', 1974: 99. Helsinki: Valtion painatuskeskus.

6

THE BRITISH INDUSTRIAL RELATIONS SYSTEM

1. GENERAL SITUATION AND BACKGROUND

1.1. The Status-Quo of political power

The immediate post-war period was initially one of socialist reform and innovation, until in 1951 the Conservatives came to power on the wave of disenchantment with austerity. The Labour Party returned to office again in 1964, when in turn the tide turned against the 'you never had it so good' affluence of the Conservatives. In 1970 there was once a more swing, although not very marked, against the Wilson Government; and the Conservatives were able to govern until 1974 when the Heath confrontation with the miners during their national strike led to the return of Labour. The agreement between the main political parties should be made explicit; they accepted such broad strategies as the mixed economy, the welfare state, and the North Atlantic alliance, although disagreeing about tactics for the most part (see Rose, 1964). Employers, through the CBI, and trade unions, through the TUC, also broadly reached a pragmatic dialogue with the government of the day. The post–1945 era had been for the most part one of political accommodation in spite of the rhetoric, although the consensus is now breaking up, given the ascendency of right-wing policies.

The main political parties are the Conservative, Labour and Liberal parties. Their respective share of the vote in selected general elections over the decades since 1945 were:

Table 6.1.
Share of Votes in Selected Recent Elections.

%	1945	1955	1966	1974
Conservative	39.8	49.7	41.9	38.2
Liberal	9.0	2.7	8.5	19.3
Labour	47.8	46.4	47.9	37.2
Others	2.8	1.1	1.7	5.4
Turnout	72.7	76.7	75.8	78.2

Sources: Butler & Freeman, 1969; and *The Times.*

1.2. Recent political events of nation/region-wide significance

Political events, other than the general elections discussed earlier, most of which led to new governments, include:

(a) the absence in 1968 of the political and industrial upheavals associated with the 'long hot summer' experienced in mainland Europe;

(b) from 1969 the violence and civil strife in Northern Ireland;
(c) the Referendum and entry of the UK into the Common Market in mid-1975;
(d) growing pressure for devolution for Scotland and Wales, culminating in political debate over specific legislation in late 1976 and early 1977, but which burst after the devolution referendum;
(e) the Social Contract and extension of tri-partite consultation and the implementation of an incomes policy from 1975 to 1979;
(f) change of Labour leadership with the election of Callaghan and the sterling crisis of mid- and late 1976;
(g) and then a Conservative government, elected in 1979.

The UK 'first-past-the-post' electoral system makes for two-party government. The parties may change over time, as Labour took over the Liberals' role in the 1920s, but it is a slow process as very big electoral swings are needed to move a third party into prominence (see Haseler, 1976).

1.3. The Economic Situation

Since the end of World War II, the United Kingdom has sharply dropped in the European economic league-table, and its share of world trade, has been reduced to half its level in the immediate post-war period. It has been menaced by balance-of-payments crisis, recurrent 'stop-go' economic policies, a fall in the return on capital (see Glyn & Sutcliffe, 1972) and in the value of sterling to under $2.00 in 1978, recovering since then to a much higher level. Great hopes are pinned on North Sea Oil, which promises to make Britain the only European country self-sufficient in energy by the end of the 1970s. The gradual dismantling of the sterling balances, and the achievement of substantial payments surpluses may or may not allow the industrial regeneration of Britain over the next ten years (see N.I.S.E.R., 1976), in the context of late entry into Europe (see Shonfield, 1972). However, the latest figures are disappointing; the 1979 visible trade deficit of £3,233 m is more than twice the 1978 deficit, though there was a sharp improvement in the oil balance – a deficit of only £804 m in 1979, as against the 1978 figure of £2,022 m – all the benefit was lost in the deterioration in other traded goods.

The population rose by around 10 per cent for the twenty year period as can be seen in Table 6.2.

At present, Commonwealth immigration is reduced to a trickle, however. The percentage of the population which was active was, on average, 47.4 per cent in 1951; 48.1 in 1961, 47.7 in 1966, and 45.8 in 1971, 41.8 in 1975, and 41.6 per

Table 6.2.
Population 1951–1971 (UK – mid-year estimates)

1951	50.6 million
1961	53.0 million
1971	55.7 million
1976	56.0 million

Source: Social Trends 1977.

cent in 1976. The rate of unemployment which was 1.2 per cent in both 1945 and 1955, rose slightly to 1.5 per cent in 1965, and by 1975 had jumped to 4.1 per cent rising even further subsequently. By 1978 there were over one and a half million unemployed, with around 6 per cent out of work: a level not known since the Second World War (see *Social Trends*, 1977). The social impact has been considerable, especially regionally. The final feature to be reviewed is the Gross Domestic Product which at 1970 constant market prices moved up fairly slowly (see Table 6.3).

Table 6.3.
GDP at Constant Market Prices (1970 = 100)

1966	1970	1975	1976
90.4	100	109.1	111.5

Source: Annual Abstract, 1977.
Notes: Measured in total home costs, GDP (at factor cost) was 58.0 in 1955; 84.1 in 1966; 100 in 1970; and 196.3 in 1975 (see Kempner, 1977: 12).

1.4. Social Stratification, Social Policy and Living Conditions

Since 1900, British society has changed considerably (see (ed.) Halsey, 1972). More specifically since 1945, Britain has pursued a policy of welfare statism, with an increasing proportion of GNP going into public expenditure. The provision of full employment, following the Beveridge Report of 1944, and the subsequent legislation to include a National Health Service, as well as educational reforms to extend equality of opportunity, may be said to have eroded the stratification of British society and improved the living conditions of its workers. Various studies have suggested that the picture can be painted in over-rosy colours as notions of class still remain valid. Although the workers have been labelled 'affluent' by some observers (see Goldthorpe *et al.*, 1969; Giddens, 1973; Moorhouse, 1976), with the return in recent years of large-scale unemployment, living standards of both wage and salary-earners may now be threatened.

Whether the distribution of wealth has changed substantially has been keenly debated (see Atkinson and Harrison, 1978). The very rich's share of total wealth has probably declined (as Table 6.4 shows) over the last fifty years:

Table 6.4.
Top one per cent's share of total wealth.

	%
Mid-1920s	60
Mid-1930s	55
Mid-1950s	45
Mid-1960s	33
Mid-1970s	24
(Population aged 18 and over.)	

Source: Observer, 19 March 1978.

But it is difficult to conclude that the share held by the next four per cent of the population has altered much. Moreover the share of GNP going to salaries and wages appears to have remained fairly constant over the period — just over 70 per cent. Wage differentials both before and after tax have however declined dramatically, although the statistics are not over-reliable. Average weekly earnings have however increased. In 1950 (taking 1955 = 100) they were 68.1, by 1965 they were 174.8, and had jumped to 549.7 in 1975, 643.2 in 1976 and 706.2 in 1977; prices, however, had risen accordingly from a 1950 level of 76.5 to 169.4 in 1970, 214.7 in 1973, 249.4 in 1974, rapidly climbing to 309.9 in 1975, 361.2 in 1976 and 422.5 in 1977 (see Kempner, 1977: 13). Though inflation fell for a period, it has since advanced considerably.

Very few British workers gain their living from the land. The percentage of the labour force outside agriculture continued to rise from 95 per cent in 1945, to 97.0 per cent in 1955, 97.5 per cent in 1966, and 98.5 per cent in 1976; the percentage of the labour force in white-collar employment also rose considerably over the period; the proportion of workers in manufacturing, however, which was 38.2 per cent in 1949, fell to 33.4 per cent in 1974 (see *Social Trends*, 1977), and is still falling amidst talk of the 'de-industrialization' of Britain. The share of GDP going to public expenditure had risen to over half, from 37.0 per cent in 1955, to 39.9 per cent in 1965, to 51.5 per cent in 1975 (see Kempner, 1977: 28). The share of capital owned by trade unions was negligible. The ratio of unskilled, semi-skilled, and skilled varied little, being approximately 1 : 3 : 3 overall. The proportions were not available industry by industry, but the metal trades probably had a higher ratio of the latter two categories, while the service sector such as banking and insurance had a much higher percentage of employees who left school after the age of 16.

Secondary-school population rose by almost a third between 1961 and 1974; and the university population grew sharply between these dates (see Table 6.5) to reach nearly 17 per cent of the working population. Illiteracy is now rarely found. The British read more newspapers per capita than most countries, and ranked third in the world league-table in the mid-sixties (a circulation count of 479 per 1,000 persons).

Table 6.5.
Higher Education in the UK (full-time)

	(thousands) 1965–6	1972–3	1975–6
Universities	128.1	170.5	178.1
Colleges of Education	24.2	37.5	4.0
Further education (advanced courses)	39.1	78.1	119.2
	191.4	286.1	301.3

Source: Social Trends, 1977.

2. THE NATIONAL INDUSTRIAL RELATIONS SYSTEM

2.1. The legal basis and main ramifications of the overall Industrial Relations system

There is no 'written' constitution in Britain, unlike most other EEC countries. It has no overall Labour Code — the main acts stem from almost the last quarter of the nineteenth and the early part of the twentieth century. Because common law was mainly formed when unions were illegal conspiracies, it has always acted to control union activities rather than support them (see Taylor, 1965).

The last Conservative government attempted a comprehensive legal reform in the Act of 1971 but this is mostly defunct. The subsequent legal basis (see Clegg, 1975: 478 ff.), in the main, derives from legislation of 1974 and 1975. The Trade Union and Labour Relations Act (TULRA) and related laws, such as those dealing with Health and Safety at Work, Employee Protection, etc. became operative (see especially *Dept. of Employment Gazette* for October, November, and December 1975). The main relationships in the industrial relations system are depicted in Figure 6.1.

The 1971 Industrial Relations Act was seen by the unions as a reinforcement of common law rather than as a statute delineating their role in society. Since 1974, three major acts have been passed which have both supported the unions and clarified their position. Based on an industrial tribunal system which had grown up out of an old social security system and is to a great extent divorced from the old common law and the high courts, this supportive, legitimating law had been completely accepted by the unions. Its inadequacies, however, have been highlighted by the Grunwick case in which the Appeal Court ruled, firstly, that it is inequitable for the tri-partite Arbitration Conciliation, and Advisory Service (ACAS) to require an employer to recognize a union without taking an adequate survey of his employees' wishes, and, secondly, it is legal for the employer to deny access and otherwise prevent such a survey being taken, 'the biggest blow to the trade union cause' in recent years (see *Financial Times*, 25 March 1978). Furthermore, of the 76 recommendations for union recognition issued up to February 1978, only 12 companies have granted recognition. New Conservative 'union reform' legislation is pending; TUC opposition is most likely.

2.2. Membership Growth and Union Density

The British Industrial Relations System is a rather special one. As Kendall (1975: 180) points out 'The British labour movement is the oldest in the world. The product of the first industrial revolution in history, of the unique political and economic circumstances under which this revolution took place' (see also Pollard, 1965). Further, the labour movement in the United Kingdom 'is different because the cultural experience of the British people has been different too', (1975: 181). There is not, however, sufficient space here to elaborate the history of the British labour movement, and it is documented in detail elsewhere (see, for example, Pelling, 1969). None the less, the recent years has seen the recovery of the trade union membership lost after the attempted General Strike of 1926

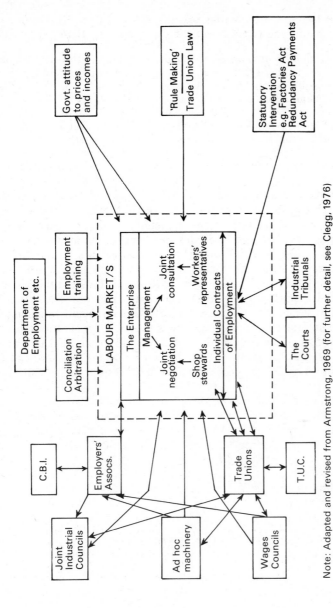

Note: Adapted and revised from Armstrong, 1969 (for further detail, see Clegg, 1976)

Figure 6.1. A view of the British Industrial Relations System
Note: adapted and revised from Armstrong, 1969 (for further detail, see Clegg, 1976).

and the Great Depression soon after, and this recovery had reached more than twelve million by the end of 1977. As has been observed by Halsey (1978: 144):

There were two million union members at the beginning of this century, out of a total potential membership of nearly 16 million. In other words, only one-eighth of all possible recruits had, in fact, been recuited. Put more technically, the density of membership was 13 per cent in 1900, and this figure rose rapidly to reach 45 per cent by 1920. Since the date, unionisation has had fluctuating fortunes, but did not attain a higher density than it had in 1920 until the 1970s, when, for the first time, it reached the present 50 per cent mark.

The main organizational principles of union and employers' bodies are based on historical roots (see Clegg, 1975 edn., and Donovan Report, 1968). Suffice to say that the bulk of British unions are a mixture of general, craft, and industrial structures which belong to a single federation the TUC, which is basically social-democratic in orientation. Out of the 12 million trade union members, the largest six unions contain over half this number. Although over half of the labour force is unionized, less than this proportion belongs to TUC affiliated unions: unionization is high in manufacturing as we shall see, especially in the metal trades for example, and rather low in service industries, although white-collar and women employees are the fast growing categories. The closed-shop principle is now established on a legal basis. In Britain, 'multiple unionism of highly diverse structures, including separate white-collar organizations, prevails' in the metal-working industries (Derber, 1976: 23). The main trade union in the metal trades is the Amalgamated Union of Engineering Workers (AUEW), commonly known as the 'Engineers'. It now has over one and a half million members.

Integration into the industrial system at company level still depends on union power derived from density of membership, while integration at the national and local government levels is complete and the unions closely participate at these levels – the current members' position can be seen in Table 6.6.

Table 6.6.
UK Trade Unions – 1975

Union members	12 million plus
By sex	8.5 million men and decreasing
	3.5 million women and increasing
By unions	60.8 per cent of members in 11 largest unions
	77.5 per cent of members in 25 largest unions
Number of unions	488 (of which just over 100 affiliated to the TUC)
Number of federations of unions	46

Source: Dept. of Employment Gazette, November 1976.

A Department of Employment survey of 1973 of manufacturing firms found 60 per cent were unionized; and in 50 per cent employees were represented by shop stewards. In one in four firms, stewards regularly held meetings during working hours from which managers were excluded. Few union officers had frequent, *direct* contact with ordinary members. Again 60 per cent of companies were members of an employers' association; and 70 per cent had joint committees of employees and managers; on half of those, all the employee representatives were shop stewards. On the whole, managers preferred not to have employees in unions, but few were strongly opposed and many approved. There is reason to think that attitudes have polarized since 1973, with many large-firm managers joining unions themselves and some small-firm employers and service-industry firms becoming more strongly anti-union.

2.3. Representative Bodies of Trade Unions and Employers

Trade unions vary in so far as their officials may be elected (newer general unions have largely vacant-post elections while older craft bodies have periodic elections) or newer white-collar unions have appointed officers for the most part. All have elected executive committees, and most have shop stewards elected, formally or informatlly, at the base. Their patterns of representation are complex, heterogeneous and difficult to summarize, let alone set out in a concise schema (for fuller details see Edelstein and Warner, 1975; Kendall, 1975; Carew, 1976; Clegg, 1976). The employers' associations have no common model, but like other voluntary bodies have elected councils, and often appointed officials. The TUC is a federal body, with elected representatives on it from member unions and officials appointed for the duration of their career, and the same goes with the CBI, the main employers' body. The Arbitration, Conciliation and Advisory Service (ACAS) is jointly sponsored by the employers, unions and government. The voluntary organizations described above are in theory responsible to their members, whom in the short term they are expected to control, but whom in the longer run they are supposed to be controlled by.

The employers' body, the Confederation of British Industry (CBI), is of fairly recent creation, being an amalgam of a number of bodies. It is not considered as being overly influential, especially when there is a Labour government in power. It has not always been happy either with Conservative government, especially when they introduce policies which limit industry's 'freedom', or squeeze the industrial sector during a 'stop' period in the 'stop-go' cycle, to help balance-of-payments pressure. The employers' side in Britain has not to date been able to develop a cohesive lobby as such, and at the level of specific industries many employers' associations are weak, with the largest firms often standing outside. The Engineering Employers' Federation is probably one of the stronger; their counterparts in the service sector, e.g. in banking and insurance, are less so. (See also Donovan Report, 1968, for the historical background of employers' associations.)

The trade unions are co-ordinated by the TUC, which was founded in 1868 and has since continued as an annual — or when necessary *special* — demonstration of the fraternity and the solidarity of trade unionists. Its full-time General Secretary, its staff of permanent officials, and its wide spectrum of specialist committees can act at all times in its name, offering a wide range of facilities to members. It is regarded as the collective voice of the unions and it was consulted on this basis by government. While unions are affiliated to it— and to do so must prove that they are *bona fide* independent associations for the furtherance of work-people's interests — its only sanction is to exclude a union from membership should it transgress. Under the Trade Union Act of 1913 (following upon the Osborne Judgment), it has been legal for trade unions to have political objectives and to have a political fund for use in pursuit of these objectives provided that it is raised by a separate levy from which members have the right not to contribute. These funds go partly to support the Labour Party, through the practice of sponsoring MP's.

2.4. The Industrial Relations Climate

By the early 1970s, the industrial relations climate developed to a high level of conflict. Confrontation diminished particularly over the next few years, partly because of the onset of the economic slow-down, and partly because of the Social Contract; but strike statistics are often to be treated with care (see Silver, 1973).

Table 6.7
Official and Unofficial Strikes (by decade. m = million)

Total wk. pop.	Date	No. of Strikes	No. of Strikers	Days Lost
21.60m	1945	2,293	0.45m	2.84m
23.90m	1955	2,419	0.60m	3.78m
25.50m	1965	2,354	0.67m	2.93m
25.40m	1975	2,282	0.79m	6.01m

Note: about half of the days lost in 1965 and 1975 were in the metal-related trades.
Sources: Kendall, 1975: 371; and also *Dept. of Employment Gazette,* October 1976.

Although the reporting of strikes may underestimate the problem, Britain, in spite of the so-called 'English disease', is in the middle, rather than the top of the industrial conflict league-table for advanced industrial societies. Industrial accidents, some have argued, caused an even greater loss of working days. In manufacturing industries, for example, there were 670 accidents per 100,000 workers in 1970, 540 per 100,000 in 1975, according to official sources (*Social Trends*, 1977).

The figures by decade above do not, however, represent the recent high points of strike activity, as the number of days lost, in round figures, rose in 1970 to 11m, and in 1972 to 24m, but in 1973 they fell to 7m. Due to the Mining dispute, they were again in 1974, 15m; but by the next year were down to 6m. They then fell again to 3m in 1976, and most recently were up to 11m in 1977. (Silver, 1973; *Department of Employment Gazette.*) *Ex post* explanations can be given for each year's strikes and incidence. When the highly unionized public sector is involved, strike incidence can go up dramatically. Such involvement is most likely to occur after erosion of relative earnings due to incomes policy (1970 and 1974) or when government tries to use its own employees to support or maintain an incomes policy (1971 and 1972, and most recently, in early 1979).

The industries most vulnerable to strike-activity were mining and quarrying, vehicles and shipbuilding. Those least prone were the distributive trades, agriculture, fisheries, insurance and banking. Few establishments (often around 2 per cent) are affected by industrial stoppages. Nearly all small plants (under 100 employees) are almost totally untouched but only just over half of large plants (with over 1,000 employees) are not involved. The notion that 'small is peaceful' is thus borne out by the official statistics.

2.5. 'Participation' via Statutory Requirements or Collective Bargaining?

There is no 'main' legal basis for participation in British companies, unlike their European counterparts (see the accompanying volume '*Industrial Democracy in Europe*'; Clarke, Fatchett, and Roberts, 1972, especially Chap. 1, for the historical background). Apart from Whitleyism, nationalization, joint consultation and work-place bargaining, British workers have seen little that compares with the German arrangements, for example, as far as *formal*, legally prescribed procedures are concerned. The more recent legislation on, for example, Health and Safety has been more significant in establishing *legal* rights for participative procedures. (cf. IDE 1980, 297–298).

Integration of unionized workers into the system at company level is mostly at a high level in the public sector, and it is often claimed that unions in the public and private sectors do not particularly wish to extend collective bargaining and thus participation much beyond the area of wage negotiations. There is more than a grain of truth in this view. Further, various surveys, the attitude of the CBI as shown in the Bullock Committee Minority Report and in press comment on the Majority and Minority Reports, might suggest that managers have little desire to extend union recognition, integration, or participation or to extend the scope of bargaining. An industrial Democracy Bill which was to have followed the Bullock Report was delayed in the face of disagreement amongst trade union leaders and opposition from employers.

The British system usually involves employees in decision-making in companies via collective bargaining. There is normally only a single channel of representation. Hence the question of unity/disunity of representation in companies concerning both unions, and employees does *not* raise itself *vis-à-vis* other European systems. True, there are problems related to collective bargaining organs for example, and to bodies involving consultation and even participation (like the recent British Leyland scheme) where this is 'voluntaristic' and *not* legally defined. The outcomes tend to follow the lines suggested by the power of the various organized groups in the workplace, and the *status quo* deriving from multi-unionism. There is very often a joint convenors' committee, representing all the senior shop stewards for the unions in the plants which bargains and is consulted. The main role of the national trade union official is therefore to act as back-up to the plant-level negotiating bodies.

National negotiations provide a framework in many industries (see Donovan Report, 1968, on the development of the 'formal' and 'informal' systems of bargaining over the post-war period, and their divergence from each other). In the public sector (employing over 25 per cent of the labour force) the role of central negotiations is more important. Recently, both public and private sector bargaining has, of course, been subject to nationally imposed limits under the *de facto* incomes policy; now cash-limits and high interest-rates constrain.

Industrial relations 'problems' have prompted various bouts of 'reformism' (see Goldthorpe, 1974, for a critique). One analysis leant heavily on the notion of 'institutional-lag' (see 1974: 422), as is clear from the conclusions of the Royal Commission on Trade Unions and Employers' Associations (see Donovan Commission between 1965 and 1968).

3. PROGRAMMATIC PERSPECTIVES, PROBLEMATIC ISSUES AND PROSPECTIVE DEVELOPMENTS

Recently there has been much public concern with the industrial relations system. However, the repeal of the 1971 Act, the introduction of the Social Contract, and the establishment of closer collaboration between unions and government have helped to reduce industrial tension and negative attitudes towards the system. Since 1974 there has been both a fairly considerable decline and, subsequently, a noticeable rise, in the number of strikes. The Labour Government set up a Committee of Inquiry on Industrial Democracy and after it reported in 1977 promised in a White Paper specific legislative proposals. Most importantly, the last few years has seen legislation to consolidate the influence and position of unions (such as the Employment Protection Act, Health and Safety Act, and Dock Labour legislation). There is also likely to be a less stringent 'voluntary' incomes policy in the future. The Conservatives are in turn seeking to legally restrain the unions (see their 1979 election manifesto) but they are also supposed to favour 'employee involvement', with individual companies being allowed a certain autonomy.

It is hard to answer precisely which outcomes are to be expected, as the debate is conducted in rather diffuse terms. Those in favour of an extension of industrial democracy argue that the worker should be more involved in decision-making in the work-place, and, through this, in the broader economy and society. Many Labour Party politicians and union leaders would agree at the level of generality, although a minority are sceptical either about the ends, or the means to achieve this. To some

'Industrial democracy thus becomes a method of increasing capitalism's productivity by burdening trade unions with responsibility without power and so reducing the independent antagonistic stance implicit in traditional collective bargaining' (Wintour, 1977: 3).

The British have no statutory system of participation; and few worker-director schemes except for a scattered incidence here and there, in British Steel for example. There are a number of so-called 'experiments' in industrial democracy (described in Hadley, in (ed.) Vanek, 1975: 238 ff.). It has been claimed that there is a growing interest in industrial democracy to improve British industrial relations. It is argued that improvements in education have led to people wanting a greater say in their destiny and this includes the work-place. It is also claimed on the basis of survey evidence that workers might want a greater control over what affects them in the immediate job.

The main groups promoting industrial democracy are important sections of the Labour movement, including the TUC and Labour Party. The other political parties have their own proposals, less far-reaching perhaps, as does the main employers' body, the CBI. The three industrialists on the Bullock Committee on industrial democracy, for instance, submitted a Minority Report dissenting from the principal conclusion to put worker-directors on boards of companies, employing 2,000 or more workers. The Majority Report, on the other hand, came out in favour of equal numbers of worker and shareholder representatives on these boards, plus a quota of independent directors to keep the balance. This is known as '2x + y' formula. The employers in general see the parity threshold as the 'rubicon' of power, and the crossing of this as the road to 'back-door nationalization'.

The TUC's original proposal (see TUC Report on Industrial Democracy, 1974; also Coates, in Vanek (ed.), 1975: pp. 92ff.) echoed the German DGB notion of 50 per cent representation on supervisory boards. The employers have argued for one-third employee representation at this level, but not on the level of single, main boards; they pressed too for direct election by the employees and not via trade union channels.

In the Majority Report, it was suggested that trade unions, in large firms over 2,000 employees (of which Britain has about 730) , where at least one in five workers were organized, can have the right to ask their members if they want to have worker-directors. Should this proportion agree, then the rest of the employees are balloted to endorse the union position and claim parity on the main board. The union members and other employees need not elect the worker-directors from their own ranks, hence national labour leaders could become prominent industrialists as worker-directors. It was not proposed to pay them the same as ordinary directors nor was it suggested they necessarily undertake executive functions as directors. The exclusion of small and medium-sized firms from this scheme could, of course, mean that the bulk of British companies would have no such type of worker-representation, although a sizeable proportion of the labour force does indeed work for large enterprises, where the degree of unionization is relatively high.

The Minority Report argued that 'It would be exceedingly unwise for the nation to disregard their practical realism and accept the theories of those who see this debate as a means of changing the structure of society in this country and who would seek to bring the boards of the private sector under trade union control' (Bullock, 1977: 170).

In terms of the national debate, decisive action was called for. 'Industrial democracy with Bullock can no longer mean all things to all men' (Wintour, 1977: 3). Only a few private sector trade unions were keen on the Majority Report proposals, and the British Left specifically often has as cynical a view of industrial democracy, at least in terms of the models in the European Community, as many British employers. The Engineering Employers' Federation have placed their unequivocal objection to worker-directors on record. The Engineering unions, particularly the AUEW, are less likely to sustain their pre-dilection for merely extending collective bargaining, although few British unions are enthusiastic about 'cosmetic' solutions, and keener on the realities of shop-floor powers. As one critic points out: 'In contrast to German unions, the British labour movement has traditionally emphasised shop-floor powers exercised through a strong shop-stewards' movement' (Garson, in (ed.) Vanek, 1975: 166).

The Left in British unions opposes the European Community model and sees 'participation' as largely irrelevant in the march to socialism, and particularly to workers' control. Even the TUC saw works councils as 'inappropriate to Britain', (1975: 167). Those in favour of workers' control have looked to the Yugoslav model, and have encouraged direct action in the form of factory occupations and the setting up of worker co-operatives, like the Meriden experiment (making the Triumph motor-cycle, largely for export to the United States). The recession and threat of further closures in the early 1970s saw a spate of such actions, in which a right to veto plant closures was claimed and the issue of workers' con-trol was raised. The Institute of Workers' Control, based in Nottingham (founded in 1968), was active in publicity, if not in direct organization, on behalf of this radical alternative. There is also a Society for Democratic Integration in Industry, which includes the oft-cited Scott Bader Commonwealth (see Hadley, in (ed.) Vanek, 1975; 238). The notion of co-ownership has also been discussed and the appeal of producer co-operatives, as a viable option, is now stronger than it has been for a long time, providing they can survive in a competitive market environ-ment. The issue came up at the time of the government assisting certain new self-managed ventures with cash grants, or loans; and for a time such support has been forthcoming on a limited scale. It had been hoped that these experiments would have a 'demonstration-effect', but this has not proved true. Some have failed (like the *Scottish Daily News*), but others still exist, to the surprise of their critics.

There was also an Industrial Common Ownership Act, passed in 1976, to help such enterprises. The question of industrial democracy in the public sector was also reviewed by another committee in parallel to the Bullock deliberations, which envisaged trade unionists elected to the boards of nationalized industries, for example. In addition, there was also a debate whether employees of local councils should have representation on these democratically elected bodies, as opposed to domination by ratepayers' representatives. Other bodies of a more moderate persuasion, such as the Industrial Society, the Industrial Participation Association, and similar groups, lead the debate for more employee consultation, even participation. Many conferences, both business-oriented as well as academic have been held on the topic: but all have been overshadowed by problems raised by the current economic recession.

The 1978 White Paper on Industrial Democracy (see Dept. of Employment, Gazette, July 1978: 795–97) presented to Parliament in the late spring of that year, will take longer to find a place of priority. The Labour government did not delay its publication because it had already reached an impasse with both the CBI and the TUC. The White Paper suggests gradual progress towards a worker-director (over 3 or 4 years) of one third representation on supervisory boards for big firms over 2,500 employees and statutory rights on employee consultation and disclosure of company information (see 1978: 795–6). It will not please *all* the parties concerned, but may avoid the sustained row that followed the publication of the Bullock Report (see Jacobs, 1977). If anything, it leans in the direction of the Minority Report. The actual implementation of these proposals is another matter. Two-tier boards are an option; joint representation committees in firms over 500 employees play a vital role towards joint discussion of company strategy: legislation is to be 'enabling'. In any case, it is too early to see signs of fundamental shifts in attitudes, gentle pressure from Brussels to harmonize our arrangements with the Community or not. The trade unions may however ultimately see the advantage of a 'foot-in-the-door' approach the decision-making processes in industry, other than through collective-bargaining and shop-steward influence, but this remains to be seen.

It is unclear if the widespread industrial unrest of early 1979 and its consequent adverse impact on public sympathy for organized labour will significantly delay the advance of industrial democracy, but that it will is now more than a possibility.

In the aftermath of the strike-wave of early 1979, the Callaghan Government was defeated by a clear margin in the General Election held on 3 May. The Conservatives promised action to curb union power, specifically to outlaw secondary picketing, to strengthen objections to the closed shop, to trim social security payments to strikers' families, to impose secret union ballots, and so on. The theme of their proposed industrial relations policy was to make the unions operate *within* the law and not *beyond* it, as they alleged had been the case during the excesses of winter 1978–9.

The unions *basically* feared an attempt to alter the industrial 'balance of power' which was now a distinct possibility — with 'great changes in the Employment Protection Act, in the role of industrial tribunals, and of the Advisory, Conciliation and Arbitration Service, which some employers have claimed is biased towards the unions' (*Guardian*, 5 May 1979). The Bullock Report, even the milder White Paper on Industrial Democracy of 1978, appeared now of mere archival interest. The reduction of public spending, of subsidies for industries and hence of jobs, began to threaten the possibility of even wider unemployment in the early 1980s.

The trade union movement reacted, however, with caution to the election of the Thatcher Government, and at once described the Concordat — a broad agreemet of mutual interests — they had made with the outgoing Labour Administration null and void. None the less, the TUC hoped to co-operate with the Conservatives, as the Government of the day, as previously had been the case from 1951 to 1964, and to a lesser degree in 1970–4, providing the former were not 'provocative' in their relations with Organized Labour. This is now rather unlikely. Many commentators feared 'industrial chaos' from a markedly ideologically right-wing government, but the Tory appointee to the sensitive Cabinet post for employment matters (Mr James Prior), has already placed himself on record as a 'moderate'.

For its part, Organized Labour has no desire to see the concrete gains of the post-1945 era whittled away. The paradox remained of public opinion expressing anxiety about 'union power', but at the same time recruitment to unions, particularly white-collar bodies, increasing to a record level.

REFERENCES

Armstrong, Eric G. A. (1969), *Industrial Relations: An Introduction*. London: Harrap.

Atkinson, Anthony B. and Harrison, A. J. (1978), *Distribution of Personal Wealth in Britain*. Cambridge: CUP.

Bullock Report (1976), *Committee of Inquiry on Industrial Democracy*. London: HMSO.

Butler, David and Freeman, J. (1969), *British Political Facts, 1900–1968*. London: MacMillian.

Carew, Anthony (1976), *Democracy and Government in European Trade Unions*. London: George Allen & Unwin.

Clarke, R. Oliver; Fatchett, D. J. and Roberts, B. C. (1972), *Workers' Participation in Britain*. London: HEB.

Clegg, Hugh A. (1975), *The System of Industrial Relations in Britain*. Oxford: Basil Blackwell.

(1976), *Trade Unionism under Collective Bargaining: A Theory based on Comparisons of Six Countries*. Oxford: Basil Blackwell.

Central Statistical Office (1977), *Social Trends*. London: HMSO.

(1976), *National Income and Expenditure* (1965–1975).

(1977), *Annual Abstract of Statistics*. London: HMSO.

Department of Employment, *Department of Employment Gazette*. October, November, December (1975), August, October, November (1976), September (1977), January and July (1978).

(1971), *British Labour Statistics: Historical Abstract, 1886–1968*. London: DEP.

Derber, Milton (1975), *The Metalworking Industry*. Research Series, No. 1, Geneva: International Institute for Labour Studies.

Donovan Report (1968), *Royal Commission on Trade Unions*. London: HMSO.

Edelstein, J. David and Warner, Malcolm (1975), *Comparative Union Democracy: Organisation and Opposition in British and American Unions*. London: George Allen & Unwin.

Garson, David (1975), 'Recent Developments in Workers' Participation in Europe'. In Vanek, J. (ed.), *Self-Management: Economic Liberation of Man*. Harmondsworth: Penguin Books.

Giddens, Anthony (1973), *The Class Structure of the Advanced Societies*. London: Hutchinson.

Glyn, Andrew and Sutcliffe, B. (1972), *British Capitalism, Workers and the Profits Squeeze*. Harmondsworth: Penguin Books.

Goldthorpe, John H.; Lockwood, D.; Bechhofer, F.; Platt, J. (1969), *The Affluent Worker in the Class Structure*. Cambridge: CUP.

Goldthorpe, John H. (1974), 'Industrial Relations in Great Britain: A critique of reformism'. *Politics and Society*. 4.

Hadley, Roger (1975), 'Rowen, South Wales: Notes on an experiment in workers' self-management'. In Vanek, J. (ed.), *Self-management: Economic Liberation of Man*. Harmondsworth: Penguin Books.

Halsey, A. H. (1972), editor. *Trends in British Society: A Guide to the Changing Social Structure of Britain.* London: MacMillan.

———— (1978), 'The rise of party: Reith lecture on change in British society'. *The Listener,* 2 February.

Haseler, Stephen (1976), *The Death of British Democracy.* London: Elek.

Jacobs, Eric (1977), 'Thumbs down for workers on the Board'. *Sunday Times,* 9 January.

Kempner, Thomas (1977), 'The Economic Environment'. The Administrative Staff College, Henley-on-Thames.

Kendall, Walter (1975), *The Labour Movement in Europe.* London: Penguin Books and Allen Lane.

Macbeath, Innes (1975), *Power-Sharing in Industry.* London: Gower Press.

Moorhouse, Harold F. (1976), 'Attitudes to clan and class relationships in Britain'. *Sociology.* 10.

National Institute of Social and Economic Research (1976), *National Institute Economic Review.* London: N.I.S.E.R., No. 78. November.

Pelling, Henry (1969), *A History of British Trade Unionism.* London: Mac-Millan.

Pollard, Sidney (1965), *The Genesis of Modern Management.* Harmondsworth: Penguin Books.

Rose, Richard (1964), *Politics in England.* Boston: Little, Brown & Co.

Silver, Michael (1973), 'Recent British strike trends: a factual analysis'. *British Journal of Industrial Relations.* 11.

Shonfield, Andrew (1965), *Modern Capitalism.* Oxford: OUP.

———— (1972), *Europe: Journey to an Unknown Destination.* Harmondsworth: Penguin Books.

Taylor, Alan J. P. (1965), *English History, 1914–1945.* Oxford: OUP.

Trade Union Congress (1974), *Report on Industrial Democracy.* London: TUC, Congress House.

White Paper on Industrial Democracy (1978), Cmnd. 7231. London: HMSO.

Wintour, Patrick, (1977), 'The Social Contract's last stand'. *New Statesman,* 7 January.

7

THE GERMAN INDUSTRIAL RELATIONS SYSTEM

1. GENERAL SITUATION AND BACKGROUND

1.1. The political context

The particular historical experience of Nazi dictatorship, of the Second World War, and the complete breakdown at the end of the war, formed the extraordinary background for the emergence of a new social and political life in divided Germany after 1945. Its impact was felt on all levels and functions of society, including the development of the federalized system in the Federal Republic of Germany, and in the context of our study, on the developing industrial relations system.

The need for a comprehensive, collective and co-operative effort of all to rebuild at least a partially, if not wholly reunited Germany out of the ruins of total disaster has during the last three decades had its lasting effects on the mental state and attitude of politicians, union and economic leaders, and the majority of the German population alike. It is marked by the concern for consensus and everyone holding social and political responsibility, even though bargaining and vociferous articulation of divergent interests may precede it in periods of political contest and collective bargaining. This concern carries over into a common interest in safeguarding the jointly created and shared system of social institutions.

This tendency towards consensus can be demonstrated in the trend of the three main political parties which present themselves to the electorate as 'people's parties' reflecting a broad range of ideological, economic, and social orientations and interest. In spite of these overlapping features, the parties differ, of course, in certain historical, programmatic, and social dimensions. The Social Democratic Party (Sozialdemokratische Partei Deutschlands = SPD), being the oldest of the three main parties, traditionally reflects worker and unionized labour constituencies; it was always seen as a membership organization with substantial strongholds in urbanized, industrial areas. The Christian Democratic Union (Christlich–Demokratische Union = CDU) with its Bavarian branch of the Christian Social Union (Christlich–Soziale Union = CSU), was founded after 1945 mainly to rally middle class, bourgeois, agricultural, catholic and protestant voters, although it has a small but articulate employee interest group. For the purposes of national elections, the CDU and CSU formed a coalition up to now. The Free Democratic Party (Freie Demokratische Partei = FDP) has during the last fifteen years successfully stripped itself from its original bourgeois–liberal medium-sized business background and changed its policies to appeal to mainly white collar, intellectual, and urban groups.

The overall thrust towards national concentration is also reflected in the trend of national elections to concentrate more and more on only these three parties, with a relatively high level of voter turn-out. In 1949, 27.8 per cent of the voters voted for other than the three largest parties: CDU/CSU (31 per cent), SPD (29.2 per cent) and FDP (11.94 per cent) — with a turn-out of 78.5 per cent, whereas in 1957 this amount was reduced to 10.3 per cent, with a voter turn-out of 87.8 per cent (*Statistisches Jahrbuch*, 1975). In the national elections of 1976, the turn-out was 90.7 per cent, of which only 0.9 per cent of the voters cast their vote for other than the three main parties — (CDU/CSU 48.6 per cent; SPD 42.6 per cent; FDP 7.9 per cent; the last two forming a coalition government). (*Deutscher Bundestag*, 1977.)

One of the consequences of past experience was a strong constitutionally backed federalization of the Federal Republic in its division into ten states with their own governmental, legal, and administrative responsibilities and institutions. This was to ensure the representation of regional interest on a national level and to counter potentially strong central governments. The constitution prescribes a Federal Parliament (*Bundestag*) to be instituted by direct votes in a national election and a Federal Council (*Bundesrat*). Its members are appointed by state governments. Thus, the members, of the federal parliament and federal government are concerned with matters and problems of national significance, whereas the Federal Council as a second chamber is supposed to ensure that the specific interests and concerns of the respective ten federal states are considered (Grundgesetz, 1975). At the moment, the power relationship between the three bodies could best be described as a situation of uneasy balance, sometimes resulting in deadlock.

The national elections of 1969 offered for the first time in the history of the Federal Republic of Germany the possibility of forming an SPD/FDP government, an opportunity readily seized by Willy Brandt and Walter Scheel, the respective party leaders. Expectations were high that important bills relating to the influence of employees in companies would be submitted to the legislative bodies. As will be seen below, these expectations were not unwarranted although major unanticipated obstacles occurred in the process.

1.2. The Economic and Social Situation

The Federal Republic of Germany with its population of roughly 60 million has over the first 25 years of its existence enjoyed a remarkable economic growth with relatively low inflation rates (Table 7.1).

Table 7.1.
GNP (in million DM) and over-all price index (private households)

	1960	1965	1970	1974		
GNP	302,300	448,800	685,600	995,500		

	1970	1971	1972	1973	1974	1975
GNP	685,600	761,900	834,600	930,300	995,500	1040,5
Price index	100	105,1	113,5	129,7	132,5	144,6

Source: Statistisches Jahrbuch (henceforth SJ), 1976.

The gross national product expanded from 302,300 millions in 1960 to 1,040,400 millions in 1975, which amounts to a real rise from 100 in prices of 1962 to 144.6 in 1975 (*SJ*, 1976). While the average annual rise of prices for private consumption from 1950 to 1973 was 2.8 per cent (Bergmann *et al.*, 1975: 343). Similarly, from 1960 to 1974 the German economy was marked by full employment conditions with a relative increase in female labour force which grew from 37.2 per cent out of the total working population in 1960, to 43.3 per cent in 1975 (*SJ*, 1976) and a large contingent of foreign workers: 8.6 per cent out of the total working population (slightly above 25 millions in 1975; *SJ*, 1976). A drastic increase in unemployment only started with the recession of 1974, which particularly affected the female labour force, as well as young and foreign workers. The over-all rate of unemployment rose from 0.7 per cent in 1970 to 4.9 per cent in 1977 (Jacobi *et al.*, 1978). This was due to various reasons: structural changes in the whole economy, sectors, and subsectors respectively, and organizational changes at company or plant level — as for instance rationalization in compliance with a heavy cut in the number of employees. The composition of the total labour force in various sectors of the economy underwent some considerable changes in the field of employment during the period of 1961 to 1975.

Table 7.2.
Structure of labour force (in per cent)

	1961	1975
Agriculture, Fisheries	13.5	6.6
Energy, Mining	3.0	2.0
Industry	45.2	43.8
Trade	11.8	12.0
Other Services	16.8	20.8
Banking, Insurance	1.7	2.9
Regional administration and Social security	5.5	9.6
Others	2.4	2.2

Source: SJ, 1966; 1976.

From 1960 to 1974, in agriculture, energy, and mining, the labour force decreased considerably (down 45.6 per cent and 45.7 per cent respectively). The private and public service sector had a notable increase in work-force, amounting to 53.2 per cent in banking and insurance, and 42.3 per cent in the regional public administration and social security institutions, while the number of people working in the industrial sector only increased by 3.8 per cent (*Bundesministerium für Arbeit und Sozialordnung*, 1975: 182; Probst, 1975: 73). More than 85 per cent of the work-force employed in the metal engineering industries in 1975 worked in establishments of between 50 and 1,000 employees, the ratio being quite similiar for the three size categories of 50–99, 100–499, and 500–999. Work-related accidents have been decreasing since 1961, when a peak of 131 accidents were reported per 1,000 full-time employees (0.20 per 1,000 workers' accidents being fatal). Accidents dropped to 99 in 1973 and to 84 in 1977 per 1,000 full-time workers (0.16 and 0.12 fatal, respectively).

Real income of German employees over the last 10 years has slowly but steadily increased since income rises were usually slightly above the rate of inflation. It can be seen that wage differentials for various employee groups have more or less remained stable over the decade from 1965 to 1975 (Table 7.3 (i) and (ii)).

Table 7.3(i).
Average weekly DM-earnings of different worker categories (male)

	Average All Workers	High Skilled		Medium Skilled		Unskilled
1965	205	218	(1.10)[1]	197	(1.12)	175
1975	430	460	(1.13)	406	(1.12)	361

(ii) *Monthly DM-earnings of white collar employees (male)*

Year	Average	Upper Middle-Management		Lower Middle-Management		Experienced Employees		Unskilled Employees
1965	1055	1392	(1.33)	1044	(1.36)	763	(1.17)	652
1975	2317	2942	(1.34)	2189	(1.33)	1642	(1.11)	1477
1975[2]	2183	2802	(1.33)	2101	(1.31)	1596	(1.08)	1476 Banking Insurance

[1] In brackets are ratios of income from one group to next.
[2] Banking and Insurance.
Source: SJ, 1966; 1977.

The student enrolment in universities or equivalent institutions of higher learning increased steadily from a meagre 337,00 in 1966 (about 3.3 per cent of total student population) to 790,000 in 1974 (about 6.0 per cent of student population − *SJ*, 1976). Newspaper circulation (papers appearing more than once weekly), after minor increases in recent years, seemed to stabilize around 23.3 million in 1975 (*SJ*, 1976). While private consumption oscillated between 53 and 57 per cent of GNP in the period of 1960 to 1975, the stake of public consumption during the same time enjoyed steady increases from 13.6 per cent to 21.3 per cent which has been accompanied (particularly since 1970) by decreases in investments (from 28.6 per cent in 1970 to 20.8 per cent in 1975, *SJ*, 1976).

2. THE NATIONAL INDUSTRIAL RELATIONS SYSTEM

2.1. Legal Framework

Various legal bases provide the setting for the German Industrial Relations System. Some are written into the constitution, some stem from labour law or labour court decisions, and some are specific laws governing the behaviour of companies, employers, and employees. Although the relevant legal elements of the IRS are marked by an integrating intent, they are nevertheless quite fragmented, sometimes contradictory and far from constituting a stringent 'labour code'. In consequence, against all traditions of Roman-Germanic jurisprudence, the rulings of courts constitute an important source of German labour law (Däubler, 1976). The constitution defines the right to free association (Art. 9) and labour disputes, the right to equal treatment in work organizations (Art. 3), and the right of free choice of occupation (Art. 12). Thus, it is the constitution that sets the legal conditions for the formation of unions, employer associations, and collective bargaining (Grundgesetz, 1975).

The Civil Code (*Bürgerliches Gesetzbuch,* 1977) and company law regulate the formal aspects of owner–employer–employee relationships (e.g. the right of employees to adequate wages). The general 'right to direct' of the entrepreneur/manager is based on one of the oldest regulations in this field (*Gewerbeordnung,* 1869), which was replaced by a new one in 1976 (*Gewerbeordnung,* 1977). Relations between owners and management are treated also by the Civil Code and by Corporate Laws. Another set of legal regulations deals with social security issues and the mitigation of the consequences of bankruptcies and shut-downs for employees (Söllner, 1974).

Existing and proposed regulations on vocational training and continued vocational education are intensely debated at the moment. They detail rights and duties of trainers (Meister, Ausbilder) and apprenticeship, conditions, curricula, and final examinations; similar regulations are provided for training and retraining of workers already on the job (Hase *et al.,* 1974). All these laws which relate to the industrial relations systems in Germany are characterized by the principle of social protection: safety and health provisions, minimum income policies, and job security guidelines predominate.

2.2. Collective Bargaining Structure and Organizational Framework of Bargaining Parties

Special laws on collective bargaining (*Tarifvertragsgesetz,* 1974) regulate the form, contents, and procedures of bargaining as well as rights and duties of bargaining parties. The only recognized collective bargaining parties are unions on the one side, and employers' associations or single employers on the other. Issues for bargaining are wages, usually agreed upon at yearly intervals and minimum working conditions, types of employment contracts, training, humanization of work, and employee participation in decision-making, usually agreed upon at, and regulated for longer periods of time. Bargaining agreements oblige the parties to observe industrial peace during the agreed period of time. Stipulations of bargaining agreements have the binding quality of regular laws. Although only unions represent employees in bargaining, union membership is voluntary, and bargaining agreements are usually extended to cover also non-unionized employees (the 'negative' coalition right). Closed-shop principles are illegal for both bargaining parties, that is, no employee can be forced to join a union, or any employer to join an association, that organizes employers or industrial plants as institutions. The legally guaranteed autonomy of employers and labour creates a considerable space for negotiations among individual companies over working conditions and standards, holidays, and social benefits. The Industrial Relations system, as far as non-public, communal, municipal, or governmental employees are concerned is further structured and characterized by the specific structural principles of unions and employers' associations (Schneider, 1965).

Employers' Associations

Employers' organizations are fragmented into a great variety of sub-groups according to such principles of association by technological orientation, representation of economic interest, collective bargaining, and by regional organization. The most comprehensive employers' interest representation is found in the 'joint Committee of German Industries' (Gemeinschaftsausschuß der deutschen gewerblichen Wirtschaft): it is constituted by the 14 leading industrial organizations. The strongest and most influential ones being the Confederation of Employers' Associations (Bundesverband der Deutschen Arbeitgeberverbände – BDA) and the Federation of Industries (Bundesverband der Deutschen Industrie – BDI).

The Bundesverband der deutschen Arbeitgeberverbände (BDA) is composed of 56 member federations, grouped by trade and region, which in turn represent about 720 smaller sub-associations, covering roughly 90 per cent of all private enterprises. Internally rather hierarchically structured (this goes for the BDI as well), the BDA with its sub-divisions controls a wide net of regional and local offices and institutions. Thus, the BDA appears to be in command of an efficient communication and influence structure with considerable leverage *vis-à-vis* public authorities. In consequence, the BDA and its members are effectively represented in a number of government and other public committees, such as radio and television supervisory boards, scientific foundations, and expert committees. The main function of the BDA is to represent employers' interests in the area of social policy. As the one collective bargaining party, it is the principal antagonist of unions in collective bargaining.

The Bundesverband der Deutschen Industrie (BDI), similarly organized to the BDA, is composed of a considerable number of member-organizations and concentrates on representing interests of German industries in the field of national and international economic policy. The interrelatedness of social and economic policies suggests close organizational links between BDA and BDI; and in fact recent developments tend to institutionalize these links. BDA and BDI both draw most of their strength from big business, although middle- and small-scale industries strongly defend their programmes and policies as well. Because of the principle that influence is distributed according to dues paid or number of employees, leaders of both organizations are usually recruited from large-scale enterprises. Financial support of employers to election campaigns of conservative parties has been publicly acknowledged in the past.

Unions

After the last war, unions were rebuilt as 'unitary' unions – that is they include all occupations, political ideologies or creeds, and are organized by sectors or industries. Thus, only 16 industrial unions constitute the German Confederation of Unions (Deutscher Gewerkschaftsbund – DGB). About 34 per cent of the German work force is organized in the DGB-unions (1975), while only an additional 2-3 per cent of the work force are organized in separate unions (German Union of White Collar Employees – DAG, German Union of Civil Servants – DBB, Christian Federation of Unions – CGB). The average level of unionization varies substantially from industry to industry: in retailing 7 per cent (1975), in the banking and insurance sector 11 per cent, in iron and steel industries 79 per cent, in coal mining 92 per cent (Streeck, 1978). Moreover, there are substantial differences between individual establishments. The degree of over-all unionization has slowly but steadily increased from 1970 (30 per cent) to 1975 (37 per cent). Individual unions are organized in regional sub-divisions with individual union headquarters. On a regional level all existing DGB unions form a permanent administrative joint headquarters with full-time staff who have become increasingly professionalized (Streeck, 1978) in order to join forces in those matters which are general problems relating to several industries − that is, when various employers' associations or the local or regional authorities for that matter − stand as the opposing bargaining party. The loosely centralized organization on a regional and national level among the various DGB unions, counteracts the sometimes central domination within one union (and of the Trade Union Congress/DGB as a whole) in important matters relating to the interests of the whole working population (such as investment regulation, development of new technologies, or energy policies).

The basic organizational unit of an individual DGB union (e.g. the metal-workers' union, Industriegewerkschaft Metall − IGM), is the individual firm. All union members of one plant belong to this group and, as is the case in most DGB unions, are represented *vis-à-vis* management by elected shop deputies who constitute a formal union committee. This committee does not have the legal status of a participatory organ in the strict sense: the action-space of unions within a company is a matter of bargaining between unions and management. Union members include all occupations and professions within a given firm, so that there is only 'one factory − one union', as far as a member union of the DGB is concerned. If more than one union is in the company, as for instance in the banking and insurance sector, the German Union of white collar employees (DAG) as well as the particular DGB-union for that sector (*Industriegewerkschaft Handel, Banken, Versicherungen*), it depends on the amount of bargaining power within the plant that determines which union takes the lead. (Bargaining between works councils and a firm's management have a separate status from these collective bargaining structures. This will be discussed below.)

Formally, unions are politically neutral, i.e. they are independent from political parties. Yet links to the Social Democratic Party have a well-founded basis in the history of the German labour movement, and the trade-union faction within the parliamentary party and the SPD as a whole plays an important political role. However, union members are also to be found among the Christian Democrats and form a small but vociferous group. In the economic field, unions hold great stakes as potent entrepreneurs in banking, construction, retailing, insurance, and tourism with a total capital of roughly 1,300 millions DM (Bank für Gemeinwirtschaft, 1976: 37).

Given the historical experience and consequent general attitude of German unions and employer federations, the German economy was characterized by a phase of heavy conflict in the first years after the Second World War, a relatively peaceful period of industrial relations from 1953 to the beginning of the sixties and a growth of potential and actual conflict since 1967. The actual number of strikes, working days lost, and number of participants, however, is lower than in many other countries within the European Community, such as Great Britain and Italy. A rough estimate of participants in official strike counts from 1951 to 1970 show 4,192,000 in Great Britain against 231,000 in Germany; and of working days lost, 10,275,000 in Great Britain against 1,280,000 in Germany (Bergmann *et al.*, 1975: 297). It should, however, be pointed out that German official and unions labour dispute statistics are unsystematically kept and are bedevilled by a host of distorting factors with an inbuilt bias towards minimizing the magnitude of strikes (Kalbitz, 1972).

2.3. Participation in Companies*

Differentiating the general term 'participation' from the term 'codetermination', as used in German labour law, is not easy. First, 'participation' refers to the rights of employees and works councils in the context of a particular site or specific job in an enterprise. This is the area where the 'works constitution' (*Betriebsverfassungsgesetz*), providing rights of initiative, consultation, and advice in social, personnel, and economic matters comes into play. Furthermore, it constitutes the right for genuine codetermination in a series of social issues that are enumerated in the law. Second, since the last war the term 'codetermination' has been used *vis-à-vis* the dual board-system of the German corporate law as a label for the representation of employees and their unions in supervisory boards of stock-holding companies and large firms (*Mitbestimmungsgesetz*) and enterprises in the mining and iron- and steel-generating industrial sector (*Montan-Mitbestimmungsgesetz*). Third the term 'codetermination' is relevant in the context of long-standing considerations regarding 'codetermination beyond the enterprise', even to co-determination in comprehensive economic policy. This implies a special form of institutionalized participation of social partners and interest groups in federal and state legislation. What follows is an abbreviated description of the main features of the codetermination system in the Federal Republic of Germany.

Main Legal Base and Scope of Regulations

Co-determination within companies is regulated primarily by law and not by collective bargaining. The laws and the respective stipulations (only the more important ones are mentioned here) apply differently to the following four categories of companies:

(1) All private companies, profit or non-profit making, with at least five employees, are subject to the general 'works constitution act' of 1972 (updating and expanding the 1952 works constitution act, the first after World War II). This laws affects, depending on the business sector, from 75 per cent (wholesale and retail sector) to 98 per cent (manufacturing industry) of the total sectoral business work-force. Its regulations include the election of works-council members by all employees (jointly or separately for groups of blue- and white-collar employees) in each firm or in independent units of a company, such

---

*Part of this section appeared in (Wilpert, 1975), and (Lux and Wilpert, 1977): permission is gratefully acknowledged.

as separate production units (the number of members elected by employees for three years varies according to the grand total of employees in a firm). Unionization of works-council members and especially of their chair persons is usually above 80 per cent. Around 17 per cent of works council members are women and 4 per cent foreign workers (Schneider, 1978). The works constitution act facilitates works council meetings during working hours, the formation of works-council committees for certain tasks, the election of youth representative committees, quarterly works assembly meetings during working hours, with the possibility of outside union representatives being present. In firms with more than 300 employees, at least one works-council member can work full-time on works council matters (number of 'full-timers' increases with the size of the firm, up to eleven or even more). The works council can call trade union representatives from outside the firm into the firm in order to consult with them on existing issues. An arbitration committee between works council and management for conflict issues can be formed. (Fitting *et al.*, 1977.)

All these organizational prescriptions, on the basis of the general works constitution act, would mean little without the role-expectations spelled out in the law which are associated with the various functional units; e.g. an important expectation is that the monthly meetings of works councils with management will deal with contentious issues with the serious intent to reach agreement. The works council's approval is needed to such matters as piece-work remuneration, company remuneration schemes, intra-firm training measures, extra-ordinary firings; the works council's rights cover prior information by management on issues such as individual hirings and ordinary firings as well as major planned changes (technical or commercial) affecting the company. The rights of individual employees include the right to hearings, to complaints, and to see, upon request his personal file.

The formal representative organ of employees within a company for intra-firm matters is the works council. It has the formal right to influence the composition of employee representatives of all other joint employee–management bodies. Even though the German system formally distinguishes between blue-collar and white-collar employees, who mostly have a specified number of representatives in the works councils, *vis-à-vis* management, the works council speaks only with one voice. (The relationship between unions, their representatives and the council members, who very often are identical in personnel, will be described within the section on the main bargaining structure.)

(2) Medium-sized companies, that is those with more than 500 employees, are governed by additional special clauses of the works constitution act, which require one-third of the votes in the supervisory board for employee representatives. The functions and responsibilities of the supervisory board are regulated by the general corporate law (*Aktiengesetz*, 1977). Among the tasks of a supervisory board are appointment, supervision, and control of the management board as well as *ex post* on the basis of periodical reports, as *in actu* on the basis of special reports of the management on request by the supervisory board, as well as *ex ante* on the basis of planning proposals to be submitted by the management.

(3) Large companies; the new codetermination act of 1976 (*Mitbestimmungs-*

gesetz) stipulates that the supervisory boards of companies with more than 2,000 employees must have numerical parity between employer and employee representatives. However, the unions point out, that this will hardly ever amount to actual parity, since there is on the bench of the employees' representatives one member of the group of high-salaried white-collar employees with management functions. The chairman of the board must be elected by two-thirds majority in a first cast of votes. If a second vote is necessary, a simple majority of the respective interest groups is sufficient to elect an employer's representative as chairman and an employees representative as his deputy. Appointments to top management positions also require two-thirds majorities which — in case of deadlock — in a second ballot can be replaced by even votes and the deciding vote of the chairman. Roughly 450 companies, with about 4 million employees, are affected by the new law of 1976. 95 per cent of elected employees' representatives on supervisory boards in 1978 were unionized (*Unterhinninghofen,* 1978).

(4) The 'Montan' sector of coal, iron, and steel industries is governed by both the works constitution act (*Betriebsverfassungsgesetz*) of 1972 and the co-determination act for the *Montan*-industries (*Montan-Mitbestimmungsgesetz,* 1965) of 1951 which was revised in 1965 in order to cover subsidiaries which also have certain characteristics of Montan-enterprises. In July 1969, the Montan sector comprised 62 companies employing 8 per cent of the industrial work-force. The regulations on the basis of the codetermination act for the *Montan*-Industries state, among other things, that the supervisory boards of all *Montan* companies must be composed of 50 per cent of representatives elected by employees, 50 per cent named by stockholders and one additional 'independent' member (here, as in the case of 'large companies', the functions of the supervisory board are defined by the general corporate law). A 'works director' must be appointed as a full member of the management board, and this appointment must be with the employees' representatives' concurrence.

The intended net result of such stipulations for 'co-determination' is 'to ensure a leadership style by institutional means which is characterized by an obligation to give arguments and reasons' (Biedenkopf, 1972) and to preclude management or stockholders taking arbitrary actions on important matters without obtaining a consensus from employees or their representatives. The term 'codetermination' implies an equality of partners in decision-making over the whole range of issues occurring in a firm. But given the legal limitations on the range of issues open for 'participation', 'codetermination' exists only in a restricted sense. In a way, codetermination, too, is marked by social prevention principles and is therefore a continuation of the protective labour legislation. The crucial policy issues in the management of a firm are either excluded (in small firms) or (in large firms) frequently not fully accessible to all parties on equal terms. And yet, on the whole, the codetermination model has provided a rather effective institutional framework and a viable mechanism of the resolution of conflict in German companies.

The Main Bargaining Structure

The issues of bargaining at firm level are limited at the margin characterized, on the one hand, by general rules and legal regulations to be applied in general, and collective bargaining agreements at a regional level on the other hand. These regulations and agreements can be bargained upon but only in so far as further agreements are an expansion of existing regulations and agreements. The expansion has to be such that it relates to the interests of the employees in a positive way. It follows that within this framework the scope of participation is influenced by the power of unions and the specific power-play at plant level, where the bargaining parties are the works council and the unions, represented by shop-stewards, opposing the employers interests, as represented by management.

(1) Within this general bargaining structure the relationship of unions and works council is of special importance. The members of the council in a firm, elected by the employees, form a body which is legally prescribed by the works constitution and which has the right and opportunity to a certain amount of intra-firm participation. But these participation rights and possible opportunities may not be conceded or simply hindered by management. In the latter case, the works council as such has hardly any other instrument to enforce its legal and legitimate demands than to institute legal proceedings against management. This rather weak standing of the council against management is frequently strongly influenced by the fact, that the council-members are often identical with union shop stewards (*Vertrauensleute*). In their council function they are not allowed to initiate or take part in strikes or disputes; in their function as shop-stewards they may very well initiate, take part in, and try to influence as much as possible any conflict within the firm. Similarly, they can use information provided by the union and bring pressure from the union to bear upon management. Depending on the competence of council-members and the present power-distribution this splitting of functions as a strategic operation can be one of the pillars of the councils' activities besides the mobilization of employees, backing 'their' council so that their interests prevail (Hoffmann, 1972).

Slightly different, as Schmidt (1973) points out, is the situation in which the works council is able to gain personal influence by bargaining with management on special firm contracts while cutting out shop-stewards and local unions. In the long run this may be useful for management, since such contracts may be more limited in scope than contracts agreed upon after considerable pressure from union, shop-stewards, employees, and works council combined.

(2) As mentioned already, most collective bargaining takes place at a regional level (the two notable exceptions being the federal bargaining arrangements for public employees and for employees of the insurance branches). Bargaining agreements are binding for all member firms and employees, yet there are some modifications. Firms may not be a member of an employers' association; they then either sign a contract with the respective union which automatically extends the bargaining contract to their firm as well, or they will have to bargain on their own. Big firms or conglomerates like VW and Philips usually bargain on their own and sign special firm contracts with their unions (not works councils!), which are sometimes slightly more favourable for their employees. Wages and basic social arrangements being agreed upon above the firm level leaves limited bargaining space in companies.

Some of the few opportunities for works councils to bargain in wage matters are wage groups, changes in piece-rates, and details of performance-evaluation procedures. Bargaining over welfare and matters of technical change within the firm start in the management's favour, since it is management's initiative that brings those issues on to the agenda. Management is often in the position to calculate in advance 'acceptable bargaining gains' for the works council. These 'gains' may increase a works council's standing among employees, but at the same time indebt works councils to management. This may result in agreements that are at odds with broader union policies. In such situations, where the council is not able or willing to interact with and combine forces with the union and shop stewards, it is often restricted to reacting on facts produced by the entrepreneur. It has then only a chance to prevent an abuse of entrepreneurial powers and at most to enforce the principles of due process — but its creative initiating possibilities would be limited.

As collective bargaining for wages and general working conditions is organized regionally, issues and procedures of collective bargaining are relatively removed from the factory level. This goes both for the input- and the output-aspect of collective bargaining. Information, decision problems, and strategies on the regional level are often different from the factory level; on the other hand, the oucome of a bargaining process will not necessarily meet concrete demands of the labour force in a given factory. The alternative of individual-firm bargaining is being put forward from time to time and justified by growing structural and economic differences at the firm level. But as neither social partners is sure about possible effects of firm bargaining on bargaining powers or internal organizational solidarity, this idea has not yet been successful. The base-line for wage agreements within this system is logically given by what small- and medium-size firms can afford, which in most cases is less than what large enterprises, which may concede better conditions in specific firm contracts, could afford. Such contracts are, however, easily put off in times of recession (Schmidt, 1972; Bermann et al., 1975).

In spite of the separation of intra- and extra-firm bargaining, committees of both social partners for collective bargaining purposes are recruited partly from companies and partly from full-time union and employers' association staff. Besides, union members and employers may be at the same time members of a bagaining committee and of particular company supervisory bodies. Thus, there is a direct input from firms into supra-firm committees. Another feature of the bargaining situation is the previous orientation towards wage policies. Only during the last few years, since resources for redistribution have decreased, a move towards non-monetary issues has been indicated, as for instance, enforced by strikes, the agreements on conditions of work organization in the metal industry (1973), the collective agreements on the ruling out of lay-offs for certain groups of employees in the metal engineering industries (1975), iron and steel generating industries (1974), and in the insurance sector (1975) (Jacobi et al., 1975: 267-70).

Enforcement and Sanctioning Possibilities

Differing degrees of access to resources in case of management–labour disputes make them expensive for works councils and employees and relatively inexpensive for management (20,000 DM in severe cases of violation of laws).

Besides, it is management that can create facts; bargaining and juridical procedures start often only thereafter. In some cases of dispute the decision of an arbitration body (parity membership) will replace a management–works council decision. But often the labour court is the last resort.

The three levels of the German labour court system are made up of 113 Local Courts, 11 State Labour Courts, and the Federal Labour Court. The State Labour Courts function as Courts of Appeal on points of law and fact, the Federal Labour Court accepts only appeals on points of law. All courts deal only with individual or collective disputes of rights, and not with disputes of interest (e.g. wages). The number of complaints brought to the attention of labour courts has steadily increased over the last ten years with peaks always in times of recession. The cases before Local Courts increased by 83 per cent between 1969 to 1975 (91 per cent for State and 65 per cent for Federal Labour Court). About 90 per cent of disputes are submitted by employees, unions, or works councils. Local Courts settle about 30–40 per cent of all cases by conciliation. In 1972 Local Labour Courts settled 71 per cent of the cases within three months, 17 per cent within 6 months, and 9.5 per cent within twelve months (European Industrial Relations Review, 1977). Some cases drag on up to two years before a final ruling is handed down. As experts have said, such extended court cases may amount to a denial of constitutional rights. Since laws on industrial relations tend to be political compromises they are often formulated quite loosely. Hence, it can be expected that the number of labour courts cases are heading for a new peak after the laws of 1972 and 1976. This has forced legislators to contemplate a streamlining and speeding-up of court procedures.

2.4. Participation on the regional/national level

Anticyclical global (governmental) economic policies in the Keynesian tradition and collective bargaining strategies of unions alone proved inadequate to resolve various economic, social, manpower, and income-distributive goal conflicts. This recognition led to the creation of the institution of 'Concerted Action', a periodical meeting of government, top union, and employers' representatives to exchange views on the general economic and prices and incomes policy needs of the German economy. This meeting has no policy or decision powers; chaired by the Federal Economics Minister, it works under the assumption that a common attitude to the situation will lead to rational behaviour, that is, policies that are not mutually defeating but Pareto-optimal.

Beyond these mainly economic aims covered by the 'Concerted Action', German unions pursue their objectives of influencing social and economic policies above the company level and beyond the realms of traditional collective bargaining. They succeed, in part, through informal and formal channels; in part, issues are still contained in programmatic statements. Informal influence is exerted on legislative processes through parliamentarians close to, or even actual members of unions. Increasingly, the institution of hearings before major social or labour legislation provides a new opportunity to voice union (and employer) concerns. The institutions of social security, obligatory health and accident insurance, and the Federal Agency for Work (functions of which include unemployment insurance, labour statistics, job placement, vocational guidance) all have at least a tripartite (government, employer, union) representation in their policy-making bodies. Nationalized enterprises (train and postal services) have a 25 per cent union representation in their policy-making bodies. The DGB in 1971 adopted a new programmatic stance for the introduction of Federal, State, and Regional Economic and Social Councils, with parity composition of membership. They are seen to be sounding-boards and discussion forums for governments and parliaments for their socio-economic plans. However, their implementation seems still far off.

2.5. The Industrial Climate

The present contractual relationship between an employer and his employees is such that the employer pays for labour services. Implicit in this basic legal relationship, is the governance relation of employers over employees. This means that the basic principles of private ownership are only affected indirectly, to the degree that control over productive means is affected and influenced by codetermination. On the whole, codetermination as a legal system of institutionalized employee interest representation in company decision-making is an accepted element in German social policy among employers as well as employees. In spite of the hot political debates, however, its place in the priority list given by the population as a whole is rather low (ranking ninth in a list of twelve items), security of jobs taking the lead. The close connection with labour legislations and the works council as a catalyst to the application of the provisions of codetermination laws and labour laws provide a pacifying effect and an institutionalized regulation of conflict. As pointed out before, striking is really a last resort, and relatively rare as compared to other countries within the European community. The dominant issues are wages and occasionally working conditions; broader political issues hardly appear when a strike does take place, it is usually conducted within the boundaries of legality. Wildcat, spontaneous strikes, and work stoppages can lead to monetary fines and forced compensation for damages or losses occurred in consequence of strikes.

3. PROGRAMMATIC PERSPECTIVES, PROBLEMATIC ISSUES, AND DEVELOPMENTS

3.1. Developing Co-determination

The new codetermination law of 1976, based on the 1952 *Montan* law with parity provisions in the supervisory boards, had been a major policy aim of the Social Democratic/Liberal coalition government. Under the influence of the general economic and political situation and the policies of the minor coalition partner (Liberals), the proposal has finally also received the consent of the opposition parties. Although many models, starting with the Biedenkopf-commission (*Mitbestimmungskommission*, 1970), had been presented, there was only one contentious issue: the union demand for parity in the supervisory boards of big enterprises, based on the *Montan* model and the employers' demand for sub-parity. The unions, always drawing on the *Montan* regulations, argued that only participation in the top decision-making organs guaranteed effective representation of workers' interests in the firm, while employers' associations maintained that more participation would hamper flexible and economic decision-making and would in the end even bring it to deadlock. This, in turn, would be disastrous to the international competitiveness of German industry. Somewhere in between, the Liberal party's goal was to keep external union representatives out of the codetermination organs. With some minor (mostly verbal) differences this was the position of the Christian Democrats as well; yet a minority of the CDU still demands a parity solution. The Social Democrats, after favouring the extension of the *Montan* model in the beginning, made the whole issue a subject of bargaining with their junior coalition partner.

One year after the passage of the compromise, while elections for supervisory boards were already being conducted, a group of nine large firms and thirty employers' associations affected by it challenged the legality of the new law of 1976 before the Federal Constitutional Court on the grounds that the law impinged, among other things, on constitutionally guaranteed property and coalition rights (Kaßler, 1977: 107). This action of the employers prompted the unions to cancel their participation in the 'Concerted Action' for the time being. The decision of the Constitutional Court will have a major impact on the German industrial relations climate and the further development of co-determination. The Federal Constitutional Court turned down the employers' plea (in March 1979) and upheld the constitutionality of the law of 1976.

A parliamentary commission has worked for several years on a bill to reform the traditional corporate law. No final proposal has reached the public as yet although it is quite clear that the proposal must confront also the question of employees as a constitutive part of the institutional system of a company, beyond the mere wage-labour relationship.

3.2. General Living and Working Conditions

Assuming that the political fight over the extension of codetermination in companies will have died down for some time after the passing of the law of 1976 and the related decision of the Federal Constitutional Court, one can foresee the emergence of new and significant points of contention in the social policy debates of the 1980s: unemployment, the degrading of skilled labour and rationalization within firms, humanization of work, and income distribution.

Two basic models of income distribution are already propagated: the distribution of income via the promotion of each employee's co-ownership of productive means in the form of individually owned and tradeable property titles (possibly in shares in a central fund) and co-ownership by way of non-tradeable ownership titles in autonomous funds; unions favour the latter and employers the former (see IDE 1980, ch. 11).

In pursuit of extending the influence of employee organizations in matters of national and regional socio-economic policy, the 1971 programme of the DGB for the introduction of Social and Economic Councils at Federal, State- and Regional level will in all likelihood become of increasing significance in public debate. The long-standing tradition of these concepts, which trace their ancestry to pre-1884 social theorists (Teuteberg, 1961), may thus experience a rebirth. The Federal Trade Union organization considers this as an instrument to influence the investment of private industry, capital and investment flows of government or communal and municipal authorities in such a way that the high unemployment rate will be cut down. Another development which has far-reaching consequences and could precipitate conflict is the technological development, which in many instances enables management to replace a well-trained and therefore relatively expensive labour force by complex machinery of a high technological standard and a smaller, less well-trained, and therefore less expensive, work-force. In 1976 the union that organizes employees within the printing and publishing industries – including newspapers (*Industriegewerkschaft Druck und Papier*) – went on strike, in order to ensure a minimal protection against a lay-off of printers caused by the introduction of such machinery. The strike was backed by many other unions and people of the work-force, if not by public opinion, which had access to news events for the time of the strike only via television, radio, and occasional special issues of newspapers. The importance of this strike was indicated by the reaction of the employers' associations in general and the respective association in particular, which locked the employees out in almost all regions and plants. Similar problems to these in the printing industries can be anticipated for office and clerical work which is threatened by new developments in automation technologies.

Another means of decreasing unemployment is widely discussed: the cut in daily, weekly, or annual working-time, as well as the retirement age. Since the consequences of the various models on the economy and the labour force in general is not yet clear, no specific stand has been taken and no specific model favoured either by unions or by employers or government. Positions are only slowly emerging. The government's 'humanization of work' programme with its projected investments of several hundred million DM amounts to one of the largest efforts of a government to improve working conditions for workers and employees in industry and the service sector. Differences in the frequency of permanent injury among various categories of employees point to the fact that manual labour in particular remains dangerous in terms of hazardous working conditions. The governmental initiative is therefore timely but most likely still inadequate.

There is in Germany a general consensus among all main parties concerned that the codetermination system has had its positive results by providing an institutional framework for conflict regulation, and the articulation of workers' interests. Some of these results may even have contributed to the relative industrial peace and economic viability which Germany has enjoyed over the last twenty-five years. However, this inevitably raises the question of what is cause and effect, a query still unanswered and, it appears, as yet unanswerable.

REFERENCES

Aktiengesetz (1977), München: Deutscher Taschenbuch Verlag.
Bank für Gemeinwirtschaft (1976) (ed.), Materialien Gemeinwirtschaft, Fragen und Antworten. Frankfurt/M.

Bergmann, A. E. (1975), 'Industrial Democracy in Germany – The Battle for Power', *Journal of General Management*, 2.

Bergmann, J., Jacobi, O., Müller-Jentsch, W. (1975), *Gewerkschaften in der Bundesrepublik*, Frankfurt/M.-Köln, Europäische Verlagsanstalt.

Betriebsverfassungsgesetz (1977), 1972, in Fitting, K., Auffarth, F., Kaiser, H., *Betriebsverfassungsgesetz mit Wahlordnung, Handkommentar*. München: Franz Vahlen.

Beyme, K. von (1979), *Trade Unions and Workers' Organizations in Industrialized Nations*. London: Sage Publications.

Biedenkopf, K. (1972), 'Deutsche Mitbestimmungserfahrungen in der schweizerischen Mitbestimmungsdiskussion', in: Lattmann, Ch. and Ganz-Keppeler (eds.), *Mitbestimmung in der Unternehmung*. Bern, Stuttgart: Paul Haupt.

Bundesministerium für Arbeit und Sozialordnung (1975), (ed.), *Arbeits- und sozialstaatliche Mitteilungen* (AsM), Bonn 6.

Bürgerliches Gesetzbuch (1977), München: Goldmann.

Däubler, W. (1976), *Das Arbeitsrecht*, Reinbek b. Hamburg, Rowohlt Taschenbuch Verlag.

Deutscher Bundestag (1977), (ed.), *Amtliches Handbuch des deutschen Bundestages*, 8. Wahlperiode, Rhein Greitbach, Neue Darmstädter Verlagsanstalt.

European Industrial Relations Review (see under West German . . .).

Fitting, K., Auffarth, F., Kaiser, H. (1977), *Betriebsverfassungsgesetz mit Wahlordnung, Handkommentar*. München: Franz Vahlen.

Gewerbeordnung (1977), München: Beck Verlag.

Grundgesetz der Bundesrepublik Deutschland (1975), von 23.5.1949. München: Deutscher Taschenbuch Verlag.

Günter, H. (1972), *Future Industrial Relations. Federal Republic of Germany and Austria*, International Institute for Labour Studies, Geneva. (Research Project on Future Industrial Relations, Document No. 3.)

Haase, H., Richard, H., Wagner, H. (1974), *Berufsbildungsgesetz*, Köln, Bund-Verlag.

Hoffmann, R. (1972), *Rechtsfortschritt durch gewerkschaftliche Gegenmacht*, Frankfurt/M., Europäische Verlagsanstalt.

International Labour Organization (1971), 'Basic Agreements and joint statements on Labour–Management Relations', *Labour–Management Relations Series* No. 38, Geneva.

Jacobi, O., Müller-Jentsch, W., Schmidt, E. (eds.), (1975), *Gewerkschaften und Klassenkampf, Kritisches Jahrbuch 1975*. Frankfurt/M.: Fischer Taschenbuch Verlag.

———— (1978), *Gewerkschaftspolitik in der Krise. Kritisches Gewerkschaftsjahrbuch 1977/78*, Berlin: Rotbuch Verlag.

Kalbitz, R. (1972), 'Die Streikstatistik in der Bundesrepublik', *Gewerkschaftliche Monatshefte*, 23.

Kaßler, E. (1977), 'Die Verfassungsklage der Unternehmer', in *Das Mitbestimmungsgespräch*, 7.

Lux, H.-J., Wilpert, B. (1978), 'Co-Determination: Worker Participation in the Federal Republic of Germany', in Wilpert, B., Kudat, A., Özkan, Y. (eds.), *Workers Participation in an Internationalized Economy*, Kent, Ohio: CARI-Publication.

Mitbestimmungsgesetz (1976), 'Gesetz über die Mitbestimmung der Arbeitnehmer vom 4. Mai 1976', in *Das deutsche Bundesrecht*, Lfg. 376, Bd. 1.

Mitbestimmungskommission (1970), *Mitbestimmung in Unternehmen*, Stuttgart, Berlin, Köln, Mainz: W. Kohlhammer.

Montan-Mitbestimmungsgesetz 1965 (1977), in Fitting, K., Auffarth, F., Kaiser, H., *Betriebsverfassungsgesetz mit Wahlordnung, Handkommentar*, München: Franz Vahlen.

OECD (Manpower and Social Affairs Directorate) (1972), *Recent Trends in Collective Bargaining*, International Management Seminar, Castelfusano 21–4 Sept. 1971: Final Report, Paris.

Probst, A. J. (1975), *Arbeitslosigkeit und Wirtschaftskrise in der BRD in den siebziger Jahren*, Frankfurt/M.: Institut für marxistische Studien und Forschungen. Informationsbericht Nr. 19.

Schmidt, E. (1972), 'Zur Strategie der betriebsnahen Tarif politik', in Jacobi, O., Müller-Jentsch, W., Schmidt, E., *Gewerkschaften und Klassenkampf. Kritisches Jahrbuch 1972*, Frankfurt/M.: Fischer Taschenbuch Verlag.

 (1973), 'Die Rolle der Betriebsräte in der BRD', in Jacobi, O., Müller-Jentsch, W., Schmidt, E., *Gewerkschaften und Klassenkampf. Kritisches Jahrbuch 1973*. Frankfurt/M.: Fischer Taschenbuch Verlag.

Schneider, H. (1965), *Die Interessenverbände*, München, Wien: Olzog.

Schneider, W. (1978), 'Betriebsratswahlen 1978 — eine zusammenfassende Bewertung', *Gewerkschaftliche Monatshefte*, 29.

Söllner, A. (1974), *Arbeitsrecht*, Stuttgart, Berlin, Köln, Mainz: W. Kohlhammer.

Statistisches Jahrbuch, 1966, 1974, 1975, 1976. Stuttgart, Berlin, Köln, Mainz: W. Kohlhammer.

Streeck, W. (1978), 'Politischer Wandel und organisatorische Reformen', *Gewerkschaftliche Monatshefte*, 29.

Tarifvertragsrecht (1974), in Söllner, A., *Arbeitsrecht*, Stuttgart, Berlin, Köln, Mainz: W. Kohlhammer.

Teuteberg, H. (1961), *Die Geschichte der industriellen Mitbestimmung in Deutschland*, Tübingen: J. C. Mohr (Paul Siebeck).

Unterhinninghofen, H. (1978), 'Aufsichtsratswahlen 1978: Erfolge und Probleme', *Gewerkschaftliche Monatshefte*, 29.

Warner, M., Peccei, R. (1978), 'Management Decentralization and Worker Participation in a Multi-National Company Context', in Wilpert, B. *et al.*, *Workers' Participation in an Internationalized Economy*, Kent, Ohio: CARI-Publication.

West German Labour Court System: A Review (1977), *European Industrial Relations Review*, 37.

Wilpert, B. (1975), 'Research on Industrial Democracy: the German Case', *Industrial Relations Journal*, 6.

Zachert, U. (1976), 'Die Arbeitnehmervertreter im Aufsichtsrat — Rechtliche, praktische und mitbestimmungs-politische Aspekte unter Einschluß des Mitbestimmungsgesetzes vom Juli 1976 I–IV', in *Das Mitbestimmungsgespräch*, 8/76, 10/76, 11/76.

8

THE DUTCH INDUSTRIAL RELATIONS SYSTEM

1. GENERAL SITUATION AND BACKGROUND

1.1. Introduction

Developments in the Netherlands after the Second World War were originally determined by the need to rebuild society. The government, the major political parties, and the employees' and employers' associations worked together harmoniously to achieve rapid industrialization.

Increased productivity and national income made it possible to aim at 'a welfare-society'. This was also reflected by increased legislation in the area of social security.

A very special aspect of the Dutch situation is found in what may be called 'vertical segregations' between religiously defined groups i.e. Roman Catholic, Protestant, and non-denominational organizations. In non-denominational groups furthermore, one can sometimes distinguish between liberal- and socialist-oriented organizations. This historical division along vertical lines is decreasing in importance, but can still be found in almost all areas, and is reflected not only in political parties, but also employers' associations, unions, schools, broadcasting corporations, voluntary associations, etc.

The post-war years can be roughly divided into three periods:
(*a*) Joint rebuilding (up to about 1960), when political parties, employees' and employers' associations supported a type of economic system that can be characterized by the term 'guided economy'. Wages and prices were almost completely controlled to promote the rebuilding of Dutch industry.
(*b*) Re-evaluation of existing relations (1960s) when because of the economic growth and the development of the welfare state the arguments for co-operation and discipline lost their strength. Criticism of existing relationships in all kinds of areas began to be heard and to grow. Even at the end of the 1950s there were protests in union circles against the guided economy. In the course of the 1960s, free collective bargaining was increasingly tolerated by the government. Conflicts between employers and unions became more acute. Also more fundamental criticism concerning the socio-economic order was growing. An example of this is the student protest movements of the 1960s, but the same held for established organizations. These developments were accompanied by more insight into the effects of the western economic system on the Third World, the environment, and the natural resources.
(*c*) Transition (1970s) when many of the above-mentioned trends continued. There are, however, also signs which seem to suggest that in recent years some of the more radical reactions have been moderated by the economic crisis and the unemployment problems.

1.2. The political situation

Although The Netherlands has always had a profusion of both large and small political parties, there are three main groups:

(*a*) The political *right* wing comprises, apart from some very small parties, the liberal party (the VVD), a party which, in view of its programme would in countries like France or Germany probably be considered a centre party.

(*b*) Politically more or less in the *centre* are the large Roman Catholic party (KVP) and two somewhat smaller Protestant parties (CHU and ARP). For the 1977 elections these three parties joined to form a Christian Democratic Party (CDA).

(*c*) The *left* wing is made up of the large Labour Party (PvdA) and some smaller parties including the Communist party.

Table 8.1.
Main parties (expressed as % of seats in Parliament).

	1946	1956	1967	1977
Conservative Party	–	9	11	18
Roman Catholic and Protestant parties	52	50	44,5	32
Labour Party	28	33	23,5	34
Others (including Communist Party)	20(10)	8(4)	21(3)	15(1.3)

Traditionally the strength of the Roman Catholic Party lies in the southern part of the Netherlands — 'below the rivers'. The northern provinces are mainly protestant. Both areas and in particular also the eastern Netherlands, are less heavily populated and have much less industry than the western provinces.

Before 1971, voting was compulsory. In the elections of 1971 and 1972 attendance was 87 per cent and 82 per cent, respectively, in the 1977 elections 89 per cent. None of the three largest groups has ever been strong enough to form a government by itself. Consequently, since 1946, there has been a series of coalitions between the Christian Democrats and either the Socialist Party (1946 to 1955 and 1973-7) or the Liberal Party (1959-65, 1966-73, 1977-).

1.3. Economic situation and the labour market

The post-war Dutch economy showed a steady growth until recently. Since 1946, the average annual increase in the national income has amounted to about 10 per cent, but under inflation conditions the real average increase (up to the 1970s) has been about 4.8 per cent.

Table 8.2.
Some indicators of economic development

	1948	1955	1965	1974
National income (net, market prices) (in mln. Dfl.)	13,442	27,528	62,547	170,890
Real National Income* (1970 = 100)	35	49	76	113
Average income per capita	1,372	2,561	5,088	12,500

*In constant prices.
Source: Central Bureau of Statistics; *75 jaar Statistiek van Nederland.*

During the last five years this increase has dropped considerably (Table 8.3).

Table 8.3.
GNP and inflation over the 1971-5 period

	1971	1972	1973	1974
GNP (market prices in mln. Dfl.)	129,550	147,230	166,480	187,040
Real national income (1970 = 100)	105	108	113	113

Source: CBS: *Statistical Yearbook.*

An important factor in the economic development was the discovery of huge amounts of natural gas.

Since the Second World War the population has increased and the composition of the labour market has changed considerably. The total population was 9.3 million in 1945 and increasing to 10.8 million in 1955, 12.4 in 1965 and 13.7 in 1975. It is predicted that it will level off at about 15 million in the next twenty years. The portion of the population living in urban areas (towns with more than 100,000 inhabitants) has remained fairly stable at about 30 per cent.

The working population decreased from 40 per cent of the total population in 1955 to 35.7 per cent in 1975. While shortly after the Second World War still 20 per cent of the total working population was working in agriculture and fishing, this decreased to about 6 per cent in 1975, the major shift being to the manufacturing and mining industries.

Table 8.4.
Change in composition of total working population (in %)

	1947	1955	1965	1974
Agriculture/fishing	17	13	9	6.5
Industry/mining	17	31	31	24
Construction	7.5	9	10	10
Services	35	34	38	46
Government	13	12	11	13

Source: CBS: *75 year statistiek van Nederland.*

Unemployment has been until recently, quite low:

1947	1955	1965	–	1971	1972	1973	1974	1975	1976
2.8	1.3	0.8		1.4	2.4	7.4	3.0	5.1	5.4

Source: Statistical Yearbook.

Unemployment has not increased much in the last few years, but it is expected that it might do so again in the near future. There is, however, much 'hidden' unemployment that these figures do not show, partly because many women who are in principle willing to work do not register as unemployed and partly because many who are at least partially able and willing to work are covered by one of the social security acts, for example, those concerning pensions or disabled persons. The part of the net national income under taxes and social security premiums has grown spectacularly from 30 per cent in 1955 to 39 per cent in 1965 and 50.5 per cent in 1974.

Unemployment in one sector can be accompanied by a labour shortage in another. This is due to the composition of the work-force in terms of education levels. Table 8.5 shows a strong increase in average education levels over the last 30 years.

Table 8.5.
Education levels of several groups (in %)

	1950	1955	1965	1973
12–19 yr. group in college/high school	16.3	20.5	27	39.4
12–19 yr. group in occupational schools	28.9	34.3	36.4	43.3
18–25 yr. group in university	2.3	2.3	4.0	6.5

Source: CBS: *75 jaar Statistiek van Nederland.*

A further indication of decreased social stratification is the fact that the top 5 per cent income bracket accounted for the following shares of the national income: 1930 – 30 per cent; 1950 – 25 per cent; and 1967 – 21 per cent. A recent report (WRR, 1977) has, however, argued that in the last ten to twenty years, social inequality in several areas has not decreased substantially.

2. INDUSTRIAL RELATIONS

2.1. Structure of the system

Introduction

Although the Dutch economic system is basically a free market system, it exhibits quite a few characteristics of both a planned economy and a corporative system. The government plays a prominent part, on the one hand through its authority (which is sometimes used) to control wages and prices or at least influence the bargaining process; and on the other hand through legislation concerning not only the rights and duties of enterprises but also participation structures. However, on the national level, in industrial sectors and in individual enterprises, decisions are often taken or prepared in councils and committees composed of both employers and employees' representatives. During the last ten or fifteen years, relations between the three main partners of the socio-economic system – i.e. the government, the employers, and the trade unions – have been changing. Before these changes can be analysed, the system and its processes must be described at both the national and company levels.

Four main characteristics of this system are:

(*a*) *Differentiation.* Both employers' and employees' associations are to a high degree divided, not only according to industrial sector but also within these sectors, into three segregated groups: Roman Catholic, Protestant, and non-denominational.

(b) *Integration.* Despite these segregations, there has been close co-operation between the different unions and the same applies to the employers' associations. And until the 1960s there was relatively harmonious co-operation between employers and unions.

(c) *Centralization.* A unique feature is the emphasis in the industrial relations system on national-level agreements in which the government plays a large part. Parallel to this there is also a fairly high degree of centralization within the employees' associations; and to a lesser degree within the employers' associations.

(d) *Consensus.* Until the 1960s, the three partners held very similar views on the objectives and implementation of industrial relations.

Institutional Framework

There are two consultative bodies at the national level: the Social and Economic Council — SER and the Foundation of Labour.

(a) The Social and Economic Council (SER)

The principle of self-determined group activity which is constitutionally based, took concrete shape in the Netherlands in the 1950 Industrial Organization Act. This Act gave birth to the Social and Economic Council and also opened up the possibility of establishing public regulatory bodies — industry boards — for industrial sectors. The SER, which is financed jointly by all Netherlands enterprises, is the principal body advising the government on social and economic problems. It is composed of 45 members — 15 each from employers' federations and the trade unions and 15 independent experts appointed by the government. The members serve in a private capacity.

The SER prepares semi-annual reports on the economic situation and anticipated economic developments. Secondly, the government can ask the SER for advice on specific social and economic matters. A third function of the SER is supervision of the formation and organization of Industrial Boards. These boards, formed mainly in some of the smaller industrial sectors and in agriculture, are comparable in their operation to the Wage Councils in the United Kingdom. The only sector where these boards really function is in agriculture.

The SER became the most important body in the social and economic consultative system. Recently, however, it has been argued that it is outdated, because it belongs to an industrial relations climate of co-operation and harmony, whereas the Dutch system is tending more and more toward a 'coalition' model.

(b) Foundation of Labour

The Foundation of Labour was established in 1945 by employers' associations and unions, and was accepted by the government as an important advisory body on socio-economic developments. Originally, the governmental commission for the control of collective agreements was even obliged by the law to consult this Foundation, but when the SER was founded in 1950, the Foundation of Labour lost its official advisory function. It remained in existence, however, because the employers and employees considered 'their' foundation a useful place to consult each other without official representatives of the government (as in the SER). The government also valued the possibility for informal contact with both groups. The Foundation can even put pressure on the government (which is impossible for an official advisory body). Moreover, the employers and employees in the Foundation of Labour are true representatives, with a mandate from their respective organizations. This means that real bargaining and also the establishment of a central agreement is possible.

Besides these two official bodies there are other consultative bodies in certain sectors. In these 'councils' the discussions often pertain not only to wages and related issues but also to general developments in the particular sector.

Relevant legislation

The Civil Code provides procedures and instruction for the execution of labour contracts, describes the obligations of the employer and of the employee, and regulates job-termination terms in the event of discharge.

The Law on Wages (1970) stipulates that employers (associations) and unions are free to decide on the contents of collective agreements. The government, however, derives the following qualifications from the Law on Wages:

(*a*) The Minister of Social Affairs can, at the request of both parties and after consulting the Foundation of Labour impose a wage regulation with the same legality as the collective agreements. This occurs for instance when the bargaining process reaches a deadlock.

(*b*) The Minister of Social Affairs can impose a wage-regulation on a particular category of industries. The approval of the Foundation of Labour is required.

(*c*) The Minister of Social Affairs can suspend individual collective agreements if required by the general social and economic situation. (The unions usually bring pressure to bear on the government not to apply this article. So far it has never done so.)

(*d*) The Minister of Social Affairs can, after consulting the SER and Foundation of Labour, prolong all collective agreements by at most six months. This would be called a 'wage freeze'. Again, the union federations have usually intervened and the 'wage freeze' was changed into a 'wage modification' (1970, 1975).

Dismissal and the Regional Labour Exchanges Act dating from 1945 stipulated that neither an employer nor an employee may break a Labour contract without the approval of the Regional Labour Exchange (GAB), unless there is mutual agreement or a pressing reason. On the basis of the EEC Social Action programme, starting in 1975 the GABs wait a month before dealing with a dismissal request covering twenty or more employees. There are eighty-six GABs scattered over the country, headed by a director and a bipartite advisory board composed of employers' and employees' representatives. The GABs also serve as local employment exchanges, promote (re-)training and vocational guidance, supply employment statistics, etc. At the moment, the GABs are trying to become modern and effective labour-market information centres.

The (1919) Labour Act (from time to time adjusted to current conditions) deals with, for example, the age at which people may start working, the hours of work and rest, and specific conditions for young employees and women. For young employees aged 15½–16½ years, education is obligatory two days a week, and at the age of 16½–17½, one day a week. Maximum working time per week is forty-five hours divided over five days. The new 1980 Safety Act provides strict regulations in the domain of safety in companies. An important factor here is formed by the Labour Inspection Services, which supervise the application of this law. The 1980 Act makes the establishment of a safety committee obligatory for companies that do not have a works council.

Although social insurance acts lies outside the scope of this chapter, it should be mentioned that the Netherlands have closely interwoven provisions for national as well as employee insurance. The legislation covering the latter category includes acts providing for health insurance, occupational disability insurance, unemployment insurance, family allowance for wage-earners, and a compulsory illness-fund. The bodies (*bedrijfsverenigingen*) charged with the execution of these Acts are bipartite.

The SER merger code, based on voluntary co-operation between business and government, stipulates that companies planning a merger must inform the union federations as soon as the merger is decided on (but not yet implemented). Since it is not an Article of law, the merger code does not dispose of legal sanctions; the only sanctions the code has at its disposal are public notification and public reprimand.

The employees' and employers' associations

(a) Employee associations

Dutch employees are organized according to two criteria: religious affiliation and company sector. In addition, there is a decreasing number of specific trade unions and a now increasing group of managerial associations. Out of a total wage-earning working population of 4.1 million, about 1.6 million employees belong to trade unions.

All of the major unions organized on an industry-wide basis belong to one of the three large federations:
1. The Netherlands Federation of Trade Unions (NVV), which has about 700,000 members. This organization is non-denominational and has some association with the Socialist Party.
2. The Netherlands Catholic Labour Federation (NKV) which has about 350,000 members.
On January 1st, 1976, these two federations formed the League of Dutch Federations of Trade Unions (FNV) with more than 1 million members.
3. The (Protestant) Christian National Labour Federation (CNV) which has about 250,000 members.
The originally highly differentiated unions have undergone a process of increasing concentration. In particular the pressure of greater efficiency brought small unions together. This process resulted a few years ago in the merger of metal, textile, and other unions into large 'manufacturing unions'. The non-demoninational manufacturing union now has about 195,000 members (almost 30 per cent of all the non-denominational union members) and is the largest union in the Netherlands.

Co-operation has also increased between the three federations and particularly between the Roman Catholic and the non-denominational federation, both on the top level and on the level of the unions themselves. The smaller Protestant federation has always remained separate but this has not prevented close co-operation and consultation, e.g. in a joint research organization and a joint office concerning developing countries.

The Labour federations generally worked closely together in negotiations. In 1954, they drew up a common set of rules on identical union dues and benefits for members. Since 1957, there has been a Consultative Body for the three trade unions. This body formulated a Common Action Programme for the 1971–5 period. This Action Programme comprised not only wages and working-conditions but also such matters as the structure of the company and employee participation in general, as well as a large number of general political points such as education, housing construction, price policies, and assistance for developing countries.

Talks concerning unification of the three federations have been going on for some years. At the end of 1972, both the Catholic (NKV) and the Protestant federations agreed in principle with the NVV to form a joint federation. In 1974, however, the Protestant federation (CNV) postponed the unification programme because they held the opinion that there were not enough possibilities for maintaining their own identity, which is based on religious conviction. Moreover, because of their small size they would have difficulty preserving this identity in a larger federation. Early in 1975, relations between the CNV on the one hand and the NVV and the NKV on the other became more strained. Thus, in the course of 1975, the latter two decided to form a federation of their own (in anticipation of a possible merger). This federation, which came into effect on January 1976, also resulted in the abolition of the Consultative Body and the joint Research Foundation.

These developments run parallel with symptoms of differentiation. The differences between blue-collar and white-collar unions had been diminishing since 1945. Most of the white-collar unions became part of the general (sectorially organized) unions, although some of them kept separate. In 1974, the last of the latter even left their union federation. In the meanwhile there had been considerable growth in the unions of managerial personnel, which co-operated with some white-collar unions in the Council for Consultation of Middle and Higher-level Personnel. Their membership increased to about 130,000 and they are now acting more and more independently. They require a separate position in the regular bargaining processes, and have recently received a seat in the SER. Apart from this council, about 250,000 employees are organized in smaller, often profession-oriented, unions.

The tendency towards centralization caused by the merger of the large federations is to some extent countered by a shift in power from the central federation to the separate unions and, within the unions, to lower levels of membership (Windmuller, de Galan, 1977, II, 148). The unions generally have a strongly centralized hierarchical structure. Most unions are nationally organized and their members work in a particular industrial sector. All unions are divided into districts and local departments on a geographical basis.

The formal decision-making power usually resides in a general assembly composed of representatives of the districts. This assembly, however, often has fifty to a hundred members. In actual practice, policy is formulated by the Executive Board consisting of full-time officials with great powers.

The geographical plan of organization (A-line) often results in a lack of involvement of the ordinary member. The manufacturing Unions have there-fore also introduced a company-wide organization for the 'trade-union work in the company' (see 2.2). This means a 'company-member group', which can elect 'mandatories'. The mandatories can also, like local departments, send representatives to the district councils.

(b) Employers' federations

Employers' federations too are divided along denominational and along sectorial lines. The result is shown schematically in Fig. 8.1.

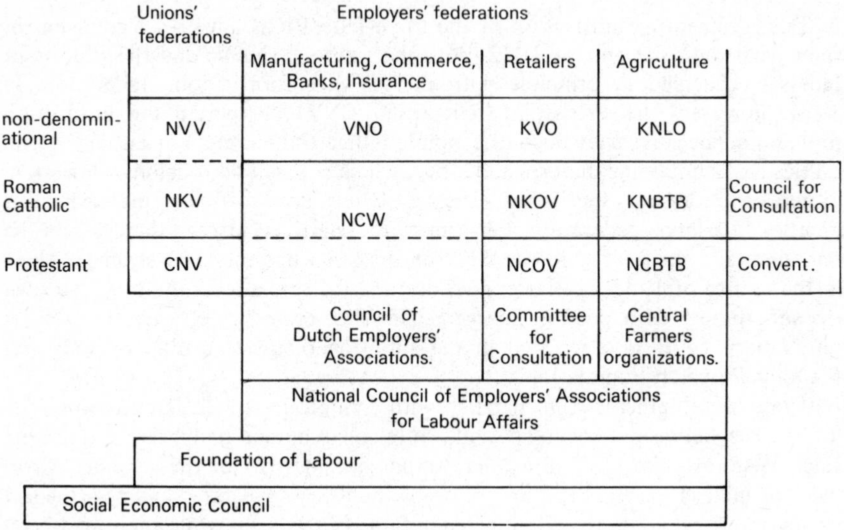

	Unions' federations	Employers' federations			
		Manufacturing, Commerce, Banks, Insurance	Retailers	Agriculture	
non-denomin-ational	NVV	VNO	KVO	KNLO	
Roman Catholic	NKV	NCW	NKOV	KNBTB	Council for Consultation
Protestant	CNV		NCOV	NCBTB	Convent.
		Council of Dutch Employers' Associations.	Committee for Consultation	Central Farmers organizations.	
		National Council of Employers' Associations for Labour Affairs			
	Foundation of Labour				
Social Economic Council					

Source: Albeda (1975)

Figure 8.1. *Classification of employers' and unions' federations and consultative bodies.*
Source: Albeda (1975).

The main federation of employers' associations is the Federation of Netherlands Industries (VNO). This federation represents a considerable number of large- and medium-sized companies (about 600 enterprises represented in about 90 employers' associations). In addition, there is the smaller Dutch Christian Employers' Federation uniting a Catholic and a Protestant employers' federation. A high percentage of their members also belong to the above-mentioned VNO.

Both employers' federations work closely together in the Council of Nether-lands Industrial Federations, and together with the retailers and agricultural federations in the national Council of Employers' Associations for Labour Affairs. This Board is important because it negotiates with the union federations to reach Central Agreements.

In Figure 8.1 mention is also made of a body for contact between Protestant employers and employees called the Convent of Christian Social Organizations.

Its function is not bargaining for working conditions but religiously orientated reflection on general socio-economic developments. Roman Catholic federations have a similar organization.

Developments since 1945

The first ten to fifteen years after the war can be characterized by the term integration, in the sense that there was a great deal of consensus between the parties about the goals of socio-economic policy. These aims included rebuilding of the national economy, full employment, and a strong expansion of social legislation in connection with the formation of a welfare state.

The consensus concerning goals meant that discussions and bargaining were focused on ways and means. The three parties had frequent and intensive contact, particularly in the Social and Economic Council and the Foundation of Labour. Conflicts were rare, and when one occurred a solution was reached by consultation. Increases in wage levels were not based on free bargaining by unions and employers, but were controlled by the government on the basis of econometric calculations made by a government planning bureau (Windmuller, 1969).

These harmonious relations were also reflected in a decreasing number of strikes and other labour conflicts. According to Albeda (1975), this was an indication of the generally accepted and important role of the unions which were (fairly) well established in society and which had strong ties with important political parties. Moreover, the general post-war situation characterized by an emphasis on reconstruction and influenced by the Cold War, encouraged this integration.

At the end of the 1950s, this situation changed. The pressures promoting integration — for example, post-war reconstruction and the Cold War situation, were disappearing. The standard of living and level of education were rising and a more critical attitude developed towards existing norms and values in general, and towards the basic premises of the economic system in particular. Fostered by a tight labour market, the trade unions adopted a more independent attitude and the tendency to decentralization of industrial relations became stronger.

One of the effects of this changing situation was a process of reorientation of the trade unions, which is still continuing. Key issues in this process are, firstly, less concern about economic growth and more about the interests of the workers; and secondly, more attention to activities at the company and shop-floor levels. This became apparent not only in the field of wages and employment conditions, but also in the field of participation and power relations within enterprises.

As a matter of fact, not only the trade unions but also the employers contributed to the change in the industrial relations system. In times of a tight labour market the latter proved quite willing to get round the collective wage agreements by using so-called 'black' wages and labour brokers (recruiters or *koppelbazen*). All these developments can be characterized as a change to a coalition model, and perhaps even to a conflict model. The main features of these models are illustrated in Table 8.6.

Table 8.6.
Three models of industrial relations

MODEL	Consensus of goals	Extent of co-operation	Level of conflict	Mechanism for conflict-solution
Harmony	strong	large	low	consultation
Coalition	partial	partial	moderate	bargaining
Conflict	weak	small	high	fighting and hard bargaining

Source: Peper, 1973.

The coalition model is typified by a separation of responsibilities and by equal power between parties. The three parties – employers, trade unions, and government – put their demands on the table, those of the employers and trade unions being based on their own interests, those of the government on the national interest. By articulation of their demands, they try to reach a compromise between their own and the general interest. In this process, instruments ranging from strikes and lock-outs to consultation might be used, but there are still certain 'rules of the game'.

Presentation of the trade unions as one party should not be taken to imply that there are no disagreements between them; there are, particularly between the federated Catholic and Socialist unions, the Protestant–Christian unions, and the white-collar unions.

The Dutch industrial relations system is not one of these ideal types. Evidence that it is moving away from the consensus model can be seen in:

(*a*) the increased number of people and firms involved in strikes and the longer duration of strikes (e.g. in the metal and construction industries and, in 1970, in the Rotterdam harbour). These strikes were initiated by the trade unions or – where they started as a wild-cat strike – were taken over by the unions. Nevertheless, in the 1960s there was no increase in the number of official or unofficial strikes. (See Figure 8.2.)

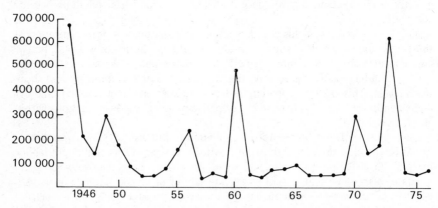

Figure 8.2a. *Number of workdays lost through strikes.*
Source: Albeda, 1975.

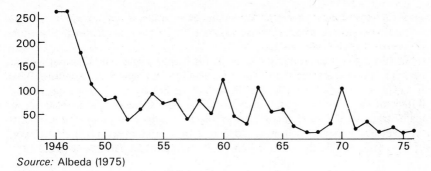

Source: Albeda (1975)

Figure 8.2b. *Number of labour disputes.*

(*b*) A shift in the content of collective bargaining agreements, more and more emphasis being put on non-economic issues. At the same time there was a change in strike tactics: fewer strikes in industrial companies or branches and more nationwide 'selective' strikes (i.e. the unions pick special companies as 'spear-points' of the general strike). A major strike in 1973 concerned income equalization, and some issues in the co-ordinated strikes early in 1977 concerned union influence on investments and the relation between profits and employment.

(*c*) Increasing toughness in the bargaining process, trade unions resorting to strikes and occupation of plants, and on the employers' side, a tightening of organization and the creation of defence funds.

(*d*) The demand that the managing director should no longer be a member, let alone chairman, of the works council.

These developments are accompanied by a tendency toward decentralization. Evidence of this can be seen in the increasing number of collective agreements at the company level, more power — at least according to the new law — for the works council, development of trade-union work in the enterprise, and the origin of conflicts on the shop floor, which are then supported by the trade union (de Jong, 1974).

All these developments do not and did not imply an abandonment of centralized bargaining and decision-making by the top layer of the three parties: government, employers, and employees' federations. Particularly with the less favourable economic situation and increased unemployment, since the beginning of the 1970s the unions once again gave attention to top-level contact and general political issues. This is reflected in the joint Policy Programme 1976-7, which was presented to the government by the three trade-union federations in July 1975. This document contains a summary of all the demands and suggestions of the unions concerning such issues of socio-economic policy as investments, taxes, social security, incomes policy, environment, education, international co-operation, and industrial democracy. The approach was favoured by the relatively good relations between the trade unions and the (partially) Socialist government which has been in power from 1973 till 1977. This situation perhaps helps us to explain why the rather conflict-ridden years between 1970 and 1973 were followed by two years without many strikes. Other reasons can, however, be sought in the oil crisis and the introduction of an Act, which gave the government a certain mandate concerning income control. The reorientation of the trade unions was not limited to suggestions concerning concrete socio-economic issues.

Within a growing economy, demands for higher wages could be met without changing the wage structure or, in general, the socio-economic structure. When the economy stopped expanding, however, the cry for a 'fundamnetal redistribution of income, knowledge, and power' became stronger. In recent years the major trade unions have therefore formulated a long-term policy for a socialist-type society in which self-managed companies function within the framework of economic guidelines – decided on by government and parliament (see 3.1).

Developments in wage policy

(a) Strict control (until 1959)

After the Second World War, wages were established in a central consultation between employers' associations, union federations, and the government, on the basis of guidelines given by the governmental planning bureau. In this period the wage policy was aimed at keeping wages and prices so low that the Dutch firms could compete successfully with other countries. Another aim was to invest as much as desirable in industrialization. The government had four types of instruments to control developments in the area of wages.

(1) *Preventive*: the guidelines of the Central Planning Bureau served as a basis for the level of wages (until 1959) or the latitude of increases (1959-68).

(2) *Supervisory*: a government Commission determined whether individual collective agreements were actually compatible with the guidelines.

(3) *Checking*: the wage-control Service checked whether the collective agreements were properly carried out.

(4) A special Act gave the government authority to nullify an existing collective agreement.

(b) Towards more freedom (1959-1968)

At the end of the 1950s, the general socio-economic situation changed. Relevant factors in this change were a tightening of the labour market and the higher national income resulting from the increase in productivity. After 1959, the wage policy became differentiated. Firstly, wage increases per sector were allowed to be based on increases in productivity. And starting in 1961, much was left to central agreements between employers' associations and unions. The government, however, still had instruments 1, 2, and 4 at its disposal. When a wage explosion in 1963 and 1964 appeared not to be disastrous for the economy, the pressure for even more freedom in bargaining increased. In 1968, the government yielded and kept only the authority to nullify collective agreements (which was used in 1968 with respect to a collective agreement in the construction industry).

(c) Developments since 1968

In the meantime, a new Wage Act was being drafted. Increasing inflation underlined the necessity for the government to have some control over wage developments. The new Act (1970) formulated conditions giving the government authority to interfere. This Wage Act was actually applied several times, e.g. when a wage freeze was issued in 1971.

The inflation, however, continued to increase, and this caused the partners to try again to come to a central agreement. But the climate was very different from that of the harmonious 1950s, and consequently the conflicts between employers' associations and unions did not decrease. As had happened before, in 1974, they could not come to a central agreement, and the international oil crisis forced the government to interfere. The government did not want to restrict only employees' wages. They therefore proposed a 'Mandate' Act giving the government the authority to curb all incomes. The oil crisis forced Parliament to pass this Act. Armed with the Wage Act and the Mandate Act, the government could limit the development of wages and other incomes to a very high degree.

2.2. Worker participation in the enterprises

Developments since 1945

Although the main focus here will be on representative participation in the works council, some attention will also be given to the institutionalization of direct consultation and participation on the shop-floor. Recently, both issues have been the subject of heated debates. The former because the government in 1973 had asked the Social and Economic Council for advice concerning the desirability of changing the nature, the composition (whether the managing director should be a member), and the co-decision rights of the works council. The latter because the government has given two and a quarter million guilders to subsidize experiments on the participation of workers in plant management. A sub-committee of the Social and Economic Council, again consisting of employer and union representatives, supervises these experiments (Van der Moolen, 1977).

The works council

In 1950, the first Works Council Act became effective. In this Act the works council is described as a consultative body concerned primarily with the common interests of the enterprise rather than with the interests of the employees or the employer. This did not allow for either decision-making power by the lower-level employees or for the idea of promotion of interests.

Since the beginning of the 1960s, numerous research studies have been completed (e.g. Drenth, 1973). They showed that works councils are very often misused, for instance as a substitute for the normal hierarchical lines of communication or as a kind of complaints desk. Moreover, according to most lower-level employees, the council is a place where their interests should be promoted. And in spite of the old idea that representation of interests would make it possible to have confidential consultative discussions, the works council actually appeared to function optimally where its interest-promoting function is recognized. Active representative consultation presupposes appreciation of the fact that an organization comprises groups with specific interests that do not necessarily always coincide with those of other groups.

Accumulated experience supported the growing opinion that the existing structure of the works council was based on an erroneous assumption of a complete consensus of interests and purposes. This led to the new Works Council Act of 1971, which specifically states that the task of the council is consultation and representation of employees' interests. The Act therefore provides for the following modifications:

(a) Improved opportunities for codetermination and advice.

(b) The possibility for individual members to consult groups of employees and external experts.

(c) The right of council members to obtain training.

(d) The right to nominate candidates for the Supervisory Board and to veto the choice of new members by the Board.

(e) Sanctions when the law is not compiled with.

In March, 1975, an amendment was proposed which stated that the works council should have the right to appeal to the court against a management decision that could not be considered to have properly weighed all interests concerned.

According to the Explanatory Memorandum to the 1971 Act:

This new Act reflects the substantial change in the views of not only trade unions and social scientists but also of the government, on the nature of companies (and other organizations) and on the relationships between groups within these organizations. Employees are not only looked upon as people who sell their labour for money and by that very act accept subordination. They are now formally recognized as a party which in principle has the right to a say.

As already mentioned, at the end of 1973 the new government asked the Social and Economic Council to advise it concerning the task, composition, and competence of the works council. The reason for this was that the afore-mentioned changes in ideologies and viewpoints had brought some unions, political parties, and other groups to the conclusion that the council should be a body representing *only* employees, rather than a consultative body. The report of the council was issued in October 1975, and reflected the wide differences in the viewpoints of the parties concerned, as well as differences between the unions (see also 3.1).

Participation at the shop-floor level

Since the end of the 1950s there have been several experiments concerning the restructuring of individual and group tasks, not only in the technical sense, but also in the way in which decisions were taken and leadership was exercised. In the 1960s these experiments acquired political meaning, because some social scientists and also union members came to look upon the institutionalized con-sultation experiments as possible steps toward power equalization and demo-cratization in organizations (see IDE 1980, ch. 10 and 11).

At the end of the 1960s some of the reports were, however, quite sceptical about the effects of these experiments, at least as far as democratization of the organization was concerned (e.g. Ramondt, 1974). Very recently it was further confirmed, for example, that:

(a) The initiative usually lay with top management, and experiments were often started because of problems (turnover, absenteeism, etc.);

(b) The workers themselves were often not involved in setting the rules and

conditions of the participation process;
(c) The experiments were sometimes stopped by the management when it appeared that the group wanted participation not only in such decisions as the assignment of tasks, but also in wider issues.

These findings have made some of the more radical unions very suspicious of these experiments (they regard them as 'tools of management'). Most of the parties concerned now urge that such experiments should be conducted very carefully and only after many conditions have been formulated in a written agreement. Three parties – the unions, the employers' federations, and a group of social scientists – have recently formulated their ideas and viewpoints in connection with the government grant mentioned above. An agreement between the parties was reached in 1976; and in 1977 the first experiments started.

Industrial relations at the company level: the present situation

The industrial relations system at the company level has three major components:
(a) legal provisions concerning the top managerial level of the enterprise, particularly the Supervisory Board;
(b) the Works Council;
(c) the trade-union work in the enterprise, at the worker level.
These components are presented here in their most recent forms. The developments leading to the present situation have been discussed in the preceding section.

(a) The top level

Three new Acts are relevant for the industrial relations system at this level.
(1) The 1971 Act concerning the *structure* of relatively large *companies* (more than 100 workers, more than f1.1 million capital). This Act made the installation of a Supervisory Board compulsory and gave this Board much more power than it had previously. The Board, which must include at least three persons who are not employees of the company or members of a trade union, has the authority to appoint and discharge managing directors (previously, this was done by the shareholders) and has the right of consent to import decisions, such as mergers, issue of shares, and large-scale dismissal. New members are co-opted on to the Board. Neither employees nor union officials can become Board members. The shareholders, managing directors, and works council have, however, the right to nominate candidates, and the shareholders and works council can veto an appointment. In case of a veto the Board can submit the issue to the SER, which can nullify the veto. The actual functioning and composition of these boards is at present the object of research.
(2) *Annual accounting*: relatively large private limited-liability companies have to publish their balance sheets. Public limited-liability companies also have to publish their profit-and-loss accounts.
(3) *The right of enquiry*: shareholders, the trade unions concerned, and a court of justice, can ask for an investigation into the affairs of a company in cases of alleged mismanagement. This being established, the courts can take strong measures.

(b) The works council

According to the 1971 Act, every work-organization (i.e. not only companies but also, for instance, hospitals) with at least 100 employees must have a works council. And since August 1977 councils are also obligatory for decentralized welfare organizations of more than 25 employees. This council consists of one of the directors as chairman and between 3 and 25 members (depending on the size of the company) chosen by the employees for terms lasting two or three years. Unions and also other groups of employees have the right to nominate candidates. Larger companies and concerns sometimes have a system of councils at plant or company levels, as well as a central works council at top level.

In every industrial sector there are bipartite 'sector committees' which supervise the proper functioning of the works councils and also have a dispute committee to arbitrate in conflicts between members of works councils.

Before 1971, the works council was meant to be a consultative body; but the 1971 Act explicitly states its double function: not only consultation but also representation of the employees' interests. The new Act gives co-decision rights to the council in a number of personnel and social matters and stresses the need for greater worker involvement in economic matters affecting the organization. This is realized by the following provisions:

(1) Management must inform the works council at least twice a year of the general economic condition of the enterprise.

(2) Management must give the works council an opportunity to give advice on any important decision concerning the organization, such as mergers, reorganization, and the dismissal or transfer of workers.

(3) The same obligation holds for decisions concerning work rules, wage systems, employment policies, training, and social work.

(4) The consent of the council must be obtained for any decision concerning the adoption or modification of pension schemes, profit-sharing or profit-savings plans, working hours, holiday arrangements, and safety and health measures.

(5) The right to nominate candidates to the Supervisory Board. The final choice of candidates (who can also be nominated at the shareholders' meeting and by the directors) lies with the Supervisory Board. The shareholders' meeting and the works council have the right of veto (which can be nullified by the SER).

The aspect of 'promotion of interest' is institutionalized, for instance, by the right to hold meeting without the director-chairman and to invite external (e.g. union) experts to attend.

The 1971 Act* also provides for certain guarantees for adequate functioning of the elected members: — they can invite experts (also from outside the company); hold meetings without the director–chairman, and force the employer to fulfil his obligations, by appealing to a district court; they are also protected against arbitrary dismissal, and have a right to training (in works council matters).

(c) Trade unions in the enterprise

In the last few years the trade unions have been trying to introduce this system,

---

*At the time of writing (1978), the third Act (1979) on works councils was not yet accepted by Parliament. It is further discussed below.

and it is currently found in most of the larger enterprises in the industrial sector. The aims are firstly to promote better communication between the members and the trade unions, which previously were mainly active on the national level, and secondly to promote workers' influence on company decisions, particularly concerning the work situation. A third, less explicit, objective is to shift emphasis from participation in decision-making to retrospective control of decision-making (Van Vliet, 1973).

At first sight there seems to be a certain resemblance between this intramural union work and the British shop-steward system, but they are quite different both functionally and operationally. In the Dutch arrangement, a so-called contact-man leads a trade-union action committee in the plant. Some enterprises have up to three of these structures originating from the three parallel trade unions: Catholic, Protestant, and non-denominational.

The function of the contact-man is to represent the union locally, for example by passing on complaints to the works council or to the trade union. In some cases he has been known to be the local organizer of a strike called by the unions. Relations between the works council and these contact men vary. Sometimes they are very positive, for example when the contact man passes complaints on to the works council members, consults with them before and after council meetings, and in general lobbies the council's constituency. Sometimes, however, relations are strained, for example when the trade union concerned is afraid that the works council is weakening the union's influence by usurping its functions, or when the works council is — in the eyes of workers and trade union — too much on the side of the management.

Particularly the largest federation, the *FNV*, adheres to the principle of the 'binding mandate', which means that the members of the works council belonging to this federation are restricted by the mandate defined by the trade union committee.

Theoretically, the works council can be seen as part of an 'electoral democracy' model functioning through representatives. In contrast, the contact-man system tends towards a 'participatory democracy' model functioning through delegates. In practice, it appears to be difficult to prevent the contact men from joining the 'labour *élite*', i.e. becoming part of the small group of workers' representatives who are informed about and involved in all kinds of activities.

In recent years, a feature of company-level industrial relations has been the increasing tendency to resort to industrial tactics such as strikes and the occupation of factories. In most cases these tactics are based on one of the following two objectives:

(1) To support union activities, e.g. strengthening of their bargaining position. Such actions are mainly initiated and terminated by the unions, and are sometimes spread throughout the industry. One of their side-effects is a strengthening of the relationship between the union and the members in individual organizations.

(2) To solve a problem of workers in a particular company, e.g. large-scale dismissals. These actions are more defensive in character, and often occur as a reaction to a reorganization of a company.

Disunity of representation

By now it will be clear that employers' or union representatives can be found at three levels in a company: (*a*) on the Supervisory Board (strictly speaking, the members of this Board who represent the employees are not genuine representatives, because they are not responsible to the employees and cannot be replaced by them); (*b*) on the works council; (*c*) the trade-union work within the company (at the shop-floor level). Of these three levels the works council will be given the most attention here. There are very few employees' representatives on the Supervisory Board, because such representation is not compulsory. In some places there is, however, a tendency toward closer contact between some members of this Supervisory Board and the works council, partially because the works council is legally empowered to nominate candidates for Supervisory Board.

Trade-union work within the company exists in most medium-sized and large manufacturing enterprises, but the role of this trade union presence in the company is still not very clear.

Types of employees (and their form of representation)

Although the distinction between white-collar and blue-collar employees can be made on the basis of external characteristics, their interests often do not conflict. Both can be and often are members of the same trade unions and are represented together on works councils and other participative bodies. Both categories are also treated similarly in collective agreements. In this respect, the Dutch situation is rather unusual particularly because these collective agreements are applicable to high hierarchical levels. The employees or functionaries above this level (say, in terms of money, above an annual income of 35,000 guilders) have become increasingly active in their own unions, especially since the inception of the discussion about income redistribution.

Main bargaining structure

The Collective Agreement Act of 1972 defines the rules for the collective bargaining process. Only officially recognized unions (federations) can participate in the process. The same holds for employers' associations, although individual employers can join too (see also 1.1).

There are two kinds of industry-wide agreements: those with a minimum character, which may be improved upon at plant level, and those with a standard character, which cannot be altered at a lower level. The unorganized employees are also covered by collective agreements, but unorganized employers are not committed by agreements reached in their industries, although the government can involve them as well via, for example, the Law on Wages (see 2.2).

Most collective agreements (CAOs) lie at the company or plant level, but the industry-wide CAOs cover more employees, i.e. 80 per cent of the Dutch labour force.

The contents of CAOs pertain firstly to such traditional issues as rates of pay, overtime, and holidays; working hours and special leaves of absence; apprenticeship and training. Recently, however, these agreements have included more and more articles on what are called non-material issues, such as participation (e.g.

through works councils), income redistribution, investments, and policy concerning hiring and dismissal. The collective-bargaining-process starts in the Foundation of Labour, where employees' and employers' representatives meet and, after consultation with the government, attempt to reach a central agreement concerning wage developments, etc. Negotiations then move to the branch level, with a tendency for each agreement to cover a large number of workers. There is also an appreciable number of enterprises which conduct their own bargaining.

If a central agreement is not reached, the bargaining process can start either on the sector level or in companies having their own collective agreements. Nevertheless the employees' federations and the government have a preference for centralized agreements. In general, the whole bargaining process, in which unions play an important role, is strongly institutionalized. Although the unions represent only about 40 per cent of the wage earners, they have a strong position in society which is enhanced by their (unofficial) right to strike. The strikes which occured early in 1977 confirmed this.

2.4. The role of public powers

As we have seen earlier, one-third of the SER membership is formed by independent experts appointed by the government (called the Crown members). Many (sub-)committees of the SER also have a tripartite or multipartite composition.

The Board of the Labour Market is composed of representatives of employers and employees and Crown members appointed by the municipalities and by the provinces. This is also the level at which the settlement of disuptes by dispute committees (committees of 'wise men') occurs.

During the present economic recession, a growing governmental (financial) influence on companies and industries (e.g. shipbuilding and textile) is developing.

3. PERSPECTIVES, PROBLEMATIC ISSUES, AND DEVELOPMENTS

3.1. Designs for the future

In the discussions on all matters concerning power and participation at and above the company level, three viewpoints or 'designs' can roughly be distinguished.

The first 'design' is that of the employers' federations. In their view top management should have and keep the right to make the major decisions in particular those concerning new investments and the like, according to the chairman of the employers' federation (Van Veen, 1977). Neither the works council nor industrial bodies should have more than advisory rights (FME, 1977) and participation must always be limited by the decisiveness necessary given international competitiveness. They consider that the 1971 Works Council Act allows more or less the maximum acceptable representative participation. In a report (VNO, 1975), they argued against increasing the co-decision rights or changing the structure of the works council. From the 1975 SER report concerning a new works council it is also evident that they consider the works council merely an advisory body that should not have even the present rights of co-decision on regulations affecting pension schemes, holidays, and working hours. It is understandable that the exclusion of the managing director from the works council is bitterly opposed by the employers. In their view this would result only in increased polarization and conflict (VNO, 1978). They did give, however, suggestions on procedures, guarantees, and education, which could — in their opinion — improve the functioning of the council.

Their viewpoint on the shop-floor participation experiments is that these should be continued, because they can bring about a greater involvement, satisfaction and motivation, a better utilization of human resources, and a more flexible and adaptive organization.

The second 'design' is put forward by groups who, in principle, accept the present economic order and its distinction between — but not the inevitable opposition of — capital and labour within the enterprises. This viewpoint is held, for example, by the Protestant–Christian Trade Union Federation (CNV) and by white-collar unions. The CNV considers the organization to a certain extent as a community. This implies that all members should participate in the power-structure, in their opinion realized not only through the works council but also through the Supervisory Board. This Board should be the centre of gravity of the power and participation structure, and consequently should have a far-reaching influence on the policy of the organization. It should also appoint and dismiss top managers. At least half of the Board members should be employee representatives, directly chosen by the workers (Lanser, 1977).

The works council can be maintained, more or less with its present tasks and functions. These concern partially the promotion of interests of workers, and partially consultation with, and advising of, management. It is therefore highly desirable that a managing director should be a member of the council, although not necessarily the chairman. The works council should have more co-decision rights than it has now; co-decision on all kinds of issues concerning internal company matters and even certain wage regulations (which other unions claim should be restricted to employer–union bargaining). Really important decisions should, however, be taken by the Board. On these issues, the works council should only have advisory rights.

A third function of the council is to serve as a link between the Board and a network of participative groups, the basis of which is direct participation and the trade-union work on the shop floor. It is not surprising that this viewpoint also includes a more or less positive attitude toward shop-floor participation, the introduction of which should be made obligatory by law.

The third group is more heterogeneous in composition than the other two. All of those belonging to it want fundamental changes in the economic order and in the structure and functioning of enterprises. Some of these groups, including the research bureau of the largest Dutch party, the Labour Party (WBS, 1975) or the Radical Political Party, have clearly defined ideas about the future. These imply a kind of workers' self-management within a socialized society, which would establish — at the national and international levels —

directives for production. They opt for possibly a Yugoslav or a parliamentary type of system for companies.

While the post-war years witnessed a loosening of the traditional ties between trade unions and churches or political parties the Roman Catholic union federatin NKV in particular has 'deconfessionalized' considerably — new ideological perspectives have developed in recent years (e.g. IBNVV, 1974; NKV, 1975). Although less specified, the ideas of the largest union federation, FNV, tend to be rather similar to those of the above-mentioned groups. In the future the works council has to develop towards being the company's top authority to which management is responsible (Spit, 1978). As a first step the works council should really be a 'personnel council' consisting only of elected members. This viewpoint is incorporated in the 1979 Works Council Act.

In this view, real participation in the present power structure is very difficult because of the characteristics of our entire socio-economic system at the national and company level. Particularly, the largest (relatively) radical metal and textile unions held the opinion that responsibility should not be taken for parts of a policy which cannot really be influenced (IBNVV, 1974, 1978). The task of organized labour should be to keep a critical eye on management and evaluate managerial decisions from the point of view of labour interests. This opinion was and is still reflected in the following words, which have become a standard expression: 'Do not accept a pound of responsibility for an ounce of participation' (IBNVV, 1978). According to this view, having retrospective control of company decisions contributes more to structural change than participation in decision-making. They are also opposed to electing employee representatives for the Supervisory Board. At the moment the board should give account of its activities to the works council (WIK Weekly, 27/4/1977). The Council of the largest union federation, FNV, with the exception of the previously mentioned metal and textile union, has recently opted for a more gradual development. In the long run the Supervisory Board should be replaced by the works council. For the time being, however, the works council should be able to appoint at least as many members of the Supervisory Board as the shareholders do. These two groups of Supervisory Board members should be allowed to co-opt other Board members, up to a third of the total membership. To keep responsibilities separate, the members appointed by the works council cannot be works council members or union members.

Shop-floor participation experiments are regarded with great suspicion. Some do not want to be involved in these experiments at all; others are reluctantly prepared to co-operate, but only under very strict conditions. The union federations are, however, co-operating within the SER-committee which supervises some of these experiments, on condition that the experiments are not confined to the shop floor.

3.2. Problematic issues

In the area of industrial relations in general and employee participation in particular there have been a number of important developments. Regarding employee participation, there are the new Works Council Act and the SER discussion concerning employee representatives on the Supervisory Board. With respect to other areas, mention may be made of the proposal concerning a capital growth sharing system, the development of union influence on company decisions, the merger code, and the Strike Act. All these developments are part of a general socio-economic climate which is being influenced by diminishing economic growth, a relatively high rate of unemployment, and the resources and energy problem.

(1) The 1979 works council act

After the SER, in 1975, gave its recommendation on the composition and competence of the works council, the debate became even hotter. It seemed almost impossible to reconcile the viewpoints described in the preceding section. Nevertheless, the government, which was at that time based on a coalition of parties having links with all the three viewpoints described above had to bring about a compromise or, in all probability, fall. It reached indeed a solution which seemed to be acceptable to most of the political parties. This proposal represented a real compromise between the works council as a consultative body and as a body for the promotion of the workers' interests. The main points are:

(*a*) the works council consists (like the German version) only of elected members; the managing director is no longer chairman or even member of the council;

(*b*) the council is nevertheless still considered a body of and for the whole organization, not just for the employees' interests;

(*c*) the competence and rights of the works council are increased; for instance, it must now also be able to give advice on investments and the appointment or dismissal of directors; and its consent is required for decisions concerning shop-floor participation schemes and working conditions;

(*d*) at least six times a year there will be consultations with the director during which advice of the council is discussed or during which some kind of agreement has to be reached concerning those issues which need the consent of the council.

Consideration of this proposal was interrupted by the change in government. The new government, in power since 1977 and more right-wing than the previous one, has, however, not changed the proposal substantially.*

Not only the powers and rights of the works council are being extended, but also the areas in which these councils are applicable. In 1977, the 1971 Act was extended to cover welfare organizations (SER-bulletin, 24/8/1977). And in the beginning of 1978 the SER issued a memorandum on the applicability of works councils or equivalent bodies to organizations of less than 100 employees (at present the lower limit for establishing works councils). Although there is no consensus between the partners in the SER on specifics there appears to be a consensus concerning the usefulness of legally based participation structures for small organizations.

(2) The Supervisory Board

As discussed previously there are various ideas concerning the composition and powers of the board. The Protestant Union Federation wants the Board to be

---

*In summer 1979, this new Works Council Act was accepted by Parliament.

nominated by the employees, as in Germany. The largest union federation, FNV, recently opted for a Supervisory Board of which a third of the members are nominated by the works council, a third by shareholders, and the remainder by those already nominated. This is fairly close to the proposal of the Fifth Directive of the European Community. This directive prompted the government, in the beginning of 1978, to ask the SER for advice.

According to the 1971 Act on the structure of companies works councils now have the right to nominate candidates to the Supervisory Board. Elected Board members who had been nominated in this way formed a contact body (overlegorgaan Vertrouwens Commissarissen) in May 1978.

(3) Union influence on company decisions

Since about 1977 the unions have been pressing for collective bargaining clauses in 'employment agreements' (APO − Arbeids Plaatsen Overeenkomst). Although sometimes seen as guarantees against dismissal, they can contain agreements concerning all aspects of the employment policy of a company (hiring, selection, allocation), on the quality of work and on investments to the extent that they affect employment. Most of the collective agreements arrived at in 1978 appear to include some APO-clauses, according to FNV chairman Kok (SER bulletin, 7/6/1978). He stressed that these APO clauses might be used in a more equal redistribution of existing employment opportunities. The importance of these APO clauses to the unions is illustrated by the fact that the powerful metal and textile unions are prepared if necessary to forego part of the automatic wage increase that compensates for higher prices, in order to make the application of the clauses financially feasible (Trouw, 23/12/1977).

To enable works council members or unions to influence company decision making, it is necessary for them to have more information about the company. Union representatives are increasingly stressing this point and the union federation FNV has issued a memorandum giving concrete specifications (FNV, 1976).

Unions desire involvement not only in company decisions but also in industrial sector decisions. In some sectors bi- or tripartite committees already exist. Proposals have been made to institutionalize them in all sectors. A recent public poll showed that the idea of unions having influence on investment decisions is not confined to a few union officials: 39 per cent wanted union influence, 25 per cent did not, and 36 per cent didn't know (SER bulletin, 17/5/1978).

(4) A system of capital-growth sharing (VAD)

In May 1975 the government proposed such a system, according to which a certain part of surplus company profit would be assigned to employees: a part to the individual employees of the company and a part to all Dutch employees collectively.

This proposal is still being hotly discussed in particular the question of who would administer the collective fund − the unions alone or a bipartite body. The system is partly comparable with the proposed German Vermögensbeteiligung and more so with the French *Réservé Speciale de Participation, RSP.*

Criticism of various aspects of this proposal has been very strong for reasons of both practicality and principle. The Christian Democrat Party, the Liberal

Party, and the Protestant trade union federation emphasize the aspect of the growth in individual property. The Socialist Party and the trade union federation FNV expect this system to be an instrument for income redistribution and the control of wages and prices. They consider the collective fund, administered by the union, the most important part of the system. The 1977 Christian Democrat and Liberal coalition government presented a new proposal, limited to the section affecting individual employees, in May 1978. Both employers' and employees' associations have strongly protested against this proposal, although for different reasons.

(5) Right to strike

In the Netherlands this is still judicially controlled. Since 1969, a draft bill has been under consideration but both the trade unions and the employers' associations are opposed to it. At the moment, the organizing of a strike is allowed; a prohibition can be issued only on the grounds of attendent circumstances. If an employee cannot work because of a strike, the employer is obliged to pay his wages.

(6) Merger code

The SER is preparing a memorandum on legal implementation of the SER-merger code. This would mean that companies planning a merger would be legally obliged to inform the unions.

3.3. Conclusions

The above-mentioned developments have to be understood within the framework of the general socio-economic changes in the western world in general and in the Netherlands in particular. Many consider that the economic depression and under-employment are not temporary but are the product of an economic system which is focused too narrowly on productivity increases and economic growth. Other aspects of this problem are environmental pollution and difficulties related to natural resources and energy. The optimism of the 1960s that these problems could be solved in a fairly short period either through technical and economical innovation (the right-wing solution) or through a fundamental restructuring of society (the left-wing solution), has disappeared. In recent years the large socialist-oriented trade union federation has, nevertheless, advocated more strongly a long-range programme for a type of self-management by workers within a socialized society. Both the long-term prospects and the short-term situation of stagnant economic growth have resulted in increased attention being given by unions to issues such as worker participation, union influence on employment and investment decisions within companies, and union involvement in industrial and national decision-making on major economic issues.

At the same time the role of the government in the economic area is increasing through, for instance, financial support for companies and because of it being itself the major employer.

The general picture is one in which all three partners in the industrial relations system play an increasingly active role, in company, industrial and national decision-making. It is quite logical that this has also resulted in a higher rate and intensity of conflict. One can therefore expect that the slow but steady development towards more participation and democracy in industry will continue.

REFERENCES

Albeda, W. (1975), *Arbeidsverhoudingen in Nederland,* Samson, Alphen a/d Rijn.

Drenth, P. J. D. (1973), 'The Works Council in the Netherlands. An experiment in participation', in Pusić, E. *et al.* (eds), *Participation and selfmanagement,* 5, Zagreb.

FME (1977), *Annual report,* Federatie Metaal en Elektrotechnische Industrie, Den Haag.

FNV (1976), *Open boek.* Federatie Nederlandse Vakbeweging, Amsterdam.

IBNVV (1978), 'Distantie, van nabij bekeken', in: *In Kader,* May.

(1974), *Fijn is anders.* Industrie Bond NVV, Amsterdam.

(1977), *Breien met een rode draad,* Industrie Bond NVV, Amsterdam.

Moolen, R. A. J. van der (1977), *Het COP Programma experimenten medezeggenschap.* Mens en Onderneming, 31; 6.

NKV (1975), *Een visie ter visie,* Nederlands Katholiek Vakverbond, Utrecht.

Peper, B. (1973), *De Nederlandse arbeidsverhoudingen, kontinuiteit en verandering,* Universitaire Pers, Rotterdam.

Ramondt, J. (1974), *Bedrijfsdemocratisering zonder arbeiders,* Samson, Alphen a/d Rijn.

Sociaal Ekonomische Raad (1975), *Advies over samenstelling en bevoegdheden van de Ondernemingsraden,* Uitgaven van de SER.

Spit (1978), *Medezeggenschap,* Studium Generale, Vrije Universiteit, Amsterdam.

Vliet, G. E. van (1973), *Het bedrijvenwerk en de veranderingen binnen de Nederlandse vakbeweging,* Mens en Onderneming, 27.

WBS (1974), *Op weg naar arbeiders zelfbestuur,* Wiards Bechman Stichting, Deventer, 1974.

Wetenschappelijke Raad voor het Regeringsbeleid (1977), *Sociale ongelijkheid, Staatsdrukkerij,* Den Haag.

Windmuller, J. P. (1969), *Labour relations in the Netherlands,* Ithaca, New York.

Windmuller, J. P., Galan, C. (1977), *Arbeidsverhoudingen in Nederland,* Spectrum, Utrecht.

9

THE BELGIAN INDUSTRIAL RELATIONS SYSTEM

1. GENERAL SITUATION AND BACKGROUND

Constitutionally, Belgium is a parliamentary democracy. Parliament, the King, and his ministers each carry out a series of different tasks which can be roughly divided into two kinds: the first purely legislative, the second a democratic control of government policies.

1.1. Status quo of political power

The Parliament consists of two Houses: the Senate with 182 members and the House of Deputies with 212. Both Houses are composed of members of the different political parties: the Christian Democrats (CVP-PSC), the Socialists (BSP-PSB), and the Liberals (PVV-PLP). Besides these, there is also the Belgian Communist Party (KPB-PC) and, moreover due to the specific Belgian language situation, three nationalist parties namely: Volksunie (VU-Flemish nationalists), Front des Francophones (FDF), and the Rassemblement Wallon (RW-Walloon assembly), the latter two being Walloon nationalist parties.

In this way the political power-play is basically determined by the representatives of the different political parties in Parliament, on the one hand; and by those of 'splinter parties' on the other hand. The present government (see Table 9.1) is the result of a coalition between two out of the three traditional parties and the three nationalist parties. The Cabinet is composed in line with over all language parity, except for the Prime Minister.

Table 9.1.
Seats in the cabinet

	CVP	PSC	BSP	PSB	VU	FDF	FDF RW	TOTAL
Ministers	6	4	5	4	2	1	1	23
Secretaries of State	2	–	1	2	1	1	–	7
TOTAL	8	4	6	6	3	2	1	30

Source: Crisp Hebdomadaire: Centre de Recherches et d'Études Socio-politiques.

As to the evolution in the number of votes for the different political parties, we can state that there is a slight over-all increase for the three traditional parties. This must be interpreted as a gain for the Christians in Flanders and as a gain for the Socialists in the French-speaking part of the country. The parties aiming

at federalism (nationalist parties) and the Belgian Communist Party seem to have
lost a certain number of votes.

1.2. Recent political events

As indicated above, Belgian political life is fundamentally influenced by its
specific 'language situation'. This causes a regionalization on the economic level
and even a decentralization on the political level. In fact, the Christian and the
Liberal Party were subdivided into Flemish and Wallonian sections. It is quite
clear that this situation influences all actions taken or proposed by the government. We can even say that the stability of Belgian political life greatly depends
on the actions undertaken by one of the two language-groups. In this light, we
see that the nationalist parties play an important role in the present government.

Another important characteristic of the Belgian government is the great com-
plexity of the governmental structures. For almost every problem committees
are formed.

More and more, the industrial relations system is becoming influenced by the
political situation. This influence is due to the relationship between unions and
political parties. This does not imply, however, a lack of interactions between
unions and political parties. In fact, some specific union objectives can only be
realized by using political power and this of course implies negotiations with
different political parties.

1.3. Economic situation

Immediately after the Second World War, the economic situation was characterized by a period of austerity (1944-7) in which the government tried to rebuild
the economy as soon as possible. From 1948 till 1959 a period of moderate
liberalism followed. During this period the government relaxed certain control
measures. Nevertheless, a Price Commission was established to look at the evolution of prices and salaries. During a period of expansion and planning (1959-73)
an attempt was made to introduce the system of a cyclical budget.

From 1973 onwards, Belgium, as most other European countries, found itself
in a period of recession, characterized by high inflation rates, heavy taxes, and
high unemployment. Although the economy is essentially 'free', there has been
governmental intervention on specific issues such as the stimulation of the production of some goods, the distribution of goods, and the recent, but growing,
governmental involvement in the management of firms with financial difficulties.

Most of our Belgian enterprises are grouped in professional associations which
are all members of the Union of Belgian Enterprises (VBO) or of the Union of
Non-Industrial Enterprises of Belgium. At the regional level, the enterprises are
merged into Chambers of Commerce. In 1948 the Central Economic Council
was established. This institution has the power to formulate propositions or to
advise parliament or the government. It is composed of an equal number (22) of
representatives of the most important employers' and employees' associations.

On top of that a number of experts (e.g. from universities) can be consulted for solving specific problems.

In 1960 the National Committee for Economic Expansion was established. The main task of this committee is to safeguard the direct communication between the government and the other 'social' partners.

In 1970, Separate Economic Councils (Flemish, Walloon, and Brussels) were established by law.

Population

See Table 9.2.

Labour Market

It is obvious that the evolution of technological knowledge, the equipment of a country, and the GNP are determined by a wide variety of factors. As far as the importance of the different industrial sectors is concerned, we can easily see the dominance of the manufacturing sector for the Belgian economy. At the same time, a steady growth of the number of people employed in the 'tertiary' sector can be observed. The general level of unemployment follows the cyclical state of the economy. The number of unemployed is very high (see Table 9.3) but it seems that, proportionally speaking, mainly women-workers and young workers are hit.

Table 9.3.
General level of unemployment

	1945	1955	1965	1975(I–VI)
MALES	1,230,100	118,400	55,400	162,000
%	–	5.8	2.4	6.1
FEMALES	519,100	55,900	36,800	89,100
%	–	2.7	1.6	3.5

Source: Yearbook of Labour Statistics, ILO, Geneva.

The figures are based on the compulsory unemployment insurance statistics. The numbers indicate the annual average of the unemployed persons registered at the end of each month (for 1975: the average of the first six months). The percentages are the result of the comparison between the number of insured unemployed workers and the total number of insured workers.

The evolution of the Belgian economy up to 1975 was very similar to that of other European countries. In 1973, already, there was a clear indication of the decline in economic activity. This trend has been confirmed in 1974 and 1975 by a slow growth and even a decrease of the GNP. At the very end of 1975 an upward movement has been noticed which seems to continue in 1976 (about 5.5 per cent at 1970 fixed prices). It is clear that the continuity of this movement greatly depends on the evolution of the inflation rates. By reducing the increase in salaries, we can reasonably foresee an improvement of the financial situation of enterprises, and the structural unemployment can be eliminated partly by stimulating new investments and by efficiently rationalizing the production process. The austerity measures of government will certainly help to realize these

Table 9.2.
Total and economically active population (1945–1975)

YEAR	MALES			FEMALES			TOTAL		
	Tot. popul.	Econ. act.	%	Tot. popul.	Econ. act.	%	Tot. popul.	Econ. act.	%
1945	4,007,418	2,757,935	68.8	4,084,586	992,330	24.3	8,092,004	3,750,285	46.3
1955	4,199,728	2,660,111	63.3	4,312,467	820,916	19	8,512,195	3,481,027	40.9
1965	4,496,860	2,579,638	57.4	4,692,881	932,925	19.9	9,189,741	3,512,463	38.2
1963*	4,571,125	2,558,560	56	4,757,001	1,135,900	23.9	9,328,126	3,694,400	39.6
1970	4,712,866	2,559,731	54.2	4,929,078	1,078,087	21.9	9,650,944	3,637,818	37.7
1972*	4,759,900	2,650,168	55.7	4,966,900	1,318,674	26.5	9,726,800	3,968,842	40.8

*Official Estimates.
Source: Yearbook Labour Statistics, ILO, Geneva.

objectives. It is, however, very important to notice that the competitive position of the Belgian products on the world market is vital to maintain a high standard of living for the Belgian people. The inflation rate (taking 1971 as 100) was 137.9 in 1975; 147.1 in 1976, and up to 154.2 in 1977.

1.4. Social stratification, social policy, and living conditions

Looking back at the period 1970-5, we can ascertain that the real increase in private consumption can be neglected. Salaries have risen but so have prices. Public consumption, however, increased considerably. Moreover, goods and services are more and more produced for governmental use. The gross national investments increased to stimulate the economy. At the same time, several measures have been taken to attract foreign capital investment.

Another element which certainly influences the living conditions is the level of wages. Generally, two main conclusions can be drawn: the huge rise in salaries after the Second World War and the difference in wages of specific branches of industry.

A third element which clearly illustrates the social-stratification process is the distribution of the economically active population over the various spheres of work. The percentage of the economically active population in the agricultural sector is decreasing considerably (from 6 per cent in 1945 to 3.5 per cent in 1975). This illustrates the phenomenon mentioned earlier: the importance of manufacturing industry and the growing importance of the 'tertiary' sector.

Other signs of the state of social welfare are:
(1) The number of enrolments at university or high school level. The growth of the student population at this level clearly indicates the process of democratization which took place in the Belgian educational system. This is also confirmed by the decreasing number of illiterates.
(2) The democratization process (on national level) has also progressed by a better distribution of information and communication; in fact the huge growth of the Belgian press for the period 1945-75.
In general, living conditions in Belgium are quite favourable. However, at the moment there is a difficult economic situation which might hinder investment in new participatory structures.

2. NATIONAL INDUSTRIAL RELATIONS SYSTEM

2.1. Legal basis and structure of the Industrial Relations System

The constitution defines such basic rights as: equality, personal freedom, and the right to free association.

Legally speaking the national Industrial Relations System is based on collective bargaining agreements (CAO). These bargaining agreements are prepared, discussed, and agreed upon in institutions which are established by Belgian law. Although most of the CAOs pertain to the industrial level, the CAOs at national and even at company level are becoming substantially more important. Generally, a CAO can be defined as follows: 'an agreement between unions, employers and employees to decide upon working conditions and to determine rights and duties of the signatory parties.' So a CAO has the two fundamental options of regulating working conditions, and determining the rights and duties of the parties involved. However, this distinction is not very clear in Belgium. Discussions generally lead to the elaboration of specific works laws and agreements.

As already indicated, different institutions have been established to regulate industrial relations. The two sides of industry can be involved at national level in four main ways (see Harrison, 1976). First, they can be involved in an administrative way such as in the management of the social security system. This implies that they take part in the establishment of administrative rules and their practical application. Second, they have been concerned with social programming. This provides the opportunity for the VBO (employers' association) and the unions to negotiate inter-industry collective agreements (e.g. concerning working-hours, work conditions in general, salary level, etc.), since 1960. Third, the two sides take part in an advisory role on government bodies like the CRB and the National Committee for Economic Expansion (tripartite consultation on social issues). Fourth, both sides are equally represented under an independent chairman in the NAR which has wide powers, on industrial relations and social issues and which is usually consulted by the government on legislative proposals. It is also concerned with national-level collective agreements made binding by Royal Decree for private sector industry.

As we can deduce from the above scheme three institutions are created at the company level: Works Council, a Health and Safety committee, and the Union Delegation. In practice, the same employees are often representative on all three bodies.

The organizational principles of unions/employers' associations and their historical roots

Unions

In Belgium almost all trade unions are 'associations *de facto*'. Although two laws are available to the unions to obtain legal status (March 3 1898: on professional unions; June 27 1921: on non-profit-making associations) they do not take advantage of them in order to avoid certain obligations which, in their opinion, might endanger their rights. However, they are recognized by the government which has associated them with the management of numerous para-statal bodies as well as with the elaboration of parliamentary bills. Nowadays, about 70 per cent of the working population is a member of a union.

Belgian trade unionism is characterized by its pluralistic structure. The trade unions organize the workers according to industry (e.g. metal industry) or profession (salaried employees). Another characteristic is its strong centralization. As a matter of fact, most representative trade union movements have developed in such a way that they consist only of national unions federated in a national trade union organization. Most of these national unions are founded on an industrial basis. Others however are constituted on a professional basis and group e.g. commercial or clerical employees or public service workers.

There have been attempts to set up a single union that would replace the national centres and group all the workers in a single inter-industrial and inter-professional organization. However, these attempts did not succeed and nowadays a balance has been reached between the tendency for all-out centralization and the wish for independence of the national centres. The system of the single trade union worked best in the General Centre of Liberal Trade Unions of Belgium.

The Confederation of Christian Trade Unions (CSC) is of a Catholic tendency. It is the outcome of the merger in 1912 of two confederations: the Federation of Christian Professional Unions of Belgium (Verbond der Christene Beroepsverenigingen van België) for the Flemish part of the country (1908) and the Confederation of Christian and Free Trade Unions of the Walloon Provinces (1909). Its constitutional aim can be phrased as follows: 'to concentrate to the maximum the Christian trade union forces so as to realize the organization of professional and economical activity and a society based on Christian principles'. (By 'Christian principles', one must understand the doctrine of the Catholic Church.)

The Belgian General Federation of Labour (FGTB) union professes a socialist ideology. The FGTB succeeded the CGTB which in turn emerged on January 1 1938 from the Trade Union Committee created by the Belgian Workers' Party in 1898.

The General Centre of Liberal Trade Union of Belgium (CGSLB) was founded in 1930. It is based on the liberal doctrine:

It aims to create understanding between the givers and takers of labour, based on mutual respect of reciprocal rights and duties in accordance with essential liberal principles of freedom, solidarity, progress, justice and social peace.

The Independent Trade Union in the Public Services was set up for the public sector in 1926. The Confederation of United Trade Unions of Belgium was created in 1963.

Employers' Associations

In 1895, the first national employers' association was established: the Comité Central du Travail Industriel. (European Studies, 1972.) They stressed the solidarity between employers and employees and underlined the fact that, in the long run, their interests are not in conflict. This principle still guides the actions of the employers' body.

In 1913, the Central Industrial Committee for Belgium succeeded the Comité Central du Travail Industriel. It had to cope with the difficult economic periods and two world wars. In 1946, the Union of Belgian Industry (VBN) succeeded the Central Industrial Committee for Belgium. The change of name involved an extension of competence and a broader sphere of concern.

The structure of the organization was simplified and the association worked efficiently with the other social partners: government and unions.

After economic decentralization, the VBN was split up into different regional sections:
(1) Vlaams Economisch Verbond (VEV) for the Flemish part;
(2) L'Union Wallonne des Entreprises (UWE) for the Walloon part;
(3) Verbond van Ondernemingen te Brussel (VOB) and Union des Entreprises de Bruxelles (UEB).

In 1973, one national association was established to cope with the huge variety of problems of an economic and social nature. The goals of this Union of the Belgian Enterprises (VBO) can be summarized as follows:

(1) to group the employers' associations of different industrial sectors (e.g. Fabrimetal, Febeltex) to favour solidarity between different branches;
(2) to take care of the economic, social, and moral interests of the enterprises;
(3) to represent the enterprises;
(4) to study and to stimulate the development of the enterprises;
(5) to look for social peace and economic and social development in harmony with the government and the unions.

The Union of Belgian Enterprises has, on the one hand, to study in depth all the problems of the enterprise; and on the other hand, to take concrete action in discussions with the other partners. This implies of course, an extensive information and communication programme.

Unions and employers' associations and their potential influence on the government

As already indicated, collective bargaining agreements are the result of discussions between the different partners: government, employers' association, employees' association. It is obvious that all the laws and, in consequence, the industrial relations system will be determined by the philosophy of the employers' association and the unions.

The Union of Belgian Enterprises examines in depth the variety of problems, it faces in order to bring them as effectively as possible into the discussion. This implies that it has a direct impact on all the proposed solutions.

As far as the trade unions are concerned, we can see a historical evolution in the influence they exert on the other partners. It is indeed true that several factors have helped to strengthen the authority of the most important trade unions. Among these can be quoted the problem of the general strike, which goes beyond the competence of one single national centre, and the attempt to set up a single central strike fund. Another factor is the arbitration role which these organizations have played in questions of union demarcation (areas of competence of the national centres). It is clear that the setting up of regional sections has reinforced their authority on this level.

Industrial Climate

Several indicators can be found to describe the industrial climate. The available statistical material reveals different trends (see Table 9.4):

(1) the number of social disputes increased considerably the last years (1965: 43; 1977: 220);
(2) recently, the most important causes for strikes have been wage-discussions on the one hand, and employment problems on the other hand;
(3) it seems that a great number of disputes are solved by compromises or by victory for the employers.

Generally speaking, we can say that the Belgian industrial climate is characterized by a latent tension. This is probably caused by the general labour market situation; considerable unemployment (especially for women and younger workers) and the general economic situation, which includes the closing-down of enterprises.

Table 9.4.
Number of Strikes

	Number of disputes	Workers involved	Workers days lost
1945	160	147,417	563,173
1955	143	118,578	1,001,769
1965	43	18,774	70,131
1974	235	55,747	580,032
1975	243	85,801	610,186
1976	281	106,654	896,446
1977	220	65,761	658,757

Sources: Yearbook of Labour Statistics: ILO, Geneva. *Statistisch jaarboek voor België,* NIS, Brussels.

2.2. Participation in companies

Main Legal Basis

The industrial relations at the 'enterprise' level are based on the following organs created by law: the works council, the union delegation, and the health and safety committee.

Works Council

Composition of the Works Council

Established by the law of September 20 1948, the Works Council (see Harrison, 1976), has been modified by several national agreements or Royal Decrees. The most important modification was the 1973 law concerning the right of information. The law applies to any private sector enterprise and it was extended in January 1975 to cover non-profit-making bodies and similar organizations. A works council must be established from the moment a firm has 150 employees, and it can only be abolished when the work-force goes below 150 employees. It is a joint body, chaired by the head of the enterprise or his representative. Employee representatives vary according to the total number of employees. There is a minimum of four representatives for enterprises with 50 up to 100 employees, to a maximum of 22 representatives for enterprises with over 8,000 employees. The representatives are elected in a secret ballot, of all employees, apart from management staff. Elections are held every four years, and receive extensive news coverage. There is usually a very high turnout. Trade unions submit lists of candidates, in proportion to their numbers. To be eligible to stand, a representative must not be part of the management, must be over 21 years of age, employed for at least six months in the firm and three years in the industry, and below retirement age. Young workers' representatives must be over 16 and under 25 (see Coetsier, 1966; Harrison, 1976: 17).

Protection of the Members

As a recent view points out:

Representatives and candidates cannot be dismissed other than on grounds of serious misconduct, or of redundancy on economic or technical grounds which must have been previously recognized by the relevant *commission paritaire* (industry level joint negotiating body). Where a dismissal does occur in violation of these provisions, the dimissed employee shall be re-instated without prejudice, or shall receive compensation equal, to between two and four years current remuneration according to length of service. (Harrison 1976: 17.)

Powers and Role of the Works Council

The Works Council has three main tasks: consultation, codetermination, and the communication of information. It has the right to be *consulted* on all areas affecting work organization and conditions, vocational training and productivity, projected redundancies, and it can examine redundancy provisions and the criteria of selection for redundancy. *Codetermination* on hours of work, job evaluation, holidays, welfare, and work rules are normally agreed on unanimously by the Council. If there is no agreement, the issue is normally referred to a government conciliation officer and then to the appropriate *commission paritaire*. The Royal Decree of 27 November 1973 brought new and radical rules on the regular disclosure to Councils of *information* concerning the economic and financial position of the undertaking, e.g. balance-sheet, general budget, research, cost-calculation, market-position, productivity, governmental aid, etc.

The Union Delegation

Composition of the Union Delegation

The union delegation or *délégation syndicale,* represents the members of all three main unions at plant level. White-collar and blue-collar delegations, are separated. This was originally established immediately after the last war, with general guidelines established in 1947, amended in 1971 by General Agreement, and applied through its adoption by the *commissions paritaires* (see Coetsier, 1966; Harrison, 1976).

Powers and Role of the Union Delegation

The Union Delegation is often compared with the British shop steward committee, though the delegation has less independence and less scope for bargaining. It deals personally with the head of the enterprise, and is the main channel for employment problems and grievances. Individual grievances however have initially to follow the established procedure. In practice, however, one can state that participation on the shop-floor passes through the Union Delegation. At the end the union delegates fulfil a central role in the democratization process of Belgian enterprises. In collective bargaining, the Union Delegation is not allowed to negotiate over general issues such as wages but may, however, negotiate plant-level agreement on such issues as bonuses for productivity. The Union Delegation must also look after the rigorous implementation of the collective bargaining agreements. If there is no Works Council, the Union Delegation assumes certain of its rights and functions, particularly those concerning information and consultation on the general prospects of the enterprises and on personnel issues (see Willems and Coetsier, 1975; Harrison, 1976: 19).

The Health and Safety Committee

This is mandatory under the Act of 1952 in any firm with more than 50 people. The provisions are similar as for the Works Council, and worker-members have the same protection on dismissal as works councillors. The committee has a wide scope of responsibilities relating directly to the implementation of security regulations within the enterprise. This body only has a consultative power and tries to alert the working-force for the safety problems via accident- and safety statistics and via specific safety-campaigns (see Harrison, 1976: 20).

Unity and disunity of Representation in Companies

As far as the unions are concerned, one of the main purposes of the trade union is the defence of the interests of the employees. Although there is a difference in numerical representation of the different Unions — Flanders: ACV (Christians) and Wallonia: ABVV (socialists) — we might say that — generally speaking — the unions pull together whenever problems concerning the general interest of the employees are discussed. It is clear, however, that the different political and ideological backgrounds of the trade unions sometimes lead to different action programmes.

As to the representation of different types of employees, we may say that the Belgian situation is characterized by a discrepancy. Indeed, on the one hand only workers are for the great majority members of a trade union. Only few higher-level employees are members of a union. (There is, however, some change in this situation.) On the other hand, the unions have a monopoly on the presentation of candidates for the participatory organs at the enterprise level. Thus, it is clear that in many cases the group of 'higher' employees has very few representatives.

Main Bargaining Structure

Interrelation of firm bargaining and extra-firm bargaining

In Belgium the main bargaining structure is determined by the actions taken by three different groups: government, trade union representatives, and employers' association representatives.

The bargaining process is conducted at three different levels: enterprise level, branch or sector level, and national level. At the enterprise-level the bargaining process resulted in the setting-up of participatory organs. In fact, these organs have little executive power. They can only give advice (except for some specific, less important problems) and exert control on the application of the agreements subscribed at the 'branch' level. Even in cases of serious conflict at the enterprise level they have to make an appeal to higher institutions. In fact, all important decisions are taken at the national or branch level. This is one of the reasons for the uni-directional character of the main bargaining structure: all bargaining at the enterprise-level is determined in advance by the decisions taken at the higher level.

This does not mean, however, that workers on the enterprise-level have no influence on decisions taken at the higher level. Through a system of representative participation, they can exert a certain influence. One can of course ask how effectively this system works and especially whether the representatives have the power to influence fundamentally important national decisions. Although, at first sight, one might be rather sceptical of accepting this, it does seem that workers at the lower levels and these workers representatives (e.g. union delegates) influence fundamentally important decisions. The evolution itself in Belgian social relations can be used as an illustration of this fact: e.g. the Works Council has the right (via a voted law) to claim specific financial and social information.

Issues involved on different levels

While describing the functions and competences of the main bargaining institutions we already indicated the problems they generally discuss.

As far as the kinds of problems discussed at the enterprise-level are concerned recent research (Coetsier, 1966; Gevers, 1973) has indicated that in the Works Council the following problems occur:

(1) economic and financial problems;
(2) functioning of the Works Council itself;
(3) organization of labour;
(4) application of industrial and social laws;
(5) working conditions;
(6) dismissal of workers;
(7) holidays.

In the C.V.G.V., the problems discussed mainly have to do with the improvement of the work conditions, while the Union Delegation is basically occupied with problems concerning wages and social premiums. They also work considerably at the preparation of the discussions about the collective bargaining agreements.

2.3. The role of public powers in the NAR

It is clear that the public powers — via the voting of specific laws — can exert a considerable influence on the industrial relations scheme e.g. in case of conflict at the enterprise level the government intervenes by referring to specific laws or by trying to reconcile the opposed parties. Also in the case of problems of a general nature, the public power can enter as another partner with specific interests and specific claims. The intervention can even be very radical e.g. the taking-over of an enterprise.

3. PROGRAMMATIC PERSPECTIVES, PROBLEMATIC ISSUES, AND POSSIBLE DEVELOPMENTS

3.1. Programmatic Perspectives

At present, one of the government's main tasks consists in the creation of solutions to resolve economic problems. Indeed, the actual economic situation vitally needs action and the whole of society must take up its responsibilities.

Outcomes expected in individual cases

It appears that the welfare of individuals in our present economic system will be determined basically by a strategy of full employment. This strategy must take into account its effect on inflation. Thus, one must not create full employment by arbitrarily supporting some specific industries. On the contrary, the enterprises with a large number of employees must be supported in particular. Even a structural reorientation could be a valuable alternative (see e.g., the options of the socialist union). Basic sectors, such as building must be supported.

As indicated above, employment constitutes a real problem for some categories of workers e.g. women, younger workers, foreigners. Structural changes will be the only solution. Looking at the programmes promulgated by the government, one might say that the problems surrounding full employment are considered seriously.

Outcomes expected for industrial organizations

First, we must stress the fact that the Belgium economy is based on both private initiative and investments, as well as governmental initiative in specific branches. Thus, one might expect serious governmental efforts, as well as private initiatives.

On the other hand, we also see that many enterprises are in great financial difficulties. To lighten their burden, the government must answer not only questions about the effective control of enterprises, but they must also decide whether to intervene whenever it seems to be necessary. In this way, the financial problems of most enterprises can be anticipated and eventually solved.

Outcomes for the economy and the social system at large

From the mid-seventies we have lived in an economy characterized by inflation and recession. To get out of this situation the government has to propose some measures concerning wages, salaries, and prices. In fact, these two elements essentially determine — particularly in the Belgian system — the costs of the end-product and consequently the position of Belgian products on the world market. Everybody agrees on the principle of the reasonable distribution of incomes. This could be realized by using different strategies:
(1) revision of the system of direct and indirect taxation, especially the control of the payment of taxes must be revised;
(2) the system of the social security must be revised and expanded in favour of the lower income groups;
(3) revision of the system of determing wages through special committees.
As far as prices are concerned, it seems vital to relate wages to the cost of living in an efficient way. On May 1 1975, the government announced a price-freeze. This price-freeze slowed-down the inflation-rate and stabilized the prices of a great number of goods and services. In 1976 the price-measures were relaxed slightly and proposals are being studied to relate wages to prices as effectively as possible.

3.2. Main Implications of the System

As can be deduced from the general industrial relations scheme, a clear distinction is made between social problems on the one hand, and economic problems on the other hand. This distinction does not apply to the company-level where the different participatory organs have a concurring competence in different matters.

In view of the current pattern of social evolution, it is clear that this distinction between social and economic problems is quite arbitrary. In fact, economic expansion and social welfare cannot be separated. All this implies a change in the competence of the different legal institutions which make up the industrial relations system.

3.3. Problematic Issues and Possible Developments

The present economic situation seems to stimulate behaviour which aims at changes in the industrial relations system. As mentioned above, people became aware of the necessity to consider economic and social problems along the same lines. This could lead to a change in the specific legal institutions above the company level. Some studies (for example, Harrison, 1976) have indicated that the Works Council does not in practice exercise its limited powers of codetermination, but seems to act as an official arena for information and consultation. The Union Delegation then takes up issues on which no agreement can be reached. Critics argue that the Works Council does not exercise its powers of codetermination fully. But there is general agreement that the Works Council is a valuable vehicle for consultation, particularly since the 1973 law on information. The unions are also undecided about employee representation at board. It is further rather peculiar that in Belgium the different unions have different attitudes *vis-à-vis* the role the Works Council should play in organizations. In 1974 Catholic Union proposed to extend the power of the Works Council (consisting only of employees' representatives). The socialist union is more in favour of 'workers' control' without direct responsibility for decisions taken.

Here again, the Catholic union wants the Board to be composed equally of representatives of the employees, the shareholders, and the public interest. It even stresses the fact that the law should intervene to extend the power of employees in the process of decision-making. The socialist union wants to have more information about the decisions which have to be taken. It stipulates further that the union should have the right of veto on a number of specific issues.

The CGSLB pleads for a 'German-like' codetermination system. The new law of 19 December 1974 was intended to extend employee participation to the public sector. It applied to central and local government employees, and the staff of other bodies working in the public sphere but does not cover the police or armed forces. Implementation of this law has run into difficulties with the unions pulling out in early 1976 from a working-party looking at draft implementation orders.

By way of conclusion, we might argue that the main problem of the government presently consists in drawing-up of acceptable solutions for the current economic problems which involve revival of the economy. These must be guided by two fundamental principles, namely, the determination of a very rigid and specific economic programme; and economic decentralization which can alter the general economic strategy to meet specific needs of regions and industries.

To sum up, the Belgian system dates from the 1948 Act, and has been since extended, especially in 1973 and 1975. The Works Council is consulted over a wide area of decisionmaking, in close relationship with the *commission paritaire*, the main organ of the industrial relations system in the firm. The Union Delegation is often compared with the British shop steward system. The Health and Safety Committee also plays a central role. Bargaining is at three levels (enterprise, sector and national). How the system will evolve in the adverse economic conditions of the early 1980s remains to be seen.

REFERENCES

ACVLB (1975), Statutair congres, Gent.
Blanpain, R. (1961), *De collectieve Arbeidsovereenkomst,* Universitaire Boekhandel Uystpruyst, Leuven.
Bolle de Bal, M. (1966), *La vie de l'entreprise,* Editions de l'Institut de Sociologie, Université Libre de Bruxelles, Brussels.
Coetsier, P. (1966), *Organismen voor medezeggenschap in de onderneming,* Standaard wetenschappelijke uitgeverij, Antwerpen/Gent.
Congrès ACLVB (1969), *Medezeggenschap en interessering.* ACLVB, Gent.
European Studies, Trade Union Series (1972), *The Trade Union Movement in the European Community,* European Press and Information, Brussels.
Fafchamps, J. (1961), *Les conventions collectives en Belgique,* 2 Vols., Ed. La Pensée Catholique, Brussels.
Gevers, P. (1971), 'Works Council in Belgium', *Sociological Contribution from Flanders.* 3
        (1973), *O.R. Randverschijnsel in de Belgische Industriele Democratiseringsbeweging,* Een Sociologische Studie, Université Catholique de Louvain, Louvain.
Goemare, J. (1976), 'La Participation dans l'Entreprise', *Annales de Droit,* 2.
Harrison, R. (1976), *Workers' Participation in Western Europe,* Institute of Personnel Management, London.
Horion, P. (1956), *Les relations collectives du travail,* Les Presses Universitaires de Liège, Liège.
Chantrenne, A. (1972), 'Concertation et participation: Dispositions Légales en Belgique', *L'Entreprise et l'homme,* 44.
Ministerie Van Economische Zaken (1976), *De Belgische Economie in 1975,* Brussels.
Molitor, M. (1971), 'De stand van het Belgische Vakbondsleven', *Synopsis,* 129.
Piron, J. (1970), *Les Relations Collectives du Travail dans les Pays de la CEE,* Fédération des Industries Belges, Bruxelles.
Rombouts, J. (1975), 'The Belgian industrial relations system – Outline of a sociological approach', *Sociological Contribution from Flanders,* 8.
Spitaels, G. (1967), *Le Mouvement Syndical en Belgique,* Études de l'Institut de Sociologie, Université Libre de Bruxelles, Brussels.
Stroobant, M. (1969), *De medezeggenschap van de werknemer in de onderneming,* Wetenschappelijk uitgeverij Story, Brussels, Gent.
        (1971), 'La Participation des Travailleurs à la Gestion de l'Entreprise', *Revue du travail,* 3.
Van Outrive, L. and Moons, A. (1969), 'De Patronale Beroepsorganisaties', *Synopsis,* 11.

VBO (1976), *De Belgische Ondernemingen,* Verbond Belgische Ondernemingen, Brussels.

Willems, A.-M. and Coetsier, P. (1975), *Formalized Workers Participation in Belgium,* Laboratorium voor Toegepaste Psychologie, Rijksuniversiteit Gent.

10

THE FRENCH INDUSTRIAL RELATIONS SYSTEM

1. GENERAL SITUATION AND BACKGROUND

1.1. The Status-quo of political power

In order to understand the general debate about industrial democracy, one must see it in a double historical perspective.

First, one must keep in mind that because of widespread class consciousness, French working-class organizations have always stood out in marked contrast to those in other western countries. They were dedicated to revolutionary ends and resolutely opposed to reforms within the capitalist system. The consequence of class-consciousness has been the creation of a working-class movement — in which left-wing parties and trade unions serve the same community of wage-earners, their activites complementing each other. This latter idea is still very much alive despite the variety of ways in which unions and parties relate to each other. In fact, three major types of relationships have been identified according to their political label: a communist tradition, a social-democratic tradition, and a syndicalist tradition (see Reynaud, 1976). An illustration of this fundamental consensus in French society lies in the fact that most of the improvements for the working class had to be won in situations where the political climate was in favour of the Left (1936, 1946, 1968). Despite this basic class division, the French working-class movement has now reached a stage where unions have institutionalized both the 'social question' and industrial conflict.

The second characteristic of the context of the problem of industrial democracy, consists in the fact that two conceptions of change have always co-existed in France: on one hand, a type of change which would emerge from the bottom, i.e. civil society (supported by the Orléanist right and part of the socialist Left), on the other hand a type of change initiated by the State (supported by the Bonapartist right and the Leninist Left). Until very recently, changes were imposed from outside, by political forces, whereas nowadays one can observe changes generated by civil society and encouraged by the 'auto-gestionnaire' Left (as opposed to the centralizing Left).

Against this general background, France has been the scene of a slowly changing party system: in 1947–58, when political parties were numerous, the dominant orientation being the centre (MRP); 1958–69, when a major liberal-conservative party (UDR) was created which over-lapped the centre, and the Left to a certain extent; and in 1969–77, when as a reaction to the strong UDR, a bipolarization occurred opposing an alliance of the Right to an alliance of the Left, which made the lack of consensus more obvious.

Since 1972, when the Socialist Party and Communist Party formed a common governmental platform, the Left has been striving to come to power. One can observe that the legislative elections of 1973 and the presidential elections of

1974 are characterized by the closeness of the outcome but a victory of the Right occurred in the last elections (March 1978), in spite of the '*cantonales*' of March 1976, which gave a majority of the votes to the Left. Both major unions (CGT and CFDT) gave their support to the common platform and the Left coalition for the elections, but wanted also to keep a certain autonomy from the parties.

The FO refused to endorse the agreement (see Reynaud, 1976). The main feature of the French party-system has been its lack of political alternation — France having kept a liberal–conservative government for twenty years (Duverger, 1971). The main representative bodies are the National Assembly and the Senate, with the former dominating.

Table 10.1.
Voting Statistics (in %)

	1945	1956	1967	1973
Abstentions	20.0	17.0	19.1	18.8
Communist Party	20.4	20.6	17.7	16.9
Socialist Party	18.2	12.1	16.5	20.0
Centre and Right	38.8	45.3	55.5	39.9
Others	0.1	1.3	3.7	2.2

Source: Goguel and Grosser, 1975.

Table 10.2.
Elections results, March 1978 (in %)

First turn		Second turn	
Communist party	20.55		
Socialist party	22.58		
Extreme left	3.33		
Radical left	2.11	Left	49.36
Gaullists	22.62	Right	50.74
Union of the French Democracy	21.45		
Majority of others	2.39		
Ecologists	2.14		
Others	2.78		

Source: Ministry of Domestic Affairs.

1.2. Recent political events of national and regional significance

In May 1968 students' demonstrated following the crisis in the university system. A general strike occurred with sit-ins and other self-management practices. No political party, however, canalized the movement. In April 1969 the government resigned after the negative referendum on regionalization and reform of the Senate, and De Gaulle withdrew from politics. Pompidou was elected in June 1969 President of the Republic, and in August 1969 the devaluation of the Franc was announced which improved the balance of payments. In December

1969, Chaban-Delmas (Prime Minister) launched the 'contractual policy' and the *'contrats de progrès'* in the public sector (gas and electricity, national railways, coal-mining). In December 1970 the CGT and CFDT (the two biggest unions) agreement on a common platform was reached. The Congress of Epinay of June 1971, which unified the socialist forces and created the new Socialist Party with Mitterand as its First Secretary. In April 1972 the enlargement of the EEC was approved. In June 1972 the Common Platform by the Socialist and Communist Parties was ratified. In March 1973 parliamentary elections were held with a serious setback for Gaullism, following the growth of the united Left after the losses sustained in May 1968.

A strike of banks and Stock Exchange employees occurred in 1974. In May Valery Giscard d'Estaing (Independent Republican) was elected as President by a narrow margin of less than 1 per cent of the votes (d'Estaing 50.6 per cent, F. Mitterand 49.3 per cent). In the same year a Ministry for the Quality of Life and for Women's Affairs was created. 1975 saw the publication of the Sudreau Report on the Reform of Enterprise. In October 1976 the Prime Minister Barre brought in his austerity plan against inflation. This plan was received with strong protest, with a national strike organized by the CGT and FEN. A year later, the united Left broke up and in March 1978 parties from the Right in Parliamentary elections gained victory.

1.3. The Economic Situation

Between 1945 and 1972 the French economy has been characterized by a rapid and continuous growth, which brought it out of its pre-war stagnation. The average growth rate of the GNP in volume has been 5.8 per cent between 1960 and 1972. This rate has been the highest (after the Japanese) among the OECD countries. Which explanatory factors have been put forward to interpret this high rate preceding the crisis? First, the increase of the active population became an important factor from 1963, with the arrival on the labour-market of post-war generations, Algerian repatriates, and immigrants. The increase of the total population, for the whole period: the whole population rose from 40.50 millions in 1946 to 42.77 millions in 1954, 48.75 in 1965, and 52.74 in 1975, the percentage of the active population (see Table 10.4) being respectively 50 per cent in 1946, 44.4 per cent in 1954, 50.3 per cent in 1965, and 42.6 per cent in 1975. Second, if the total work-day duration has been a negative factor in the growth rate, on the contrary the quality of work, related to the level of education, accounts for half a point of the growth rate, and this tendency seems to continue to increase. Finally, the changing of activity from agriculture to industry accounts for another half-point in the growth rate. All factors related to labour have contributed one point to the rate, whereas factors related to capital have contributed one and a half points. The remaining half of the growth rate (2.5 per cent) must be due to less tangible factors such as technical progress etc. (See Carré *et al.*, 1973.)

This rhythm has been affected since 1974 (the growth rate being only 3.8 per cent that year). The break has affected internal demand, foreign exchanges, and the pace of growth:

(*a*) The growth of the purchasing power of available income fell from 6.8 per cent in 1973 to 3.3 per cent in 1974, to an even lower level in 1975;

(*b*) imports (in volume) rose 17.2 per cent in 1972, 4.9 per cent in 1974, and diminished by 12 per cent in 1975; exports (in volume) showed a decline, too: before 1974 their rate of growth was 14 per cent, 8.8 per cent in 1974, 4.4 per cent in 1975;

(*c*) growth in production fell to 3.5 per cent in 1974 and to minus 2.5 per cent in 1975.

The GNP at market prices (see Table 10.3) in current Francs (billions) (on a 1962 basis) was Fr.88.1 in 1949; Fr.173.2 in 1955; Fr.489.8 in 1965; Fr.1324.8 in 1974. In the period 1970-4 it moved from Fr.808.4 in 1970 to Fr.898.6 in 1971; Fr.1007.7 in 1972; Fr.1,143.9 in 1973; and Fr.1,324.8 in 1974.

Despite the break described earlier, the French economy benefits from positive factors: first, a reservoir of labour with a high level of education, and second, the growth in labour productivity which reached 5.5 per cent between 1970 and 1973 (a tendency which may stick).

The two major problems from which the French economy suffers at present are: the drop in the rate of return on investments and the difficulties on the present labour market. The proportion of the active population looking for a job was 250,000 (1.3 per cent) in 1955, 303,729 (1.5 per cent) in 1966, 737,000 (3.5 per cent) in 1975, and 978,000 (4.3 per cent) in 1976. Among the unemployed in 1976, one counts 47.3 per cent of people under 25 and 54.3 per cent women, the rate being highest in the services and trade industries, and geographically speaking in the South of France. The rate of unemployment has not stopped growing since 1964: in other words, the crisis is only one cause of it, the increase of the active population in absolute terms being another one. The indices of retail prices on a basis 100 in 1938, were 393 in 1945, 2,429 in 1955, 3,871 in 1965 and 7,330 in 1975. The average annual growth rate of the retail price indices was 5.6 per cent between 1955 and 1960, 3.5 per cent between 1960 and 1967, 5.6 per cent between 1968 and 1970, 6.4 per cent between 1971 and 1972, 8.5 per cent between 1972 and 1973, 15.2 per cent between 1973 and 1974, and a slight deceleration later on, to 9.8 per cent in 1976 and 9.7 per cent in 1977.

1.4. Social stratification, social policy, and living conditions

Public expenditure amounts to 20.5 per cent of the GNP, the most important part of it going to education and culture, defence to the social sector and employment. This percentage has been constantly regressing, the high point being 31.8 per cent in 1953. Between 1963 and 1975 the amount going to education has increased from 30 per cent to 40 per cent within the structure of the budget (*Tableaux de l'Economie Française*, 1976). Like most countries, France has experienced a wage-price spiral and has been trying to protect workers' earnings, and to diminish inequalities due to basic wages, by redistribution. In order to protect the purchasing power of the less privileged, the SMIG (a minimum wage) was introduced in 1950, with the intention of linking its development to that of prices. But very soon, other salaries (apart from the

SMIG) went up much more rapidly than prices and the SMIG was no longer a relevant notion: this problem was at the core of the social crisis of May 1968, and in 1970 the original SMIG was replaced by the SMIC, the latter being based not only on the evolution of prices but also on the evolution of all wages.

On the other hand, the French government, like most conservative ones, has tried to diminish inequalities by monetary redistribution — through the distribution of different sorts of allowances and through tax deductions. In fact, a study carried out by the CREDOC shows that, as a result, the only beneficiaries of this monetary redistribution were those not working. Indeed, whereas the income tax is progressive (and thus helps to diminish inequalities), the social assessments and VAT are regressive (*Tableau de l'Economie Française*, 1976). The share of GNP going to salaries increased from 45 per cent in 1965 to 51 per cent in 1974. In 1959 salaries were, in billions, Fr.117,615; in 1965 they were Fr.233,072; and Fr.681,220 in 1974. Both the share of the wages and the social assessments went up. In the national income salaries have increased to the detriment of companies' income (in 1959 salaries counted for 60 per cent in the national income; in 1974 they count for 66 per cent). (See also Table 10.3.)

Table 10.3
GNP at market prices in current Francs (1962 basis)

	(billions)		
1949	88.1	1975	1,309.78
1955	173.2	1976	1,599.00
1965	489.8	1977	1,850.00
1974	1,324.8		

Source: Tableaux de l'Economie Française, 1976.

Purchasing power has risen each year on average by 4.7 per cent between 1959 and 1974. Despite this rise, wage differentials remain very strong. (A recent study reveals that they are the same nowadays as they were twenty years ago.) In 1954, a top manager earned (on average) 4.1 times more than a worker (on average), a middle manager twice as much. In 1975 (and 1976) these proportions are still operative. In 1976 a top manager earned Fr.8,400 a month, a middle manager Fr.4,100, a foreman Fr.3,800, a white-collar worker Fr.2,400, a worker Fr.2,200 (*Le Monde, L'année sociale et économique*, 1976). The range of salaries was at its greatest before 1968. The only element which has moved is the salaries of white-collar workers compared to blue-collar workers: the former earned 13 per cent more than the latter in 1954, 10 per cent more in 1967, and only 4 per cent more in 1974. Skilled workers earn on average 32 per cent more than unskilled ones (on an hourly basis). Hourly wages for workers are the highest in printing, chemicals, metalworking, and lowest in catering and in the clothing industry. The gap between salaries in Paris and in the provinces has remained relatively constant, around 44 per cent.

As Table 10.5 shows, the labour force outside the agricultural sector stood at 78 per cent in 1960, 86 per cent in 1970, and 89 per cent in 1975. The percentage of the labour force in manufacturing remained constant around 40 per cent,

Table 10.4.
Members of active population seeking a job

1955	–	250,000
1966	–	303,729
1975	–	737,000
1976	–	978,000

Table 10.5.
Proportion of population outside agriculture (%)

1960	78	:	1970	86	:	1975	89

Source: Tableaux de l'Economie Française, 1976.

the one in the service industry rose considerably, up to 49 per cent. The proportion of workers within the active population has increased drastically from 30 per cent in 1950 to 37 per cent in 1974. In 1954 the skilled workers represented 14.8 per cent of the active population, the unskilled 15.3 per cent; in 1962 the skilled workers represented 12.2 per cent, the unskilled workers 20.2 per cent; and in 1968 the skilled workers represented 12.5 per cent, the unskilled workers 20.8 per cent. As it appears through these percentages, a movement towards dequalification has affected the workers' population. It is only in printing and in clothing industry that the skilled count for more than 50 per cent of the work-force.

Paradoxically, beside this dequalification, the number of students and of secondary school pupils has gone up impressively. The primary school population rose gradually from 4¾ millions in 1948 to 7½ millions in 1974. The secondary school population rose from three-quarters of a million in 1948 to 4¾ millions in 1974; the university population rose from 123,313 in 1948 to 9,000,000 in 1974. Together pupils and students constituted 12.9 per cent of the whole population in 1952 and they represent 25 per cent in 1974. Illiteracy was hardly to be found. However the French read less newspapers than one would expect: only 23 per cent read a daily paper.

2. THE NATIONAL INDUSTRIAL RELATIONS SYSTEM

2.1. Formal, structural bases and main ramifications of the Industrial Relations System

The preambles to the Constitutions of 1946 and 1958 have laid down a certain number of principles concerning industrial relations – the right to a job, to belong to a trade union and defend one's interests through it, to go on strike, to have representatives (employee delegates and enterprise committees provided with powers of information, consultation, participation), the right to the *Sécurité Sociale*. This social legislation can be initiated by law (incorporated in the *Code du Travail*) or by statutory governmental power and regulates such issues as the national minimum wage, the length of the working week, paid holidays, and provides procedures for bargaining and for settlement of disputes. What has traditionally characterized the French system of industrial relations is that among the different methods of external job regulation, priority has been given to social legislation as opposed to collective bargaining. This preference for social legislation and institutional participation explains why collective bargaining did not take root until the passing of the Act of 11 February 1950, with the exception of brief bursts of activity (1919–20 and the Popular Front, 1936) and why collective bargaining constitutes a new practice.

Of course there are areas where collective bargaining was considered justified: to improve the minimum advantages fixed by law or to regulate on questions ignored by the law. But as a consequence of the preference for the law, the type of bargaining which was to follow was 'regulated' bargaining, and the level at which it was preferably to take place was the 'highest level' possible i.e. the industry-level. But as J. D. Reynaud points out, this situation has somehow changed; the legislator has left more room for the autonomy of the parties and one can observe also that it is increasingly difficult to decide whether an issue is the outcome of a law or of a collective agreement (Reynaud, 1978).

Organizational principles of unions/employers

The development of trade unionism has not matched the nation's industrial and economic growth. Precise figures are not available but it is estimated that the trade-union membership represents only about 20 to 25 per cent of the total labour force. This low membership can be explained. First, there is the fragmentation of unions on ideological and political grounds. Second, employers have often opposed any extensions of trade-union influence. There is a continuing paternalistic tradition, particularly in small firms, which argues in favour of direct communications rather than union representation. Third, the absence of anything like the closed shop relieves the pressure on the individual worker to join a union. Trade-union membership is lowest in the retail, building, and textile industries; higher in expanding industries such as electronics and oil; highest in the public sector. The influence of the unions is however much greater politically and professionally than their low membership would imply. The trade-union movement developed rather late and it was not until 1884 that trade-unions obtained recognized legal status.

The CGT (Confédération Générale du Travail) is the oldest among the trade-union confederations and was set up in 1895. Its philosophy is based on marxist doctrine and some of its leaders are Communist Party members. Within the CGT itself, the difficulty of coexistence of a marxist group with anarchist and social reformist elements, led to a split in 1921 and to the marxist defection into the Confédération Générale du Travail Unifié. The two wings were reunified at the time of the Popular Front in 1936, but split again in 1947 when the marxist group remained in control and the other group became the CGT-FO (Force Ouvrière). Although the latter is basically socialist, it follows a policy of collective bargaining.

Catholic trade-unionism was introduced in 1919 with the formation of the CFTC (Confédération Française des Travailleurs Chrétiens). Its main objective was to promote peaceful collaboration between capital and labour. The Christian union became schismatic in 1964 when the majority decided to emphasize its independence from religious control and became the CFDT (Confédération Française Democratique du Travail). The latter adopted a policy of left-wing democratic socialism, whereas the minority group retained the Christian connection and the title of CFTC.

There are two other major unions – the CGC (Confédération Générale des Cadres) formed in 1945, a professional union. Their philosophy is one of moderation and participation – the FEN (Fédération de l'Éducation Nationale) which was originally affiliated to the CGT, but which chose to form an autonomous unified federation and represents the teachers.

In France it is very difficult to know precisely the membership of each union. If one takes the figures given by the unions themselves one has to interpret them because they are often exaggerated. Membership of the various bodies is estimated in Table 10.6.

Table 10.6.
Trade Union Membership

CGT	2 million members (strongest in manual workers – skilled and semi-skilled, particularly in the metal, building, and chemical industries, and railways).
CFDT	800,000 members (spread among manual and non-manual workers, particularly in chemicals, textiles, steel, and banks).
CGT-FO	600,000 members (strongest among white-collar and professional groups, particularly in the public sector).
FEN	450,000 members (teachers in nationalized establishments).
CGC	200,000 members (caters for qualified engineers, senior executives, representatives and agents, foremen, and technicians).
CFTC	150,000 members (strongest among public servants, bank employees, and non-industrial workers).

Sources: Various Estimates by Unions concerned.

Besides the unions listed above, there are also a number of independent and autonomous bodies, but those mentioned above are the main ones, 'representative' at the national level. The criteria for representativeness of a union are: its membership, its independence from management, its financial strength, its experience and seniority, and its patriotic attitude during the war. The fact of a union being representative or not is very important because it determines the union's rights.

Despite their ideological differences there is considerable similarity in the structure and organization of the three main confederations (CGT, CFDT, FO). All are based on industries rather than crafts or professions (apart from the CGC and FEN)! They have a dual structure, part-horizontal (geographical) and part-vertical (industrial). Each union contains about 30 to 40 federations and 90 UDs (union départementales). It must be added that some federations have their own UDs (metal workers and builders, for instance). The day-to-day management of the confederation is vested in a four-tier structure of organization: (1) a congress, held normally every two years, is constitutionally empowered to formulate policy; (2) a confederal committee representing all local unions and federations, meeting about twice a year; (3) an executive commission of about 35 representatives; (4) a confederal bureau of full-time officers which is the organization's standing executive committee; about 15 members.

The organization of the CFDT differs slightly from that of the CGT and FO. The Act of December 1968, which confers recognition on the plant-based section syndicale as a fundamental unit of union organization may prove to have great significance for the future of the union organization.

Employers are grouped together in local trade organizations affiliated to industrial and regional organizations and also in multi-industry associations with their own regional federations. The most influential association is that for the engineering industry, the UIMM (Union of Metal and Mining Industries). The different associations are affiliated to a single national body; the CNPF (National Council of French Employers) formed in 1946 (for historical background, see Reynaud, 1975).

The Industrial Climate

Recognized since 1864, the right to strike is guaranteed in the 1946 Constitution. Although some strikes are in theory illegal, it becomes more and more difficult in practice to draw the line between lawful and unlawful strikes. What characterizes French strikes since 1945 is that they are essentially short-term affairs, and that the number of strikes as well as the number of strikers show contrary tendencies. This explains why the number of days lost has remained constant since 1954, oscillating on average between 1 and 6 millions from one year to another.

Table 10.7.
Recent Strike Statistics

Date	No. of Strikes	No. of Strikers	Days Lost
1955	2,672	792,000	3,078,000
1965	1,680	688,000	980,000
1975	3,888	1,827,000	3,869,000
1976	3,247	–	3,278,000
1977	4,298	–	2,146,000

The number of days lost was highest in the metal related trade (in 1975, 66 days lost per 100 workers).

Source: Ministry of Labour.

The recent period is characterized by the fact that strikes take place simultaneously at plant-level, throughout an industry, or even at national level. Among the strikes at local level we can observe two types of strikes: first, strikes of a defensive nature take place in traditional industries or depressed areas where the major claim is the refusal to accept closure of firms and massive redundancies e.g. Rateau, Annonay, Titan-Coder, Everwear, Teppaz, Socotamec, etc. Strikers reject the inevitability of unemployment and try to set up alternative plans to prove that these firms are viable even according to a capitalist logic. By doing so they safeguard their jobs as well as demonstrate 'from within' that the system is incoherent and adopts strategies contrary to workers' interests. Second, strikes of a more offensive nature in more advanced sectors where the major claim is the improvement of conditions of work: banks, the Post Office, etc.

The function of strikes at the national level is to preserve a certain unity in the labour movement which could be threatened by grass-roots movements. The strategy of the CGT has favoured the national strike whereas the CFDT has favoured the local strike. Both strategies are complementary and the fact that one or the other prevails depends on circumstances. As far as the means are concerned rather than exerting economic pressure of the employers, the employees pressurize them by obtaining public sympathy. The strike methods have become more radical (repeated short stoppages which stop production, often accompanied by sit-ins) and new categories of workers (either highly qualified, or the least privileged: women, young workers, immigrants) have got involved in them.

The rate of industrial accidents has remained the same since 1949 (40 accidents per million hours worked): they were 1,011 million in 1955, 1,267 million in 1965, and 1,137 million in 1973. Altogether the count on average for 6.8 millions of lost days. The rate of accidents is the highest in the building industry (29 per cent) and in the metal industries (30 per cent).

2.2. Participation in Companies

Main legal basis

For the moment, there is in France no joint decision-making model, that is, no codetermination giving equal weight to both parties. Concerning participation at board level, in limited companies the enterprise committee has the right to appoint two of its members to attend all meetings of the supervisory board or *conseil d'administration.* One member represents the managerial and technical grades, and the other the manual workers and junior grade white-collar staff. Nationalized industries have a tripartite supervisory board, with one third for government representatives, all of whom have the same voting rights. In fact, the formal provisions whether in the private sector or in nationalized industries do not give the CE (*comité d'entreprise*) representatives any role in the decision-making process; moreover very often major issues have been discussed informally without the trade unions before the formal meeting takes place. Up till very recently, most employers and their organizations have been clearly opposed to any workers representation at this level. The CGT and CFDT have also rejected any idea of codetermination or co-operation with the capitalist system.

Following the two-tier structure proposed by the EEC a Bill has been tabled by the government on the *Réforme de l'Entreprise* — Rapport Sudreau, February 1975 — which suggests that firms should give to representatives of all employees a third of the seats on the supervisory board (the latter being appointed by shareholders) or on the present board of directors. The representatives of the employees would be directly elected by them provided they have been in the firm for at least two years, and they would not have to be necessarily members of a trade-union. The board would have to meet at least each term and the members nominated by the CE could stay with the newly elected members — only the latter having voting rights. Employers have not shown great enthusiasm for the Bill. Trade Unions too have expressed reservations and remain suspicious (see *Le Monde,* 15 February 1975). The Bill aims also at developing the existing profit-sharing schemes introduced by the Ordinances of 1959 and 1967. The measure of 1959 encouraged workers to share the fruits of the expansion of the enterprise, and with the measure of 1967 such a scheme became compulsory in all firms with more than 100 employees. This participatory legislation has not been welcomed by any of the three main confederations which have been inclined to condemn the measure as an endeavour to integrate the workers within the system. This reluctance is shown by the fact that 80 per cent of the profit-sharing schemes have been signed by the employer and the works council and not by the unions directly (for the different ways of operating the scheme, see Camerlynck, Lyon-Caen, 1973).

Unity and disunity of representation in companies

The analysis of the representative bodies within the firm set up between 1936 and today shows that there is no unity among the different representative institutions but that several bodies coexist. They have been successively set up, simply added to each other without any logical order between them, and their aims and functions are not necessarily coherent. Indeed, they developed as a result of social pressures at different points in time. To start with we must examine the representatives elected by the employees.

Employee delegates (*délégués du personnel*), instituted by the Popular Front in the Matignon Agreement in 1936, put forward grievances of the individuals who elected them. They were often perceived by management as 'soviets' within factories because they dealt with employees'–employers' divergent interests.

The enterprise committee, more or less equivalent to a works council, was set up by an Ordinance in 1945. The CE has specified powers of decision, consultation, and information which differs widely on whether the issue concerned is social or economic. The committee is responsible for social welfare schemes within the firm. It has consultative power on the other social issues such as work rules, determination of the period of paid holidays, arrangements under the profit-sharing legislation. On economic and technical matters it can express its opinion about the economic and technical performance of the firm, major investment proposals, changes in the organization and conditions or work, more recently about employment questions. This implies that it must be informed. It has the right to quarterly reports on the order book, the general employment situation and annual reports on the company's activities. Its role was to achieve participation between the parties who have common interests.

A Health and Safety Committee must also be established as a sub-committee of the CE in all industrial concerns employing more than 50 workers and in all concerns with more than 500 employees. The Act of December 1973 reinforced the powers of such committees and provided for other sub-committees to deal with more general problems of improving working conditions and works organizations, as well as training.

The *Sections Syndicales* and trade-unions' representatives set up by the Act of December 1968 are nominated by each of the 'representative' unions within the firm. Their role is to defend all professional interests and to negotiate plant-level agreements.

Despite this multiplicity of institutions, it is often said that trade-unions have a 'monopoly' over the representation of professional interests and this should have helped to unify the different institutions. Indeed, for the first ballot of the election of the CE and employee representative only the most 'representative' unions can present candidates for these posts. It is only for the second ballot (if there is one) that any employee can stand as a candidate. Another example to illustrate this monopoly is the union's right to send a nominated representative to the CE. But in fact, they do not always exert such a monopoly because, for the election, representativeness of a trade-union is judged within the firm regardless of its representativeness on a national level. It may result from this that a trade union which is representative within a firm can present candidates *and* designate union representatives, whereas a union which is only representative on a national level can only designate union representatives but not present candidates for the CE and employee representative elections (such cases may occur but are rare).

The diversity of institutions, despite criticism, seems to fulfil certain functional needs: the most important being, that it is well suited to a situation where a multiplicity of unions exist — should a union be in a minority situation it can have a say, thanks to the trade-union section and perhaps thus improve its membership.

Despite what is foreseen by the legal framework, points of view diverge in practice between management and unions as to the role the elected institution should play as opposed to the nominated one. For the CGT and CFDT the *section syndicale* should play a predominant role and co-ordinate the activities of elected institution, and negotiate on its own with management. The two elected institutions are still indispensable in the sense that their role consists of providing information to the union on the economic situation of the firm and on the collective and individual grievances of employees. For management on the other hand, the nominated institution should be subordinated to the elected one or at least not interfere in their activities. The different views on the relationship between the elected (especially the CE) and the nominated institution then became a stake between management and unions.

Trade Unions

In France, an employer has very often to meet four different unions speaking for the same bargaining unit. This is so because they do not represent a particular craft or industry (apart from the CGC) but they represent all categories of employees and find themselves competing in the same areas for recruiting members. This multiplicity can be explained by the fact that unions do not only represent the immediate interests of the workers but also their long-term hopes, which is bound to lead to differences. The consequences of such a situation are especially felt in collective bargaining. Competition between unions may lead to a lack of consensus on the relative importance of the different claims put forward or to a 'highest bidder' situation of which the employer often takes advantage. On the other hand, multiplicity can also lead unions to complement each other. More and more unions gather their strength, principally CGT and CFDT. There is some empirical evidence that in firms where three unions are present, negotiations take place more frequently than in firms where they are more or less unions (see Bachy, Dupuy, Martin, 1974).

Type of employee

There are two systems to elect the representatives. First, the members of the CE are elected by a proportional representation system of votes of all employees in up to three electoral 'colleges' — manual and lower clerical grades; technicians and supervisory staff; and technical and managerial staff. Originally the third college was allowed only where the cadres represented over 5 per cent of the labour force, but since December 1972 it has also been possible where there are 25 cadres only. The distribution of seats between the three colleges or of employees within the colleges is regulated by collective agreement or by the departmental labour inspection in the case of disagreement.

Second, the *délégués de personnel* are represented in two colleges only: technicians and supervisory staff vote with the managerial staff. It follows from this that very often there is no unity within colleges including different categories. Coalition occur then which can completely alter the balance of power. (For any further legal specification concerning the CE and employee representation see Camerlynck, Lyon-Caen, 1973).

The main bargaining structure

Traditionally (since 1950) industry-level bargaining has been prevalent in France. Nevertheless local structures have been maintained for the least unionized industries (such as agriculture). For the engineering industry too, collective bargaining takes place at a regional level (mainly because the employers' associations are better organized at this level). Both parties expressed their preference for the industry level. For the union, it had the advantage of covering a maximum of employees — important when union membership is low. The employers were protected against unfair competition, only minima being agreed at this level. This preference showed an obvious lack of mutual recognition between the parties and was taken up by the legislator in the Act of February 1950, which distinguished three types of agreements: first, ordinary agreements at industry, regional, or local level; second, agreements which can be extended to other firms in a whole industry, although they were neither present nor represented when the agreement was signed; and third, plant-level agreements which were simple wage agreements.

Between 1960 and 1970 new bargaining levels have started to develop: multi-industry level and plant-level bargaining. As a consequence the Act of 1950 was brought up to date and modified by the Act of July 1971 which had three objectives: to organize plant-level and multi-industry bargaining (since 1971 plant-level agreements can deal with a wider range of issues), to widen the field covered by collective bargaining, and to strengthen the 'contractual' basis of negotiation. The parties have not yet adopted a definite position regarding the level at which bargaining should take place. Of course, there are tactical reasons which lead them to favour one level over another. But the question still remains as to whether it is possible in practice to co-ordinate the different levels and which will be the level to prevail (see Adam, Reynaud, Verdier, 1972). First of all, very often the level is more or less dictated by the nature of the issue under discussion. Conditions of work, bonuses, promotion, job evaluation, etc., because of their technicality can only be dealt with at plant-level, whereas complementary unemployment benefits have to be dealt with at multi-industry level. But apart from such issues there remain others for which the level is uncertain. Some are being shifted from one level to another — the most problematic being wages settlements.

At a time when the bargaining structure is changing it is very often difficult to say what are exactly the relationships among the different levels. Usually multi-industry agreements set up principles which lead afterwards to industry-level agreements (for instance the multi-level agreement on *mensualisation* for hourly paid workers was taken up by the different industries). As far as plant-level agreements are concerned, they have sometimes constituted innovatory agreements and been taken up by the law (e.g. fourth week of paid holidays in the Renault agreement in 1955) or at industry-level (reduction of the number of working-hours without any loss in wages), or at multi-industry level (complementary old-age pension benefits in the Renault agreement). But in general they tend not to be innovatory and take up or adapt a law or an agreement signed at a higher level, like the right for a trade-union section to be recognized within a firm or length of the working week (see Bachy, Dupuy, Martin, 1974).

Role and strength of unions in bargaining

Legally speaking, unions play a fundamental role in collective bargaining and at all levels. The importance of their role is made obvious in two ways as the outcome of their bargaining applies to all employees, unionized or not; and in a second way, as it is possible for an agreement to be extended to a whole industry which allows unions to bargain for firms not involved in the bargaining process. In practice, the strength of the union in bargaining depends on the balance of power (especially at plant level). At the latter level, it is determined by structural factors such as trade-union membership, competition among unions, militancy and education of workers, working of the representative institutions, type of management, etc., and more immediate contingencies such as the economic situation. This balance of power will determine the possible success of a strike. Concerning the latter point, one characteristic has been that in France unions did not have any strike funds. The CGT has choosen consciously not to have any, so that in case of need strikers would ask the public for help, and thus create a certain solidarity. Nevertheless, FO and CFDT have started to create such funds in order to exert pressures of a more realistic nature on employers.

Enforcement and sanctioning possibilities

This section deals with grievances which could not be refused to be satisfied through the normal channel, i.e. the employee delegate and collective agreements whose interpretation or implementation is problematic. Grievances may be taken to the *Conseil de Prudhommes* which has jurisdiction over a wide variety of issues arising out of the individual contract of employment or to local labour inspectors who are responsible for enforcing compliance with all labour legislation. But very often (see Reynaud, 1975) the awards made by the court concern the conditions of separation of an employee and not the problem of an employee who remains in the firm.

All collective agreements being legally binding, sanctions are foreseen in case an employer or a union does not respect them. Most frequently, the problem is not one of breach of contract but one of divergence of interpretation of some clauses by the parties (the first are usually dealt with by courts whereas the latter are dealt with by a *commission paritaire* in which both sides are equally represented). Lawsuits can be individual or collective (see Camerlynck, Lyon-Caen, 1973). But one must notice that it is often difficult to determine what falls within the *commission paritaire*'s competence and within the judge's competence. The recent tendency to increase the parties' autonomy suggests that the commission has to take the lead from the judge. There is no link between the grievance procedure and negotiations at plant level. First, negotiations at this level are still rare. Second, even when they exist it is not a 'permanent' type of negotiation and it is difficult for the agreement to take the day-to-day grievance into account.

2.3. The role of public powers

Three procedures for the resolution of conflicts of rights and of interests — at company level or above company level — are available by law. The Act of 11 February 1950 has established compulsory conciliation and optional arbitration and created a Superior Court of Arbitration. In 1955 this system was completed by a mediation procedure. The whole system was slightly modified in July 1971. To attempt conciliation through the conciliation procedure is obligatory but does not necessarily precede to a strike. Such procedures must be included in every collective agreement at national level and failing that or a settlement under such procedures, the dispute must be taken before a state conciliation commission. The latter is a three-party institution, whose members are nominated by the Minister of Labour following unions' and employers' suggestions. If conciliation succeeds then the outcome becomes similar in every way to a collective agreement. But conciliation does not have to succeed: the parties have to appear before the commission but do not necessarily have to reach a settlement.

If conciliation fails optional arbitration may take place. The award may be given by the arbitrator which is binding on the parties and against which an appeal may be made in the Superior Court.

Mediation is an intermediate and optional procedure between conciliation and arbitration. It is more of an amicable settlement and differs from arbitration by the fact that the mediator's recommendations are not binding on the parties. This procedure encourages the parties to make concessions because even in the event of the mediator's failure his recommendations are published, and public opinion may judge the parties' goodwill or insincerity.

Most industries traditionally refused to use any of these formal procedures (except during the period 1936-8). For about ten years, conciliation has been attempted on average for about 39 conflicts a year out of a total of 3,500 conflicts — in 1972, there were 29 attempts of conciliation. There were 5 mediations in 1970, 8 in 1971, 3 in 1972, and 2 in 1973. Arbitrations stood at 1 in 1971, 2 in 1972, and none in 1973.

The reasons why the parties fail to use such procedures are numerous. An important one is the fact that they are no more adapted to the present practice of industrial relations between the state, the unions, and the employers' associations (see the Sudreau Report which suggests some reforms relative to this topic). But the fact that such legal procedures are no longer used does not mean that the state intervenes less. On the contrary, the state intervenes more and more in conflicts and thus in different ways. At first sight, this can appear contradictory at a time when the government policy initiated by Chaban-Delmas consists of giving more autonomy to the respective parties. But precisely by leaving more freedom to the parties for solving their problems, the likelihood of the number and politicization of conflicts increases. The intervention of the state then becomes inevitable.

2.4. Participation on the regional and national level

The French Plan has, for about ten years, been the means through which consensus could be expressed on the main objectives of the economy, but this is no longer the case. Indeed, from 1960 onwards in particular, workers' and employers' associations have shown great interest in discussion and participation in planning. They could participate through representation in the 'modernizatin committees' which are of two types: first, the horizontal committees each of which deals with a problem common to several branches of the economy; and second, the vertical committees which study all the problems arising in a particular sphere. There are also two other institutionalized forms of discussion in which they participate as *de facto* representatives of social and economic groups — the Economic and Social Council and the Regional Economic development committees.

During this period, while criticism was being made of the procedures, information showed the growing importance attached to the plan by the unions. The employers' association took on the whole a favourable attitude, especially the Young Employers' Group who saw in the proposed system of participation the germ of a third way leading to peaceful resolution of the conflict between communism and capitalism. But in recent years, while the attitude of employers' associations has become more and more favourable, that of unions has become more and more reluctant. The CFDT's attitude has changed most. In 1960, it invested great hopes in the Plan and gave support to the idea of 'democratic planning'. However, its attitude changed, and in 1970 it temporarily withdrew its representatives from the modernization committees. CGT participation has always remained more or less limited, except during a period of active collaboration after the war. According to the CGT the Plan 'is the mere translation of the aims and wishes of the monopolies'. FO too, but for different reasons, expressed reservation and considered the plan no more than a starting-point for discussion. Although participation in planning has lost some of its importance for workers' associations and plays only a secondary role in their strategy, it still remains a means through which they can obtain information and express their points of view.

3. PROGRAMMATIC PERSPECTIVES, PROBLEMATIC ISSUES, AND DEVELOPMENTS

In the present situation, none of the social partners wants a complete transformatin of the Industrial Relations System. The two dominant unions (CGT and CFDT) consider that the industrial relations system cannot change without a corresponding change of society. This latter position has been reconfirmed, although the Left lost the elections in March 1978. Nevertheless this failure has provoked great disappointments among the militants and led the unions to adapt their strategies to the new situation. Whereas before the elections claims were somehow subordinated to a potential victory of the Left, it became clear after March 1978 that both unions were very keen to remain (for the CFDT) or become (for the CGT) more independent from the parties of the Left. They are now pressing the government and the employers' associations very strongly for the opening of negotiations at all levels and they both give a new priority to daily claims of workers in order to satisfy their immediate interests.

The most enlightened fringe of the employers and the government — conscious of the new demands and the spirit of May 1968 — had undertaken for a while a contractual policy — with the *contrat de progrès* — and several reforms. In this context, one event is of major importance: the Reform of the Enterprise i.e. the Sudreau Report which we shall examine below. After the elections of 1978 the government has also shown its willingness to improve the social climate by encouraging negotiations between the different unions and employers' associations.

The Sudreau Report

The committee created in July 1974 published its report in February 1975. Numerous collaborators participated in it: experts, twelve working groups, several unions and employers' associations. This report, continues the new law on collective bargaining of July 1971 which fostered negotiations between the partners, and it translates this latter orientation into limited but concrete proposals and suggestions. The Report starts with a diagnosis. This first part deals with the obstacles preventing complete change within the enterprise i.e. productivity, hierarchical relationships, the difficulty of a social dialogue due to the plurality of unions, ideological clashes, the ambivalent role of the State (indeed the State tries to introduce laws, but by doing so, does not take into account the diversity of French industrial structures). The second part contains a series of reforms (rather than one reform of the Enterprise) which can only be realized, according to the Report, in the following framework: local solutions have to be developed in order to give autonomy to the partners, and reforms can only be progressive and optional. Three types of problems are examined: the situation of the workers, the reform of company law, and new means for solving eventual bankruptcies and conflicts.

Concerning changes related to the workers, the Report advocates improvement of working conditions and more generally of living conditions (like housing and public transport). It puts emphasis too on a better functioning of the works councils and their sub-committees and argues that the representative unions should in fact and once for ever be recognized by employers. Finally, it encourages experimentation through which people could participate (i.e. autonomous work groups, etc.) and the diffusion of such experiments. But the most audacious proposal concerns the two-tier structure.

As far as company law is concerned, efforts have been made for the extension of the formula which was introduced by a law in 1966. It has been observed that this juridical form has not been very successful until now: one of the reasons being that the idea of collegiality in the Directory is not adapted to the French mentality. According to the 1966 law, the Directors and the President have to be nominated by the Supervisory Board. The Report suggests that from now on, the Directors (and their attributions) should be nominated by the President, after proposition by the Supervisory Board.

Other measures have also been taken to render this new system more flexible. For limited companies, several recommendations are expressed: one aims at separating the management function from the control function by distinguishing the role of the President and the role of the General Director, the former assuring the liaison between the Board of Directors and the General Director. Another measure tends to ameliorate the functioning of the Board of Directors, to reduce the number of people who hold a plurality of offices, and to advocate the more frequent change of Directors. Finally, shareholders' means of expression will be increased in two ways: stable shareholders would get more rights (such as the right to propose Directors and to vote by post) and specific protection will be introduced to safeguard the interests of shareholders in the minority. Both a modernization and a diversification of juridical statutes for firms should help the creation of enterprises and the elimination of certain anomalies. A last outcome of the Report, for industrial companies, which are in a state of bankruptcy, suggests the creation of a warning procedure for employees, shareholders, and creditors, with a right of intervention for these groups, as well as the creation of an assistance body, helping the firm in its diagnosis, its recovery and reconversion plans; these latter proposals are very relevant to the present economic situation.

What should one conclude from the Report? 'What is certainly most innovating concerns changes of daily relationships within firms: for once the expression of workers has been at the core of experts' preoccupations.' (Reynaud, 1975.) But nevertheless a major theoretical critique can be made of the Report: how can one speak of reforms within the enterprise without at the same time envisaging a transformation of the economic system, in which the enterprise develops a system which conditions it and which is at the same time originated by the enterprise? For this reason CFDT and CGT expressed great reservations about the Report.

As to the promoters of Industrial Democracy in the enterprise, one has to specify that the definition of the problem is hampered by each political group and its own terminology, which depends on 'whether the political thrust is working class or bourgeois, reformist or revolutionary' (see Bornstein, Fine, 1977). The three terms which cover the problem are *participation, autogestion*, and *gestion démocratique*. Whereas *participation* refers to employees' involvement in decision-making and is the word favoured by the Right and the Centre, the term *autogestion* is used by the Socialist Party and the CFDT who, since 1968, have put emphasis on the learning and development of workers' consciousness through symbolic strikes like LIP. The PCF and the CGT speak of *gestion démocratique*; they are more suspicious about self-managed experiments (despite recent talks) and situate the debate more directly in questions of political change (for further details on the theoretical approaches of each group see Bornstein and Fine, 1977).

Among employers' associations, the two most progressive bodies – the *Centre des Jeunes Dirigeants* and *Entreprise et Progrès* – have favoured experimental schemes, as well as a transformation of the juridical statutes of the enterprise. Besides, some study groups have developed which look upon Industrial Democracy in more theoretical and critical terms than parties and unions do – like the Group for Self-management Studies whose journal is entitled *Autogestion et Socialisme*.

Concerning the public in general, one can acknowledge that social conflict and Industrial Democracy problems no longer lie only in the firm, but also within social movements of consumers, feminists, ecologists, regionalists, urbanists, etc. These new movements which struggle against different types of domination exerted by certain groups within society are not yet channelled into a real social force. The great issue is whether trade unions can and will play the role of political 'operators' for such movements (Touraine, 1976).

REFERENCES

Adam, G., Lucas, M. (1976), 'Les institutions de représentation du personnel en France: bilan et perspectives', *Revue de Droit Social*, 1.

    Reynaud, J. D. (1978), *Conflits du travail et changement social*, Paris: PUF.

    Reynaud, J. D., Verdier, J. M. (1972), *La négociation collective en France*, Paris: Editions ouvrières.

    Bon, F., Capdevielle, J., Mouriaux, R. (1970), *L'ouvrier Français en 1970*, Paris: Colin.

Bachy, J. P. (1976), 'Evolution des modes de règlement des grèves en France', *Revue de Droit Social*, 1.

    Dupuy, F., Martin, D. (1974), *Représentation et négociation dans l'entreprise*, Sceaux: Publication du CRESST.

Barjonet, A. (1968), *La CGT*, Paris: Seuil.

Bergounioux, A. (1975), *FO*, Paris: Seuil.

Bloch-Laine, F. (1963), *Pour une réforme de l'entreprise*, Paris: Seuil.

Bornstein, S., Fine, K. (1977), 'Worker Control in France: Recent Political Developments', in G. David Garson (ed.), *Workers' self-management in Industry: the Western European Experience*, New York, Praeger.

Bourdet, Y. (1974), *Pour l'autogestion*, Paris: Anthropos.
Brizay, B. (1975), *Le Patronat*, Paris: Seuil.
Caire, G. (1971), *Les Syndicats ouvriers en France*, Paris: A. Colin.
  (1973), *Les relations industrielles*, Paris: Dalloz.
Camerlinck, G. H., Lyon-Caen, G. (1973), *Droit du Travail*, Paris: Précis Dalloz.
Crozier, M. (1963), *Le Phénomène bureaucratique*, Paris: Ed. Minuit.
Collectif (1971), *La CFDT*, Paris: Seuil.
Centre des Jeunes Dirigeants (1974), *L'autorité dans l'entreprise*, Paris.
Carre, J. J., Dubois, P., Malinvaud, E. (1973), *Abrégé de la croissance française*, Paris: Seuil.
Delamotte, Y. (1971), 'Les tendances recentes de la négotiation collective en France', *ILO Review*, 103.
  (1959), 'Conflict industriel et participation ouvrière', *Sociologie du travail*, 1.
Dubois, P., Durand, C., Bose, S. (1976), 'Décentralisation Industrielle et Relations de travail', *Travaux et Recherches de Prospective: La Documentation Française*, No. 61.
Dubois, P., Durand, C. (1975), *La grève*, Paris: A. Colin.
Durand, M. (1977), *Les conflits du travail*, Sceaux: Publication CRESST.
  Harff, Y. (1976), *Mouvement écologique, mouvement ouvrier*, Paris: Mouton.
Duverger, M. (1971), *Institutions politiques*, Paris: Presses universitaires de France.
Erbes-Seguin, S. (1972), *Sociologie du Travail*, Paris: Dalloz.
  (1971), *La démocratie dans les syndicats*, Paris: Mouton.
Friedmann, G., Naville, P. (1964), *Traité de Sociologie du travail*, Paris: A. Colin (2 vols.).
Goguel, F., Grosser, A. (1975), *La politique en France*, Paris: A. Colin.
INSEE (1976), *Tableaux de l'Economie Française*, Editions INSEE.
Javillier, J. C. (1976), *Les conflits du travail*, Paris: PUF.
Lefranc, G. (1969), *Le mouvement syndical de la libération à Mai 68*, Paris: Payot.
  (1976), *Les organisations patronales en France*, Paris: Payot.
Le Monde (1977), *L'année économique et social*, Dossier.
Reynaud, J. D. (1975), *Les syndicats en France*, Paris: Seuil (2 vols.).
  (1976), *Evolution et tendances de la négociation collective en France*, Paris: Ed. Ouvrières.
  Dassa, S., Madorf, P. (1971), 'Les évènements de Mai 68 et le système des relations professionnelles', *Sociologie du Travail*, 13.
Sallon, M. (1976), *L'autogestion*, Paris: PUF.
Sellier, F. (1976), *Les relations industrielles*, Paris: PUF.
Sudreau, P. (1975), *La réforme de l'entreprise*, Paris: Seuil.
Touraine, A. (1976), 'L'avenir du syndicalisme', *CFDT aujourd'hui*, 19.
  (1969), *La société post-industrielle*, Paris: Denoel.
Weiss, D. (1978), *La democratie industrielle: cogestion ou contrôle ouvrier?*, Paris: Ed. ouvrières.

THE ITALIAN INDUSTRIAL RELATIONS SYSTEM

1. GENERAL SITUATION AND BACKGROUND

1.1 Political and socio-economic background

Since the late 1960s, Italian politics have been characterized and conditioned by a profound crisis in the Christian Democratic Party (DC) — Italy's largest party which has been in power since the early post-war years. This crisis, which began with the by now famous 'hot autumn' of 1968-9, came to a head in 1975-6 with the major electoral gains obtained by the Italian Communist Party (PCI) first in local and then in national elections (see Table 11.1).

An indication of the PCI's recent electoral gains and of the profound changes which have taken place in the balance of power in Italy's representative institutions (parliament, regional, and local government) is given by the fact that most major Italian cities — Milan, Turin, Rome, Florence, Naples — are now governed by left-wing coalitions. The exclusion of the Communist Party however, at national level has led to a period of great political uncertainty and instability. Over the past few years the Christian Democrats have found it increasingly difficult to put together a working majority in Parliament and have recently turned for support to the Italian Socialist Party. At the same time the PCI's participation in government has come to be regarded by many observers as the only effective guarantee of socio-political stability, particularly in view of the grave economic situation of the country. Italy's economic difficulties in recent years fall within the context of problems affecting the world economy since the general crisis of 1973. The difficulties faced by the Italian economy in the mid 1970s, however have been particularly acute due to the country's backlog of unresolved socio-economic problems (see Arnato and Runci, 1974).

The 1950s and early 1960s were a period of rapid economic growth for Italy. Between 1955 and 1962, in fact, the Gross Domestic Product grew at an average annual rate of approximately 6 per cent while industrial production increased at an average annual rate of 9.4 per cent (see Table 11.2).

Italy's so-called 'economic miracle' came to an end with the recession of 1964-5. Since 1963, in fact, the Italian economy has not been able to achieve or sustain the same high levels of performance as in the early 1960s (Salvati, 1974). Thus, in the period between 1963 and 1970, the average rate of growth in the GDP declined to approximately 5 per cent per year. At the same time, the average annual rate of increase in industrial production declined to 6.2 per cent. As can be seen from Table 11.2, the 1970s saw a further, and yet more drastic, decline in the general level of economic performance.

During the course of the 1970s, and particularly after 1973, there was also a serious deterioration in the country's balance of payments situation. Starting in 1973, there was also a dramatic rise in Italy's annual rate of inflation which

Table 11.1.
*Percentage of Valid Votes and Number of Seats obtained by Major
Political Parties in Parliamentary Elections 1958-1976*

	1958		1963		1968		1972		1976	
	% votes	seats	% votes	seats	% votes	seats	% votes	seats	% votes	seats
Christian Democratic Party (DC)	42.3	273	38.3	260	39.1	266	38.7	266	38.7	262
Italian Communist Party (PCI)	22.7	140	25.3	166	26.9	177	27.1	179	35.4	228
Italian Socialist Party (PSI)	14.2	84	13.8	87			9.6	61	9.6	57
Italian Social & Democratic Party (PSDI)	4.6	22	6.1	32	14.5	91	5.1	29	3.4	15
Italian Republican Party (PRI)	1.4	6	1.4	6	2.0	9	2.9	15	3.1	15
Italian Liberal Party (PIL)	3.5	17	7.0	40	5.8	31	3.9	20	1.3	4
Italian Social Movement (MSI)	4.8	24	5.1	27	4.5	24	8.7	56	6.1	25
Others	6.3	30	3.0	12	7.2	32	4.0	4	3.4	14
Total	100.0	596	100.0	630	100.0	630	100.0	630	100.0	630

Source: Annuario Statistico Italiano.

Table 11.2.
*Average Annual Rate of Growth of Real Gross Domestic Product at
Market Prices and Average Annual Rates of Change in Total Industrial
Production (expressed in percentages)*

Period	Gross Domestic Product	Total Industrial Production
1955–1962	6.2	9.4
1963–1970	5.1	6.2
1971–1077	2.7	2.9

Sources: GDP figures calculated from data reported in United Nations, *Yearbook of National Accounts Statistics;* Total Industrial Production figures calculated from data reported in OECD, *Industrial Production: Historical Statistics.*

currently remains among the highest in Europe. Thus, for example, the annual rate of increase in consumer prices went up from approximately 5 per cent in 1970 to 10 per cent in 1973, and to 19 per cent in 1977. (See Table 11.3.)

Italy's precarious economic position and high rate of inflation has prompted the government, under pressure from the IMF, to introduce a series of deflationary measures (cuts in public spending, increased taxation, etc.) over the past couple of years which have had serious repercussions on employment levels. (See Table 11.4.)

Table 11.3.

Annual Rate of Change in Consumer Prices and in General Prices 1970–1977 (expressed in percentages)

Year	Consumer Prices	General Prices
1970	5.1	7.3
1971	5.0	3.4
1972	5.6	4.0
1973	10.3	17.8
1974	19.4	40.8
1975	17.2	17.1
1976	19.6	16.5
1977	19.0	18.0
Average Annual Rate of Change for Period 1960–9	3.7	2.0
Average Annual Rate of Change for Period 1970–7	12.6	15.6

Source: Figures adapted from data reported in *Annuario Statistico Italiano.*

Table 11.4.

Rates of Unemployment* – 1960, 1970–78

Year	% Unemployed Out of Total Labour Force
1960	4.0
1965	3.6
1970	3.2
1971	3.2
1972	3.7
1973	3.5
1974	3.9
1975	3.3.
1976	3.5

*Includes people currently unemployed, underemployed, or in search of employment.
Source: Annuario Statistico Italiano.

There is a real danger, however, that the deflationary policy currently being pursued by the government, besides leading to a further major rise in unemployment, might actually bring about an economic recession. Because of this danger, it is now generally agreed that there is a pressing need to boost domestic demand and to encourage major programmes of capital investments.

In the medium-to-long-term, however, this is not likely to prove an easy task. Among other things, such a policy implies a fundamental restructuring of Italy's industrial system. Over the past two decades, there has been a relative contraction in the country's industrial base, as manifested, for example, by the growing shift in resources from productive to non-productive activities (Paci, 1973; Salvati, 1975), Table 11.5, showing broad shifts in patterns of employment between different sectors of the economy, provides an indication of this tendency.

Since the last war, there has been a major shift away from agriculture. The full magnitude and significance of this change can best be appreciated if we consider that in 1950 over one in three of Italy's working population gained its living from the land, while by 1975 less than one in seven of the labour force was employed in agriculture. As can be seen from Table 11.5, however, over the past twenty years, the service sector has grown even more rapidly than industry as a whole. Over this period, in fact, some industries have actually experienced a contraction in employment. The industries which have probably been most affected in this respect have been textiles, steel, and chemicals (Arnato and Runci, 1974).

The contraction experienced by these industries has further contributed to the general deterioration in the state of the labour market in recent years (Salvati, 1976). The effects of the crisis have been felt most deeply in the economically weaker, marginal areas of Southern Italy — areas with a long history of chronic unemployment and underemployment and with a predominantly low-skilled labour force. This, in turn, has further accentuated the imbalance in development between the North and the South, an age-old problem of the Italian economy (Salvati, 1976).

Table 11.5.
Changes in the Structure and Distribution of the Labour Force 1960-1970

Year	Agriculture		Industry		Other Activities		Total Active Labour Force	
	*	**	*	**	*	**	+	% of Total Population
1960	6,567	32.5	7,388	36.6	6,181	30.6	20,136	41.1
1965	4,898	25.7	7,659	40.3	6,446	33.9	19,003	37.3
1970	3,613	19.3	8,117	43.4	6,963	37.2	18,693	35.4
1975	2,964	15.6	8,305	43.7	7,727	40.6	18,996	34.5

*Annual Averages in thousands.
+Annual Averages in thousands excluding unemployed, undermeployed, or people in search of employment.
**As % of total active Labour Force.
Source: figures adapted from data reported in *Annuario Statistico Italiano.*

2. NATIONAL INDUSTRIAL RELATIONS

2.1. Legal Framework

The basic legal framework of the Italian system of Industrial Relations is provided by (a) the Republican Constitution of 1948, (b) certain sections of the Civil Code drawn up during the last years of the Fascist era (1938-41), and (c) basic labour legislation passed by Parliament at various stages during the post-war period (see Ichino, 1975).

The Italian constitution contains a number of articles referring to certain fundamental labour rights and principles. The most important ones are those relating to: the right of employees to an adequate remuneration, to annual holidays, and to weekly rest (art. 36); equal rights for women and juveniles and the protection of working mothers and minors (art. 37); the right to adequate social assistance and security (art. 38); freedom of association (union rights and collective bargaining as a means of regulating employment relations (art. 39); and the right to strike (art. 40).

Many of the articles contained in Volume V of the Fascist Civil Code regulating various aspects of work relations have now been repealed as unconstitutional. A number of sections, however, are still in force. The most important among these is the section which attributes to employers/managers the exclusive power to manage, organize, and run productive activities within an enterprise (art. 1986, 2104, and 2106). These general powers, however, have now been curtailed by the enactment of more specific legislation (particularly the 1970 Statuto dei Diritti dei Lavoratori) aimed at limiting the power of employers/managers *vis-à-vis* labour.

The relevant post-war legislation covers a number of different areas. Among the most important laws which have been passed are those relating to: unemployment and lay-off benefits and 'guaranteed' incomes (laws of 1945, 1949, 1968, and 1975); the protection of minors, juveniles, invalids, and working mothers (1967, 1968, 1971); apprenticeships (1955 and 1968); national holidays (1953); domestic work (1958 and 1973); individual dismissals (1963 and 1966); accident insurance, pensions, and social security (1965 and 1969). Lastly, there is the 1970 law known as the Statuto dei Diritii dei Lavoratori. The *Statuto* – which is a sort of Labour Bill of Rights – is probably the most important piece of labour legislation of the post-war period. It is a comprehensive attempt to limit the scope of managerial power by defining a set of basic rights and freedoms to which both employees and unions are entitled within the place of work (see Pera, 1975).

It is worth noting that even though the law plays a fairly important part in regulating employment relations in Italy, the content of this legislation tends to reflect existing collective bargaining agreements. Usually, in fact, the law does no more than generalize and formalize rights and norms already won or established through collective bargaining (e.g. the 1966 law regulating individual dismissals followed an inter-confederal agreement on dismissals signed the previous year, while the 1970 Statuto incorporates and formalizes some of the labour gains obtained during the 1969 round of industry-wide negotiations, particularly in so far as union rights at plant level are concerned). In other words, in Italy the law seldom introduces completely new principles or sets down norms and deals with questions which have not already been the subject of negotiation between unions and employers (see Guidi *et al.*, 1974).

2.2. Structure of the Industrial Relations System

Historical Roots of the Industrial Relations System

The Italian movement dates back to before the First International of 1864. It was not until 1906, however, that the first national trade union, the General Confederation of Labour (CGL), was established as the labour arm of the Socialist Party. The first collective agreements between employers and workers and between unions and employers also date back to this period. Both the

Socialist party and the trade unions were outlawed during the Fascist era and remained illegal until the Liberation of 1943-5 (Horowitz, 1963).

The 1944 Pact of Rome between Communist, Socialist, and Christian Democratic union leaders provided for the establishment of a single labour confederation, the Confederazione Generale Italiana del Lavoro (CGIL). With the outbreak of the Cold War, however, the Christian Democratic faction and the right wing of the Socialist faction split off from the Communist-dominated CGIL. By 1950, there were three major confederations of trade unions divided along ideological and political lines: the CGIL, tied to the Communist Party and the left-wing Socialists, the CISL, tied to the Christian Democrats, and the UIL, aligned with the Republican and the Social Democratic parties. The CGIL was and still is by far the largest of the three confederations (Horowitz, 1963).

The strong political orientation of Italian unionism in the immediate post-war period and the 1950s is both a cause and an effect of the close ties which existed between the confederations and the various parties during these early years. These ties were maintained through a system of interlocking directorates. The confederations were also dependent on the parties for financial support and for personnel at the national and local level which further strengthened the position of the parties in relation to the unions. As a result, the parties were in a position to influence and, if need be, determine union policies which often reflected purely party political concerns and ideologies.

Trade Union Structure and Organization

Each confederation encompasses a number of separate unions and has two cross-cutting organizational structures; a horizontally or geographically based structure and a vertically or category-based structure. This distinction between vertical and horizontal structure tends to coincide with a distinction between structures oriented towards specific industrial problems and more politically oriented structures.

Unions in Italy are organized on an industrial basis. In the immediate post-war period there was no formally recognized union organization inside the plant. It was not until 1954 that the unions began to establish factory-level organizations. Plant-level unionism, however, still remained at an embryonic stage of development by the late 1950s (La Palombara, 1957). The basic unit of union structure remained the category organization staffed by full-time officers (provincial secretariat and executive committee). In each locality or area, whenever a sufficient number of workers in a given sector of industry (e.g. metalworking or textiles) had been organized, a provincial organization was formed (Horowitz, 1963). Above the area level is the national organization, the apex of which is the national secretariat and the national executive committee. The category unions concern themselves primarily with the occupational interests of workers and with collective bargaining.

The individual category unions are in turn affiliated to the confederations. Each level of the union organization is affiliated with a corresponding confederal unit so that the confederal structure parallels the union structure.

At the area level there are the confederal chambers of labour to which are affiliated the various provincial union organizations. Traditionally, the chambers of labour have constituted the main local headquarters of the labour movement. The chamber secretariat outlines broad policy for the various provincial organizations and until not too long ago it also provided these units with technical assistance relating to strikes, negotiations, and contract interpretation. At the apex of the confederal structure are the national confederal committees (national confederal congress, confederal secretariat, and confederal executive committee). The purpose of these supreme policy-making bodies is to work out the broad, largely political, outlines of labour policy and to integrate and co-ordinate the goals and efforts of all the category unions and provincial chambers which are encompassed by the confederation. Traditionally, the horizontal confederal structure has been the dominant one. Over the past fifteen years, however, there has been a general strengthening of the vertical organization at the expense of the horizontal one, so that individual category unions have become increasingly independent *vis-à-vis* the confederations (Cella, 1977).

System of Collective Bargaining

In the immediate post-war period, politicized and horizontally-based labour organizations were accompanied by a highly centralized system of collective bargaining based on national all-industry (so-called inter-confederal) agreements between the labour confederations and the employers' association (*Confindustria*). These all-industry agreements set wage rates in a number of basic skill classifications, and established a sliding scale cost-of-living allowance for the entire country with zonal differentials. They also dealt with lay-off policy and with grievance procedures. In addition, there were also national industry-wide (category) agreements for each main branch of industry (metal-working, textiles, mining, etc.) which sometimes improved upon the standards fixed in the inter-confederal agreements. By the late 1950s, in spite of the resistance of the Confindustria, these industry-wide agreements had become the main feature of the Italian system of collective bargaining, which virtually excluded any negotiations at plant level (see Giugni, 1969; Garavini, 1977).

Plant-Level Participative System in the 1950s and 1960s

The main representative body at company level up till 1970, was the Internal Commission (Commissione Interna or CI). General Elections for the CI were held on a yearly basis with both unionized and unorganized employees voting on lists of candidates drawn up by the unions. Inter-union competition for seats on the CI was always intense. The commissions, however, did not form part of the union structure and in this sense they were similar to works' councils. During the 1950s, the main function of the CI was to deal with individual grievances and in general to represent employees in their relationships with management. After 1960, however, against the strong resistance of employers, the commissions gradually began to play a more clearly defined bargaining role and to negotiate plant-level agreements with management over a limited set of issues (e.g. production bonuses, piece-rates, etc.). (See Bianchi, 1969; Giugni, 1969.)

Employers' Associations

Private employers in the industrial sector are mainly organized in the Confindustria. The Confindustria is a national confederation encompassing a series of separate federations and has local units at the regional and provincial level representing private employers in small, medium, and large firms in a variety of industrial sectors. Parallel to the Confindustria is the *Intersind,* the employers' association representing public enterprises. Employers in agriculture and commerce are affiliated with the *Confagricultura* and the *Confcommercio* respectively.

Trends and Developments Since the Early 1960s

Over the past 15 years the Italian industrial relations system has undergone some major changes. In most cases the process of change began gradually but became particularly pronounced from the late 1960s. The late 1960s and early 1970s, in fact, marked an important turning-point for the Italian system of industrial relations. The major changes which have taken place since the early 1960s, summarized here, occured in six areas:

(1) Relations between unions and political parties, where an increased autonomy of confederations and unions from political parties in terms of organization, ideology, and policy-making occurred (Tronti, 1977).

(2) Inter-union relations, where the gradual process of unification of trade-union movement with a substantial *rapprochement* between the three main components of the labour movement took place in the late 1960s and the early 1970s. After 1970, the close organizational ties between the CGIL, CISL, and UIL, with the creation of unitary (federal-type) structures at all levels, accompanied by a significant decline in the level of inter-union conflict and competition, particularly at plant level, were established. (Baglioni, 1977).

(3) Relations between cateogry unions and confederations, where autonomy and independence of individual unions *vis-à-vis* national confederations increased.

(4) Increasing Union Membership. Union membership is still optional and varies considerably between regions and industries. In industries such as engineering, chemicals, and textiles, however, over 70 per cent of the labour force is unionized.

(5) Trade union structure which was strengthened and consolidated at local and grass roots level. Particularly,

(*a*) the emergence of new forms of representation and organization at plant level, i.e. the election of shop-floor delegates, and the creation of Factory Councils as basic units of union structure at the company level to replace the CI and the plant level union locals (Sezione Aziendale Sindacale in 1970); and

(*b*) the establishment of zonal organizations in the 1970s linking plant-level units and provincial organization.

(6) Collective bargaining structure, which was gradually decentralized, with an increasing emphasis on plant-level negotiations in addition to industry-wide contracts, as evidenced in the growing number of company agreements between management and the CI or the provincial unions (1970), and between

management and the Factory Councils (1970s). (See Giugni, 1969; Guidi *et al.*, 1974; Giugni, 1977).

2.3. Worker Representation and Trade Union Organization at Plant Level

Main legal basis

In Italy there is a considerable body of legislation regulating employment relations. At the same time, though, there is no legally defined, detailed institutional framework for participation at plant level, as in some other European countries. In Italy, in fact, there is no system of codetermination nor are there works councils or other legally defined bipartite (labour-management) bodies at company level. The main representative body at plant level is the *union* Factory Council (CdF), the internal structure and functions of which are not regulated by law. Consultative-participative types of institutions comprising representatives from both management and labour are essentially alien to the Italian system of industrial relations. After the War, a type of codetermination scheme was introduced in Italy; but this experiment failed and was abandoned by the early 1950s (see Zanzardo, 1977). The negative experience with the so-called Consigli di Gestione caused widespread disenchantment with the idea of co-partnerships and reinforced the unions' ideological opposition to 'participation'. This general rejection of bipartite type of institutions is reflected in the kind of legislation which has been passed over the past twenty years and serves to account for the fact that in Italy there are no legally prescribed channels and procedures for participation and consultation at plant level. The main emphasis of legislation during the post-war period has been to establish a broad framework for industrial relations. This legal framework sets limits on the absolute power of management but at the same time it allows for a large element of voluntarism in labour-management relations and allows for the two sides to develop substantive and procedural norms, relatively independent of specific legal constraints.

The basis of this framework is contained in legislation safeguarding certain basic labour rights and freedoms. Probably the most important legislation in this respect is the Statuto of 1970 (law No. 300) relating to collective bargaining as a means of regulating employment relations, to union rights, and to individual freedom. In addition, the Statuto also prohibits employers from supporting or financing 'company' unions and formally recognizes the right of elected representatives within the plant to carry out their union activities during company time without management interference. More specifically, the Statuto sets down the minimum number of hours which employers are required to put at the disposal of union representatives for the fulfilment of their functions, establishes the right of unions to hold group or mass meetings at the plant during working-hours (a certain number of these meetings can be held on company time), and requires employers to provide the CdF with a permanent meeting-place within the plant and with adequate space for the posting of union notices and communications.

The Statuto also includes a number of other articles which limit the freedom of action and power of employers *vis-à-vis* employees. Among the most important of these articles are those that restrict the use by management of company guards who control and monitor the behaviour of employees; which prohibit employers from conducting private medical inspections in cases of absenteeism; regulate the application of disciplinary measures and set down appropriate appeals procedures; and limit the scope of managerial discretion in the assignment of tasks and in the transfer of employees. The above legislation, together with the 1966 law regulating individual dismissals (law no. 604) provides the basic legal framework for plant-level industrial relations in Italy.

Worker representation at plant level: shop-floor delegates and factory councils

In recent years, there have been major changes in the system of representation at plant level with the emergence in 1969–70 of shop-floor representatives (delegati) and the creation of Factory Councils (*Consigli di Fabbrica* or CdF). The new system of representation at plant level is directly linked to the system of trade-union organization. Usually, there are three main unions at plant level, each affiliated with one of the three main labour confederations. Each union is organized on an industrial basis and recruits its membership from all sections of the work-force (both blue- and white-collar workers). In addition to the unions, a number of more overtly political, left-wing groups such as Lotta Continua, Potere Operaio, Manifesto, etc., may also be active at plant level.

Each homogeneous group of either blue- or white-collar workers (i.e. employees performing the same or similar tasks within an establishment) elects its own representative. The size of these constituencies varies but on the average, in the metalworking industry, for example, they consist of between 60 and 100 workers. An establishment with 1,000 employees, therefore, could have anything between 10 and 20 delegates. The method of election of shop-floor representatives varies within and between industries. Usually, however, the delegates are elected by secret ballot. Elections are often preceded by a lot of canvassing on the part of the unions and, once elected, there are usually strong informal pressures on non-union representatives to join one of the main unions. Election is generally on the basis of a simple majority. The term of office usually lasts between one and two years, but delegates are subject to recall by the group at any time (a recall motion requires the signatures of an absolute majority of the group). Shop-floor delegates are the backbone of trade union organization at the grass-roots level. As such, they perform two main functions which at times may be difficult to reconcile: (a) to represent the interests of the union at shop-floor level and (b) to represent the immediate interests of members of their work-group *vis-à-vis* management. More specifically, and allowing for considerable variations in actual practice and performance, the function of delegates is to keep workers informed about trade-union policies and implement these policies at shop-floor level, to deal with individual and group grievances and disputes, and to enforce the day-to-day application of existing collective bargaining agreements and in general to insure that the rights of employees are not infringed upon by management (see Sedi, 1977; Anderlini, 1977).

All delegates are automatically members of the CdF which is the main representative body at plant level. As such, the CdF is composed of representatives from all sectors of the work force. The CdF does not necessarily meet at regular intervals. Usually, however, it meets at least once a month or even more frequently if the need arises. All meetings of the CdF are held at the plant during working-hours (company time). Generally speaking, the functions of the CdF are to formulate and to implement trade-union policies at plant level and to represent the work-force to the management. More specifically, the CdF is responsible for co-ordinating and directing the activities of shop-floor delegates and for negotiating plant-level collective bargaining agreements on terms and conditions of employment.

The CdF in turn appoints an executive committee which varies in size depending on the size of the CdF. In theory, the function of the executive committee is simply to co-ordinate the activities of the CdF and to carry out its decisions. In practice, however, the executive is the main decision-making centre of the CdF, usually playing a direct and active role in the formulation and initiation of policy. The executive Committee usually meets slightly more frequently than the CdF, has the power to convene the CdF, and reports directly back to it. The proposals of the executive are subject to the approval of the CdF as a whole. Appointment to the executive committee is generally for a period of between one and two years. Members of the executive are usually not allowed to hold office for more than one term at a time, so as to insure a certain amount of rotation. New members of the executive are nominated by out-going members, but are subject to the approval of the CdF as a whole.

Under recommendation of the executive, the CdF selects two or three full-time officials (*membri fissi*), i.e. delegates who are permanently detached from production and who are responsible for conducting the day-to-day business of the CdF. These full-time officials often are, yet they need not necessarily be, members of the executive committee. Their term in office usually lasts one year, after which they are generally not allowed to serve as full-time officers again for a given period (sometimes as long as two years).

Inter-union conflict and competition at plant level

The degree of inter-union conflict at plant level varies considerably depending on the situation and, in any case, is difficult to assess on an absolute scale. There is little doubt, however, that over the past few years, and particularly since the late 1960s and early 1970s, there has been a marked improvement in inter-union relations at plant level. Evidence of this change can be seen at both the institutional and the behavioural levels. The establishment of factory councils is particularly important in this respect. The CdF, in fact, is essentially a joint or unitary structure, in the sense that it is composed of delegates belonging to all three unions. A union still retains its own identity within the plant. But instead of there being three completely separate and often hostile union organizations as in the past, there is now a single federal type of institution in the form of the CdF. At the behavioural–attitudinal level, the trend towards increased co-operation is reflected in a far greater readiness on the part of the unions to co-ordinate their policies, to engage in joint action, and to present a united front against management, e.g. development of common collective bargaining platforms, adoption of common bargaining strategies and tactics, and joint negotiation and acceptance of plant-level agreements (Sedi, 1977).

On the whole, one could argue that there is now quite a high degree of co-operation between the three main unions. It is difficult to say whether this type of co-operative relationship will continue in the near future due to the uncertainty of the present political situation. Barring any major political and economic changes, however, any increases which might occur in the level of inter-union conflict are likely to be only of a temporary and localized nature.

The development of closer inter-union ties clearly does not mean that there no longer is competition or disagreement between the unions. Inter-union competition is particularly evident during membership drives and at election time. In addition to competing for members and for seats on the CdF (and in the various committees of the Council), the unions also frequently disagree over major policy issues at plant level. Often, however, superimposed upon these inter-union divisions are major intra-union cleavages over policies and tactics.

In this type of situation, the coalitions which do form within the CdF tend to be more unstable and to shift depending on the nature of the issues at stake so that the divisions which do emerge often cut across union lines. In any case, over the past few years there has been a broad convergence in union policy. This convergence has been accompanied by a greater readiness on the part of the unions to compromise for the sake of union unity, thus resulting in a substantial decline in the level of inter-union conflict at plant level.

2.4. Developments in the System of Collective Bargaining

Over the past fifteen years there has been a general trend towards the decentralization of collective bargaining in Italy. Until 1960–3, national agreements were the main source of regulation of working conditions in Italian industry. After 1960, plant-level agreements were gradually introduced and became increasingly more important. This trend has accelerated since the mid–late 1960s so that in the past few years there has been a significant shift in the locus of collective bargaining (see Giugni, 1969; Giugni, 1973; Guidi et al., 1974; Giugni, 1977).

Main bargaining structure

The Italian system of industrial relations is essentially characterized by a two-tier system of collective bargaining. This system — known as 'articulated bargaining' — became established in the early 1960s and combines industry-wide agreements with plant-level bargaining. Industry-wide agreements cover an entire industrial sector (e.g. metalworking) and are renegotiated approximately every three years. These national agreements serve to fix minimum wage rates and general conditions of employment for the industry as a whole. More detailed supplementary negotiations covering piece-rates, rest periods, production bonuses, increases in basic wages, job evaluation, grading, etc. are then carried out at company level in an attempt to improve on the terms of conditions established in the national agreements. Company agreements usually have no fixed term of duration, i.e.

terms and conditions of employment may be renegotiated at any time. Sometimes one or even two agreements are negotiated during the three-year duration of an industry-wide contract.

The two sets of negotiations are interrelated and complementary in the sense that there is a close co-ordination of union action at the national and local level. From the unions' point of view, the national agreements not only serve to establish minima for the industry as a whole but they also serve as a basis for formulating more detailed and advanced demands at plant level. The gains obtained at company level in turn become a point of departure for the formulation of the next national claims and a basis for the next round of industry-wide negotiations. Thus, even though the system of articulated bargaining allows much greater scope for local negotiations than did the more centralized system of bargaining of the late 1940s and 1950s, national-level agreements still play an important part in the Italian system of industrial relations.

Scope of bargaining and content of demands

In Italy there is no formal legislation defining the scope or limits of collective bargaining at either national or plant level. Whether or not a given type of issue enters the collective bargaining arena depends on the relative power of unions and employers.

Over the past 15 years and particularly since the mid-1960s along with the decentralization of collective bargaining, there has also been an enlargement in the scope or area of bargaining to decisions which were once the sole prerogative of management. In other words, collective agreements now tend to cover a broader range of issues and to provide a more detailed and intensive regulation of employment relations than in the past. (Guidi *et al.*, 1974; Romagnoli, 1977). Alongside these developments, in recent years there has also been a change in the actual content of union demands or claims. Two of the most important developments in this respect have been: first, a growing emphasis on greater egalitarianism, reflected for example, in demands for across the board (flat-) wage increases aimed at reducing pay differentials both within and between different categories of blue- and white-collar workers, demands for automatic promotion aimed at increasing career mobility, and demands for a reduction in the number of grades and for the adoption of a single grading system encompassing both white- and blue-collar workers, aimed at reducing status differentials between different categories of employees; and second, a decreasing emphasis on the monetarization of work, reflected, for example, in demands for the introduction of day-wage payment systems in lieu of individual and group-incentive schemes and systems based on payments by results. With the recent economic recession there has also been a growing emphasis on greater job security. This concern has manifested itself in demands for a guaranteed income as a form of insurance against short-time working and in demands for greater job guarantees as a hedge against redundancies etc.

In addition to these issues, in recent years there has also been a renewed concern on the part of the unions with broader socio-economic questions. In particular, the unions have pressed for basic reforms in the health system, housing, agriculture, education, etc., and for a redirection of economic policy aimed at reducing unemployment and increasing investments in traditionally depressed areas such as the south of Italy (see Giugni, 1973; Romagnoli, 1977).

Role of unions in bargaining at national and plant level

As should be apparent from the above discussion, unions play a crucial role in bargaining at both national and plant level. Industry-wide bargaining platforms are developed at national level on the basis of previous meetings and discussions held at regional and provincial level. Prior to the opening of negotiations, the platform is submitted for approval to a national conference of full-time officials and shop-floor delegates. Formal negotiations with employers are carried out jointly by full-time national officials from each of the unions concerned. The final agreement is subject to the approval of the work-force at large. Voting on the agreement is carried out by a show of hands at mass meetings held at factory level.

Similar procedures are followed in the case of local bargaining. Plant level bargaining platforms are prepared by the CdF, usually in close co-operation with outside full-time union officials. Negotiations with management are usually carried out by members of the executive committee. Often, however, the negotiating committee is expanded to include 'regular' delegates. In smaller plants or when particularly important issues are at stake, it is not unusual for outside union officials to be directly involved in the negotiation process. The final agreement is then submitted for approval to the work-force. Voting is carried out by show of hands at either group or general meetings held at the plant during working hours.

Strength of unions in bargaining

In periods of relative union weakness management is more likely to be able to resist union demands and to prevent certain issues from entering the collective bargaining arena. The recent trend towards a more intensive regulation of employment relations, therefore, provides a rough indication of the increasing bargaining strength possessed by the unions both at national and at plant levels. A second measure of their increased power is provided by the fact that, on the whole, in recent years the unions have been able to achieve fairly favourable settlements at national and plant level (both in terms of wages and in terms of general improvements in other conditions of employment). The current economic recession has tended to undermine the power of the unions. On the whole, however, the unions can still be said to be fairly strong in the sense that they are often capable of resisting managerial policies which go against their interests. What this means essentially is that in spite of the adverse economic situation, the unions in Italy are still sufficiently powerful to set severe restrictions on the freedom of action of employers. In this connection, it is worth noting that, traditionally in Italy there has been little reliance on the courts as a means of redressing grievances and enforcing rights in the field of industrial relations. Since the introduction of the Statuto dei Diritti del Lavoratore (1970) it has become more common for unions and employees to have recourse to the courts in case of an infringement of rights on the part of employers. Such recourse to external agencies of control however, still remains fairly infrequent in Italy. The very fact that it is now possible for labour to bring employers to court for infringing upon certain specific rights and freedoms set down in the Statuto, however, has tended to act as a general deterrent against managerial abuses of power. In particular, it has tended to discourage employers from actively pursuing discriminatory and repressive policies at plant level. The main deterrent in this respect, however, is the potential power of labour rather than the existence of legislation backed by formal sanctions. There is little doubt that in Italy it is the unions themselves which play the major role in the process of norm-enforcement and control. In attempting to defend acquired rights, redress grievances, and enforce the application of existing agreements, labour tends to rely primarily on its power. This power, in turn, rests on the unions' readiness to mobilize the work-force and their capacity to impose negative sanctions of management through various forms of industrial action.

Patterns and levels of industrial conflict

The Italian system of industrial relations has always been highly conflictual. Italy, in fact, has traditionally had one of the highest strike rates in Europe. As can be seen from Table 11.6, in the past there have been a number of fluctuations in the level of industrial conflict. Over this period, however, there also has been a general increase in the level of conflicts measured in terms of the number of strikes and the number of hours lost in strike activity.

Equally important is the fact that over this period the proportion of plant-level strikes (as opposed to industry-wide and general strikes) has increased, as has the proportion of hours which have been lost in plant-level conflicts. In other words, since the early 1960s not only has industrial conflict tended to increase, but it has also become more decentralized, reflecting the decentralization in the system of collective bargaining discussed above.

2.5. Role of the Government in the System of Industrial Relations and Role of the Unions at Societal Level

Role of Government

In Italy the government plays both a direct and an indirect role in the system of industrial relations through the enactment of labour legislation, in its capacity as mediator in labour disputes in both the public and private sector, and in its role as employer. In recent years the government has played an increasingly active role in these respects. Government intervention in the system of industrial relations essentially takes place through three Departments: the Department of Labour, the Department of Industry, and the Department responsible for the Public Sector. The Department of Labour, like other government departments, does not have formal powers of arbitration. Its function is essentially one of mediation between unions and employers in the private sector when national negotiations break down or in the case of major or prolonged disputes. There is no formal legislation, however, regulating this process of mediation. Whether the government intervenes in favour of the unions or of the employers, therefore, tends to depend on existing power-relations, government policy, and the immediate political situation. Major labour disputes in nationalized industries,

Table 11.6.
*Total Number of Strikes and Number of Hours Lost through
Strike Activity*

Year	Total Number of Strikes	Total number of hours lost. (Thousands)
1955	1,981	44,978
1959	1,925	73,523
1960	2,471	46,289
1961	3,502	79,127
1962	3,652	181,732
1963	4,145	91,158
1964	3,841	104,709
1965	2,191	55,943
1966	2,387	115,788
1967	2,658	68,548
1968	3,377	73,918
1969	3,788	302,597
1970	4,162	146,212
1971	5,598	103,590
1972	4,765	136,480
1973	3,769	163,935
1974	5,174	136,267
1975	3,568	181,381
1976	2,706	177,643

Source: Annuario Statistico Italiana.

on the other hand, are handled through the Department responsible for the public sector. The process of mediation in these cases tends to be more overtly political in nature, given that there often are close political ties between Board members of state-controlled enterprises, government officials, and local trade-union leaders. This department also plays an important role in the public sector through the financing and running of the main state-controlled industrial corporations (IRI, ENI, etc.), from which individual enterprises in turn depend. *Role of Unions in Italy* – unlike in some other European countries, there is no formal incomes policy. Both unions and employers' associations, however, are actively involved in socio-economic questions at the national and regional level. Legislation passed in 1968, for example, makes provision for periodic consultations between government, unions, and employers over economic planning and over problems relating to employment, investments, technological change, etc. In any event, since the late 1960s it has become common practice for the government to consult with both unions and employers before the introduction of any major new socio-economic programme. As a result, those which have been adopted in recent years have often been the outcome of an intense process of bargaining between government, unions, and employers. In this connection it it worth noting that even though the influence of the unions at national and regional level has increased during the course of the 1970s, their relation with the government has often been of a conflictual nature. The unions, have frequently been highly critical of government programmes and have often engaged in militant forms of socio-political action (e.g. general strikes) as a means of protesting against government policies and of putting pressure on the government to introduce fundamental socio-economic reforms at the national level.

3. PERSPECTIVES, PROBLEMS AND ISSUES

The question of participation and of industrial democracy, interpreted in its traditional sense, has not been a central topic of socio-political debate in Italy. Of late, however, there has been an increasing awareness among both employers and labour leaders of the need to take a fresh look at this whole issue, due also to the possible introduction of EEC legislation in this area. The new awareness and interest is reflected in the increasing public debate on this issue over the past year or so.

A number of other problems and issues have also been at the centre of debate such as:

(1) General debate on the flexibility of the labour force. In particular, employers have complained that the Statuto and recent collective bargaining agreements have made it increasingly difficult for them to manage and control the labour force and to take full advantage of economic opportunities (e.g. high rates of absenteeism, restrictions on deployment of labour, limits on overtime, introduction of strict output norms). Related to this is the debate on the interpretation, and application of the Statuto and on the role of legislation in the system of industrial relations.

(2) Employer demands for a tighter regulation of plant-level collective bargaining. In particular, demands for the introduction of agreements with fixed terms of duration excluding interim renegotiation of terms and conditions of employment, as well as demands for the introduction of peace clauses in collective agreements to increase stability and predictability and facilitate long-term planning.

(3) Union demands for tighter control over subcontracting and over systems of contracting-out and of 'homework'.

(4) Continuing debate within the labour movement on questions of the relation between unions and political parties (i.e. degree of autonomy and co-ordination and respective functions of unions and parties).

(5) Continuing debate on questions of unification of labour movement and on problems of achieving closer organizational ties between the three main components at both national and local level.

(6) Debate on exclusive bargaining rights for the three main unions, spurred by emergence of break-away or autonomous unions, particularly in certain areas of the public sector (e.g. railways, airways, health service, etc.).

(7) Continuing debate on the broader socio-political role and function of unions and problem of translating general socio-economic demands (e.g. social reforms, employment, investments, work humanization) into specific policies and of developing effective strategies of action.

REFERENCES

Anderlini, F. and Sechi, S. (1977), 'Dalle Sezioni Sindacali ai Consigli di Fabbrica', *Fondaxione Giangiacomo Feltrinelli: Annali*, 16.
Antinolfi, R. (1974), *La Crisi Economica Italiana: 1969-1973*, Bari: De Donato.
Baglioni, G. (1977), 'Il Cammino e le Difficolta dell'Unita Sindacale', *Fondazione Giangiacomo Feltrinelli: Annali*, 16.
Bianchi, G. (1969), *Sindacati e Impresa*, Milano: Franco Angeli.
Cella, G. P. (1977), 'Stabilita et Crisi del Centralismo nell' Organizzazione Sindacale', *Fondazione Giangiacomo Feltrinelli: Annali*, 16.
De Masi, D. and Fevola, G. (1974), *I Lavoratori Nell'Industria Italiana: Basi Teoriche e Contesto Strutturale*, Milano: Franco Angeli.
Garavini, S. (1977), 'La Centralizzazione Contrattuale e le Strategie del Sindacato', *Fondazione Giangiacomo Feltrinelli: Annali*, 16.
Giugni, G. (1969), 'Articulated Bargaining in Italy', in: Flanders, A. (ed.), *Collective Bargaining*, Harmondsworth: Penguin Books.
    (1973), *Il Sindacato Fra Contratti E Riforme: 1963-1973*, Bari: De Donato.
    (1977), 'Critica e Rovesciamento dell'Assetto Contrattuale', *Fondazione Giangiacome Feltrinelli: Annali*, 16.
    Valcavi, D., Salvarani, G., Gimabarba, E., La Porta, A, Drago, F., Vinay, G. (1974), *Movimento Sindacale E Contrattazione Collettiva 1945-1973*, Milano: Franco Angeli.
Horowitz, D. (1963), *The Italian Labor Movement*, Cambridge: Harvard University Press.
Ichino, P. (1975), *Diritto Del Lavoro Per I Lavoratori*.
Instituto Centrale di Statistica (1977), *Annuario Statistico Italiano*, Rome.
Lanzardo, L. (1977), 'I Consigli di Gestione nella Strategia della Collaborazione', *Fondazione Giangiacomo Feltrinelli: Annali*, 16.
La Palombara, J. (1957), *The Italian Labor Movement: Problems and Prospects*, Cornell University Press: Ithaca, NY.
Organization for Economic Co-operation and Development (1977), Industrial Production: Historical Statistics, Paris: OECD.
Paci, M. (1973), *Mercato del Lavoro e Classi Sociali*, Bologna: Il Mulino.
Pera, G. (1975), *L'Applicazione dello Statuto dei Lavoratori: Tendenze et Orientazione*, Milano: Franco Angeli.
Quaderni di Mondoperaio (1977), Democrazia Industriale e Sindacato in Italia.
Quaderni di Rassegna Sindacale (1969), 'I Delegati dei Reparto – No. 24.
    (1970), Le Organizzazioni degli Imprenditori – No. 27.
    (1971), L'Unita Sindacale – No. 29.
    (1971), I Contratti di Lovoro – No. 30.
    (1972), Il Sindacato in Italia – Nos. 31-2.
    (1972), Sindacato e Partiti – Nos. 33-4.
    (1972), Sindacato e Riforme – No. 36.
    (1973), I Consigli di Zona – Nos. 39-40.
    (1974), Il Sindacato e le sue Strutture – No. 49.
    (1977), Sindacato e Controllo dell'Economia – No. 62-3.
Regalia, I., Regini, M., Reyneri, E. (1978), 'Labour Conflicts and Industrial Relations in Italy', in Crouch, C. and Pizzorno, A. (eds), *The Resurgence of Class Conflict in Western Europe since 1968*, London: MacMillan.
Romagnoli, U. (1977), 'La Scelta dei Contenuti Rivendicativi', *Fondazione Giangiaco Feltrinelli: Annali*, 16.

Salvati, M. (1975), *Il Sistema Economico Italiano: Analisi Di Una Crisi,* Bologna: Il Mulino.

Sechi, S. (1977), 'Strutture Aziendali e Potere Sindacale', *Fondazione Giangiacomo Feltrinelli: Annali,* 16.

Shalev, M. (1978), 'Lies Damned Lies and Strike Statistics: Trends in Industrial Conflict', in Crouch, C. and Pizzorno, A. (eds), *The Resurgence of Class Conflict in Western Europe since 1968,* London: MacMillan.

Treu, T. (1971), *Sindacato e Rappresentanze Aziendali,* Bologna: Il Mulino.

(1975), *L'Uso Politico Dello Statuto Dei Lavoratori,* Bologna: Il Mulino.

Tronti, M. (1977), 'Sindacato, Partiti e Sistema Politico', *Fondazione Giangiacomo Feltrinelli: Annali,* 16.

United Nations (1977), *Yearbook of National Accounts Statistics,* New York: UNO.

12

THE YUGOSLAV INDUSTRIAL RELATIONS SYSTEM

1. GENERAL SITUATION AND BACKGROUND

The People's Liberation War (1941–5), in which Yugoslavia arose as a new socialist country, was led by the Communist Party. The popular movement was established in the Liberation Front during the War, and after the War was re-named the Socialist Alliance. Whereas the Party was a very ideologically homo-geneous and centralized organization of the political élite, the Liberation Front was a pluralistic and decentralized organization.

The historical association of Party and Front, which is characteristic of the development of Yugoslavia from 1941 to today, prevented the degeneration of the revolution. Even though after the War, there emerged a certain bureaucratiza-tion of society and increasing domination of the Party over the Front, the state-Party apparatus nevertheless did not attempt to liquidate the popular movement. As the successor of the Liberation Front, the Socialist Alliance was the main target of Stalin's attack on Tito and on Yugoslavia. Stalin insisted that the Yugoslav Communist Party was 'drowning' in the Socialist Alliance and thus losing its dominant position in society. Stalin was partly right: even though the Yugoslav Party was a party of the Leninist type, it was never Stalinized exactly because it remained integrated in the popular movement (Rus, 1967).

Self-management, which began to be constituted after the break with Stalin, was in fact the continuation of the popular movement. Even though the initia-tive for self-management originated from above, it was not a system of 'imposed democracy' because it had its own real social base in the liberation movement. Thus, self-management was not only the voluntary act of the political élite, which would in this way acquire legitimization for its struggle against Stalin and the Comintern, but was at the same time a transformation of the liberation movement, based on political participation, into a labour movement, which was henceforth based on the economic participation of those employed.

With the introduction of self-management after 1950, a process of liberaliza-tion of Yugoslav society was begun. This period is characterized by the separa-tion of the Party from the state apparatus, the transformation of the Party into the League of Communists, the abolition of Party organizations in work organ-izations, the decentralization of state management, the development of the market, the transformation of imperative planning into indicative planning, and the incorporation of the Yugoslav economy into the international division of labour. The consequences of liberalization were manifested in very rapid economic growth, and increasing regional and social differentiation. This period of liberalization lasted approximately from 1950 to 1972 and concluded in a fairly anarchical state of affairs, in tendencies toward the separatism of various national groups, extensive unemployment, emigration of a part of the labour force to Western European countries, the rapid growth of individual consumption, and inadequate development of social services.

Since 1972 attempts have been made to transcend this inordinate liberalism and to re-establish the integrity of Yugoslav society. This period is termed the era of socialization, because it is directed toward the increasing social integration of the society, which would thus avoid the centralization of the state apparatus and bureaucratic planning of the economy. To a great extent the role of the League of Communists has increased, but not so far that it has been integrated into the state apparatus, but rather so that it is integrated with the Trade Unions and with the Socialist Alliance.

Political and ideological integration of the society is therefore based not on coercion but on persuasion. This kind of integration also holds for economic integration, which is based not only on greater state intervention (via the regulation of prices), but first of all on the integration of smaller enterprises into large companies, mutual agreements between the branches of the economy, and on economic planning developed on the basis of mutual agreements between the economic organizations themselves (Bilanžić, 1973).

POLITICAL STRUCTURE

The Socialist Alliance prepares and carries out elections for the representative bodies, which incorporate political organizations including the League of Communists, the Trade Unions, the youth organizations, the Veterans' Federation, etc. The Socialist Alliance organizes conferences of candidates and prepares lists of candidates for individual representative bodies. In the early years the candidates' lists usually were composed of only as many candidates as were to be elected, while in later years there has been more and more insistence that there be competition between candidates.

Participation of voters in elections has been quite high since the first post-war elections in 1945 (see Table 12.1). More than 90 per cent of the voters participated in all these elections, which is proof of the high political mobilization of Yugoslav citizens.

Table 12.1.
Percentages of voters who participated in elections for the Federal Assembly

Year of election:	1945	1953	1958	1965	1974
% of voters voting:	95.3	90.3	94.5	95.0	*

Note: We have cited here only the percentage of voters who participated in elections for the Federal Assembly and not for other chambers of assembly because these were replaced and a comparison is therefore not possible (*see text).

Since the 1974 elections were held under the new delegate system, these elections were not compared with previous ones. This new system means that voters now elect delegates only within the framework of their own work organizations, and within the framework of their local commune. Delegates are thereupon organized in delegations, which then elect the corresponding Chambers at the level of the Commune. The delegations chosen at this level elect the corresponding Chambers at the level of the Republics, and each chamber at the level of the Republican Assembly again elects delegations which make up the two chambers at the level of the Federal Assembly (see Fig. 12.1). Furthermore, only

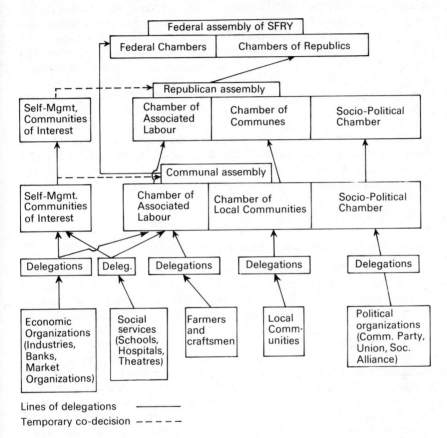

Lines of delegations ————
Temporary co-decision — — — — —

Figure 12.1. *Scheme of the Delegation System*

the delegation in work organizations and in local collectives are directly elected, while all bodies at the Community, Republican, and Federal level are elected through corresponding delegations. Delegations and delegates do not have an imperative mandate, as had, for example, delegates in the Paris Commune, but before every significant session they are obliged to consult with their electorate concerning the issues to be decided at that session. Thus delegates do not receive directives as to how to vote, but they do receive instructions from the electorate which must be followed. In the 1974 elections, 72,521 delegates were elected, which is evidence of the mass character of the delegate system.

Voters do not elect delegates and delegations of political organizations; they are appointed by mutual agreement. The delegations of political organizations then elect the Socio-Political Chamber at the level of the Communal Assemblies and at the level of the Republican Assemblies. The function of these Socio-Political Chambers is to guarantee the realization of the long-range interests of the working class throughout the entire institutional system, and to oppose all possible decisions of the other Chamber which contradict this principle. In this way the entire delegate system is realized as a special form of the dictatorship of the proletariat, as described in the 1974 Constitution (Yugoslav Survey, 1974).

The special Socio-Political Chamber does not exist at the federal level. The only federal organ in which political organizations are directly represented is the Presidency of the Socialist Federal Republic of Yugoslavia (SFRY). This collective organ, which succeeded Tito as President of the Republic, is composed of one representative from each Republic and the President of the League of Communists. Executive bodies such as the federal and republican government are subordinated to representative bodies, as evinced both by the powers which these Assemblies have and by the fact that the most prestigious politcal leaders are almost entirely concentrated in the representative rather than in the executive bodies. The fact that political organizations are included in the representative bodies (Socio-Political Chambers) is an additional reason for the domination of these representative bodies over the executive bodies.

ECONOMIC SITUATION AND SOCIAL STRATIFICATION

Yugoslav society is essentially different from western European society in that it is extremely voluntaristic. The institutional structure in Yugoslav society stimulates and even forces economic and social development, especially the development of industrial democracy. On the other hand, because the economy is relatively less developed, a gap is created between norms and possibilities, between that which should be, and that which is. Thus, the main problem of further social development is the development of economic and social conditions for the realization of the existing institutional structure and, first of all, for the realization of self-management as a specific form of industrial democracy.

Even though it is still insufficiently developed, in the entire post-war period Yugoslavia had a very large and at the same time constant growth in its G.N.P. In the period from 1947 to 1972 the G.N.P. increased 4.8 times, with a yearly rate of growth of 6.6 per cent. The yearly rate of growth in the G.N.P. was not even: the lowest rate (2 per cent) was in the first five post-war years when the economy was governed by the centralized state apparatus, and the fastest rate of growth was in the following decade when the society changed over to a decentralized market economy and self-management of working organizations. In this period the average rate of growth was 8.5 per cent. In the last period the rate of growth was somewhat less, but nevertheless amounted to 7 per cent annually for the 1963–72 period. With this level of growth Yugoslavia ranked behind only Romania, Bulgaria, and the Soviet Union among European countries.

The economic development of Croatia and Slovenia in this period was approximately the same as the national average: in Croatia it amounted to 6.6 per cent, in Slovenia to 6.9 per cent of the average yearly growth. But because both Republics were initially more developed, this rate of growth caused a situation in which the per capita G.N.P. in Slovenia was 84 per cent and in Croatia 23 per cent greater than in Yugoslavia as a whole.

The rapid growth of the G.N.P. was mainly the result of intensive industrialization, which can be appreciated in the fact that the yearly rate of growth in industry averaged 10 per cent, while in agriculture it was only 3 per cent. The growth of the metal industry was somewhat faster than that of industry as a whole, so that we can speak about the 'normal' development of this branch of industry (see Table 12.2). The period in which we conducted the analysis of metal enterprises can in the same way be designated as a normal period or as a period of slower conjuncture which is evident in the fact that the growth in the entire economy for the period 1974–5 amounted to 3 per cent while in the metal industry it was 13 per cent (see Table 12.2).

Table 12.2.
Growth of the G.N.P. in the economy as a whole and in the metal industry

Index	1965–75	1971–2	1972–3	1973–4	1974–5
For the entire economy	176	104	105	109	103
For industry	188	–	–	–	–
For the iron and steel industry	197	103	107	113	113

The rapid economic development gave rise to difficulties which were manifested in the decline of the active population, in the growth of unemployment, and in inflation. The proportion of the active population in relation to the entire population has declined constantly over the last 20 years: from 49.1 per cent in 1949 to 46.3 per cent in 1955, to 45 per cent in 1965, and finally to 43.3 per cent in 1975. This decline of the active population is partly a consequence of the greater number of educated young people, the greater number of pensioners, as it is also a consequence of the greater unemployment of women in those families which emigrated from the village to the city. The large migration from the village to the city on the one hand made possible this rapid industrialization, but on the other hand it formed a surplus work-force. This surplus is manifested not only in the gradual increase in the number of unemployed (see Table 12.3), but also in the significant emigration of peasants abroad for temporary work. According to

Table 12.3.
Growth of unemployment

	1957	1964	1975
Number of unemployed	116,000	212,000	502,000
Percentage of unemployed in relation to all employed	2.7	7.9	12.0

the 1971 official census there were 670,000 Yugoslav workers abroad, and of these 45.3 per cent were peasants.

The extensive migration of peasants to the city and industry created therefore an even greater surplus labour force which had a negative effect on industrial relations and on the evolution of democracy within industrial enterprises. In some periods inflation was another source of insecurity, but in the last period inflation has been relatively stabilized (see Table 12.4).

Table 12.4.
Indicators of inflation

	1956	1965	1970	1972	1973	1974	1975
Rate of inflation in percentage calculated on the basis of retail prices	3.3	39.1	10.7	16.7	18.7	24.7	18.6

In 1976 the rate of inflation was only 6.7 per cent; in 1977 it was expected to be approximately 12 per cent.

The rapid economic development, based first of all on industrialization, required especially large investment. This investment was borne by the industrial workers, particularly because of the shortage in the import of foreign capital and also because of an economically weak agriculture.

The growth of personal income of the employed for the entire economy was for this reason significantly lower than the growth of the G.N.P. through 1963. Only from this period onwards did personal spending grow in parallel with the G.N.P. (See Table 12.5.)

Table 12.5.
Percentage of the G.N.P. spent on personal income

	1952	1956	1965	1975
Net proportion of personal income of persons employed in industry in relation to the entire G.N.P.	25	38.5	41.3	45.3

While earlier management together with political organizations within enterprises strongly insisted on as great as possible investments and as low as possible salaries, the situation today tends towards negotiating and compromise. The reason that greater social unrest did not develop in the earlier periods, despite relatively low incomes, may be found, among other things, in the relatively great equality of personal incomes for varous categories of workers (see Table 12.6). Although we do not have data for earlier periods, it is possible to see that the differences in personal income even in the last period are relatively small, so that we can speak of 'levelling' (equal pay for different work).

In 1968 the salaries of highly educated workers were 2.58 times greater, and in 1971 they were 2.63 times greater than the salaries of unqualified workers. In earlier periods these differences were even smaller: in 1964 the salaries of highly educated workers were only 1.9 times larger than those of unqualified workers (Jurancic, 1975).

Table 12.6.
Personal incomes by qualifications and education (in dinars)

YEAR	College: 4-years	College: 2-years	High-school	Elementary school	Highly skilled	Skilled	Semi-skilled	Non-skilled
1968	1,705	1,252	1,065	871	1,119	863	700	660
1971	2,836	2,138	1,730	1,428	1,905	1,456	1,140	1,079

In spite of all the above-mentioned difficulties, industrialization had one great advantage: it created a widespread mobility of the labour force, both with regard to intensive employment in the social sector and with regard to the intensive development of schooling. The number of employed increased 2.5 times in the last twenty years. Every year there were on the average 124,000 new job vacancies, so that the total number of employed grew in this period from 1.7 to 4.2 million.

This process of intensive employment had two simultaneous effects, de-agrarianization, and socialization of economic activity, because the majority of new jobs appeared in the non-agricultural and public sector, that is, in the social sector. Table 12.7 shows how the proportion of the active peasant population declined in relation to the entire active population, and in Table 12.8 it can be seen that the proportion of the active population which is employed in the social, that is, the public sector has grown. De-agrarianization and socialization occurred relatively painlessly, partly because of the large possibilities of employment, and partly because of the relatively great social equality and efficient social control which was made possible by social ownership of the means of production.

Table 12.7.
Decreasing of the active peasant population

	1953	1961	1971
Total active population	7,848,000	8,340,000	8,890,000
Peasant active population	5,360,000	4,691,000	3,903,000

Table 12.8.
Disposition of the active population with regard to ownership (in percentage)

	Private sector	Co-operative sector	Public sector
1953	63.7	8.9	27.4
1971	43.5	1.8	54.7

The parallel intensive development of schooling made possible major advances in the qualifications of the employed and their vertical mobility. In 1953 elementary schools encompassed only 70 per cent of children, but in 1971 they encompassed already 90 per cent. In the last fifteen years the number of teachers in middle schools increased 2.5 times and now amounts to approximately 40 per cent of the total. The number of colleges and universities also increased: in 1952 there were only 30, but by 1972 there were 238. The number of students in this period increased from 22,000 to 232,000.

But in spite of the large growth in schooling, the number of illiterates has remained considerable. In 1953 the number of illiterates amounted to 25.4 per cent of the entire population over 10 years of age, in 1961 19.7 per cent, and in 1971 it was still 15.1 per cent of the entire population over 10. The number of illiterates is greatest in Kosova where they compose almost a third of the population, and the number of illiterates is lowest in Slovenia (1.2 per cent) and in Croatia (9.0 per cent). Thus the rate of illiteracy in these two Republics does not present an important obstacle to industrial democracy.

A relatively greater handicap to direct participation is presented by the relatively low qualification structure of workers which, characteristically, does not improve (see Table 12.9). The reason for this can be found in intensive employment, which produces an uninterrupted flow of unskilled workers. Thus the level of qualifications remains approximately the same despite intensive schooling: in the last ten years the number of highly skilled and skilled workers increased by 6.2 per cent across the entire industry, and by only 2.3 per cent in the metal industry — which means a long-term stagnation. These trends bode ill for the development of industrial democracy. Probably they are conditioned not only by the above-mentioned processes of massive de-agrarianization and industrialization, but also by the character of industry and by the division of labour which dominates in industry.

Table 12.9.
Qualification structure of blue collar workers (in percentage)

Qualification structure of workers	Entire industry		Metal industry	
	1964	1974	1964	1974
Highly skilled	5.6	6.1	6.1	7.6
Skilled	27.3	33.0	28.3	29.1
Semi-skilled	17.6	17.0	16.0	20.3
Unskilled	33.9	18.5	32.5	23.9

More intensive political work, the great number of journals which are published within enterprises, and the increase in circulation of daily newspapers (see Table 12.10) stimulate to some extent the greater social activity of workers. But on the other hand these trends cannot have such an influence on the growth of industrial democracy as does the existing division of labour.

The number of daily newspapers has not seen a major growth; in the last ten years it has remained almost the same. But the circulation of these newspapers grew 2.5 times. The growth of local and factory newspapers is particularly large:

both the total number and the circulation of these newspapers is four times greater than it was twenty years ago.

Table 12.10.
Daily and other newspapers

	1955	1965	1975
Number of daily newspapers	18	23	26
Circulation of daily newspapers (in thousands of copies)	801,000	1,507,000	1,896,000
Number of all newspapers	493	1,171	1,939
Circulation of all newspapers (in thousands of copies)	3,559,000	9,817,000	9,629,000

2. NATIONAL INDUSTRIAL RELATIONS SYSTEM

With the new Constitution of 1974 the National Industrial System became completely integrated in the political representative system, as the Delegate System (which is outlined in Table 12.2) is at the same time integrated in the political and self-management system. Thus the Federal, Republican, and Community Assemblies are in this context as self-management bodies and at the same time they are the highest organs of government. The 'self-management' character of the Republican and Community Assemblies is most clearly manifested in the work of the Chambers of Associated Labour. The Community chambers are composed of delegates who are regularly sent by the delegations of their own work organizations. The Republican Chamber is composed of delegates from the Community Chambers of Associated Labour. These delegates have a four-year mandate and have the right of immunity in their activity as delegates. Managers and other administrators cannot be delegates either in the Community or in the Republican Chambers of Associated Labour. The substance of the work of the Republican Chambers of Associated Labour is defined by the Republican Constitution. These Chambers first of all make decisions concerning: laws which concern labour relations and labour protection; laws which concern the organization of banking and the Office of Social Accounts; laws which regulate the growth of regional economy or of branches of the economy; laws which concern the quality of production and service.

The Chambers of Associated Labour do not decide independently on issues such as the economic plan, fiscal policy, the social control of prices, and other problems of general social significance; rather these matters are decided upon in conjunction with the other Chambers of the Republican Assembly. However, the Chambers of Associated Labour have veto power in these questions.

The other system of regulating the relations between economic organizations and social services is based on the so-called Self-Management Associations of Interest (SMAI). These SMAI's are required by law in the fields of education, health, social security, science, and cultural activity, at the community and republican level. They are administered by delegates from economic organizations which finance social services, and by delegates who are employed in the corresponding social services. Collectively and on an equal basis, both sets of delegates decide about yearly and middle-range plans of work for the social services, as well as about finance for the realization of these plans. Thus social services are not budgeted by the state administration, but are agreed upon by the work organizations according to their own efforts and financing of them. In this way the work organizations, through their own delegates, have a direct influence on the development of social services, and through this on the development of the wider social environment (Džodžević, 1975).

The third system in the framework of industrial relations is the system of Social Compacts and Self-Management Agreements. This system was introduced in the New Constitution with the intention of regulating by agreements both the plan and market relations between work orgnanizations, and thus to negate both the hierarchy of the state plans and the ungovernability of the liberal market. Social compacts are contracted between government organs, economic chambers, and trade unions and concern pricing policy, the policy of personal incomes, employment policy, and planning. Social compacts are therefore agreements between the government, the economy, and the trade unions about questions of wider social interest. The Self-Management Agreements regulate relations between work organizations, whether these relations concern production co-operation, the business integration of larger enterprises into a Company, the instituting of banks on the part of work orgnaizations, the instituting of economic chambers, or even the penetration (of Yugoslav enterprises) in foreign markets. Economic relations between work organizations and some other relatins which encroach on the policy of salaries and on personnel policy in work organizations are also regulated by self-management organs of enterprises, but must also be accepted by the majority of workers of the corresponding work organizations.

The fourth industrial relations system was also established with the new Constitution. This is the special system of Courts of Associated Labour, which arbitrate all controversies in relation to the Social Compacts and Self-Management Agreements. All controversies which concern labour relations in work organizations are resolved through the 'Social Attorney of Self-Management' which is included in the composition of the Courts of Associated Labour. These courts are formed by the Communes or the Republican Assemblies. They have eight-year mandates.

TRADE UNIONS

The trade unions are organized according to the territorial and functional principle. On the Federal and Republican level the trade unions are differentiated by industry and on the commune and work organization level they are unified i.e. all employees in a work organization belong to the same union. The trade union organization exists in every work organization and includes more than 90 per cent of all those employed.

The social function of the trade unions has changed during the post-war period. In the early post-war years the trade union was the 'transmission belt' of the Party, that is, the instrument with which it was attempted to encourage workers towards greater political participation, more intensive work, and more intensive education. After the installing of self-management it became more widely believed that the trade union was no longer necessary since all its traditinal functions, particularly the protective function, were taken over by the new self-management system. According to the data of one survey, during the period of liberalism more than one-third of the presidents of local trade union organizations were of the opinion that the trade union organization was no longer needed. The influence of the trade unions on enterprises was less than that of the lower managerial personnel, and in some enterprises it was even lower than that of the skilled workers. The activity of the trade unions in this period was reduced to the collection of membership fees and the organization of the workers' recreation activity (Kavčič, 1972).

In the last five years the *de facto* and *de jure* influence of the trade unions has increased. It has become recognized that the participation of the workers cannot stop manipulation on the part of the manager, if this participation is not supported by the counter-power of the Unions and the League of Communists. It has become evident that equitable distribution of power is not the outcome of workers' participation but is, rather, the pre-condition for un-manipulated participation. Because of this recognition, the trade unions acquired the following functions in the new Constitution:

(1) they took over responsibility for proposing candidates for all self-management and administrative organs within the enterprise; they took over the role of mediator in strikes and in other conflicts which cannot be solved within the self-management bodies;

(2) they safeguard the new system of workers' control, which has the task of supervising the work of administrative and self-management organs;

(3) they took over the responsibility for criticism and initiative towards all self-management agreements which are contracted between work organizations.

As an equal partner in the concluding Social Compacts of broad social significance, the trade unions have signficantly greater influence on the government and on the economic chamber, the bodies with which they ratified these compacts.

PARTICIPATION IN ENTERPRISES

From 1950 (when the first workers' council was formed) to 1974, the institutional structure of self-management remained essentially unchanged. It was composed of: the Workers' Council, the Commission of the Workers' Council, and the Executive Board of the Workers' Council. All of these bodies of self-management had a representative character and were situated at the level of the enterprise. Attempts at developing self-management were oriented first in the direction of increasing the number of commissions of Workers' Councils, but later in the direction of enlarging the decision-making area and in the direction of creating workers' councils at a lower level. When it became clear that these efforts had not sufficiently increased the power and efficacy of self-management in enterprises, efforts were made in the direction of the 'professionalization' of self-management, which meant that the qualification and educational structure of the self-management organs were intentionally raised.

With the 1974 Constitution four essential changes were made in the enterprise system of self-management (Gorupič and Paj, 1970). The first was the formation of Basic Organizations of Associated Labour (BOAL) at the plant level. These organizations constitute the initial subjects of all economic and self-management rights. The Workers' Councils on the level of the firm or company are only associated bodies which decide about those matters delegated to them by the Workers' Council of BOAL on the basis of Self-Management Agreements. Enterprises and companies therefore are no longer classical hierarchical structures, but are associations of BOAL. Association in large organizations therefore does not mean greater centralization, but integration, with which the basic organizations lose almost none of their autonomy.

The second change is that Workers' Assemblies were created as organs of direct self-management. It is no longer the Workers' Council of the BOAL but the Workers' Assembly which directly makes all decisions concerning labour relations and personal income. With this change representative participation of the workers was replaced by direct participation.

The third change is the introduction of a special system of Workers' Control which is dependent neither on the Workers' Assembly nor on the Workers' Council. The Commission of Workers' Control supervises all self-management and administrative bodies. The introduction of the system of workers' control means the abandoning of the system of non-conflictual participation, which had ignored the inherently conflictual character of relations in work organizations, which in turn led to the informal resolution of conflicts, wildcat strikes, and manipulation by management. This theory of non-conflictual participation had been a consequence of the optimistic assumption that social conflicts between management and labour would automatically disappear with the abolishment of private property (Jovanov, 1977; Jeličić, 1977).

The fourth change is that administrators cannot any longer be elected to self-management organs. This change was the logical consequence of the recognition of conflictual relations between groups within the enterprise. Other groups must also be proportionally represented in all the organs. Members of the Workers' Council and of Workers' Control are elected directly. They have a two-year mandate and enjoy immunity. They are directly responsible to the workers, that is, to the Workers' Assembly.

Participation within the plant is in large measure defined by the Republican Constitution and Laws. It was not foreseen by the Constitution or the laws that there would only rarely be participation of the workers' or self-management organs. More often the Workers' Council (sometimes its commissions) makes decisions and in some cases workers decide directly through their Assemblies. Thus, a considerable amount of direct decision-making by the workers is anticipated by the law. Economic decisions are to a great extent under the competence of the Workers' Assembly; personnel and social decisions under the competence of the Workers' Council; and organizational-technical matters still fully at the discretion of management.

There is no bargaining structure within the enterprises. Agreements between workers and managers pass through the existing self-management organs. The law particularly emphasizes the obligation of management to give the workers and self-management organs, and particularly the organs of workers' control, all essential information related to the enterprise. Any intentional concealment of information or even any limitation of participation is punishable.

3. PROSPECTIVE DEVELOPMENTS

In 1977 and 1978 the Law on Associated Labour was implemented. This law is usually called the 'Little Constitution' because it elaborates the 1974 Constitution. The two-year implementation of the new Law on Associated Labour was conceived as a major and continuous political action in which the greater participation of workers in management, greater control of the basic organizations over the circulation of social capital, better co-ordination between work organizations, and more efficient and democratic planning, was to be realized.

Basically, Taylorism, that is, the traditional 'scientific division of work' which exists in the majority of industrial organizations will be one of the main obstacles to installing the new law. Because of the supposition that the abolition of private property and of state authority would constitute sufficient conditions for the growth of democracy, that is, of self-management in enterprises, the Taylorist division of work remains, so to speak, untouched. It remains the basis of the executive hierarchy of management which is in express contradiction to the existing self-management system in enterprises (Rus, 1979).

A second obstacle to the further development of self-management is the unresolved status of professionals and professional service in enterprise. The greater need for professional skills leads inescapably towards the greater influence of professionals and professional service, while on the other hand their influence is systematically limited because of the danger that a technocracy would render impossible the participation and influence of blue-collar workers. Under the new Constitution professionals will essentially have less work autonomy, which will certainly result in long-range economic and even social consequences. A solution must be found which would make possible professional autonomy and which would at the same time prevent its becoming the source of a political monopoly in work organizations (Rus, Burns, 1979).

A third obstacle to the development of self-management is the existing kind of massive consumption, which is expressly materialist and individualist in nature. Because of this kind of consumption a contradiction has been created between highly socialized production and highly privatized consumption. The formation of a new consumer culture which would be more social and less private in nature is one of the essential conditions for the further development of industrial democracy, that is of self-management, in Yugoslavia (Supek, 1975).

Because Yugoslavia is a 'voluntary society', the future development of self-management will be largely dependent on the role and character of political organizations — particularly the League of Communists. The democratization of political organizations will be the condition for a more general political democratization, and in this also lie the conditions for true industrial democracy. But it is not so much pluralism of political parties which is needed for such political democratization but, rather, the openness of the political centres of power to a new rising of social movements. The linking of the League of Communists with the trade unions, the Socialist Alliance, and with other mass organizations and the distancing of the League from the state apparatus may create a wide enough space for the genesis, development, and integration of new social movements within the existing environment.

REFERENCES

Bilanžić, D. (1973), *Idele i praksa drustvenog razvoja Jogoslavije od 1945 do 1973*, Komunist: Beograd.

Džordžević, J. (1975), *Drustveno politicki sistem SFRJ*, Radricka Stampa: Beorgrad.

Gorupic, D. and Paj, J. (1970), *Workers' Self-Management in Yugoslav Undertakings*, Ekonomski Institut: Zagreb.

Jeličić, Z. (1977), 'Analiza djelovanja samoupravne, radnicke kontorole u organizacijama udruzenograde, *Kuiturni radnik*, Zagreb: 30.

Jovanov, N. (1977), 'Samoupravna radnicka kontrola', in *Nas Teme*, Beograd: vol. 20.

Jurancic, I. (1975), *Organizacija in Kadri*, Kranj: 4–6.

Kavčič, B. (1972), 'Polozaj sindikatuv delovni organizaciji', in *Teorija inpraksa* Ljubljana: no. 2.

Rus, V. (1967), *Institutionalization of the Revolutionary Movement*, Zagreb.

(1979), 'Limited effects of workers participation and political power' in (ed.) T. Burns *et al.*, *Work and Power*, London: SAGE.

(1979), *Pokusaji samovpravljanja proizvodnjom*, Universa u Zagrebu.

Supek, R. (1975), 'Proizvodna organizacija i drustveni totalitet', in J. Dbradovic *et al.*, *Proizvodna organizacija i samoupravljanje*, Filozofski fakultet: Zagreb.

Yugoslav Survey (1974), Beograd: vol. 15, August.

13

THE ISRAELI INDUSTRIAL RELATIONS SYSTEM

1. GENERAL SITUATION AND BACKGROUND

1.1. The Political Situation

The roots of the political system of Israel can be found in the first Zionist Congress, which took place in Basle in 1897. The method of proportional elections was then selected in order to facilitate wide representation of all groups of the nation. The same method of election has been accepted in Israel. Some of the large political parties which existed then are the continuation of those which participated in the first Zionist Congress. Since then, until the establishment of the State in 1948, the political parties were also the foci around which part of the social and welfare activity concentrated. The parties each had a strong ideological characteristic on which their identities were based.

A relatively weak parliament and a strong executive branch are prominent features of the Israeli political system, which is based on the assumption that the same party or coalition of parties govern both the legislative and executive branches. Party leaders determine the major policies and the *Knesset* (Parliament) grants these decisions a national character. In most cases party discipline exists, which obliges the representatives of parties to vote in accordance with party decisions.

The most important fact in the analysis of the political system is that the Labour party was, until 1977, dominant, and the party around which the coalitions were built. Moreover, since this party also had the majority vote in the *Histadrut* (the Jewish Labour Federation), its leadership concentrated much power and all major decisions during nearly fifty years were made with its blessings.

The elections of 1977 caused a political 'revolution' in Israel, when the *Likud* (a bloc of right-wing parties) won the elections and formed a new coalition cabinet. The political culture of Israel has always been characterized by a high degree of involvement, reflecting the critical issues by which Israel was confronted: the establishment of peace with the surrounding Arab states, the achievement of economic independence, and the social integration of the new immigrants in the social structure.

Roughly, Israel's parties may be classified into four groups: left, i.e. Labour, Mapam, and Communists; centre, i.e. Liberals and Democratic-Change; right, i.e. Herut; and religious, i.e. Agudat Israel, and the National Religious Party. Prior to 1977 changes in the results of the elections were within factional grouping. Parties of the left never won fewer than 64 nor more than 69 seats in the 120-seat Knesset in the seven elections through to 1973. In 1973 they won 59 seats and in 1977 33 seats. The centre parties have ranged between 27 and 34 seats, and 45 in 1975. The religious parties between 15 and 18 seats, 15 in 1973, and 16 in 1977 (Arian, 1973).

Until 1977, Herut was the only opposition party in the full sense of the word: now it is the major party of the existing coalition. It grew out of re-visionist groups of the Mandate period. In the political sense, it is an activist party and economically it supports private initiative and wishes to limit as much as possible the function of the State. Though considered a right-wing party, it has among its members many workers as well as people from the lower classes. The various groups in Herut kept together because of their great nationalist drive. The religious parties do not represent all the religious sections of the population. Their very existence indicates, however, that religion constitutes one of the most complex issues of the Israeli society. A status quo principle in religious matters had been established between the parties during the pre-state period which allowed co-operation between the governing party and the religious parties. This status quo has been kept until the present day.

1.2. Significant political events

The most important recent political event was the May 1977 elections, when, for the first time in the twenty-nine year history of the State of Israel, a party other than the Labour Party won the elections. On June 20 1977, Mr Menachem Begin, head of the Likud block (Herut, Liberals, and several other small parties) became Prime Minister of Israel. Power in the Histadrut remained however, in the hands of the Labour bloc, which won the elections there. There is not much hope that bills relating to employee influence in companies would be submitted to the legislative bodies in the near future, since the right-wing parties do not support the idea in principle.

1.3. Population

Israel's citizens, including reunited Jerusalem, number 3,708,300 of whom 590,100 are non-Jews (Moslems, Christians, Druze, etc., see Table 13.1). The declaration of Independence proclaims that the State of Israel will be open to Jewish immigration and the in-gathering of the exiles. The Law of Return and the Citizenship Law of 1952 grant every Jew who so chooses an instant and automatic right to settle in Israel as a citizen. Since the renewal of statehoood the population has grown fivefold, and almost half the increment coming from immigration (*Aliyah*). The pace has varied. First (from 1948 to 1951) came survivors of the Holocaust in Europe and whole communities from Arab states; after a lull of four years, a second wave (1955-7) came mainly from Morocco, Tunisia, and Poland. The third wave (1961-4) also came from North Africa and Eastern Europe. The fourth major wave, after the Six Days War (1967) was mainly from the West and the Soviet Union.

1.4. Economic Growth

The outstanding characteristic of the Israeli economy is its almost uninterruptedly rapid growth (see, for example, Horowitz, 1967). This process was evident

Table 13.1.
Population

1948	0.6m
1965	2.5m
1970	3.0m
1977	3.7m

Source: Horowitz, 1967 and official statistics.

through the past two decades except for a few years of slowed-down economic activity (the recession years of 1965-7). The development was marked by a 10 per cent annual rise in the GNP and a rapid industrialization and development of food resources. Full employment was the rule rather than the exception. These facts are surprising because Israel has always had heavy defence costs, lack of natural resources, and a chronic water-supply problem.

A turning-point came in 1973, a year of global recession. Israel was not spared this economic decline. The balance of payments has slipped, inflation has reached annual rates in excess of 25 per cent (over 100 per cent in 1979), the currency has been depressed and there have been signs of impending recession.

In October, 1977, the Israeli Government decided on a new economic policy, the aim of which has been the recovery of the economy. It includes the termination of control of foreign currency and floating exchange-rate of the Israeli currency. Indirect taxes were continued, subsidies for goods and services were gradually cut, and the income of the poor guaranteed. The Government's expectations are that the new policy will improve the balance of payments situation, attract foreign investments, encourage growth of the GNP, limit inflation, and change the wage system. Industry accounts for 25 per cent of the national product. It has developed with exceptional dynamism, its production outpacing the growth of the GNP. In 1968, it rose by 29 per cent, in 1969 by 16 per cent, and in 1970-2 by 12 per cent. Agriculture accounts for less than 10 per cent of the national product, transportation and communication for more than 10 per cent, and services for 40 per cent. Israel's economy is pluralistic – 42 per cent is in private hands, 35 per cent is run by the State, and 23 per cent by the Histadrut-General Federation of Labour.

Manpower and Labour

The civilian labour force at 1.2 million in 1976 is four times what it was in 1949 – an average annual growth of about 7 per cent, against a population growth of 5.5 per cent. The biggest employer is the public services, with 370,000 wage-earners (see Table 13.2).

Over two-thirds of the force are employed, 12 per cent are self-employed, and 2.5 per cent are employers. The non-agricultural sector has grown steadily (see Table 13.3).

Standard of living

Private per capita consumption has risen in Israel at an average annual rate of 4.4 per cent except for the recession years of 1965-7. Generally speaking, this

Table 13.2.
Employment Structure (1977)

Public Services	370,000
Industry	280,000
Commerce & Tourism	150,000
Building	120,000
Transport & Communications	80,000
Agriculture	70,000
Electricity & Water	10,000

Source: official statistics.

Table 13.3.
Employment in the non-Agricultural Sector (1970 = 100)

1967	78.6
1968	86.0
1969	94.0
1970	100.0
1971	106.0
1972	111.0
1973	114.2
1974	115.6
1975	119.5
1976	122.7
1977	124.8

Source: ILO Yearbook, 1977.

followed closely the growth of the GNP. The rising standard of living is relected in the changed composition of commodities and services used and in assets owned by the population.

2. NATIONAL INDUSTRIAL RELATIONS SYSTEM

2.1. Legal Framework

Labour Legislation in the Mandatory Period

Due to established custom in British colonial territories, and because of the possible effects on the Arab and governmental economies, the British Mandatory Authorities (1920–48) were in no hurry to enact labour laws. They left almost unchanged the situation which they had inherited from the Ottoman Empire, in which relations between employer and employees were regulated by a section of the *Mejelle* which dealt with leases. In the first twenty years of the Mandate only a handful of labour laws were enacted: The Mining Ordinance (1925), which regulated safety conditions and prohibited, *inter alia*, the employment underground of women or children under 14, and the Law Enjoining the Fencing of Machinery, 1928. Several other laws of the early 1940s were concerned solely with meeting emergency needs. An important, if belated, step, was the establishment of a Department of Labour Affairs in 1943, mainly under pressure of economic developments during World War II. It set to work with dispatch and left before the end of the Mandate, paying more attention to the relatively advanced needs of the Jewish economy. The Accident and Occupational Diseases Ordinance (1945) which provided for compulsory notification of accidents at work or occupational diseases marked a considerable advance, as did two other ordinances issued in the same year, concerned with employment of women and children. The Factories Ordinance (1946), which established standards of safety and hygiene, was a very important and progressive addition to Mandatory Labour Legislation.

While the Mandatory Government concentrated most of its attention on safety regulations, the Jewish community had a large measure of autonomy in its labour relations (see Hyen, 1974). In the absence of adequate legislation, it established practices and customs which, though voluntary, were firmly adhered to, as attempts to violate them were frustrated by the pressure of the organized community, which was led by the labour movement. This autonomy was reinforced by the High Court ruling to the effect that accepted custom in labour relations was legally binding. An eight-hour working day, annual vacations, severance pay, allocation of work through labour exchanges according to agreed priorities, holidays on the Jewish Sabbath and Festivals, recognition of the trade unions, and collective agreements became established practice.

In the early years labour relations in the Jewish community were not chiefly concerned with wages and working conditions. Tension was due mainly to unemployment and charges of unfair distribution of the available jobs. The Labour Department of the Jewish Agency (founded in 1935) concerned itself actively in labour disputes. It was the highest authority in all such matters from its foundation until the establishment of the State. During this period, it dealt with more than 2,500 disputes, for the most part concerning collective agreements, and through its decisions it set the seal of approval on working conditions and practices worked out by collective agreements. Among other things, it developed a system for the resolution of labour disputes by arbitration or the good offices of the department, which was also recognized as a court of appeal (Hyen, 1974).

Labour legislation in the State of Israel

The emergence of Israel as an independent State in 1948 marked a turning-point in the approach to labour relations. In practice, the procedures and customs which had been accepted among the Jews of Palestine remained in force. The Government set up a Labour Relations Department in the Ministry of Labour, which inherited the functions of the Labour Department of the Jewish Agency. Before long, the Government submitted the first labour law to the Knesset: the Ex-Soldiers (Reinstatement in Employment) Law (1949), which was aimed at alleviating the difficulties caused by conscription for the War of Independence. It was followed by a lengthy series of labour laws, many of which gave legal force to procedures already established by custom and agreement within the Jewish community. They dealt, inter alia, with hours of work and rest (1951), annual leave (1951), employment of youth (1953), apprenticeship (1953), employment of women (1954), enforcement of collective agreements (1957), settlement of trade disputes (1957), penalties for excessive delays in payment of wages (1958), labour exchanges (1959), and severance pay (1969). No legal basis exists in Israel concerning workers' participation in the management of economic enterprise, except recent regulations issued by the Minister of Finance concerning State-owned industrial companies (to be dealt with in section 2.3).

Collective bargaining structure

Labour relations in Israel are based upon a system of collective agreements of Labour contracts, recognized in the Collective Agreement Law (1957). These agreements, which are signed by an employer or employers' association on the one hand and the representative of the trade union on the other, lay down conditions of work, including wages, social benefits, working hours, shifts, and labour relations, as well as the rules of conduct and discipline, engagement of staff, and termination of employment, negotiation procedures, the settlement of disputes, and the rights and obligations of the parties. Collective agreements may be 'special', applying to a particular enterprise of employer, or 'general', applying to the whole or part of the country or to a specific type of work. Collective agreements were to be registered by the Chief Labour Relations Officer at the Ministry of Labour. The Minister is empowered to issue an order extending the application of the general collective agreement to employees or employers who are not organized in a trade union or employers' organization. Can we argue that these arrangements in themselves constitute a form of industrial democracy? A debatable conceptual issue in the literature of workers' participation is whether collective bargaining and negotiations between labour and management should be considered as forms of participation. Clearly it is impossible to define finally the limits of the union-influenced areas, since they have shown a long-run tendency to expand, and if the process continues, more managerial decisions will undoubtedly be affected by the collective bargaining process. The question to be asked, however, is whether all forms of workers' influence upon managerial decisions are to be regarded as 'participation'. It seems that from an analytical point of view there is a qualitative difference between influencing management through pressure implied in the bargaining process on the one hand, or through consultation and joint management on the other. Collective bargaining is a process of accommodation and constitutes a formal mechanism through which conflicting interests of equal parties are resolved. The logics of participative management measures, joint consultation, or joint management are different. The underlying assumption is that there are objectives common to both management and labour that can provide the basis for co-operation between the two.

The participative bodies are mechanisms for the elaboration and expression of common interests. In practice, the border between collective bargaining and some forms of participation is blurred, as both seem to include elements of co-operation and conflict. The two schemes often operate side by side, since collective bargaining leaves wide areas to management discretion, and it is here that participation bodies may enter. Actually, subjects which in one country constitute an integral part of collective bargaining are within the jurisdiction of 'participation' in another. Thus, the distinction between the two forms is often more analytical than practical (see Rosenstein, 1977: 57).

2.2. Organizational Framework of Bargaining Parties

The Unions

The dominant body in the Industrial Relations System in Israel on the employees' side is the Histadrut — The Labour Federation in Israel. It was established in 1920 by several political parties belonging to the Labour movement, in order to unite all the country's workers for the realization of the ideal of a Jewish working society and to deal with the day-to-day needs of its members. The Histadrut has always been guided by four related aims: a nation-building programme of pioneering and development; the formation and development of a labour class; the creation of a just society; and the development of a high standard of living. Unique to the Histadrut is the coexistence of a powerful and virtually all-embracing trade union wing and an extensive set of economic activities. (The economic sector of the Histadrut consists of all co-operatives, *kibbutzim, moshavim,* and the so-called administrative economy — which is directly owned by the Histadrut). These two principal units are combined with a broad network of cultural and educational activities, extensive welfare services, and consumers' and producers' co-operatives. Thus, from the very beginning, the Histadrut was not a trade union in the narrow sense of the term, but an institution which fulfilled many tasks beyond those of traditional trade unions (Derber, 1973).

Membership of the Histadrut is direct. Upon joining the member is entitled to all the services, including trade union protection and social welfare. He also becomes a member of *Hevrat Ovdim* (the economic unit of the Histadrut) and automatically a co-owner of its properties.

Over the years, the Histadrut has grown into a mass organization. The growth of its membership was faster than that of the country's Jewish population. At present, over 90 per cent of the country's wage earners and salaried employees are among its members, or approximately 60 per cent of Israeli citizens above the age of 18. Its economic sector now accounts for about 23 per cent of national employment, 19 per cent of the net national product, and 19 per cent of total exports.

The Histadrut is a unique organization in many respects (Kolat, 1973; Hyen, 1974). Most unusual is its being both a powerful trade union and a major entrepreneur and owner of industry, headed by a powerful managerial wing. The entrepreneurial activities of the Histadrut were originally envisaged in terms of internal co-operation and strong national principles. The first principle was based on the belief (only rarely explicitly expressed) that Histadrut's ownership of economic enterprises provides the assurance for harmonious relationships between managing and managed. The second principle consisted of the idea that the labour community must develop its own economic activity in order to lay down and develop the economic basis for the growing Jewish community in Palestine–Israel.

Since the early 1940s, Histadrut-owned industrial plants have grown both in number and size. Moreover, the ideologically oriented workers of the early days have been gradually replaced by newcomers, who very often did not share the forward-looking social and national commitments of the pioneers. For the newcomers, a Histadrut enterprise has become just a place of work. Naturally, a process of internal differentiation gradually took place in the plants. Thus, when the importance of productivity increased, when the employment grew considerably in size, when the enterprises underwent a continuous process of bureaucratization, when production itself became more complex, when managers and workers became more distinct groups with different styles of life – it became difficult to ignore indications showing that labour-management relations in these plants did not vary substantially from those which prevailed in non-Histadrut enterprises (see Rosenstein, 1977: 57). Indeed, the Israeli economy is far from strike-free (see Table 13.4).

Table 13.4.
Industrial Disputes

	No. of Disputes	Workers Involved	Workdays lost
1967	142	25,058	58,286
1968	100	42,146	71,789
1969	114	44,496	102,162
1970	163	144,941	309,344
1971	169	88,265	178,612
1972	168	87,309	235,058
1973	96	122,338	375,020
1974	71	27,141	51,333
1975	117	114,091	164,509
1976	123	114,970	308,214

Source: ILO Yearbook, 1977.

The Trade Union department (recently called 'sector') of the Histadrut is its organizational arm. It co-ordinates and implements the trade union policy adopted by the Executive Committee of the Histadrut. It consists of approximately thirty national unions and federations of both blue- and white-collar employees (the workers of the administrative industries of the Histadrut itself have a special union). Usually, the Trade Union Department of the Histadrut and the employers' association conclude 'skeleton' agreements which are then adapted to conditions in each industry by means of subsidiary agreements negotiated by an individual national union, and the corresponding section of the employers' association. In general, the skeleton agreeements are renegotiated every two years by the Histadrut and the Israeli Manufacturers' Association. They lay down conditions of work including wages, social benefits, working hours, shift work, rules of conduct and discipline, hiring, employment termination, negotiating procedures, settlement of disputes, and the right and obligation of the parties.

Most activities of the national unions are carried out by the local unions which constitute a part of the regional workers' councils. These councils function in their respective regions as branches of the national centre of the Histadrut. As such, they represent the workers of their respective areas in local negotiations with the individual employers. The regional–local trade unions, which are an integral part of the respective regional workers' councils, are at the same time subordinate to their respective trade union federations or national unions, and represent the Centre in the area under their jurisdiction.

Within the plants the local trade unions function through the workers committees whose members are elected by the employees of the particular plant (see Tabb & Goldfarb, 1970; Derber, 1963). The trade-union department of the Histadrut speaks for about 90 per cent of wage and salary earners in the country. There was also the National Labour Federation organized in 1934 under the aegis of the revisionist party which opposed the Histadrut's socialist outlook. From the beginning, it had its own trade-union department. There are also a few independent unions, like the one of the secondary school teachers, university teachers, and other professional wage earners. It is evident that almost all trade unions in Israel are part of the Histradut and function at four related levels: the trade-union department of the Histadrut, the national federation and unions usually organized on the basis of trade, the local unions which function within the framework of the regional labour council, and the Workers Committees which function at the plant level. Co-ordination between these four levels and the exercise of authority is naturally problematic; this is especially so in relation with the Workers Committees who represent the immediate interests of the employees by whom they are directly elected.

Employers Association

The very existence of three major sectors in Israeli economy − private, state and labour economy − weakens the position of the employers in comparison with the centralized trade-union organization.

The employers in the private sector are organized in a federal structure of the Co-ordinative Chamber of the Economic Organization. This is an organization founded in 1966 in which 15 employers' associations are members. It negotiates the skeleton agreements with the trade-union department of the Histadrut. Within this organization the Manufacturers' Association, founded in 1920, is dominant. Its approximately 800 members turn out metals, electronics, textiles, processed citrus fruits, foodstuffs, electrical appliances, chemicals, pharmaceuticals, medical equipment, paper, and plastics. About 80 per cent of Israel's industry is privately owned, employing about 70 per cent of all factory labour.

Hevrat Ovdim, which founded in 1923, is the central organization for all economic undertakings owned by or affiliated with the Histadrut. It is at present made up of five components. In descending scale of their contribution to the net product of the economy, they are: (1) co-operative settlements − kibbutzim and moshavim; (2) wholly and partially owned enterprises (known as the Institutional Economy); (3) manufacturing, transportation, and service co-operatives; (4) marketing and consumer associations; (5) Histadrut non-profit-making organizations. The main influence of Hevrat Ovdim is evident in the Institutional Economy, which is owned by it and is directly under its control. The various forms of workers participation adopted by the Histadrut have been introduced into enterprieses belonging to the Institutional Economy.

The interests of the Government as an employer are expressed through its representatives in the boards of directors of the state-owned companies. The activities of these representatives in the labour relations area are co-ordinated by a special unit within the Ministry of Finance. Each of the state-owned companies signs with the Histadrut a 'special' collective agreement (a term which applies to a particular enterprise or employer in contrast with a general agreement which applies to the whole or part of the country or to a specific type of work).

Labour Disputes

The Israeli economy is far from strike-free (Michael A. Bar-El R, 1977.) In comparison with industrialized countries, Israel's relative ranking, measured by the number of days lost through strikes per 1,000 salaried workers through the economy, is not among the highest — thirteen among nineteen nations in the period 1964–74 (Histadrut Committee, 1976). But Israel is conspicious in having most of its disputes concentrated in the governmental public services. The intensity of strikes in the public services, in the context of a comparative analysis of ten industrialized countries for the years 1960–9 was second among these countries (see I.L.O., 1970).

A comparison of the rate of strikes by sector shows that in the governmental public sector the rate is significantly higher than in the private or Histadrut sectors. From 1968 through 1977 it exceeded 50 per cent of all strikes. A summary of the strikes for 1971-5 shows that the rate of strikes in the public and vital services reached approximately 61 per cent of all strikes in the economy, 74 per cent of all strikers and 67 per cent of all days lost (Galin-Harel, 1978). In 1977, 54 per cent of the strikes took place in the public sector (Government, municipalities, national institutions), 20 per cent in the private sector, and 15 per cent in the Histadrut sector. Table 13.5 enables the reader to follow the scope of strikes from 1960 to 1977 as well as the extent of sanctions or work-to-rules for 1973-7. The table reflects significant fluctuations in all indices of disputes, but, excluding 1974, from 1970 on the trend is one of growth in the number of strikers and work-days lost.

2.3. Participation in Companies

Three forms of direct-representative participation exist in Israeli companies. They are: the workers' committee, which exists in each company and plant; the Joint Productivity Council, which exists almost entirely in industrial plants, and the joint management, which exists in some Histadrut-owned industrial plants only. In addition, there are regulations for the inclusion of two worker-representatives in the Board of Directors in the state-owned industrial companies. We shall briefly examine each of the four forms of participation in companies and plant level (see also IDE 1980, 295–296).

The Workers' Committee

The basic unit of trade union representation is the Workers' Committee (*Va'ad Ha-ovdim*) which is elected by all workers in each factory, office, shop, etc. (see Shirom, 1971). It consists of three to nine members, depending on the size of the enterprise, elected every tow to three years. Voting is on an individual basis but workers often support the candidates nominated by their own political

Table 13.5.
Strikes and lock-outs; strikers and locked-out; work days lost and work-to-rules

	Participants in work-to-rule	Work-to-rules	Works days lost[1]	Strikers & locked-out[1]	Strikes & lock-outs[1]
1960			49,368	14,420	135
1964			100,912	47,168	135
1965			207,561	90,210	288
1966			147,846	85,953	286
1967			58,286	25,058	142
1968			71,789	42,146	100
1969			102,162	44,496	114
1970			390,260	114,941	163
1971			178,612	88,265	169
1972			236,058	87,309	168
1973	32,059	54	375,023	122,348	96
1974	18,363	49	51,333	27,141	71
1975	43,688	62	164,509	114,091	117
1976	114,567	76	308,214	114,970	123
1977	24,659	57	416,256	194,297	126

[1] Excluding work-to-rule.
Source: Israel Statistical Annual 1978, No. 28, Central Bureau of Statistics. Table 36 p.386.

parties. In most industrial plants, there are at least two workers' committees, one elected by the blue-collar, and the other by the white-collar employees.

As mentioned earlier, the Local Labour Council is the regional branch of the Histadrut. The Councils are elected in each region by proportional representation in the same way and at the same time as the national convention of the Histadrut, lists of candidates being submitted by the political parties. The Workers' Committees, together with the local Labour Council, represent the workers in all matters connected with the labour contracts. It negotiates supplementary agreements and takes up with the management any questions concerning working conditions or discipline that may arise from the administration of the agreement. The Committee also organizes mutual aid projects and sometimes serves as a channel for information from the management on the position of the enterprise, production plans, technological changes, and so forth. The Committees report regularly to general meetings of the workers to which it may submit matters of special importance for a dcision by majority vote. Any decision involving a strike must, according to Histadrut regulations, be taken by secret ballot and be approved by the labour council (rules which are most often not adhered to).

Workers' Committees have no standing in the Israeli labour laws. The law of Collective Agreements, for example, states that the trade union which represents a majority of the workers is party to the agreements. Thus, the formal basis for the functioning of the Workers' Committees is to be found in internal rules and regulations of the Histadrut itself as a trade union, and in some collective agreements. But these sources do not provide a clear definition of the authority of the Workers' Committees and confusion surrounds the permissible areas of their activity and mode of operation. Even the Work Rules of Histadrut-owned enterprises do not contribute much towards the clarification of the role and authority of Workers' Committees.

The Joint Productivity Councils

The Joint Productivity Councils (JPC) were first developed in several Histadrut enterprises during the mid-1940s. They were designed both to raise output and to provide a mechanism for participation in managerial decision-making in areas which were not included within the collective bargaining boundaries. The original idea did not include material rewards to those workers who would produce more, but soon after the purely psychological rewards were accompanied by premium payments. Soon after the establishment of the State in 1948, the Histadrut adopted the JPCs as a long-term instrument to raise national productivity and to raise the workers' standards of living. Since then, it has actually supported their establishment. In contrast with the enthusiasm of the leadership of the Histadrut, the idea of the JPC was much less welcomed in the early years by the workers, the Workers' Committees, and especially by the Manufacturers Association. Nevertheless, after two years of negotiation, an agreement was signed in 1952 between the Histadrut and the Manufacturers' Association in which the purpose of the committees as well as their rules and regulations were agreed upon.

The major emphasis in the agreement was on the introduction of appropriate work methods, by the committees, and of incentive payment for the purpose of cost reduction. It was clearly stated that the JPCs will not deal in any way with wages and working conditions. These will continue to be handled by the trade union organization, including the Workers' Committees. Half the Members of the Joint Productivity Council are appointed by the management of the plant whereas the other half are directly elected by the work-force. Election of a new JPC was to take place every year, but the agreement did not specify the frequency of its meetings. The JPC has an advisory capacity. Its decisions are made by a majority vote but these decisions are not more than recommendations to the management of the plant and to the Workers' Committee.

The number of the councils grew from about 100 in 1954 to the present number of about 550, almost all in industrial plants. The Councils are to be found in all three sectors of the Israeli economy: 62 per cent in the private sector, 26 per cent in the Histadrut sector, and 12 per cent in state-owned enterprises. The conditions and functioning of the JPCs in Histadrut-owned plants do not seem to differ from those existing in the other sectors. Only in very few places have the Joint Productivity Councils been introduced at the departmental level.

In 1967, a new agreement was signed between the Histadrut and the Manufacturers' Association regarding the JPCs. The purpose of both parties was to use in the new agreement the lessons which had been drawn since 1952. The capacity of the Council has been changed from advisory to compulsory but only if its decisions are made by the majority of each party. In addition, many general clauses of the old agreement were rewritten in a more concrete and specific manner. It is stated, for example, that the incentive payments system should cover as far as possible all jobs in the enterprise and it will be based on norms determined by industrial engineering methods. The new agreement also specifies the conditions under which production norms should be remeasured as a result of technological change.

On the whole the Israeli Joint Productivity Councils have proved to constitute a constructive instrument in the national effort to increase productivity. They have become, in many enterprises, an integral part of the management system and succeeded in promoting participation over a narrow, though important, range of managerial decisions. In the plants the importance and vitality of the JPCs are felt by both management and workers wherever incentive schemes are practicable (Rosenstein, 1977).

The Joint-Management System

While the Workers' Committees and JPCs discussed earlier are to be found in all three sectors of the economy, the joint-management system has been introduced only in some of the Histadrut-owned companies and plants. In the Histadrut plan for workers' participation adopted already in 1958, 'Joint Managements' were conceived as a higher stage of participation to be introduced in the future where conditions would warrant it. In the early 1960s, after it became clear that the Plant Council plan — the lower stage of participation — had failed, the Histadrut leadership was faced with a dilemma: whether or not to proceed to the higher stage when the lower one had not succeeded. The decision was to take the step. Both social and economic factors played a role in the decision: lack of participation, the leadership perceived, endangered the economic conditions and progress of the enterprise, and it also hampered the very possibility of achieving the social mission of establishing a 'community of workers' in the plants. Plant Councils were introduced in about thirty industrial plants of the Histadrut. This experience of workers' participation began in 1956 and ended for all practical purposes in 1961. These were joint councils, consisting of 5–10 elected representatives of the workers and 2–5 appointees of managements, which were to meet monthly to discuss and decide on all matters pertaining to the enterprise except wages and working conditions. Decisions approved by two-thirds of each side were to be binding on management and worker.

In 1964, the Histadrut Council endorsed in principle a joint management programme. Similarly, the 10th National Convention of the Histadrut in 1966 urged the introduction of such a programme. However, only in 1968 were the rules and regulations of the plan officially declared after a compromise was concluded beween the management groups of the Labour Economy on the one hand, and the ideologues-politicians designated by the Histadrut to administer the new programme on the other.

The programme envisages participation at two levels: the company- (central-) level and the plant-level. Very little information exists on the first level which includes both the board of directors and the central management board of the large Histadrut companies. It is estimated that in 1975 workers' representatives were included in the boards of directors in at least twelve of the Histadrut's companies.

The plant-level programme now provides for the establishment and functioning of joint-mangements in every Histadrut-owned enterprise. It also specifies the division of labour between the new joint-management body and the trade-union organization in the plant and endorses in principle the sharing of profits among employees. Figure 13.1 outlines the major formal aspects of the joint management scheme which was more generally adopted in 1968.

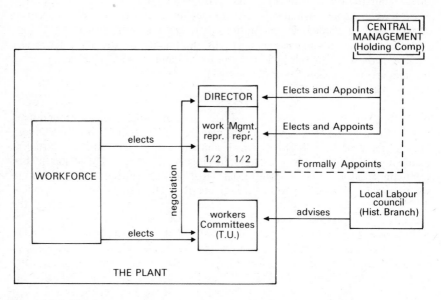

Figure 13.1. *The plant joint-management programme*

The plant level programme provides for the establishment in each plant of a joint-management board consisting of the director of the plant as a chairman and an equal number of workers' representatives and appointees of management. This board is responsible for the operation of the enterprise. It decides all issues except working conditions and wages, which continue to be negotiated between the Workers' Committee (the plant-level trade-union unit) and the general manager or his personnel manager. Election of the representatives of the workers will be by all employees in the plant, and they could not serve more than three consecutive years. The rules state that time should be allocated to the representatives of the work-force for preparatory work for the meetings of the joint-management board, which are to take place once a week. The representatives are otherwise expected to continue to work in their regular jobs. The plan encourages communication and co-ordination between the two arms of the work-force representation: the workers' committee and the workers' representatives to the joint-management board. The 1968 provisions state that up to 40 per cent of the profits resulting from the participation scheme should be shared among employees. In practice, profit-sharing has become dissociated from the existence of joint-management. It is estimated that about fifty joint-managements have been established since 1964.

3. PERSPECTIVES, PROBLEMS AND CURRENT ISSUES

Comparative case-studies of joint managements indicate that there are con-siderable differences among enterprises regarding the degree of co-ordination which exists between the channels of representation of workers. The Histadrut has been very careful in drawing a clear distinction between the subject matter of the Workers' Committee (plant-level trade-union organization) and that of the Joint-Management Board. In practice, however, there have been cases of open disputes and severe tension between representatives of workers in the two groups. Such acute disagreements are bound to occur when a functional conflict between the two groups emerges, as the developments in *Pheonicia* and in *Taim* illustrate (see Rosenstein, 1977).

Phoenicia — Israel Glass Works Inc., which in 1967 employed 700 workers, was the first plant to introduce a Joint-Management Board, but the road proved to be full of obstacles. From the very beginning, the shop stewards did not dis-play much enthusiasm over the idea of workers' participation. They were suspicious of it and feared that competition for hegemony between themselves and the representatives of the work-force in the Joint-Management Board would emerge. Out of the eight members of the workers' committee only one favoured participation: not a single committee member thought that the workers were in favour of the idea. It is not surprising that there was no support by the workers' committee in the joint-management programme.

More severe friction and rivalry between the two arms of representation occurred in *Taim* (fictitious name). This is a small enterprise of 120 employees in the food industry managed by one of the Histadrut's holding companies. Here, the shop stewards strongly disagreed with the line taken by the workers' representatives to give priority to the long-run interests of management over the short-run demands of the employees. The conflict emerged when the representa-tives started to exert pressure on the shop stewards and on the rank and file to give up, or at least to postpone their demands for a wage increase. The enter-prise, so claimed the representatives on the basis of their knowledge, of the financial condition of the enterprise, could not afford higher labour costs at that time without damaging its long-run potential for becoming a profitable organiza-tion. Therefore, in their opinion the shop stewards should not exert pressure on the chief executive to raise wages. The shop stewards on the other hand argued that the representatives of the work-force in the joint-Management Board had no right to present such claims since, by doing it, they betrayed their constituents. Moreoever, claimed the shop stewards, the representative should systematically co-ordinate their positions with the shop-stewards in order to exert more effective pressure on the management. Frictions in Taim between the two bodies fre-quently occurred during several months and culminated in the resignation of the Workers' Committee.

In principle, it seems that a clash between the two groups which represent the same work-force in the two functional areas of 'labour relations' and 'all other decision areas', is bound to emerge when the workers' representatives of the Joint-Management Board take positions in the labour relations area, which are closer to the management than to the Workers' Committee. When this happens, the latter reveals little tolerance and the outbreak of an open conflict is highly probable.

Why does it happen? There seem to be at least two reasons for the workers' representatives to back management *vis-à-vis* the plant trade-union organization: pressures exerted by top management on the representatives to help management achieve a 'common goal', e.g. not to raise labour costs till the plant becomes profitable; and the role-perception of the representatives who sometimes tend to regard themselves as part-time managers who must secure the long-range targets of the company. They, therefore, consider it their duty to restrain the demands of the workers' committee. Whether the reason is a tendency for top managers to manipulate the representatives, or the role-perception of the representatives themselves, the result would often be a clash with the workers' committee and eventually emergence of an open conflict. This in the past had endangered the very continuation of the participation system in some plants. There is, therefore, a need to draw in practice, a clear distinction between the subject matter of the two kinds of representation, and also to promote, through formal and informal means, the flow of information and co-ordination between them (see Rosenstein, 1977: 65-6).

Two general lessons seem to emerge from the Israeli scene. One major lesson is that mere ownership of economic organizations by an organized labour movement does not automatically ensure the actual implementation of participative principles. Rather, the Israeli experience seems to indicate that in order to have an effective participation programme absorbed and functioning, a considerable degree of integration among the major parties involved is required. Furthermore, the experience of workers' participation as a means of social change in Histadrut-owned plants seems to indicate that a perceived need to change the social status quo by a political and ideological leadership is not sufficient, at least when western democracies are concerned. An implementation of a participation programme designed by central official bodies for the purpose of social change depends largely on the will of the parties at the plant-level to introduce that social change. To the ideologists, the participation solution is seen as an over-all cure for the ailments of modern bureaucratized work: to the empiricist, who is sometimes also responsible for the efficient performance of the economic enterprise, this is a dubious cure. To the ideologist, the participation solution is applicable to all situations because it can cause only good: to the empiricist, such a solution should be handled with care since it might have no effect, or even a negative one. The ideologist thinks about participation in terms of harmony and integration: the empiricist is more inclined to analyse the application of such programmes in terms of self interest of the two parties. Thus, examination of the application of several participation programmes in enterprises owned by the Histradut in Israel suggest that it is the local conditions at the level of enterprise rather than the characteristics of the official programme and its underlying ideology that are crucial to the better understanding of the implementation process of participative plants.

Another major lesson from the Israeli experience with workers' participation seems to be that when a representative (or 'indirect') model of participation is not integrated with a 'direct' participation programme at the face-to-face level, the whole idea of participation is bound to have only limited success. The three programmes of participation initiated by the Histadrut (joint productivity councils. Plant Councils and Joint-Managements) were all within the boundaries of a representative model, its major assumption being that the representatives of the work-force should be given the legitimate means to exert influence on the full-time managers in the decision-making process. It seems that even if such influence is effected at the upper level, the involvement of the rank-and-file would be minimal or non-existent and, would therefore have very little impact on the relationship between the individual employee and the organization in (or for) which he works. For promoting the identification and involvement of the ordinary worker, representative or 'indirect' participation mechanisms (such as Joint-Management Boards) must be simultaneously developed and integrated with 'direct' participation mechanisms (such as consultation and delegation to the individual employee or to the group) at the shop-level where work is performed. Participation programmes implemented at both levels at the top of the hierarchy and at the immediate work group, may augment the favourable effects of each of them.

Related to the separation of the direct and indirect mechanisms of participation in Histadrut-owned enterprises, was another factor: the tradition of centralization of decision-making in the Histadrut. With regard to the institutionalization of participatory programmes this has been manifested in two areas: the participation plans as well as the rules and regulations for their implementation, were adopted by central bodies of the Histadrut and left relatively little leeway to the various holding companies to design their own schemes. Diversions from the resolutions of the central bodies were therefore often associated with bitter internal disputes between the holding companies on one hand and the special unit within the Histadrut head office responsible for the implementation of the participation programme on the other (Yudin, 1972); and, secondly, even at the corporate level, there has for a long time been a tendency to centralize decision-making in the area of participation. This can easily be interpreted by the plant personnel as a means of control, inspection, or sometimes even as an expression of lack of confidence in local management and in the workers. Centralized decision-making in the participation area may thus constitute an important obstacle preventing the development of effective participation at the plant- and shop-levels. The very obligation of a Joint-Management Board at the individual plant to adhere to outside rules with relatively little manoeuvrability decreases a priori the probability that plant and departmental institutions of participation which suit the specific local conditions will be initiated and developed. Any intention of making the participation institutions relevant and meaningful for the ordinary workers at floor-level should therefore be accompanied with a decentralized decision-making process in matters associated with the concerns, institutions, and procedures of the participation programme. On the other hand, centralization in these matters including profit-sharing programmes may deprive local management and workers' representatives alike of an opportunity to participate in a meaningful way. Naturally, the more centralized and rigid a participation programme is, the less sensitive it becomes to specific local needs.

Given the unique nature of the Histadrut as the organized labour movement of Israel, there is a very great chance that its search for an effective participation programme will continue. As an example of this, the most recent development in the area of representative participation in Israel concerns the regulations affecting the participation of representatives of the work-force on the board of directors of state-owned manufacturing companies. The Histadrut was most active in the formulation of this proposal. This scheme calls for two elected representatives of the employees to serve as part-time members in such boards. These directors, who are not to occupy elective union offices, are to be elected for a three-year period, once renewable.

Their income is to be the same as before their election and they will continue to perform their regular work, although they are to be given adequate time to perform their duties as members of the board. Top management will not be eligible for election. Basically, these are the same conditions under which worker-directors in some Histadrut companies have already been functioning for some time. Because of the political change which took place in Israel with the right-wing bloc coming into power, it is doubtful whether the new regulations will be implemented in the near future.

REFERENCES

Arian, A. (1973), *The Elections in Israel,* Tel Aviv: University Press.

Blumberg, P. (1968), *Industrial Democracy: The Sociology of Participation,* London: Constable.

Central Bureau of Statistics (1979), *Israel Statistical Annual 1978,* No. 28, Central Bureau of Statistics.

Derber, M. (1962), 'Worker Participation in Industrial Management in Israel' (Institute of Labour & IR, University of Illinois, Mimeo).

(1963), 'Plant Labor Relations in Israel', Industrial and Labor Relations Review 1963, Vol. 17.

(1973), Histadrut and Industrial Democracy in Israel: 'An interpretative Essay from an American Perspective', in Avrech, I. and Gilandi, D., *Labor and Society in Israel,* Dept. Of Labor Studies, Tel-Aviv University and Dept. of Higher Education, Histadrut, Israel.

Fine, K. S. (1973), 'Worker Participation in Israel', in Gerry Hunnius (ed.), *Worker' Control: A Reader on Labor & Social Change,* New York: Random House.

Galin, A., Harel, A. (1978), *Developments and Trends in Israeli Industrial and Labour Relations System,* Massada Ltd., Israel (in Hebrew).

Golomb, N. and Katz, D., *The Kibbutzim as Open Social Systems,* Tel Aviv: Ruppin Institute, undated.

Hyen, Z. (1974), 'Ideology of Labor', in *Society,* Israel Pocket Library, Keter Publishing House, Jerusalem.

(1974), 'Labor Relations', in *Society,* Israel Pocket Library, Keter Publishing House, Jerusalem.

Horowitz, D. (1967), *The Economics of Israel,* Israel, Oxford: Pergamon.

Kerem, M. (1969), *The Kibbutz,* Jerusalem: Israel Digest.

Kolat, I. (1973), 'The Concept of the Histadrut', in Avrech, I. and Giladi, D.,

Labor and Society in Israel, Dept. of Labor Studies, Tel-Aviv University and Dept. of Higher Education, Histadrut, Israel.

Michael, A., Bar-El, R. (1977), *Strikes in Israel,* Bar-Illan University, Ramat-Gan in collaboration with the Israel Institute of Industrial and Labor Relations, Tel-Aviv.

Rosenstein, E. (1970), 'Histadrut's Search for a Participation Program', *Industrial Relations,* Vol. 9, No. 2.

(1977), 'Workers Participation in Management: Problematic Issues in the Israeli system', *Industrial Relations Journal,* 8.

(1977(b)), 'Workers Participation in Israel: Experience and Lessons', in *Industrial Democracy in International Perspective,* The Annals of the American Academy of Political and Social Science, May 1977.

Rosner, M. (1971), *Hierarchy & Democracy in Kibbutz Industry,* Haifa: Givat Publications.

(1977), 'The Structural Conditions of Self-Management' (The Case of the Kibbutz Industry), Paper for 2nd International Conference on Participation, Workers' Control & Self-Management, Paris, 7–10 Sept. 1977.

Report of the Histadrut Committee for the Study of Labor Disputes in the Public Services in Israel, 1976, p. 27.

Shirom, A. (1971), 'Workers' committees in the Israeli Labour Relations System – an appraisal', *Industrial Relations Journal.*

Spiro, M. E. (1963), *Kibbutz: Venture in Utopia,* New York: Schocken Books.

Tabb, J. and Goldfarb, A. (1970), *Workers Participation in Management,* Oxford: Pergamon.

Yudin, Y. (1972), 'Industrial Democracy', *Histadrut Execution,* Tel-Aviv.

Zweig, F. (1959), The Israeli Worker: *Achievements, Attitudes & Aspirations,* Herzl Press, New York.

14

CONCLUDING SYNTHESIS

UNDERSTANDING DIFFERENCES AND SIMILARITIES

The reader who scrutinized — or just glanced through — the foregoing twelve national reports on the state of industrial democracy will, in all likelihood, be more impressed by the differences than by the similarities from country to country in participative structure (PS), industrial relations system (IRS), and society context. The question arises as to how far it is possible to account for the variety of participatory arrangements in terms of features of the systems of industrial relations and of the wider economic, political, and social context of the nations in question.

In the first chapter of this volume several conjectures were offered with respect to possible determinants of PS. As pointed out, the explanations distinguished there do not refer to competing theories, but rather to various factors all — or some — of which could be operative jointly. In this last chapter an effort will be made to develop a conceptual sketch integrating notions from chapter one, with the aid of which some of the results of this survey may be interpreted.

What follows obviously is in no way an analysis in line with the canons of the hypothetico-deductive method. The theory was formulated to fit the facts known and should therefore be viewed merely as a stimulus towards a new approach to the systematic, comparative study of industrial relations systems and their effects on industrial democracy.

1. THE INDUSTRIAL RELATIONS SYSTEM AS A NETWORK

Inter-organizational theory is seldom if ever applied to the field of industrial relations. This is curious indeed, for the interactions between union and management, unions and employers' associations, confederations of unions and of employers' associations furnish outstanding examples of the *accommodative* nature of such relations. In some of the early literature here, linkage-mechanisms between organizations were seen primarily as efforts on the part of organizations to achieve jointly what they could not — due to scarcity of resources — achieve all by themselves (e.g. Levine and White, 1961). However, gradually the insight developed that such arrangements and processes do not function only — and perhaps not even primarily — to attain strength by union, but rather to solve the problem of how to 'stand dividedly'. To clarify the point further: some authors (Litwak and Hylton, 1962: 409-10; Litwak and Rothman, 1970: 161-3) point out that such relations contain adjudication in addition to communication mechanisms. Others (Pfeffer and Salancik, 1978: ch. 6) stress the view that such attempts at linkage quite often are not so much devices to maximize profit, but rather strategies on the part of organizations to control their environments, in particular to manage and stabilize their interdependence with other organizations.

In other words, relations between organizations offer rather perfect specimens of what was called 'accommodation', a form of 'antagonistic co-operation' in the old American sociology (e.g. Ogburn and Nimkoff, 1946: ch. XIII).

Now, even for a casual observer of the scene of industrial relations in modern society, it will be clear that the institutionalized relations between worker- and employer-organizations preponderantly exhibit forms of accommodation between conflicting interests. Consequently, it appears quite appropriate to attempt an analysis of IRS with the aid of this kind of organizational theory.

Systems of industrial relations, according to Dunlop (1958: 7-16), comprise three parties:

(1) a hierarchy of managers and their representatives;
(2) a hierarchy of workers (non-managerial) and any spokesmen; and
(3) specialized governmental agencies (and specialized agencies created by the first two actors) concerned with workers, enterprises, and their relationships.

These parties operate in a context which involves three sets of givens: the technological characteristics of the work place and work community, the market or budgetary constraints which impinge on the parties, and the locus and distribution of power in the larger society. Furthermore, these actors between them produce a 'web of rules' consisting of procedures to establish rules, substantive rules, and procedures for deciding their application to particular situations.

It goes without saying that we can consider Participative Structures (PS) as part of that 'web of rules' and the three 'actors' in question as organized parties to an inter-organizational 'game'. In countries like Sweden, unions and employers' associations have formed at the national level organization-linking structures, or rather centralized federations with their own bureaucratic apparatus and a good deal of authority *vis-à-vis* their members (unions or employers' associations). In other countries, for example, France, unions and employers' associations are represented at the national level by loosely coupled confederacies or committees which have hardly any staff of their own and which are not in a position to initiate and enforce central policies.

Of course, there is some variety in the degree to which the parties acting on behalf of workers and employers in a certain country are well organized. None the less, in most cases both the 'hierarchy of managers' and the 'hierarchy of workers' are each represented on the national scene each either by an organization (of organizations!) or by a more loosely structured agency.

Likewise, the governmental agencies dealing with labour relations together form an appropriate new structure of mutually co-operating (or competing) organizations. On the whole, however, the governmental party can usually be presumed to constitute a centralized organization, since main policies in this field are usually decided upon by the cabinet and have to be approved by a parliament.

What Dunlop calls 'specialized agencies created by the first two actors' are obviously inter-organizational structures linking the hierarchies of managers and workers. One may add that governmental agencies also often participate in co-ordinative agencies of this kind. Evidently, it makes sense to treat such agencies as quite distinct from the governmental party.

Given the limits of this chapter, we have to forego an analysis of the intricacies of the internal inter-organizational relations of each of the parties acting at the national level and of their interrelations. We will for the sake of simplicity assume that there are just three more or less organized parties (U = some sort of confederacy of the unions; E = some sort of confederacy of employers' associations; G = government) which between them have come to a more or less lasting agreement on a 'web of rules' concerning their interactions and concerning the degree to which workers are entitled to participate in decision-making in enterprises. We are, however, aware (as can be seen from the foregoing chapters) that some countries have more than one confederacy for respectively U and E, so that there is a multiple role-playing, as will become apparent.

2. RULES ON PARTICIPATION IN ENTERPRISES

It is clear from the foregoing chapters that prescriptions as to the degree of involvement of workers in decision-making in an enterprise can refer — roughly speaking — to three levels. Rights of information, consultation, or codetermination can pertain to:
— shop-floor level (e.g. the right to be consulted in advance for a worker with respect to his vacation, transfer, etc.)
— management level (e.g. rights of a works council or a health and safety committee to participate in the formulation of specified policies);
— board level (e.g. the right of a works council or similar organ to elect a number of board members).
In theory, one could try to account for international differences in participatory arrangements for each level separately, or focus on the explanation of all occurring constellations of arrangements at two or more levels. In view of the limited number of cases (N = 12!) covered in this study, it was decided to follow a third road and concentrate on an interpretation of the degree to which, in the countries concerned, national agreements or legislation prescribe a relatively high amount of participation for workers on all three levels, on two levels, on one, or on no level.

Usually the reports on the separate countries furnish some data on the degree of prescribed involvement on these levels. In addition, in chapter 6 of the Volume 'Industrial Democracy in Europe', 1980, a quantitative account is presented of the degree to which workers and their representative organs are entitled to participation in sixteen decision-areas in the industries studied. This enables us to determine the relative ranking of all the countries investigated in terms of their 'average mode scores' for involvement at shop-floor- and at management-level. In Table 14.1 the rank-orders in terms of these two dimensions is given (1 = relatively great involvement, . . . 12 = almost no involvement prescribed).

As to the third level of participation (participation in a board or similar supervisory organ), it turned out to be relatively easy to group the countries into three categories: one where workers or their representatives have no rights whatsoever to nominate and/or elect board members, one where they do have

Table 14.1.

Relative standing of the twelve countries as to degree of prescribed involvement of workers or their representatives in decision-making in enterprises

	Direct involve-ment of workers	Involvement of representative bodies	Board-representa-tion standing	Over-all standing
Yugoslavia	1	1	1	A
Germany	4	2	1	A
Sweden	5	3	1	A
Norway	2	11	1	B
Netherlands	10	5	2	C
France	8	4	2	C
Belgium	6	7	3	D
Finland	3	10	3	D
Denmark	9	8	1	D
Israel	12	6	3	D
Italy	7	9	3	E
Great Britain	11	12	3	E

Source: Industrial Democracy in Europe, 1980, Table 6.4.

the right to elect at least a minority of board members, and one in-between category.

This latter category contains cases where workers or their representatives are entitled to elect two observers at board-meetings (France), or where the works council can nominate (but not appoint) board-members and veto the apoint-ment of new members nominated by others (Netherlands). In Table 14.1, all cases without any kind of board-participation are numbered 3; with the right of appointment of two or more members, 1; and the in-between category, 2.

The data in Table 14.1 show that Yugoslavia, Germany, and Sweden have a relatively good standing in all three respects. Yugoslavia, of course, is a case apart. One could consider the Workers' Council there as an amalgam of a super-visory board and a representative body. An alternative option would be to view the Yugoslavian Chamber of Associated Labour as roughly equivalent to a board in capitalist countries. In either case, however, the Yugoslavian system would satisfy the criterion of having at least two workers' representatives on the board.

Next in line is Norway, with relatively high scores for arrangements pertain-ing to workers' participation and board-representation, but with quite a low score for prescribed involvement of the representative bodies.

A third place in this ranking order is occupied by the Netherlands, and France. These two countries belong to the upper-half as far as involvement rights for representative bodies is concerned; to the lower half with respect to direct worker involvement on the shop-floor; and to the in-between category as to board representation. Belgium, Finland, Israel and Denmark each score above average in one respect: in the case of Finland and Belgium, for direct worker-involvement, in the case of Denmark, for board-representation, while Israel's score for involvement of representative bodies falls in the upper half.

The remaining countries — Italy and Great Britain — score average or low in all three categories.

We now have at our disposal a ranking from high (= A) to low (= E) which broadly indicates the degree to which the 'web of rules' in the countries concerned contains stronger or weaker provisions for workers' involvement at various levels in policy or administrative decisions in enterprises. This index is a meaningful instrument not only because influence at various levels supposedly 'adds up', but also because simultaneous pressure at various levels may produce a 'surplus-value' due to interaction-effects. An early investigation of *Mitbestimmung* in the German heavy industry, for example, contains indications that it is especially the interplay of workers' representatives at adjacent levels that brings about a significant impact on managerial policy (Voigt, 1962: 225, 280–1, 294, 331–2, 429).

Finally, a word of caution is in order. The ranking of the twelve countries in terms of formal opportunities for workers and their spokesmen to exert multiple-level influence on decision-making in their enterprises, is a very rough measure indeed, which glosses over quite important differences between systems of participation and representation. Also, one should keep in mind that we deal here only with the amount prescribed, not with the amount of *actual* industrial democracy in enterprises.

3. MUTUAL DEPENDENCE BETWEEN THE MAIN ACTORS

To pave the way for an interpretation of the international differences in arrangements for industrial democracy, we first have to consider the nature of their interdependence of the main actors of the IRS. Let us start with the mutual dependence between E (= the national confederation or coalition of employers' associations) and U (= the national confederation or coalition of unions).

In general, following the reasoning of Pfeffer and Salancik (1978: pp. 43 ff.), one organization is dependent on another if the latter controls resources of vital interest to the former. Labour, of course, is a vital resource for the functioning of an industrial organization. Therefore, to the extent that U — via its member unions — can withdraw, slow down, or further the labour-'input' in industry, E — an organization to defend the interests of its member-associations and ultimately of all affiliated managements — is dependent on U.

U, however, is no less dependent on E. In any kind of bargaining at the national level, it is E that has the power to resist or to grant the demands of the workers as voiced by U.

To obtain concessions from E, at least to some extent, at least once in a while, is a matter of life and death for U, since gaining benefits from E is the very *raison d'être* of U. In addition, U is dependent on E for various facilities such as provisions for:

meetings of union officials and/or in-plant unionists on the premises of the firm, during working hours; obtaining relevant information on plans, policies and problems of management and employer-organizations. In some instances unions even depend on managements and their representative organizations for the recruitment of new members (closed shop!), or for dues collection or for

contributions to funds which they control by themselves or jointly with management for the benefit of their members. Not only is E for U a source of positive
sanctions, but also of negative ones (lock-out; reprisals against union-members;
reduction of positive sanctions thus far granted).

Table 14.2 contains a short summary of the sanctions E and U in principle
have with respect to one another. In most Western countries nowadays, the
strength of E in its relation to U lies in positive sanctions, whereas U has to rely
mainly on (threats with) negative sanctions in its dealing with E. This directs
our attention to the fact that if and when certain conditions favour the use of
negative sanctions by E or the deployment of positive sanctions by U, such a
state of affairs can affect the balance of power between the actors in question.

Table 14.2.
Mutual dependence of the main parties of the industrial relations system

	Positive sanctions	Negative sanctions
Dependence of:		
E on U	U can (co-)sponsor productivity drive, stimulate other co-operative endeavours etc.	U can threaten with or initiate strikes, slowdowns, etc.
U on E	E can grant material or other demands of workers and their organizations.	E can resist demands or withdraw privileges of workers and their organizations; E can also threaten with or initiate lock-outs, reprisals, etc.
U and E on G	Legislation or policies wanted or approved of by U and/or E can be enacted by G; G can also bestow financial benefits on the constituents of U and/or E.	Legislation or policies not wanted or disapproved of by U and/or E can be enacted by G; G can also withhold or withdraw benefits from the constituents of U and/or E.
G on U and E	E and/or U can contribute to a positive image of G as guardian of the general welfare; U can render political support.	E and/or U can contribute to a negative image of G as guardian of the general welfare; U can withdraw or withhold political support.

E = Central decision-making organ or organization of employers' associations.
U = Central decision-making organ or organization of unions.
G = The government in office.

It will also be clear that the strengths of both E and U hinge upon the degree
to which these superordinate organs have the consent of their constituents for
their policies or have sufficient authority *vis-à-vis* their constituents to have them
conform to their policies. We can presume furthermore that E and U can hardly
formulate and follow any clear-cut policy at all, unless there is a fair level of consensus on the issue at stake among their constituents. Therefore, it stands to
reason to conclude that the degree of unity (among member-unions in the case
of U, and member-associations in the case of E) and the degree of centralization

in the decision-making machinery of U and E form strategically important determinants of the power which one party can bring to bear upon the other party.

Finally, one could surmise that the degree of 'coverage' of all potential members (workers in the case of U, managements in the case of E) by the affiliated unions and employer-associations also goes into the 'strength' of U and E with respect to each other.[1] Divide-and rule tactics by management, employers' associations, and their central negotiating organ at the national level (E) might be more effective, if the degree of unionization is low. In similar vein, if not all managements — and primarily those of the big firms — belong to the main employers' associations, such a lack of a common front on the part of the employers may be to the advantage of U.

Both U and E are to some extent dependent on G for enacting labour legislation in line with their views. However, if U and E can come to a formal or tacit agreement on certain matters, they can do without legislation. Moreover, it is a moot point whether a government in a western, parliamentary democracy can really enforce labour legislation. If not both E and U, and of course their members, co-operate either whole- or half-heartedly in executing the policies in question.

Apart from labour legislation, governmental laws, degrees, measures, and decisions on economic and social affairs may have a positive or negative impact on the interests of management and labour. Tariff-barriers, subsidies for distressed industries, government orders, etc. usually constitute positive sanctions for both workers and managers in the branches concerned. Other actions or policies may be perceived as beneficial or harmful by one party only, e.g. a reduction or rise in profits tax, or an increase or decrease in welfare benefits. Anyway, E and U are dependent on G, not only for its powers to regulate labour relations, and other activities of — or relevant for — industry, but also because the 'clients' of U and E can either benefit or be injured by governmental policies financially.

We may infer from all this that a government in office — especially if it is likely to remain in command for the years to come — is a valuable ally for both E and U. Its regulatory powers enable the state to facilitate or restrict the activities and functioning of industry and of workers' and employers' associations, while by pulling the purse-strings it can in a variety of ways manipulate the level of income or profit for the constituents of both parties.

Of course, there are serious limits on government making full use of these powers, for they are also dependent in various respects on the principle labour-market organizations. Rightly or wrongly — more often than not wrongly! — labour unrest and in general any reversal or slow-down in the pace of economic growth and of rising standards of living is ascribed to government policy or the absence thereof. Consequently, governments tend to presume that their chances to remain in office or be re-elected depend on the level of joint effort by workers and managers to make the economy work, grow, and thus guarantee the national welfare.

Not only 'spontaneous' reactions of parties and voters to the government's success or failure to maintain or bring about a thriving economy, but also the deliberate and explicit support or disapproval of its policies by parties on the labour front, is a factor that counts for a government. Since there are many more workers than managers in a one-man, one-vote democracy, a left-of-centre government usually is much more dependent for its votes on support from the unions than a right-of-centre government is on approval of the employers' associations.

It goes without saying that the general state of the interdependence between U, E, and G is portrayed here in a very incomplete and global sense only. Nevertheless, the analysis suffices as a basis for some conjectures about the powers of U to push for formal rules with respect to participation on the part of workers or their representatives in firm policy-making and about the conditions under which they will want and obtain this kind of rule from E and G.

4. THE ROLE OF THE MAIN PARTIES

Under what conditions will the parties in question be willing and able to introduce formal arrangements for participation in the enterprise? As suggested in Chapter 1 — the 'Organized Labour' Explanation — a strong labour movement could very well be able to push effectively for PS, either via legislation or in the form of national agreements with the organization or coalition of employers' associations. As indicated in that chapter and in the previous paragraph, a high degree of unionization of the labour force, unity of the labour front, and centralization of policy-making would enable U to exert a good deal of pressure on both E and G.

Of course, the strength of U contributes to a relatively high degree of prescribed involvement only if the unions espouse this form of participation as a goal. We will return later to the conditions under which the parties in question might want PS, and conclude for the moment that strength of U rates as one potential determinant of the chances of getting PS introduced once U has decided to strive after this goal.

It was pointed out earlier that a high degree of Organized Labour might lead to Labour or Socialist parties in office and this way promote the chances of getting PS measures on the books. This tallies with our observation in the last paragraph that G, and particularly a left-of-centre-government, is dependent on U for political support. If in addition one takes into account the general dependence of any G on U, it follows that a socialist or socialist-dominated government, will tend to be a willing coalition partner of U — especially of a strong U! — in efforts to enact PS, if that is what they want.

Furthermore, we surmise that a left-of-centre government, not only as the pawn of a strong U, but also in its own right could be a condition favourable to the rise of PS. After all, 'participation' or 'democratization' might very well be a significant objective of a labour or socialist party and an issue stressed in election campaigns. If that is the case, and if the socialist-dominated government is in office for a prolonged period, such a red or pink G would also qualify as a determinant of PS.

What kind of hypothesis can we make as to the role of the third partner in the game, that is, E? Obviously, a united and centralized employers' movement is better equipped than a weak one to oppose a coalition of U and G. Nevertheless, one could suspect that a strong E, although more able to resist the introduction of participatory arrangements, is less likely than a weak one to do so. For one thing, the chances that E endorses proposals for PS *for strategic reasons* are in all likelihood higher if E bargains with U from a position of strength than in the opposite case. Why should this be so?

In inter-organizational relationships of interdependency it is better for an organization to rely on positive than on negative sanctions. Negative sanctions antagonize opponents and often have the unintended consequence of closing ranks and thus fortifying a position. Therefore, in bargaining relations it is usually advantageous to convert negative into positive sanctions, for the latter type of sanctions have no such boomerang effects. Now, if E fiercely resists demands for PS from U, it disposes in this respect of negative sanctions only. However, as soon as E declares such demands (for PS) as negotiable, it converts negative into positive sanctions and thereby gains a tactical advantage.

Moreover, if there is a trend towards increasing the degree of prescribed worker-involvement in decision-making, a positive stance towards such a trend enables E to shape PS in accordance with its own wishes.

A positive policy on such an issue means that one can take (or hold) the initiative to some extent and that improves one's chances of codetermining the nature of the arrangements to be made as compared to a situation in which one adopts a negative and thus rather reactive policy.[2]

Now it appears plausible that only or primarily a rather strong employers' federation will recognize clearly the potential gains of a positive strategy towards demands for PS from the side of U, to formulate a policy along these lines and to carry it out. A case can be made for the hypothesis that a strong E – with a relatively high 'density' of professionals and with some authority over its member-associations – will be guided by *Zweckrationalität* (goal-directed rationality) rather than by *Wertrationalität* (value-oriented rationality), to use a famous pair of concepts suggested by Max Weber (1974: 12–13).

Perhaps one could say that professionals in general are not only more *able* to apply goal-directed rationality, but also more *inclined* to do so. Of course, the professionals' inclination towards such a cool, instrumental kind of rationality will, to a considerable extent, be due to their proficiency in this respect. However that may be, it stands to reason that professionals, also thanks to their socialization and experience, will feel more affinity for goal-directed than value-oriented rationality.

Consequently, there are reasons for believing that due to the more professional orientation of a strong E, a positive, strategic policy in connection with PS-issues will prevail there. If E is nothing but a weak confederation or committee, the delegates dominating the scene there may be more oriented towards a value-oriented rationality, inspired by common values such as insistence on 'managerial prerogatives', 'entrepreneurial autonomy', etc.[3]

We argued that E could adopt a cautious pro-PS stance with an eye towards the potential strategic advantages of such a stance in terms of the balance of power in its relations with U. In addition one could imagine that a strong E where a goal-directed type of rationality prevails, will be wise to the possible pay-off for managerial ends of such a positive policy with respect to participation (see IDE, 1980, ch. 11).

As mentioned already, the (only) positive sanctions U can offer E and its constituents, consist of attempts to stimulate co-operative endeavours at the level of the enterprise and of the branch (see Table 14.2). This kind of contribution to the welfare of the enterprise is evidently valued only by managers and the advocates of their interests, if they really believe that participation can be benefical, e.g. for productivity, to curb turnover and absenteeism, to prevent or quash various forms of labour unrest and protest. In this connection it is irrelevant whether managers or their representatives perceive participation schemes as serious 'joint ventures' of management and union, or as excellent means to play organized and unorganized labour off against each other. In both cases managers and their associations and organs are likely to initiate, or react favourably to, proposals for PS from the side of U and/or G.

If E is strong and takes a positive stance with respect to PS, this might very well motivate U to insist more forcefully on the introduction of participation schemes than it (U) would do otherwise.

In the first place, efforts to bother at all with the design of PS and with negotiating about it, will certainly be seen as more worthwhile by U, the better the indications are that there will be a positive response from E. Not only does a relatively positive policy with respect to PS on the part of E signify to U, that there is a fair chance of reaching an agreement with E, but on the basis of E's positive stance U will also assess the chances of inducing G to adopt legislation of this sort as far better than if U itself was the only sponsor of such legislation.

In the second place, union officials and their staffs are likely to recognize that the actualization of PS requires a degree of co-operation from the managements concerned. The stronger E is in relation to its membership, the better its position to 'educate' its members and to see to it that agreements made are fulfilled. Therefore, U — and particularly a U which is professionalized itself! — is bound to perceive participatory arrangements as more viable, the stronger E is.

In the third place, U can stress the positive significance of participatory arrangements for E only if E is at all willing to ponder in a rational way the possible functions and dysfunctions of PS from the point of view of managerial goals. As we noticed, in general U has to manipulate more with negative than with positive sanctions. A somewhat positive and instrumental view of participation from the side of the employers therefore implies to the unions that they can possibly amplify their assortment of sanctions. Moreover, since they would add *positive* sanctions to their assortment, the unions could find this particulary desirable given the fact that positive sanctions have, as we saw, less drawbacks than negative ones.

In the argument presented thus far, we stressed that the strength of U and that of E can be seen as positive determinants of PS. Not only can both factors contribute separately but also jointly to the institution of PS. The level of effort on the part of U to strive for PS is, we saw, to quite an extent contingent on the strength of E and the degree to which E entertains a neutral to positive outlook on the desirability of PS. The reverse — that E will push harder for PS, the stronger U is and the more positive towards PS — is probably not true, but we will not go into that.

Anyway, in trying to explain PS we should not just look at the state of U and of E, but also at the nature of their inter-organizational relations. If both actors are relatively strong, the nature of their interrelations is such as to re-inforce already existing forces to bring about PS. In addition to the effect of a strong E on efforts towards PS by U, we also pointed to the 'added value' of a kind of coalition between U and E if they jointly put pressure on G to introduce PS. Another positive effect with respect to PS could result from the interrelations between a strong E and a strong U in so far as under these circumstances professionals from both sides in boundary positions play an important role in outlining PS-policy.

In organizational theory literature (e.g. Evan, 1976: 155), the significance of the normative reference-group orientation of boundary personnel comes to the fore. The more professional and 'cosmopolitan' the outlook of boundary employees in an organization, the less loyal and committed they will be to the goals and norms of their own organization. However, the other side of the coin is, of course, that 'cosmopolitan' policy-shapers, when they negotiate with one another on behalf of different organizations, come to an understanding, work out compromises etc. rather easily, thanks to a somewhat common outlook and to their common interest in keeping the inter-organizational relations viable. We can surmise that in the relations between E and U this kind of mutual under-standing between experts from both sides facilitates joint action with respect to PS proposals. In fact, one encounters this very notion — that the presence of professionals on both sides contributes to the maintenance of E-U relations and to the production of common rules — also in the industrial relations literature (Dunlop, 1958: 15-16, 30-1).

5. THE ROLE OF CONTEXTUAL FACTORS

In the previous section we focussed mainly on the properties of the three parties and of their interrelations. How far can the societal context within which these actors operate condition their game and its outcome? Let us look first at the economic aspects of that context. In Chapter 1 it was mentioned — the 'Econo-mic Explanation' — that in times of affluence managers and their representatives might be more inclined to think they can 'afford' participation. Although there is no research evidence in support of this assumption, nevertheless such ill-advised managerial beliefs to the effect that participation is a costly affair, could very well militate against the introduction of PS. This resistance against PS would tend to be or become weaker, the richer a country is or becomes.

Furthermore, as touched upon likewise in Chapter 1, a more advanced tech-nology might require more involvement of personnel in decision- and policy-making. One could add that perhaps not only the nature of the technology, but also the kind of management system which is conducive to economic growth demands an active effort and a responsible attitude from the workforce in modern industry.[3]

This means that industrialization and economic growth in a sense raise the value of the positive sanctions U has at its disposal for E (see Table 14.2). At the same time, work-stoppages and labour unrest in general pose more of a threat for an industry in times of prosperity than in hard times. Workers and unions can 'afford' a strike better during an upswing of the business cycle than during a downswing and often the reverse is true for the industry.[4] On the same grounds it appears plausible that due to a tight labour market and the relative welfare of the labour force, employers can take less recourse in periods of economic growth than in periods of standstill or decline to their negative sanctions.

On the whole, therefore, industrialization and economic growth enhance the worth of the sanctions of U with respect to E but rather diminish the value of what E has in store for U (see Table 14.2). Consequently, the level of economic development of the countries concerned and/or their rates of economic growth during recent decades, may be conceived off as variables conditioning the effects on the introduction of PS by other factors. If, for whatever reasons, U and G push for PS, we would expect them to be more successful under conditions of (a rising level of) prosperity than under conditions of economic hardship (or of a slowdown in the rate of economic growth).

Up till now we paid attention primarily to conditions facilitating the spread or intensification of PS, once one or two parties — U and/or G — are determined to do so. But what makes unions and governments think participation by workers in their enterprises is a good thing? It is generally recognized that most participative provisions can contribute to either the representation of workers' interests and/or the welfare of the enterprise. In other words, participative arrangements can enable the workers and/or their representatives to engage in bargaining and/ or in joint consultation. Since most unions everywhere consider bargaining as their main task and prerogative, they are usually rather hesitant to initiate or tolerate any new arrangements for bargaining which are not firmly under their control. Therefore, unions will advocate the institutionalization of participation in the enterprise only, if they are convinced that these arrangements:

(a) will not undermine, but rather consolidate or fortify their bargaining position; and

(b) lead to forms of joint consultation beneficial for workers as well as for management.

In other words, U will attempt to introduce PS only, if it is confident that the employers, their associations, and, E, will be unable and/or unwilling to utilize participative structures solely for their own purposes. Various forms of participation no doubt can be tools in the hands of managers to prevent or quash labour unrest or protest, to extract relevant information from the work-force with respect to policy-formation, to legitimate managerial policies, and to motivate workers. In such cases, in terms of our inventory of Table 14.2, workers and their representatives are hindered in their effective use of negative sanctions, whereas management has the benefit of the positive sanctions of labour without offering much in return (see IDE, 1980, chs 10 and 11).

Under what conditions then will U assess the chances that its sanctions will be devaluated as a calculated risk and that instead its positive sanctions will be appreciated and yield a reasonable pay-off as a sure bet? In a general and abstract manner the answer to this question can be: whenever in a country the industrial culture stresses the value of co-operation between labour and management and upholds an image of managers and workers as partners with at least some interests in common.[5] It goes without saying that there is a whole continuum ranging from one extreme of such a 'co-operative' industrial culture to an 'oppositional' one in terms of which workers and managers are defined as belonging to divergent classes with irreconcilable interests.

In Chapter 1 it was mentioned that such a 'Cultural Explanation' in a way begs the question and calls for other explanations. Thus, the 'Social Explantion' implies that such a 'co-operative' culture originates from a society with a low or moderate level of economic and/or social inequality, while an 'oppositional' one springs from a society with pronounced class cleavages. In as far as equality of educational opportunities is either a cause or effect of economic and/or social equality, the 'Informational Explanation' would more or less coincide with the 'Social Explanation'. (See also ch. 9 in 'Industrial Democracy in Europe'.)

The 'Political Explanation' can likewise be interpreted as operative in conjunction with the cultural one. In a highly developed political democracy workers and their representatives may have sufficient experience with and faith in democratic procedures to possess a measure of 'civic competence' (Almond and Verba, 1965: ch. VI and X) and not too much fear of the manipulative powers of management. Perhaps one could say that democracy is a form of governance allowing various groups to strive after the joint optimization of their own interests and the common weal. Seen in this light, PS would then be nothing but the extension of democracy — albeit in a rather weak form — to industrial life. Such a penetration of forms of democratic governance in the industrial sphere is then, according to this hypothesis the more likely, the more firmly rooted and extensive democracy is in the political and in other spheres.

Finally, it will be clear that the cultural explanation in principle covers not only the PS-proneness of U, but to some extent that of G and even E as well. The more widespread the belief in co-operation between labour and management, the more likely that political parties — not only those of labour or socialist inclinations, but also centre parties — will fly the colours of industrial democracy and that the managerial class will pay at least some tribute to those colours.

6. THE EVIDENCE

For the sake of clarity the foregoing interpretative model was cast in the form of an *a priori* argument, although this as well as the conjectures of Chapter 1 were formulated on the basis of the existing literature on IRS and after taking cognizance of the twelve national reports. Therefore, the evidence to be reviewed now can hardly be expected to yield proof or disconfirmation of the hypotheses so far offered. In this last section we only hope to present a somewhat systematic summary of our knowledge of the twelve industrial relations systems studied with an eye to sorting out what is more and what is less plausible in the theoretical outline elaborated in this chapter.

Table 14.3 contains in the first place impressions gained from the national reports with respect to strength of U, strength of E, 'left-of-centre' orientation of governments in office, and economic growth in the post-World War Two period up till about 1975. The remaining data are derived from other sources and offer an estimate of the relative ranking of the countries concerned in terms of some contextual variables. The countries are listed in the same order as in Table 14.2 and the capitals behind the proper names designate (as in Table 14.2) the over-all standing of the countries in question as to degree of prescribed involvement of workers in enterprise decision-making.

The meaning of most of the indicators used will be clear from the text. In one respect only, there is a deviation. Originally, strength of U and of E was defined in terms of: — degree of centralization and professionalization of the central negotiating coalition or confederacy; degree of unity among the affiliated unions or associations; degree of 'coverage' of the potential constituents of unions or associations.

However, in this table the data for the strength-indicators do *not* include this last factor. The twelve national reports contain few indications as to the 'coverage' by employers' associations of managements, while in several reports it is explicitly stated that an average or rather low degree of unionization does not imply less readiness on the part of the unorganized workers to join industrial action when initiated by unions. Therefore, it was decided not to consider 'coverage' an ingredient of strength.

Our main thesis that a combination of a strong U and a strong E is conducive to a high degree of prescribed involvement of workers in enterprise policy- and decision-making turns out to be quite in accordance with the data presented in Table 14.3. Of course, it is hard to assess the 'strength' of U and E in Yugoslavia. One could argue that the Yugoslavian system is so completely different from that of all other countries in this survey, that it makes no sense to include Yugoslavia in the list. If one does decide that the Yugoslavian case is comparable at all to the other cases, one can reason that in Yugoslavia management — at least as far as formal policy-making authority is concerned — is in the hands of worker-representatives who are supported to some extent in their functioning by unions and party. In other words, instead of a strong E and a strong U, in Yugoslavia a strong 'labour movement' in coalition with a government, both sharing the goal of self-management, have been able to introduce PS at all levels most forcefully.

Sweden and Norway both exhibit the pattern of a strong and well-organized labour movement which in collaboration with a similarly well-equipped and united 'movement' of employers, and in coalignment with a socialist dominated government, have pulled off a full-fledged system of PS. The two countries are so much alike in these respects that one wonders why Norway has much weaker provisions than Sweden for PS in the way of works councils etc.

Germany has during the period in question undoubtedly had both a strong U and a strong E, a socialist-dominated government only since the late sixties.

The Low Countries, France, Israel, and the two remaining Scandinavian countries all fail to satisfy the three main criteria (strong U, strong E, 'leftist' G) as adequately as the first batch of countries. However, it is not 'predictable' from these main variables why France and the Netherlands should have more PS than the other four countries.

Table 14.3.
Relative standing of the twelve countries with respect to conditions favourable to PS (1947-1975)

		Strength of U	Strength of E	Orientation of G	Economic growth	Wealth	'Co-operativness' of IRS	Economic equality	Political democracy
Yugoslavia	(A)	?	?	L	+	–	+	+	?
Germany	(A)	+	+	L/R	+	+	+	±	+
Sweden	(A)	+	+	L	+	+	+	+	+
Norway	(B)	+	+	L	+	+	±	–	+
Netherlands	(C)	±	±	L/R	+	±	+	±	±
France	(C)	±	±	R	+	±	±	–	+
Belgium	(D)	±	±	L/R	+	±	±	±	±
Finland	(D)	±	+	L/R	+	±	–	±	+
Israel	(D)	+	–	L	+	–	±	+	–
Denmark	(D)	±	±	L	±	+	±	–	±
Italy	(E)	±	±	R	±	–	–	–	–
Great Britain	(E)	±	–	L/R	±	–	–	+	±

Strength of U and E   + = strong, ± = average, – = weak (*source*: foregoing chapters).

Orientation of G   L = left-of-centre most of the time; L/R = alternately left- and right-of-centre; R = right-of-centre most of the time (*source*: foregoing chapters).

Economic growth   + = most rapid growth; ± = rather slow growth and/or some periods of stagnation (*source*: foregoing chapters).

Wealth   relative ranking in terms of (highest = +) GDP per Capita – 1975 (*source*: ILO Yearbook, 1977).

Co-operativeness of IRS   relative ranking in terms of (least = +) days lost per 1,000 employed (av. 1967–76) due to strikes (*source*: ILO Yearbook, 1977).

Economic inequality   relative ranking in terms of (least = +) inequality of income distribution in the mid-1960s (Gini-coefficients), (*source*: Russett, 1967).

Political democracy   relative ranking in terms of an index of 'democratic history' (most democratic = +), (Hewitt, 1977: 457).

Italy, Israel, and Great Britain have it in common that at least one of the two principal actors in the IRS is characterized as weak, while the orientation of their governments is either 'mixed' or tending to the right.

If we look now at the contingent conditions, we must keep in mind that these matter only in the case of a rather strong U and E. According to the theory developed before, economic and cultural conditions can only promote or frustrate attempts of the main parties to realize PS, but are not seen themselves as driving forces capable of producing PS. We notice then that only economic growth and 'co-operativeness' of IRS look like conditions facilitating the origination of PS. At least, all countries with well-developed participation systems (category A) have generally known a steady rise in the standard of living in the post-World War Two era and a relatively peaceful industrial climate.

Economic conditions have likewise improved considerably since the late forties in the countries of medium standing as to PS (categories B and C), while their strike rates indicate an industrial climate, if less peaceful than that of the first set of countries, definitely also less conflictual than that of the remaining ones.

The indices for wealth, economic inequality, and political democracy do not bear out the expectation that the top-scoring countries in terms of PS (categories A and B) always have a relatively high standing as to these contextual dimensions. How to account for that? Wealth could be less important indeed than economic growth as a moderator variable, for there are indications that the rise and decline in the level of living have more serious attitudinal and behavioural consequences than mere differences in the absolute level of living.[6]

If we take our indicators of equality and political democracy seriously, then there are two ways of interpreting the lack of correspondence between these dimensions and the level of prescribed worker-involvement in enterprise policy-making per country. In the first place, one could suppose that the correlation between the social and political conditions, on the one hand, and the degree of co-operativeness of the industrial culture, on the other hand, is rather tenuous. In the second place, one could simply reject the cultural explanation altogether and presume that key figures of U will tend to believe in PS for strategic reasons alone whenever oganized labour and organized 'employerism' are strong.

We emphasized that U on the whole has to rely mainly on negative sanctions in its dealings with E and that in interorganizational relations in general negotiators will prefer positive to negative sanctions. Therefore, it could be that if U is strong, its policy-makers will be aware of the advantage of amplifying and 'diversifying' the stock of sanctions at their disposal by adding positive ones whenever possible. These policy-makers and their following would then also feel more competent to adopt and carry out a 'positive' strategy with respect to the introduction of PS if their position is sufficiently strong and if E is in a strong position as well (see also IDE, 1980, ch. 11).

If the correlation between strengths of U and E and the introduction of PS is not contingent on cultural conditions, the question arises as to how to explain the noted correspondence of the ranking of the countries concerned as to degree of 'co-operativeness' of the IRS and degree of prescribed involvement. Perhaps the strike rate is not really an (inverse) index of the degree to which in the industrial relations systems a 'co-operative' culture prevails, but either (like PS) an outcome of the general state of accommodation between U and E, or a consequence from PS.

To round off this section we have to pay attention to the 'deviations' noted before. Norway, Belgium, Finland, Denmark, and Israel exhibit slightly *less* PS than might have been expected on the basis of the scores of these countries for strength of U, strength of E, and orientation of G. Belgium, Finland and Denmark we can say now, would indeed tend to score lower than the Netherlands and France as to their over-all PS-standing, given the fact that the three former countries were not subject to the same high rate of economic growth and had a more conflictual industrial climate than the Netherlands and France. The same holds for Norway in comparison with Sweden.

In the case of Israel, our scheme does not provide an obvious explanation as to why this country should have a somewhat less developed PS-system than France and Holland. Similarly, for the case of Germany — which has a slightly more developed PS system than expected on the basis of our 'predictors' — our theoretical model does not quite 'fit'. Of course, these 'deviations' are comparatively minor and one might well ascribe these to special circumstances, in other words to conditions not included in the model (see IDE, 1980, ch. 9).

7. CONCLUSIONS

One way of summing up the results of this exploration is to say that we end up with two variants of one explanation, of the genesis and spread of participatory arrangements in industry. The interpretation starts from the assumption that whenever unions and employers' associations each form a centralized federation with a measure of authority *vis-à-vis* their membership, they can coalesce to promote a system of participation in the enterprise at various levels. According to the first variant, they will come to an agreement between themselves and push for legislation to this effect, provided: there is a relatively enduring government of socialist leanings in office; the country in question is experiencing economic growth; their industrial culture values co-operation between management and labour. The second variant simply relaxes this last requirement and is otherwise identical with the first one (cf., IDE, 1980, ch. 11).

NOTES

[1] The concept of 'strength' of contestants in a conflictual relationship was developed earlier, be it in somewhat different fashion, in Lammers, 1969: 567–8.

[2] In general a 'repressive' strategy which relies heavily on negative sanctions is, as compared to a 'concessional' strategy based mainly on positive sanctions, rather detrimental for the internal and the external relations of the organization that adopts such a policy. See on this: Lammers, 1977: 190–4.

[3] On the relationship between organization regime and strategies or tactics, see also Lammers, 1977: 189.

[4] See Rees, 1954, for evidence that there is more strike-activity during upswings than during downswings of the business-cycle.

[5] In the interorganizational literature, one encounters the notion that there is a 'normative context' which implies certain constraints for the ways in which the parties in question interact (Laumann *et al.,* 1978: 465-6). Likewise, Dunlop (1958: 16-18) stresses the fact the IRS usually has an overarching ideology 'that helps to bind or to integrate the system together as an entity'.

[6] The main idea — sometimes called the 'revolution of rising expectations' — dates back to de Tocqueville and comes down to the thesis that, in particular, set-backs in continuing processes of economic and political progress are experienced as extremely disruptive by groups that have come to expect improvements

REFERENCES

Almond, G. A. and Verba, S. (1965, or. ed. 1963), *The Civic Culture. Political Attitudes and Democracy in Five Nations,* Boston: Little, Brown and Cy.

Dunlop. J. T. (1958), *Industrial Relations Systems,* New York: Holt.

Evan, W. M. (1976), *Organization Theory. Structures, systems and environments,* New York: Wiley.

Hewitt, Christopher (1977), 'The effect of political democracy and social democracy on equality in industrial societies: a cross-national comparison', *American Sociological Review,* 42 (June).

IDE — International Research Group (1980), *Industrial Democracy in Europe,* Oxford, OUP, forthcoming.

Lammers, C. J. (1969), 'Strikes and mutinies: a comparative study of organizational conflicts between rulers and ruled', *Administrative Science Quarterly,* 14 (December): no. 4.

    (1977), 'Tactics and strategies adopted by university authorities to counter student opposition', *The Dynamics of University Protest,* edited by Donald Light Jr. and John Spiegel, Chicago: Nelson-Hall.

Laumann, E. O., Galaskiewioz, J. and Marsden, P. V. (1978), 'Community structure as interorganizational linkages', *Annual Review of Sociology,* 4.

Levine, S. and White, P. E. (1961), 'Exchange as a Conceptual Framework for the Study of Interorganizational Relationships', *Administrative Science Quarterly,* 5.

Litwak, E. and Hylton, L. F. (1962), 'Interorganizational Analysis: A Hypothesis on Coordinating Agencies', *Administrative Science Quarterly,* 6 (March).

Litwak, E. and Rothman, J. (1970), 'Toward the Theory and Practice of Coordination between Formal Organizations', *Organizations and Clients,* edited by William R. Rosengren and Mark Lefton. Columbus, Ohio: Charles E. Merrill.

Ogburn, W. F. and Nimkoff, M. F. (1946), *Sociology,* Boston: Houghton Mifflin.

Pfeffer, J. and Salancik, G. R. (1978), *The External Control of Organizations. A Resource Dependence Perspectivc,* New York: Harper and Row.

Rees, A. (1954), 'Industrial conflict and business fluctuations', *Industrial Conflict,* edited by Arthur Kornhauser, Robert Dubin, and Arthur M. Ross. New York: McGraw Hill.

Russett, B. M. (1967), *World Handbook of Political and Social Indicators,* New Haven: Yale University Press.

Voight, F. and Weddigen, W. (1962), *Zur Theorie und Praxis der Mitbestimmung,* Berlin: Duncker and Humblot.

Weber, M. (1947, or. ed. 1921), *Wirtschaft und Gesellschaft,* Tübingen: Mohr.

IDE-PUBLICATIONS

Collective publications of the IDE-Team

Industrial Democracy in Europe: An international comparative study, in: *Social Science Information* 1976, (15), pp. 177–203.

Participation: Formal Rules, Influence and Involvement, in: *Industrial Relations*, Vol. 18 (3), 1979, pp. 273–294.

Die Messung von Mitbestimmungsnormen — Darstellung eines international vergleichenden Forschungsansatzes, in: Bankenburg, Erhard; Lenk, Klaus (eds.): *Jahrbuch der Rechtssoziologie und Rechtstheorie*, Vol. 7, Opladen: Westdeutscher Verlag 1980.

Industrial Democracy in Europe. Oxford: Oxford University Press 1980.

Industrial Relations in Europe. Oxford: Oxford University Press 1980.

Individual or group publications

Individual team members or subgroups of the IDE-team published various books or articles directly or indirectly based on the IDE-research:

Andriessen, J. H. T. H., Meer Zeggenschap voor de Nieuwe Ondernemingsrad? Intermediair 1976 (12).

Andriessen, J. H. T. H., The Dutch Industrial Relations System. *Industrial Relations Journal,* 1976 (2), pp. 49–59.

De Corte, W., Realiteitswaarde van de notie feitelyke participatie: een studie in de variate taal van het sociopsychologisch onderzoek. *Psychologica Belgica,* 1979 (19), pp. 330–360.

Heller, Frank; Wilders, Malcolm; Abell, Peter; Warner, Malcolm, *What do the British want from Participation and Industrial Democracy?* London: Anglo-German Foundation for the Study of Industrial Society, 1979.

Laaksonen, Oiva; Kauhanen, Juhani; Kivisaari, Sirkku; Vanhala, Sinikka: *Päätöksentekoon Osaliistuminen, Arvot Ja Tyytyväisyys Yrityksissa.* Helsinki: Helsingin Kaupparkorkeakoulun Julkaisuja, 1979.

Martin, Dominique; Dupy, François: *Les Jeux et Enjeux de la Participation.* Paris, 1977.

Martin, Dominique; Goetschy, Janine: *Participation et Pouvoir dans l'Entreprise.* Paris: CRESST, 1980.

Sandberg, Thomas; Björklund, Lars; Molin, Roger: *Företags Democrati i sex Verkstadsföretag.* Lund, Studentlitteratur, 1979.

Sandberg, Thomas: Arbetornos krav och medbestammardeavtalen. In: Stahl, Ingolf (ed.): *Forskning, utbildning, praxis.* Vol. 1, Stockholm School of Economics, 1979, pp. 82–94.

Sandberg, Thomas: Hur blir medbestammandet i industriforetagen? *Ekonomen,* 1979, No. 9, pp. 30–33.

Stymne, Bengt: *Människan i organisationen.* Malmö: Liber, 1978, 199 p.

Wilpert, Bernhard: Meshing Internationality with Interdisciplinarity, in: Barth, Richard and R. Steck (ed.), *Interdisciplinary Research Groups: Their Management and Organization,* Vancouver, International Research Group on Interdisciplinary Programs, 1979.

SUBJECT INDEX

Absenteeism, 54, 95, 152, 209, 216, 261
Antagonistic co-operation, 253
Arbitration, *see* conflict, resolution of
Autogestion, 198

Beveridge Report, 106
Bullock Committee Report, 113, 114, 115, 116, 117

Centralization
  alternatives to, 31
  and co-determination, 50-3, 57-8
  in collective bargaining, 149, 157, 206, 212
  and the Communist party of Yugoslavia, 219
  in inter-organizational game, 253, 256, 257, 259-60, 268
  of labour market organizations, 23-4, 43-4, 71, 88, 142, 144-5, 241, 249
  and self-management, 225
  of state apparatus in Yugoslavia, 220
  of work-place and industry in Sweden, 36-7
Co-determination
  absence of legal basis for, 189, 208
  act on, 45-6, 47, 48, 49-53, 56-8
  debate on 34
  and economic development, 5
  differentiated from participation, 127
  legal basis of, 127-9
  levels of, 254
  impact of sanctions on, 260
  opportunities for, 152
  and other forms of industrial democracy, 2
  popularity of, 8
  recent developments in, 133-5
  right to, 74
  as task of works council, 173, 177
  see also participation
Collective agreements, *see* collective bargaining
Collective bargaining
  and co-determination, 49, 50, 127
  centralization of, 68
  debate on, 216
  and employers' organization, 43
  government involvement in, 23
  inadequacy of, 132
  and incomes policy, 91
  and industrial democracy, 3, 8-9
  as limiting factor, 73

  as problematic issue, 31
  recent development in, 149, 150, 161
  and role of the state, 77-8
  and shop steward system, 97
  and state sector, 91
  and trade union confederation, 42
  and unionization, 47
Collective bargaining, system of
  in Belgium, 168-9, 173, 174-5
  in Denmark, 63, 75-6
  in Finland, 88-9, 98-100, 101
  in France, 186, 191-4
  in Great Britain, 113
  in Holland, 143, 156-7
  in Israel, 237, 238, 242, 243
  in Italy, 204-5, 206, 207, 208, 210, 211-14
  in Norway, 24-5
  in West Germany, 124-6, 130, 131
Compulsory arbitration, 24-5
Concentration, *see* centralization
'Concerted Action' (West Germany), 132, 134
Conflict
  and accommodation in inter-organizational relations, 253
  among unions in Italy, 207, 210, 211
  and co-determination act in Sweden, 49, 50, 51
  and employers' organization in Sweden, 43
  institutionalization of, in France, 180
  of interests, 24, 29, 47-8, 68, 132
  nature of, in Sweden, 39
  and participative structure, 2
  of rights, 24, 29, 47-8, 68, 132
  role of shop steward in, in Denmark, 75
  role of trade union confederation in, in Sweden, 42
  and self-management in Yugoslavia, 225
'Conflict continuum', 93
Conflict, level of
  in Belgium, 171-2
  in Denmark, 63
  in Finland, 93-5
  in France, 188-9
  in Great Britain, 112-13
  in Holland, 147, 148-9, 151, 163
  in Israel, 237, 240, 242, 243, 247-8
  in Italy, 214-16
  in Norway, 23-4
  in Sweden, 44
  in West Germany, 126-7

INDEX OF NAMES